Managing Product = Managing Tension

First published 2020

Published under licence by Brown Dog Books and
The Self-Publishing Partnership, 7 Green Park Station, Bath BA1 1JB

www.selfpublishingpartnership.co.uk

ISBN printed book: 978-1-83952-195-9
ISBN e-book: 978-1-83952-196-6

Cover design by Rachel Smith
Internal design by Andrew Easton

Printed and bound in the UK
This book is printed on FSC certified paper

MIX
Paper from
responsible sources
FSC® C013604

Managing Product = Managing Tension

MARC ABRAHAM

BROWN DOG BOOKS

In memory of my dad,
Ernie Abraham [1947–2020]

CONTENTS

INTRODUCTION 8

CHAPTER 1. MANAGING PRODUCT = MANAGING TENSION 12

CHAPTER 2. KNOW YOUR TENSIONS 47

CHAPTER 3. THE ROLE AND IMPACT OF TENSION ON MANAGING PRODUCTS 73

CHAPTER 4. LEANING IN WITH CONFIDENCE 109

CHAPTER 5. LEANING INTO TENSION EFFECTIVELY 140

CHAPTER 6. SO, YOU WANT TO LEAN INTO TENSION COLLABORATIVELY?! 206

CHAPTER 7. MANAGING PRODUCT = MANAGING RESILIENCE AND GROWTH 241

ACKNOWLEDGEMENTS 282

CONCLUSION 280

ABOUT THE AUTHOR 283

INTRODUCTION

When consumers use a product or a service, the experience generates an emotion. Take for example, people using Uber to get from A to B; some customers will feel delighted by the experience, whilst others might be bitterly disappointed. For those of us creating those products or services, our primary focus is on the customer, helping them achieve their desired outcome and attempting to create a positive and memorable experience.

However, in our focus to satisfy customer needs, many product people or 'makers' don't spend enough time reflecting and managing their own emotions when developing products. There are so many tensions inherent in product creation and management, but we hardly ever acknowledge or talk about them.

Think of the last time you were at your wits' end when a business stakeholder completely torpedoed your great product idea. Or the sense of deflation we have all experienced when launching a product that customers seem to care less about (when we were convinced it was amazing!). We are so busy learning about customer needs and releasing products that we fail to reflect on the pressures inherent in managing products.

In striving to emulate the success of Facebook, Apple or Uber, and the people who famously contributed to their success, we've perhaps lost track of the tensions that occurred during their genesis and the accompanying blood, sweat and tears that went into creating products used by billions of people around the world. Irrespective of whether your product serves 10 people or 10 million, there will be tensions involved in building and managing it. Think of the tensions and frustrations involved in product failures, the struggle to acquire customers and anger due to endless internal debates; just some of the common product development tensions that come to mind.

I am thinking of my previous role as a Chief Product Officer at an early stage startup that did not end the way I hoped it would. Did product tensions get the better of me, or my colleagues? Licking my wounds led me to reflect on the stresses experienced, looking back at the tensions I could have managed differently and the ones I should have embraced with open arms.

HOW I FIRST STARTED THINKING ABOUT WRITING THIS BOOK ...

I had been at this early stage startup for one year exactly and this milestone coincided with a regular catch up with my boss. As part of our conversation, she asked me to reflect on my first year in the business, getting me to think about what had gone well and what had not. I shared my thoughts honestly and constructively, mentioning some of the frictions we had encountered in the year past. I explained how I could have better facilitated collaboration between the product team and the founders. Similarly, I felt that the natural trade-off between the perfect product and speed to market could have been managed more effectively.

My boss and I discussed these frictions in detail, and it made me realise the often-stressful nature of developing and managing products. My boss was clearly struck by some of the strains and trade-offs that I mentioned, asking 'so, why didn't you resolve them?'. We talked through why she felt that way, and I explained more about the nature of managing products. Unfortunately, my boss and I felt that the gap between expectations and reality was too big and we agreed to part ways amicably.

This experience made me ponder the often-frustrating nature of managing products, and the different factors that contribute to this feeling of frustration. It formed the starting point for the book that you are reading now ...

Both with the product managers that I have managed over the years and the peers I compare notes with, 'frustration' seems to be a common theme. This frustration is usually the result of tensions which are inherent in managing products; the fact that product creation is often not a linear, predictable process, and that the people involved in the process turn out to be just as irrational and unpredictable as the process itself!

Within the confines of four walls, a cup of coffee or 'Product Managers Anonymous' type of conversations, I have encountered plenty of product people who opened up about their frustrations and anxieties with respect to managing products. Whenever I talk publicly about the frustrating aspects of product management, I am always amazed at the number of people that come up to me afterwards and share their personal experiences and feelings.

There are a number of lessons that I have learned - the hard way - and which I feel other product people can benefit from. There are a number of things we can do (differently) to utilise tensions in such a way that they create great products and teams. In this book, we will examine the tensions inherent in creating and managing products. Make no mistake, tension can be a good thing! Real-life examples will demonstrate the distinction between healthy and unhealthy product tensions and how to ensure they have a positive impact.

This is, however, NOT a self-help book: I don't proclaim to have all the answers, nor will I provide you with the holy grail that will stop you from feeling frustrated ever again. This book is meant to encourage an open conversation about the strains innate to managing both digital and physical products and the frustrations or emotions associated with these tensions. I will also share a wide range of tools and techniques aimed at helping you better pre-empt and manage the challenges and opportunities that you are likely to encounter through the product life cycle. Combined with real-life examples from other product managers that I have spoken to and practical techniques by renowned authors, this book aims to give you a great toolkit to help you become aware and deal effectively with the tensions that come with managing successful products!

THE STRUCTURE OF THIS BOOK

In the first part of this book, we will look at the tensions that are built into the process of managing products. There are a number of reasons why tension and managing products are so tightly coupled, and we will take a closer look at both the underlying reasons for that and ways in which tensions manifest themselves. I have grouped these into three key components of the product management equation: mind, matter and moves. I will introduce these components in Chapter 1 and then build on them in subsequent chapters.

In the second half of the book I will make the case that the sense of discomfort associated with the product management process is not necessarily a bad thing. However, it does mean that we need to be fully aware of these frictions and their potential consequences. I will cover how you can best manage and even optimise these and share a related toolkit at the end of each chapter.

Ultimately, the main point of 'Managing Product = Managing Tension' is that tensions are inherent to products and that we as product people should find ways to embrace that.

CHAPTER 1.
MANAGING PRODUCT = MANAGING TENSION

'Discomfort causes us to think differently, to engage our brains more and in different ways, and this is how we come up with better solutions to problems.' **Shane Snow**

Product Management = Mind + Matter + Moves

In this chapter we will explore:

- How the very **nature of product management** lends itself to tension.
- The **mind** of people impacting the product.
- The **matter** that a product is made of and how it affects development.
- The **moves** people make in relation to the product.

INTRODUCTION

I call it the 'To Jump or Not' tension: deciding whether to jump into the pool because everybody else has, even though the water is absolutely freezing, and you really don't want to go in. It is the situation in which a stakeholder argues that we should be building a feature 'because the competitor already has it' whilst the product person is concerned about blindly following the competition without good reason or benefit to the customer. 'To Jump or Not' is one of many tensions we can encounter when managing products. I am, for example, thinking back to an experience I had a few years ago where a senior stakeholder brutally interfered with what I thought was a great product plan.

WHEN A SENIOR STAKEHOLDER THROWS A SPANNER IN THE WORKS …

I was excited. The new feature that the team and I had planned would drastically simplify the onboarding of new customers onto our platform. Instead of asking people for their personal details early on in the customer journey, we would demonstrate the benefits of our app first and ask for details later. We discussed our assumption that this new feature would drastically reduce the number of people leaving the app as friction would be removed. Happy days!

Then the Chief Marketing Officer interjected … He expressed his concern about missing out on valuable customer data. 'Despite some customers not signing up, we do get important customer data when they register,' he explained. 'This data is then used for our targeted marketing campaigns, and I am concerned that we might well lose this data if we stop asking people to register upfront.' I was still contemplating the CMO's words, when he then spoke in a tone that did not leave much room for dissent: 'So, I have decided that we will stick with the existing onboarding flow.' You could feel the tension starting to build in the room, with everyone turning to me to see how I would respond …

I paused and said that I understood his concerns but reiterated the need to simplify the onboarding flow for our users in order to create a better experience and increase the number of completed signups. We considered alternative onboarding scenarios which our team had explored and settled on a compromise whereby the first step of the onboarding journey both asked for a limited number of personal details and outlined the app's benefits.

This is just one of many examples that I have encountered in my career as a product manager; you have a seemingly great creative idea, but an important stakeholder is worried about a potentially negative consequence of that same idea and puts a huge spanner in the works.

Before I became a product manager, I used to be a digital *project* manager. My primary responsibility as a project manager was to ensure that projects were delivered within budget, time and scope.[1] Highly detailed Gantt charts helped planning and tracking my projects.[2] Each project would start off hopefully, confident that we would meet the deadlines and dependencies specified in the project plan.

I quickly learned that these project plans are not worth the paper they are written on. As Mike Tyson says, 'everyone has a plan until they get punched in the face'. It would quickly become apparent to me that the technology underpinning the new website was more complex than we had originally accounted for; or the client would not sign off on the new homepage design (never mind that we did deliver it on time, in scope and on budget).

I thus learned the hard way that working on technology never is a linear or predictable process. This is particularly true when we use new technologies in products or when prevailing technologies are applied in untested, novel ways. The very nature of the product management process is highly fluid and unpredictable. The mere fact that you are working with technology drives uncertainty as well as the involvement of multiple cross-disciplined people. As we will see throughout this book, the tension that we experience when managing products is the net result of a variety of - often opposing - causes and effects. Take, for example, the strains we can feel when having to satisfy both the needs of our end users and those of the shareholders of our businesses.

---

1 See for an explanation of the difference between project and product management: "What's the Difference Between Program, Product and Project Managers?," David Goulden, June 17, 2017, https://www.clarizen.com/whats-difference-program-product-project-managers/; "Product Manager vs Project Manager," Andrei Tit, Medium, March 20, 2018, https://medium.com/paymo/product-manager-vs-project-manager-b4ac603d872a; "Project Manager vs. Product Manager," Brainrants | Brainmates Blog, Updated October 2019, https://brainmates.com.au/brainrants/project-manager-vs-product-manager/.

2 A Gantt chart is a type of bar chart that illustrates a project schedule, named after its inventor, Henry Gantt, who designed such a chart around the years 1910–1915.

Does that by default make product management more pressured than other professions?! Not necessarily, but the position of a product manager does undoubtedly generate innate tension. When you are covering the commercial, experiential and technical aspects of a product and all the unknowns inherent in any of these areas, it means that you are often flying in the face of uncertainty whilst dealing with highly demanding stakeholders. All these factors combined feed into the highly pressured nature of product management.

Product Management = Mind + Matter + Moves

'A great product manager has the brain of an engineer, the heart of a designer, and the speech of a diplomat.' **Deep Nishar**

Managing products is a bit like an everlasting tug of war, with various forces pulling in lots of different directions at the same time. The three main forces we see are the *mind* of the people involved with the product, the *matter* that the product is made of and the *moves* that people make in relation to the product.

For example, you might have a product person coming up with a great product idea that customers will love, whilst the sales person struggles to figure out how to best commercialise it. Or the engineer who wants to make the software code more elegant, seemingly immune to the pressure to take the product to market as quickly as possible. These tussles can make the difference between being first to market or a product never seeing the light of day; between customer delight and customer indifference; between customer value and commercial realism.

For the purposes of this book, I define product management to include both building the product and its subsequent management and iterations throughout the product life cycle.[3] There will be parts of the book where I will zero in on developing a product or feature, and other places that highlight the continuous iterations of a product. The three core components of product management, each of which, in their own right, can cause tension are mind, matter and moves.

MIND

Tensions caused by the 'Mind' of the individuals and teams involved with the product, their attitudes, approaches and mental states.

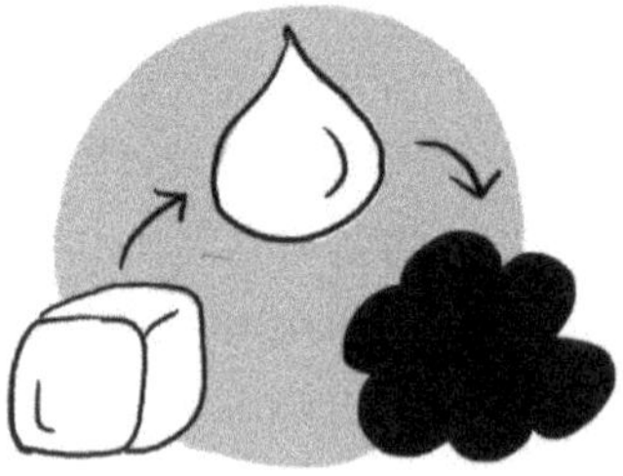

MATTER

3 "Exploit the Product Life Cycle," Theodore Levitt, Harvard Business Review, November 1965, https://hbr.org/1965/11/exploit-the-product-life-cycle.

Tensions caused by the 'Matter' of which the product is formed. Whether the matter of your product is technological or physical, it might not always 'act' the way we want or predict it to.

MOVES

Tensions caused by the 'Moves' made with respect to the product. Moves such as decisions to create or terminate a product or the processes we put in place to manage a product throughout its life cycle. Not only do we need to be aware of the distinctive tensions inherent within mind, matter and moves individually, we also encounter tension as a result of friction between different factors or due to specific circumstances. The mind of people involved in developing products, for instance, can be rather unpredictable. This doesn't have to be problematic in its own right but will lead to friction or uncertainty if the product *matter* is very unpredictable or if the moves designed to guide the product development process hinge on certainty. Or take a totally unprecedented circumstance like the COVID-19 pandemic which has caused a lot of tension in its own right. Tension is therefore the cumulative result of cause, effect and circumstances which manifests itself in a multitude of ways when managing products:

- Uncertainty
- Friction
- Creativity
- Tough decisions
- Ambiguity
- Challenges
- Constraints
- Unclear territory
- Problems
- Opinions
- Doubt
- Anxiety
- Conflict

Better understanding of both the reasons and manifestations of tension is critical if we want to improve the ways in which we manage them when creating products. Take 'people and technology', for example; this tension alone can completely derail the development of your product. In this book I will argue that tension is neither good nor bad. Tension is inevitable and it is down to us to manage tension effectively. The nature of product management gives rise to multiple tensions and, if we are not careful, it could leave a mark on the product and impact its value to the customer (See fig. 1). In this first chapter we will see the tensions heaped on the product, caused by the mind, matter and moves respectively.

Fig. 1 – How the nature of product management causes multiple tensions along the way

Product Management = **Mind** + Matter + Moves

'Since new developments are the products of a creative mind, we must therefore stimulate and encourage that type of mind in every way possible.' **George Washington Carver**

When I took on my first role as a product manager, I was very excited. One of the reasons for my initial excitement was that I expected to focus solely on products, no longer having to worry about dealing with other people, their personalities and agendas. Or that's what I thought. The reality of being a product manager could not be further removed from my initial assumptions: These days, I probably spend eighty percent of each day interacting with other people!

Don't be fooled into thinking that the problematic nature of product management is all down to products and the technologies or materials that they are made of. The *mind* of the person(s) involved in designing, building and marketing products is just as pivotal. At the start of this first chapter we talked about the inherent tension between technology and people. Collaborating effectively with other people can be just as complicated, if not more so. In this section, we will look at the following challenges to cognitive diversity and collaboration, as well as the existence of emotional triggers.

> **Product Management = Mind + Matter + Moves**
>
> Three tensions caused by the **mind** when managing products:
>
> 1. The **'Not Seeing the Wood for the Trees'** tension.
> 2. The **'Dysfunctional Family'** tension.
> 3. The **'You're Only Human'** tension.

1. THE 'NOT SEEING THE WOOD FOR THE TREES' TENSION

'What you really want is people to solve problems in diverse ways - to have a creative team, you want people to think of different types of ideas.' **Scott Page**

Product management is a team sport. When I interview product management candidates for a role on a product team, I always explore the products they have worked on. When I hear candidates talk about '*I* built_____' or '*I* acquired ______ new customers' I probe to find out about both their specific individual contribution and how they collaborated with others.[4]

The main reason why I am always keen to explore collaboration as well as individual contributions is because of my strong belief in the value of 'cognitive diversity' which occurs when different perspectives

4 "My product management toolkit (31): hiring product managers," Marc Abraham, October 5, 2018, https://medium.com/@maa1/my-product-management-toolkit-31-hiring-product-managers-4442740af77.

and problem solving approaches come together.[5] Creativity triggers a focus of critical judgement, rather than a suspension of it; as creators master their own creative process, less and less is left to explore alternatives. Instead, creators aim to try and get to their desired final result as quickly and efficiently as possible.[6] Going through such a creative process collectively therefore generates pressure and opposing points of view, starting with reaching agreement about the desired end result, let alone figuring out as a team how best to get there.

Cognitive diversity is closely linked with so-called 'healthy tension' or 'constructive conflict' which, if exercised wisely, fuels innovation and team success.[7] In both instances, people will respect each other's different perspectives and opinions, and aim to resolve issues in a productive manner. Achieving a state of productive disagreement sits in the middle of the 'Conflict Continuum' developed by business author Patrick Lencioni.[8] In this continuum, productive disagreement is flanked by artificial harmony and destructive conflict. At first glance,

5 See: "The Difference: How the Power of Diversity Creates Better Groups, Firms, Schools and Societies," Scott Page, Princeton University Press, 2008; "Teams Solve Problems Faster When They're More Cognitive Diverse, " Alison Reynolds and David Lewis, Harvard Business Review, March 30, 2017, https://hbr.org/2017/03/teams-solve-problems-faster-when-theyre-more-cognitively-diverse; "Cognitive Diversity: what's often missing from conversations about diversity and inclusion," Sara Canaday, Psychology Today, June 18, 2017, Psychology Today, https://www.psychologytoday.com/us/blog/you-according-them/201706/cognitive-diversity ; "How Diverse Leadership Teams Boost Innovation," Rocío Lorenzo, Nicole Voigt, Miki Tsusaka, Matt Krentz, and Katie Abouzahr, Boston Consulting Group, January 23, 2018, https://www.bcg.com/en-us/publications/2018/how-diverse-leadership-teams-boost-innovation.aspx.

6 Robert Fritz, *The Path of Least Resistance* (New York: Fawcett Columbine, 2nd Edition, 1989, p. 39).

7 See: "Four Questions to Spot the Difference Between Healthy Tension and Unhealthy Conflict ," Eric Geiger, January 18, 2016, https://ericgeiger.com/2016/01/four-questions-to-spot-the-difference-between-healthy-tension-and-unhealthy-conflict/; "Healthy tension in product teams," Emmet Connolly, Inside Intercom, July 21, 2017, https://www.intercom.com/blog/healthy-tension-in-product-teams/; "What is healthy tension?" Tim Arnold, Leaders for Leaders, https://www.leadersforleaders.ca/blog/entry/what-is-healthy-tension; "Thomas-Kilmann Conflict Mode Instrument," Kenneth W. Thomas and Ralph H. Kilmann, Profile and Interpretive Report (sample), CPP Inc., May 1, 2008.

8 Patrick Lencioni, *The Five Dysfunctions of a Team* (San Francisco: Jossey-Bass, April 2002).

the idea of 'artificial harmony' might sound appealing but there is often a lot of discontent hiding underneath the group agreement or it risks being based on the lowest common denominator. Equally, a state of deconstructive conflict is not desirable either. Whilst it is impossible - and as I will point out later in the book, not conducive to product innovation - for team members to always agree, we don't want teams to be in a state of conflict that doesn't move the team or the product forward (See fig. 2).

Fig. 2 – Productive Conflict: the sweet spot in between artificial harmony and destructive conflict

In reality, I see an additional dimension playing out; 'noise' caused by people sharing their viewpoints haphazardly and not listening to each other. We thus get caught up in a cacophony of split perspectives, losing sight of what really matters or what is actually happening. In my experience, cognitive diversity becomes troublesome when people don't respect or trust different views or approaches, have divergent interests or follow different goals. You might have come across companies or teams where people only pay lip service to the concept of cognitive diversity. Equally, friction rears its head when people fail to shed deeply-held biases.[9] As much as we like to see ourselves as totally rational beings, the reality is that we aren't.

Throughout our lives we develop so many different learnings and biases, some more ingrained than others. Unlearning these 'priors' can be really tough and cause friction between people and teams.[10] As a consequence this often simply creates noise, with people failing to reach agreement on anything. Wayne Greene, a highly experienced product management leader and consultant, has reflected on this noise and compared it to 'walking into a dysfunctional family'. Greene explained to me how product managers might feel like a 'mini CEO', owning the product, but the reality is that 'you almost need a degree in psychology' when working with others on products.[11] Cognitive diversity is priceless with respect to developing great products, but we need to recognise that it can also cause a great deal of friction.

2. THE 'DYSFUNCTIONAL FAMILY' TENSION

'They did not need to be close friends to work together. But they need to trust each other.' **Kirsten Beyer**

Spotify is a great example of a collaborative approach to product management. About ten years ago, they introduced their 'squad' structure, which represents their cross-functional approach to product development. Each squad is designed to act as a self-contained unit, consisting of a product person, designer and engineers. The squad should thus have all the skills and tools needed to design, develop,

9 "Why Diversity Programs Fail," Frank Dobbin and Alexandra Kalev, Harvard Business Review, July-August 2016, https://hbr.org/2016/07/why-diversity-programs-fail.

10 "The Dominant Logic: Retrospective and Extension," Richard A. Bettis and C.K. Prahalad, Strategic Management Journal, Vol. 16, Issue 1, 1995, http://213.55.83.214:8181/Economics/Economy/00539.pdf.

11 Wayne Greene, *interview by author*, San Jose, June 27, 2019.

test and release to production.[12] Naturally, Spotify's approach has evolved since its introduction, and Spotify employees are at pains to stress that they never set out to create a 'Spotify model' and that squads were only meant as an output and not as a goal in its own right.[13] In other words, it is a common misconception to think that assembling squads will automatically get people to collaborate effectively.

I have been fortunate enough to have worked in a squad-like fashion, working closely with engineers, designers and testers on a day-to-day basis. However, I have also come across businesses where collaboration wasn't a given. For example, I joined a company a good few years ago which had an impressive engineering team and a team of equally committed project managers. Notwithstanding everyone's good intentions, the two teams operated as silos, and cooperation between 'tech' and 'project management' was limited. Instead, it felt more like there was an imaginary fence between the two sides with people tossing things to each other over the top of it.

In her article 'The Collaboration Blind Spot', Harvard University researcher Lisa B. Kwan writes about why groups of people can feel threatened when they are being asked to collaborate.[14] From her research, Kwan has found that resistance to collaboration tends to emerge 'especially when those groups are being told to break down walls, divulge information, sacrifice autonomy, share resources, or even cede responsibilities that define them as a group.'[15] People can

12 "How Spotify builds products," Henrik Kniberg, Crisp's Blog, January 13, 2013, https://blog.crisp.se/wp-content/uploads/2013/01/HowSpotifyBuildsProducts.pdf.

13 See: "The Spotify Model Is No Agile Nirvana ," Ben Linders, InfoQ, October 12, 2017, https://www.infoq.com/news/2017/10/spotify-agile-nirvana/; "Why 'the Spotify model' won't solve all your problems with Product Delivery," Curtis Stanier, Medium, November 3, 2019, https://medium.com/@crstanier/why-the-spotify-model-won-t-solve-all-your-problems-4c31640c719a; "Failed #SquadGoals," Jeremiah Lee, April 19, 2020, https://www.jeremiahlee.com/posts/failed-squad-goals/.

14 "The Collaboration Blind Spot," Lisa B. Kwan, Harvard Business Review, March - April 2019, https://hbr.org/2019/03/the-collaboration-blind-spot.

15 *Ibid 14.*

thus interpret collaboration as a sign that their own importance to the company - as a team or individual - is waning. As a consequence, they become defensive and uncommunicative in trying to protect their area or role. Having seen such behaviours play out first-hand, collaboration can add an additional layer of complexity to the product management process.

'Collaboration is rarely all bliss' claims Allen Gannett in his book 'The Creative Curve', and so-called 'conflicting collaborators' are the best people to work with, according to him. You don't want to, Gannett explains, collaborate with someone who is so easy to get along with that they don't push you. Instead, you want to work with someone who will help you discover and overcome your flaws or those of your creative idea.[16]

A conflicting collaborator has specific traits which compensate for your flaws.[17] Let's say that Rosy has great product ideas but struggles to turn them into action. Kevin, a colleague of Rosy, isn't necessarily the best at coming up with ideas; his forte is the practical execution of other people's ideas. Paired together, Rosy and Kevin form a great team, and complement each other well.[18] Their productive partnership is then thrown off track when Mona joins the team; she brings a wealth of experience but finds it hard at times to venture beyond what she already knows. As this simple, fictitious example shows, collaboration is hardly ever straightforward, and putting complementary skills together will not create a high-performing team overnight. However, if managed well, collaboration can act as a strong source of creativity and innovation.

16 Allen Gannett, *The Creative Curve*, (London: Ebury Publishing, June 2018, p. 171).

17 *Ibid 16*, p. 182.

18 See also "The AEM-Cube: A Management Tool, Based on Ecological Concepts, in Order to Profit from Diversity," Peter Robertson. Presented at the 43rd Annual Conference of the International Society for the Systems Sciences, 1999, Pacific Grove, CA.

3. THE 'YOU'RE ONLY HUMAN' TENSION

'Our emotions have a mind of their own, one which can hold views quite independently of our rational mind.' **Daniel Goleman**

As Sylvester Stallone's character once said in the film 'Rocky', 'In the boxing ring of life it's not how hard you can hit, but rather how many times you can get hit and keep moving forward.' This quote is spot on when it comes to emotional triggers; you will feel a blow each time your weak spot is hit; however, the test is whether you have the resilience to continue. Before you 'feel', you are likely to experience an emotion first.[19] Emotions are effectively a survival mechanism, an instant response which in turn triggers a certain feeling.[20]

Emotional triggers are people, words, opinions or situations that provoke a strong emotional reaction within us. In her famous TED talk, neuroscientist Lisa Feldman Barrett explains that emotions are rooted in predictions.[21] She explains that emotions are primal, helping us to make sense of the world in a quick and efficient way.[22] It's our past experience that our brain uses to predict and trigger associated emotions.

Emotions that can be triggered include anger, rage, sadness and fear.[23] For example, when other people disagree vehemently with my view of the world, I will often feel sad and lonely. Over the years I have at least become aware of this trigger and its impact, but it can nevertheless affect the way in which I collaborate with others or the

19 Antonio Damasio, *Looking for Spinoza: Joy, Sorrow and the Feeling Brain* (London: William Heinemann, 2003, pp. 29 – 30).

20 Marcia Reynolds, *Outsmart Your Brains: How to Master Your Mind When Emotions Take the Wheel* (Arizona: Covisioning, 2nd Edition, August 2017).

21 "You aren't at the mercy of your emotions - your brain creates them," Lisa Feldman Barrett, TED @ IBM, January 2, 2018, https://www.ted.com/talks/lisa_feldman_barrett_you_aren_t_at_the_mercy_of_your_emotions_your_brain_creates_them/.

22 *Ibid 21.*

23 See: *The Ekmans' Atlas of Emotions*, http://atlasofemotions.org/.

ways in which I behave.

I once worked with a colleague who other colleagues described to me as 'a tough cookie'. Granted, he was a bold character who wasn't afraid to stand up for his opinions and take drastic action. I realised, however, that my colleague was still susceptible to what other people thought of him, often asking 'what do people think of me?' or 'what did they think of my decision?' A clear example of someone who appeared to be made out of Teflon, whilst in reality having his own emotional triggers to deal with.

When your emotions are triggered, Dr. Marcia Reynolds explains in 'Outsmart Your Brain', a host of neural, biochemical, and hormonal actions are initiated based on what your brain perceives you need to feel happy or satisfied.[24] Psychology professor Michael Gazzaniga argues that people have a built-in system which creates a narrative about why we do the things we do and which helps decide how we respond to certain triggers. Both Gazzaniga and Reynolds explain how we react emotionally if the following needs or desires are not being met:[25]

- To be liked
- To be understood
- To be in control
- To be included
- To feel valued
- To be right
- To feel needed
- To be respected
- To feel safe

24 *Ibid 20.*

25 *Ibid 21* and "Who Is in Charge?" Michael S. Gazzaniga, BioScience, Volume 61, Issue 12, December 2011, pp. 937–938.

Understanding your emotional triggers is essential in any walk of life. But when you are managing products and the level of collaboration that comes with that, recognising your own and others' emotional triggers is absolutely imperative. Even if the number of people involved with a product is small, these people will most likely have diverse backgrounds, disciplines and perspectives. Their emotional triggers and personal styles will most likely vary too.

When collaborating with others we need to be aware of these differences and be respectful of dissimilar emotional triggers - our own and those of others. People's failure to recognise and manage emotional needs or triggers - their own or those of others - can introduce an extra level of frustration to the already uncertain endeavour that is product management.

Product Management= Mind + **Matter** + Moves

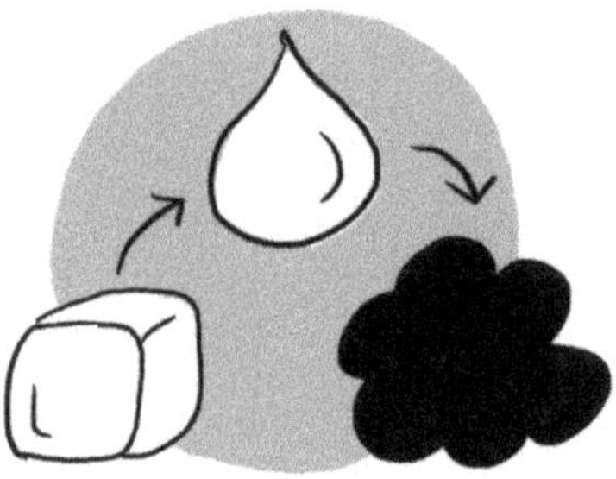

MATTER

'The test of the machine is the satisfaction it gives you. There isn't any other test. If the machine produces tranquility, it's right. If it disturbs you it's wrong until either the machine or your mind is changed.'
Robert M. Pirsig

LEARNING ABOUT THE DEFINITIVE NATURE OF SOFTWARE CODE ...

I am not a software engineer myself and perhaps that is one of the reasons why I have always been in awe of engineers and the work they do. When I started my career in the digital space, I remember a colleague explaining to me that 'coding is pretty black and white', as she showed me the code that she had just written. It took me a while to make sense of her code, but I could see how she had created a set of instructions and rules for when to apply them.

My colleague then taught me about basic 'if statements' in a common coding language, meaning that you need a set 'condition' to be true for a specific instruction or 'statement' to be executed. If the condition is false, then the statements get ignored:[26]

```
if(condition_1) {
 /*if condition_1 is true execute this*/
 statement(s);
}
else if(condition_2) {
 /* execute this if condition_1 is not met and
 * condition_2 is met
 */
 statement(s);
}
```

In short, get an instruction wrong and the product won't behave in the way you expect it to!

The story above illustrates the certain character of software programming, with the onus on the software engineer to make sure

26 "If else Statement in C++," Chaitanya Singh, BeginnersBook, August 2017, https://beginnersbook.com/2017/08/cpp-if-else-statement/.

that the instructions put in are (a) the correct ones and (b) executed as expected. Until machine learning takes hold fully, computers will be dependent on humans feeding instructions, and those humans not messing up their commands.

Craig Strong, Global Speciality Practice Advisory Lead for EMEA at Amazon Web Services, emphasises the effort required to develop software solutions, which can be high in cognitive load and complexity. 'Changes which seem simple to some people can in fact be a lot of technical work.' For instance, code inheritance, domain logic, rules and technology dependencies. Strong adds: 'I've witnessed many people with little knowledge on the technology side be very dangerous in this context, manifesting disrespect for the tech. As a result, they underestimate the time something should take to develop or disrespect the proposed timelines from the tech team which can in turn can cause human conflict.'[27]

Whether the product is an app, website, API, self-driving car or smart speaker, errors in the code written can cause 'crashes' or 'bugs'. Whilst Basecamp co-founder David Heinemeier Hansson argues that 'bugs are an inevitable byproduct of writing software', most engineers will strive - as a matter of professional pride, if anything - to reduce any room for error.[28] Software development can be very complex, both when working on existing systems or implementing new technologies. This is the reason why coding is such a painstaking, almost binary discipline. Its focus is on eliminating any sense of ambiguity, aiming to make the software as repeatable and predictable as possible.[29]

---

27 Craig Strong, *email to author*, March 28, 2020.

28 "Software has bugs. This is normal," David Heinemeier Hansson, Signal v. Noise, March 7, 2016, https://m.signalvnoise.com/software-has-bugs-this-is-normal/.

29 "Software is actually extremely repeatable and predictable for the majority of business applications," Justin James, Medium, August 11, 2018, https://medium.com/@jmjames/software-is-actually-extremely-repeatable-and-predictable-for-the-overwhelming-majority-of-business-4459aa7fc0b2.

Product Management = Mind + Matter + Moves

Three tensions caused by the **matter** when managing products:

- The **'Tell Me What to Do'** tension.
- The **'Knitting Spaghetti'** tension.
- The **'Who's the Boss'** tension.

1. THE 'TELL ME WHAT TO DO' TENSION

'For good ideas and true innovation, you need human interaction, conflict, argument, debate.' **Margaret Heffernan**

Involving humans in product management can equate to opening the floodgates for the herd. Products are never developed in isolation; from making product decisions to people building and using the product, humans are heavily involved at every stage. Despite this being a good thing for the most part, the combination of technology and people can lead to clashes and frustration.

The creation of products leaves little room for ambiguity, but humans are not built like that. Products are designed and built in a highly rational and calculated manner. For instance, when designing and building a car, the different materials and components that make up the car dictate its design and build. Materials like steel and aluminum aren't particularly malleable and don't leave much room for nuance! As humans, in contrast, there will be times when we make fully rational decisions and times when we clearly don't.[30] At times,

30 Jurgen Habermas, *The Theory of Communicative Action Volume 1, Reason and the Rationalization of Society* (Cambridge: Polity Press, 1984); "Study suggests emotion plays a role in rational decision making," Kate Wong, Scientific American, November 27, 2001, https://www.scientificamerican.com/article/study-suggests-emotion-pl/.

emotional or contradictory thoughts or behaviours will take over.[31] In addition, creativity requires a healthy degree of irrationality. Would we have had the lightbulb or the automobile if people had complied with the status quo or accepted, logical ways of thinking?!

Bringing a group of people together as part of product development means introducing emotion, creativity, uncertainty, contradiction and a whole host of other behaviours. If you offset this against the more rational, predictable nature of technology products, you have got the second cause for product management tension.

2. THE 'KNITTING SPAGHETTI' TENSION

'Creativity can solve almost any problem.' **George Lois**

The world's greatest products and inventions wouldn't be anywhere without creativity, and creative geniuses spurring them on. From Thomas Edison to Steve Jobs, the most famous product people and inventors all share one key trait: creativity. Some of these visionaries are well known for displaying 'challenging behaviours': Steve Jobs and his tendency to erupt in anger or Marie Curie's insistence on working with highly radioactive materials.[32]

Creativity is an intangible phenomenon and can't be captured in checklists or fixed processes; creativity means coming up with original or unusual ideas, which can be applied to existing or fresh problems. Especially when working on problems that haven't yet been solved (successfully) you will need to think in novel and unexpected ways. Solving these problems involves uncertainty, unknowns and relentless iteration. Take British inventor James Dyson, who set out to solve the problem of

31 Julius Friedrich August Bahnsen, *The Contradiction in the Knowledge and Being of the World*, 1880.

32 Walter Isaacson, Steve Jobs: *The Exclusive Biography* (Simon & Schuster, October 2011); Barbara Goldsmith, *Obsessive Genius: The inner world of Marie Curie* (New York: W.W. Norton and Company, 2004).

traditional vacuum cleaner bags rapidly filling up with dust and losing suction power as a result. Dyson went through thousands of prototypes to finally come up with a vacuum cleaner that used centrifugal force instead of a bag, to successfully separate dirt from air.[33]

Such an evolution becomes even more of a challenge when coupling innovation with heavily regulated industries or process driven companies. Would Steve Jobs have become such a prodigy had he manufactured airplanes? How would Sara Blakely, founder of Spanx, have fared if she had worked in the pharma industry as opposed to underwear?[34]

The impalpable nature of creativity can be a breeding ground for frustration when developing products. Creativity is hard to direct and cannot be delivered on demand. In Chapter 3 we will examine the nonlinear nature of creativity, and the unpredictable outcomes of divergent perspectives coming together. This clashes with the demanding nature of all competitive and pressurised environments.

33 See: "How to Make It: James Dyson built a better vacuum. Can he pull off a second industrial revolution?" John Seabrook, The New Yorker, September 13, 2010, https://www.newyorker.com/magazine/2010/09/20/how-to-make-it; *"How James Dyson Makes the Ordinary Extraordinary,"* Shoshana Berger, Wired, November 19, 2012, https://www.wired.com/2012/11/mf-james-dyson/; "How we made the Dyson vacuum cleaner," Andrew Dickson, The Guardian, May 24, 2016, https://www.newyorker.com/magazine/2010/09/20/how-to-make-it.

34 "Interview with Sara Blakely," Guy Raz, NPR "How I Built This" podcast, July 3, 2017, https://www.npr.org/2017/08/15/534771839/spanx-sara-blakely.

3. THE 'WHO'S THE BOSS' TENSION

'Managers who do not understand people's different thinking styles cannot understand how the people working for them will handle different situations.' **Ray Dalio**

One of the things I love about being a product manager is the front row seat that you often get within a business. You will be involved in commercial and strategic aspects as well as technology and design. Product people repeatedly engage with a wide cross-section of people and disciplines, both inside and outside their businesses.

In the space of a typical working day you can have talks with the sales team, discuss a go-to market strategy with a marketeer or sit down with engineers to plan implementation. These are all 'stakeholders' that a product manager needs to engage with. Marty Cagan, an internationally renowned product management expert and author, lists the following stakeholder examples:[35]

- **The executive team** - The CEO and leaders of finance, marketing, sales and technology.
- **Sales and Marketing** - To make sure the product and the business are aligned.
- **Finance** - To make sure the product fits within the financial parameters and model of the company.
- **Legal** - To make sure that what you propose is defensible.
- **Compliance** - To make sure what you propose complies with any relevant standards or policies.
- **Operations** - To make sure that people at the front line of your business, e.g. working on the supply chain or in customer

35 "Stakeholder Management," Marty Cagan, Silicon Valley Product Group, April 30, 2013, https://svpg.com/stakeholder-management/.

support, know about your product or can work with it.
- **Business Development**- To make sure what you propose does not violate any existing contracts or relationships.

These people typically also bring their own approaches to problem solving and I strongly believe that cognitive diversity can contribute significantly to great products and high-performing teams. The downside of having such a rich diversity of views and approaches, however, is the risk of much 'noise' or 'analysis paralysis':

- **'Who makes the decisions around here?!'**- Think of the marketeer, the salesperson or the business owner all having a view on the product or how to solve a customer problem. It is plain to see how endless debates can ensue without ever reaching a decision.
- **'Can we please agree on an approach to solving the problem?'**- Similarly, if a problem has been agreed but there are a multitude of potential approaches to solving a problem, how do you identify the best approach quickly and efficiently?
- **'We're not all in the same place!'**- Especially when stakeholders are not collocated in the same place, communicating and collaborating effectively can be a thorny affair.

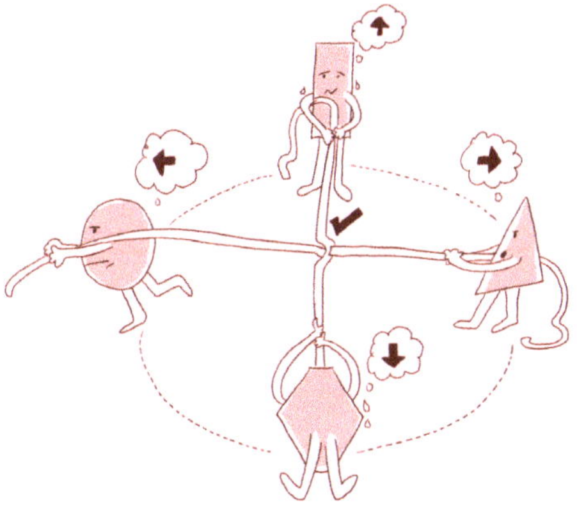

Product Management = Mind + Matter + **Moves**

MOVES

'If the path be beautiful, let us not ask where it leads.' **Anatole France**

Product Management = Mind + Matter + Moves

Three tensions caused by the **moves** when managing products:

- The **'Hold on To Your Seat'** tension.
- The **'I Love It When A Plan Comes Together'** tension.
- The **'You Can't Have It All'** tension.

1. THE 'HOLD ON TO YOUR SEAT' TENSION

'The only way to win is to learn faster than anyone else.' **Eric Ries**

Success is never guaranteed when you are developing a new product or iterating on an existing product. Unless you are a market leader or a monopolist, there are so many factors that determine product success. Will customers want the product, and pay for it? How about that pesky competitor that managed to get to market first? What about that new technology that we still know so little about? These are the kinds of factors that companies struggle to control and why product management is not a straightforward or linear process.

WAZE: THE UNEVEN PATH FROM A TINY STARTUP TO A $1 BILLION EXIT

If there only was a magic recipe or checklist with all the steps required to create a successful product ... A few years ago, I attended a lecture by an Israeli entrepreneur who told the story of the humble beginnings of a GPS navigation app, and all the mistakes he and his colleagues made in building their product. Uri Levine was the name of the entrepreneur and 'Waze' the name of the app, which was eventually sold to Google for a hefty $1 billion. From shifting focus to dealing with gnarly technology and scaling issues, Levine painted a vivid picture of the bumpy road travelled when building Waze.[36] *His story made me realise that there is no special blueprint for managing successful products. By contrast, managing products often feels more like playing a pinball machine, having to carefully navigate the multiple flippers within the machine.*

36 "Lessons learned from Uri Levine, Co-Founder of Waze," Marc Abraham, As I learn, May 14, 2017, https://marcabraham.com/2017/05/14/lessons-learned-from-uri-levine-co-founder-of-waze/.

Ever driven a car in the mountains? Going from curve to curve, without knowing what is around the next bend? That is what managing products often feels like. Successful product companies like Amazon have developed a knack for taking the mountainous curves as expeditiously as possible so that they can learn quickly what awaits around the other side of the mountain.[37] Amazon founder Jeff Bezos has said 'Our success at Amazon is a function of how many experiments we do per year, per month, per week, per day.'[38]

Learning early and often helps to minimise risk but can in turn create a huge amount of uncertainty and ambiguity. Product people will embrace this ambiguity; often out of choice or simply dictated by the circumstances they operate in. This appetite for uncertainty often conflicts with how the rest of the organisation functions. Hope Gurion, an experienced product leader and coach, pointed out to me that 'the way product works is so countercultural to how the rest of the organisation operates. Think about accounting and sales, for example, where things tend to be a lot more predictable and certain, whereas products are flying in the face of uncertainty.' Gurion went on to explain how product people often question or assume things will go wrong, 'with everybody else assuming that things will go right.'[39] Consider the scenario where we start an experiment or 'spike' a new technology, not having any certainty about outcomes of these experiments.[40] In a world where people are looking for certainty and predictability, the experimental nature of product management can introduce significant pressure.

---

37 "Product management at Amazon - What is it like?" Marc Abraham, As I learn, November 26, 2015, https://marcabraham.com/2014/11/26/product-management-at-amazon-what-is-it-like/.

38 "Why These Tech Companies Keep Running Thousands of Failed Experiments," Ben Clarke, Fast Company, September 21, 2016, https://www.fastcompany.com/3063846/why-these-tech-companies-keep-running-thousands-of-failed.

39 Hope Gurion, *interview by author*, Greenbrae, December 9, 2019.

40 "What's a spike, who should enter it and how to word it?" Andrew Fuqua, Leading Agile, September 13, 2016, https://www.leadingagile.com/2016/09/whats-a-spike-who-should-enter-it-how-to-word-it/.

2. THE 'I LOVE IT WHEN A PLAN COMES TOGETHER' TENSION

'In preparing for battle I have always found that plans are useless, but planning is indispensable.' **Dwight D. Eisenhower**

MY THINKING THAT PROJECTS WOULD MATERIALISE EXACTLY AS PLANNED ...

As I mentioned earlier, before I became a product manager, I used to work as a digital project manager. At the beginning I managed a lot of government projects, and I had to create project plans in Microsoft Project. Each time I put together such a plan for, let's say, the build of a website or an app, the world felt like a better and more certain place. In my project plans, things always happened according to plan within the set timeframes, seamless handovers between different teams, everything according to spec and all within a pre-agreed budget. Any project dependencies would be dealt with smoothly by the various people involved in executing the project ...

... sounds of breaking glass.

I have learned over the years, and the hard way, that working on technology projects or products does not follow a linear or predictable path. Plans are malleable or, as the quote by Fujio Cho, Chairman of Toyota Motor Company, goes: 'Plans are things that change'. These are just some of the things that I have seen go wrong when working on software products:

- **Unexpected complexity** - The underlying technology or workflows turn out to be way more complex than expected. As a result, thinking about, writing and testing software code takes longer than anticipated.
- **Altered scope** - We all say that we should not be doing it, but it still happens regardless: scope creep. Specific product features are agreed, often complemented with a list of things that are not in scope, upfront. As soon as we start working on a product, a request comes from left field, suggesting: 'wouldn't it be nice to have _____.'
- **Communication breakdown** - People responsible for different aspects of the product fail to communicate effectively with each other. The development process thus becomes a relay race where colleagues drop the baton in an effort to pass it on. Think, for instance, of the designer who has spent a lot of time designing an elaborate user interface, which the engineer then says cannot be implemented ...
- **Change in priorities** - Whilst the product team has committed to building a specific product or feature, a new commercial opportunity arises for the sales team and a revision of priorities is required. Or your biggest competitor has just launched a similar feature. This often means that teams have gone back to their product roadmaps to discuss whether it makes sense to deviate from the items on the roadmap.[41] This can generate significant friction if the organisation treats the roadmap as a set in stone plan, an artefact that promises certainty and predictability ...

41 See: "No more features on product roadmaps - Have themes or goals instead!" Marc Abraham, As I learn, October 1, 2015, https://marcabraham.com/2015/10/01/no-more-features-on-product-roadmaps-have-themes-or-goals-instead/; C. Todd Lombardo, Bruce McCarthy, Evan Ryan and Michael Connors, *Product Roadmaps Relaunched* (Sebastopol, CA: O'Reilly, 2018).

Managing products is an uncertain business. It is therefore an illusion to think (1) that we can fully control a successful execution of a plan and (2) that everything will go as planned. However, this does not make planning or roadmaps redundant; a product roadmap is a beneficial communication and collaboration tool, as long as we accept that we might have to deviate from what was initially planned.

3. THE 'YOU CAN'T HAVE IT ALL' TENSION

'A compromise is the art of dividing a cake in such a way that everyone believes he has the biggest piece.' **Ludwig Erhard**

A significant part of managing products comes down to successfully handling constraints and making tough trade-off decisions. As Brandon Chu, VP of Product & GM of Platform at Shopify, explains, 'product teams are constrained by the money, people, and time they have to launch a product.'[42] In project management this is referred to as the 'Iron Triangle', with its three angles occupied by cost, scope and time (See fig. 3).

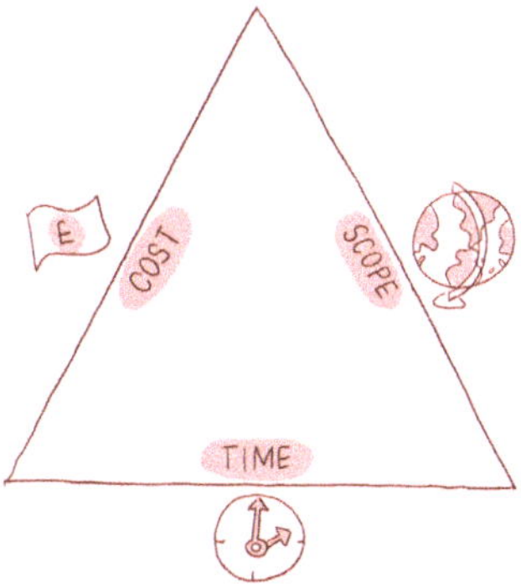

Fig. 3 – The 'Iron Triangle': constant trade-offs between cost, scope and time

42 "The First Principles of Product Management," Brandon Chu, The Black Box of Product Management, January 7, 2018, https://blackboxofpm.com/the-first-principles-of-product-management-ea0e2f2a018c.

However, when it comes to product management, teams can often have all three variables in play at one time, which continuously changes the shape of the triangle. Alex Watson, Head of Product at BBC News, says 'it is well known that if you fix two sides of a triangle, the third is what has to flex.'[43] Teams can thus be held back by all three of these constraints when working on a product, which means that you will have to compromise on cost, time and quality - sometimes one of these or all three at once - related to your product or business:[44]

People - This is often the biggest constraint, as most companies have a limited number of people that can work on a problem at a given time. It can, however, be made even worse in companies when teams lose focus as a result of switching their attention between various products.[45]John Medina, a Developmental Biologist, has studied the brain and our ability to multitask. Contrary to popular belief, he has found that our brains are not conditioned for multitasking, actually slowing us down and increasing errors by 50 percent.[46] Similarly, our instinct to simply throw more people at a problem has also proven to be inadequate, often causing delays to software projects, as it takes time for people to get up to speed and to manage communication overhead due to the increased number of people working on the same project.[47]

Cost - How much does it cost to develop a new product or to iterate

43 Alex Watson, *email to author*, December 21, 2019.

44 "Project Management: cost, time and quality, two best guesses and a phenomenon, it's time to accept other success criteria," Roger Atkinson, International Journal of Project Management, 1999, Vol. 17, No. 16, pp. 337-442.

45 "Making Trade-offs is Product Management," Wayne Greene, This Is Product Management podcast, Alpha, August 2018, https://www.thisisproductmanagement.com/episodes/making-tradeoffs/.

46 "Brain Rules: The brain cannot multitask," John Medina, March 16, 2008, http://brainrules.blogspot.com/2008/03/brain-cannot-multitask_16.html.

47 Frederick P. Brooks, Jr., The Mythical Man-Month: *Essays on Software Engineering (Boston:* Addison-Wesley Professional, 2nd Edition, August 12, 1995).

on an existing one? Typical cost components are (1) salaries to hire and pay the team (2) marketing and business development to drive the product's go-to-market strategy (3) operations to maintain a product and (4) operational and capital expenditure to enable teams to iterate on the product.

Timings - Given that time is a finite resource, you will have to make difficult decisions that will affect 'speed to market', i.e. how quickly a product or feature can be launched.[48] A team might be working on Product A, but is then asked to work on Product B. If the decision is made for the team to move its focus from Product A to B, the release timings of Product A will suffer as a result. This concept is called 'cost of delay' which can be calculated by taking the projected value of a product or feature, dividing it by the duration of its build. Businesses suck up the value of each product or feature until it and any items preceding it are delivered.[49]

Long-term vs short-term - Compromises can enable parties to achieve a desperately needed short-term 'win' that boosts morale, moves the business forward or simply generates badly needed revenue. These tend to be more short-term goals which can well be at odds with long-term business objectives.[50]Jo Wickremasinghe, Product Director at Zoopla and someone who has worked with and led numerous product development teams, describes the associated challenge for product managers and product development teams of

48 "4 Reasons Speed Is Everything in Business," Adam Fridman, Inc., July 5, 2015, https://www.inc.com/adam-fridman/4-reasons-speed-is-everything-in-business.html.

49 "My product management toolkit (21): Assessing opportunities," Marc Abraham, Medium, May 9, 2017, https://medium.com/@maa1/my-product-management-toolkit-21-assessing-opportunities-17f7f6343080; "Breaking down cost of delay: everything you need to know in a simple guide," Planview Leankit, https://leankit.com/learn/lean/cost-of-delay/.

50 "Leading Change: 3 Reasons Why Great Leaders Are Reluctant to Compromise," Aad Boot, LeadershipWatch, August 28, 2013, https://leadershipwatch-aadboot.com/2013/08/28/leading-change-3-key-reasons-why-great-leaders-are-reluctant-to-compromise-2/.

'being able to deliver against both short-term and longer term aims at the same time.'[51]

Competing customer demands - In an ideal world, we would develop products for all the people and build those features that make *all* our customers happy. Whether you work in a business-to-consumer ('B2C') or business-to-business ('B2B') environment, you will have to choose between often conflicting customer demands, simply because product resources are limited.[52]

New vs existing products - Think of it like going to the casino; as a company, which products do you place your chips on? Do you go all in on new products, or instead spread your bets between existing and new products? Not only is this important from a strategic perspective, it also determines how you allocate time, budget and people. The aforementioned Craig Strong shares how he has witnessed times where resentment surfaces between existing product teams and business units: 'the signal that these new products are the future, sends a signal to the other areas that they are the past.' Strong has seen the subsequent tension between product teams play out in pretty undesirable ways: 'I recall a time where I was in a very large tech company and I was working on the new innovative product. I heard many times from the main function in the business "that's never going to work" and off the back of that resources were limited and delayed. It thus created competition for resources or delays internally where integration was required.'[53]

51 Jo Wickremasinghe, *email to author*, January 2, 2020.

52 "Welcome to product management - a city of trade-offs ," Matthew Tse, UX Collective, April 16, 2018, https://uxdesign.cc/welcome-to-product-management-a-city-of-trade-offs-843c85a5212.

53 *Ibid 27.*

Product is a results business - At the end of the day, building and managing products is all about achieving results. For the customer and for the business. Even when we talk about creativity or building the unprecedented, both are geared towards realising specific results. Take the famous architect Frank Lloyd Wright, who when designing a house, would first conceive of the result that he wanted to create. As Wright stayed focused on the results he wanted to create, the 'how' of obtaining those results emerged organically, and only after the 'what' had been crystalised fully.[54] However, even determining product success can be a tense process. Hope Gurion explains that the friction here does not have to be a bad thing: 'This target setting creates healthy tension, because it requires critical thinking by all people involved. It fosters tension - healthy - around success criteria.'[55]

The very nature of product management is a true breeding ground for tension. Whether it is the often-uncomfortable marriage between humans and technology or the necessity to compromise, frustrations and frictions are innate to developing products.

CONCLUSION

Managing products is a strenuous business. There are three overarching factors responsible for this strain: the very nature of product management, the substance which makes up the product and the fact that people are involved in each aspect of building products. We need to acknowledge the existence and impact of these three factors before we can start thinking about how to best manage product tensions.

54 Robert Fritz, *The Path of Least Resistance: Learning to Become the Creative Force in Your Own Life* (Fawcett Columbine, revised edition, 1989, p. 69).

55 *Ibid 39.*

SUMMARY

How the very **nature of product management** lends itself to tension:

- Designing and building products is like an everlasting **tug of war**, with various forces pulling the rope in lots of different directions at the same time.
- There are three main forces that are constantly trying to pull the product into different, and often opposing, directions: the **mind** of the people involved with the product, the **matter** that the product is made of and the **moves** that people make in relation to the product.

The impact of the **mind** on the product:

- Disagreement and **friction** between the people involved with the product.
- The multiple, and often opposing, minds when **collaborating**.
- The **emotional triggers** that are sparked when managing products.

The impact of the **matter** on the product:

- Leaves little room for **ambiguity** or nuance when creating products.
- The substance of the product - e.g. software code or raw materials - puts constraints on human **creativity**.
- Multiple people working on the product matter cause friction and **'noise'**.

The impact of **moves** on the product:

- Products are surrounded by so much **uncertainty** that it is hard to predict things - as product managers we are walking an uneven path.
- Your moves in relation to the product will rarely go fully according to **plan**.
- The constant need for tough **trade-off decisions** causes a lot of tension.

CHAPTER 2.
KNOW YOUR TENSIONS!

'Every good story needs a conflict. Without conflict or tension, there's nowhere to go. All you have is a Hallmark card - something with a nice sentiment, but nothing that provokes real emotion.' **unknown**

Product Management = Mind + Matter + Moves

In this chapter we will explore:

- **Internal and external tensions** which affect your product and your management of it.
- **External tension** from moves primarily made by others; moves that we can't easily influence.
- **Internal tension** caused by us; from the friction that occurs when we collaborate to shareholders that 'pay to play'.
- How product companies **Pono**, **Airbnb** and **Twitter** managed external and internal tensions.

INTRODUCTION

Tension can come from anywhere and can rear its head in a myriad of ways. You and your team may be pursuing a common goal but can't agree on how to best achieve it. Or you may all be floundering without a clear shared goal, rushing off in different directions. In both examples, the tension is *internal* and originates from ourselves. In contrast, the pressure that you experience may be *external*: perhaps your direct competitor has been hugely successful lately, leaving you all scratching your heads, needing to respond but without any clear solution to fight back.

In the previous chapter we saw how the very essence of products and their management brings about friction. As someone closely involved in managing products you need to be fully aware of important frictions, how they originate and how you can make the most of them. If we build on our central premise that tensions are inherent and necessary to creating great products, we need to:

- Become attentive to the tensions related to ourselves, our products, teams, organisations, markets and customers.
- Figure out how and when tensions arise, distinguish between different tension types and their respective impacts.
- Understand their (potential) impact and work out how to best respond or optimise.

Let's start by having a look at two companies, Pono and Airbnb, which were set up to disrupt their respective markets, but which are now achieving radically different outcomes. Despite their contrasting fates, they had one major thing in common. They both suffered from external tension: pressures and constraints imposed on the business or the product by outside stakeholders. In the case of Pono, the major record labels were seen to be holding the product back, whilst in the case of Airbnb, local councils use their regulatory powers to constrain the expansion of homes in their areas.

External Tension = (Mind + Matter + Moves) x **<u>Others</u>**

PONO: NEIL YOUNG' S DREAM OF A BETTER LISTENING EXPERIENCE

'There are certain people that I would love to listen to, that I would love to actually hear, but I can't listen to them on MP3s or CDs, because as an artist, I know what's missing and I don't want to listen to that. It's always bothered me that people are stuck with that experience.'
Neil Young

Multi-platinum singer-songwriter Neil Young wanted to change the sound quality of recorded music dramatically. Despite being a hugely successful artist, Young couldn't help but be frustrated with the audio quality of CDs and MP3 audio files.[56] *He therefore introduced a yellow, Toblerone-shaped portable audio player called 'Pono', which means 'righteousness' in Hawaiian. His vision was to give consumers easy access to high-quality music recordings and banish poor quality audio.*

The idea for the Pono was shared with the world when Young showed an oddly shaped, yellow device to a slightly bemused David Letterman on his eponymous talk show.[57] *Apart from the device, Pono would comprise a music store with high-resolution recordings and a digital-to-*

56 "Neil Young Expands Pono Digital-To-Analog Music Service," Patrick Flanary, Rolling Stone, September 27, 2012, https://www.rollingstone.com/music/music-news/neil-young-expands-pono-digital-to-analog-music-service-126298/; "Neil Young's PonoMusic seeks to make high-quality audio portable," Melissa Locker, Fortune, April 7, 2014, http://fortune.com/2014/04/17/neil-youngs-ponomusic-seeks-to-make-high-quality-audio-portable/.

57 Neil Young on the "Late Show with David Letterman", September 27, 2012.

analogue conversion technology. It wasn't Young's intention to take on the established record industry. Instead, he was keen to work together with big record labels in improving the quality of recorded music. Young regarded the cause that underpinned Pono as a win-win situation for artists and consumers alike; the artists would allow their fans to hear studio-quality audio and music lovers would enjoy the music at the best imaginable quality.'[58]

I was working at a London-based digital music company when my boss told me enthusiastically about how he'd met Neil Young and driven around his Californian ranch talking about all things Pono. Up to that point I don't think that I'd ever seen my boss this excited; Pono was going to be the next big thing in digital music and he was convinced that we should make our catalogue of millions of digital tracks immediately available to Pono. My boss was confident that we could make things work from a technology point of view and that Neil Young would be able to get all the record labels on board.

To cut a long story short. Our company didn't end up making our music catalogue available to Pono, who went to a competitor instead (ironically, that competitor was eventually acquired by Apple). We investigated the various aspects of the opportunity thoroughly - implementation, commercial and operational - and ultimately decided it just wasn't viable to partner with them. The main rationale for this outcome was that we struggled to justify the work involved in the unknown innovation that was Pono over the ongoing focus on strengthening our existing value proposition.

Pono didn't turn the music industry on its head, nor did it topple Apple or Spotify. Instead, it sold 10,000 of its yellow music players

58 "R.I.P. Pono, Neil Young Kills Off His Digital Player," Roger Wink, Noise11, April 23, 2017, http://www.noise11.com/news/r-i-p-pono-neil-young-kills-off-his-digital-player-20170423.

after they went into production in 2015 and ended up shutting its online music store in 2016. In the four years after its unveiling Pono to the world, customer needs had evolved; people had moved away from having separate devices, rather using their smartphones to listen to music, and no longer bought records online, opting to stream music instead. Young later blamed the record labels for the demise of Pono, saying that 'They killed it by insisting on charging two to three times as much for the high-res files as for MP3s.'[59] Pointing his finger at the major record labels Young was convinced that they had continuously pressured his product by not cooperating, resulting in a product without (compelling) content. In other words, in Young's view the external stakeholders got the better of his product.

AIRBNB: HOW THREE PEOPLE DISRUPTED THE HOTEL INDUSTRY

'I want to challenge the status quo, but in a way that's constructive.'
Brian Chesky

airbnb

59 "Neil Young fights for quality streaming with career-spanning online archive," Randy Lewis, Los Angeles Times, February 14, 2018, https://www.latimes.com/entertainment/music/la-et-ms-neil-young-archives-online-20180214-story.html.

Much like Neil Young with Pono, Brian Chesky and his co-founders Joe Gebbia and Nathan Blecharczyk started Airbnb with the view of disrupting the status quo. Their target was the hotel industry, giving people alternative lodging options.[60] *Like most startups, Airbnb's success story didn't follow a linear path; the founders started with renting out three air mattresses back in 2007, creating a website that got little traction before launching a shared accommodation proposition in 2008.*[61] *Around 2009, Airbnb changed its target from shared accommodation to enabling users to book all types of accommodation through its platform.*[62]

Fast forward a few years and Airbnb hits a rapid growth trajectory around 2011, when it reaches its 1 millionth booking mark, before climbing to 10 million bookings by June 2012.[63] *The result of this was that Airbnb's founders exchanged one tension - getting traction - for another - legal problems - as Airbnb have increasingly found themselves stuck in a protracted legal wrangling with local councils in large metropolitan areas who blame Airbnb for increasing short-term lets and driving up rents.*[64]

60 "Airbnb CEO has a vision of a future where everyone shares - and Airbnb collects a modest fee," Dennis Schaal, Skift, November 16, 2012, https://www.wsj.com/articles/brian-chesky-the-8216sharing-economy8217-and-its-enemies-1390003096; "Brian Chesky, The 'Sharing Economy and Its Enemies," Andy Kessler, Wall Street Journal, January 17, 2014, https://www.wsj.com/articles/brian-chesky-the-8216sharing-economy8217-and-its-enemies-1390003096.

61 "How Airbnb Started – Infographic," Anna Vital, April 10, 2014, https://blog.adioma.com/how-airbnb-started-infographic/; "The Airbnb Founder Story: From Selling Cereals To A $25B Company," Jasper Ribbers, September 18, 2015, https://getpaidforyourpad.com/blog/the-airbnb-founder-story/.

62 "The Story No One Believed," Brian Chesky, Talk, Khosla Ventures, May 17, 2014, https://www.youtube.com/watch?time_continue=140&v=1bAT44QPPHw.

63 *Ibid 61.*

64 "Airbnb's legal troubles: what are the issues?" Will Coldwell, The Guardian, July 8, 2014, https://www.theguardian.com/travel/2014/jul/08/airbnb-legal-troubles-what-are-the-issues; "What you need to know about Airbnb's legal challenges," Jennifer Williams-Alvarez, Engadget, November 11, 2014, https://www.engadget.com/2014/11/11/airbnb-legal-explainer/; "Unwelcome guests: Airbnb, cities battle over illegal short-term rentals," Scott Zamost, CNBC, May 24, 2018, https://www.cnbc.com/2018/05/23/unwelcome-guests-airbnb-cities-battle-over-illegal-short-term-rentals.html.

The story of Airbnb perfectly illustrates my previous point that even great innovation comes with tension. As philosopher and scholar Nassim Taleb argues - to innovate, you need to get into trouble first.[65]

Despite the stark difference in outcomes, the stories of Pono and Airbnb have one thing in common: external tension. This is the pressure caused by the minds and moves of others. In the case of Pono, I witnessed first-hand how the major record labels didn't want to play ball with Neil Young and his ambitious dreams. With Airbnb, their growth has been hampered by pushback from regulators who view them as the culprit behind a rapid rise in short-term lets and rents that locals can no longer afford.

In the remainder of this section we will do a deep dive into the different ways in which external tension can manifest itself with respect to our businesses and the products that we manage.

External Tension = (Mind + Matter + Moves) x Others

How can **external tensions** interfere with our products?

1. **Uncontrollable circumstances**; think pandemics and natural disasters.
2. We can review and learn from them, but we can't influence **competitor moves**.
3. Moves made by others that we can't control and have to **comply** with.

65 Nassim Nicholas Taleb, *Antifragile: Things that Gain from Disorder* (London: Penguin Books, 2012, p. 41).

External tensions are those pressures that, as the name suggests, come from outside your organisation, team or product. Specific events, competitors, regulators, customers and shareholders are the most common sources of external tension. These pressures are typically hard to influence and manage; they sit outside our sphere of influence. In this section, I'll look at the nature of each of these external tensions and how they manifest themselves throughout the product life cycle.

1. THE 'BEYOND MY CONTROL' TENSION

'We cannot choose our external circumstances, but we can always choose how we respond to them.' **Epictetus**

At the time of writing this book, the world has been severely hit by a global outbreak of the COVID-19 pandemic or 'Coronavirus'. Thus far, there have been millions of cases confirmed globally of people falling ill with the virus, and an extraordinarily high death toll. The pandemic has affected people, businesses and institutions right across the world. From people having to work remotely, to factories or schools being shut, the virus poses an external tension which affects us all. Businesses are equally affected. Airbnb, for instance, has already had to pay out $250m in compensation to its hosts, making up for 2.5 months' worth of cancelled reservations due to the Coronavirus pandemic. The company then had to lay off about 1,900 employees, amounting to about 25 percent of its workforce.[66]

66 "Airbnb to pay $250m to hosts losing out to Covid-19 cancellations," Margi Murphy, The Telegraph, March 31, 2020, https://www.telegraph.co.uk/technology/2020/03/31/airbnb-pay-250m-hosts-losing-covid-19-cancellations/; "Airbnb drops valuation target 16% to $26b," Dave Lee, Financial Times, April 4, 2020, https://www.ft.com/content/02a-8ca9b-1ba9-4e0a-a3d5-084dd93469bb; "A Message from Co-Founder and CEO Brian Chesky," Airbnb, May 5, 2020, https://news.airbnb.com/a-message-from-co-founder-and-ceo-brian-chesky/; "Brian Chesky: These 9 weeks were the most stressful in my life", Recode Decode podcast with Kara Swisher, May 22, 2020, https://www.stitcher.com/podcast/vox/recode-decode/e/69855876.

Other similar examples of force majeure events with huge ramifications include Hurricane Katrina in 2005, the 2004 Indian Ocean tsunami and the financial crisis in 2008. These are external events that - depending on their reach - can significantly impact resources, supply chains, markets, and people. And ultimately leave their mark on businesses and products. The reality of the nature and scale of such events is that it is nigh on impossible to fully plan for such crisis scenarios, and in most cases our actions are likely to be reactive at best.[67]

2. THE 'KEEPING UP WITH THE JONESES' TENSION

'The problem with competition is that it takes away the requirement to set your own path, to invent your own method, to find a new way.'
Seth Godin

WHEN I WOKE UP TO PANICKED MESSAGES FROM MY CEO ...

It was 6am and I'd just made the mistake of opening my work email on my phone ... Quickly scrolling through all the new emails I'd received overnight, my eye caught a message from my CEO, sent at 3am and marked as 'urgent'. 'Marc, ______ (our biggest competitor in the US at the time) has just launched a mood-based recommendations feature. We should do something similar! Didn't we talk about this before? Can you please get the team all over this tomorrow morning?' When I turned on my phone, text messages from numerous colleagues who had clearly received a similar email overnight started pinging about this new feature that

67 See: "Enhancing horizon scanning by utilizing pre-developed scenarios: Analysis of current practice and specification of a process improvement to aid the identification of important 'weak signals," Emily Rowe, George Wright and James Derbyshire, Technical Forecasting and Social Change, December 1, 2017; "Planning for uncertainty," The Bottom Line, BBC Radio 4, March 30, 2019, https://www.bbc.co.uk/programmes/m0003jsm.

we now needed to build...

I don't know whether you've ever found yourself in a similar situation, but it is easy to see where knee-jerk reactions to competitors' actions come from. At the time, I made the mistake of brushing off my CEO's message as just another attempt to influence our product roadmap, but I've since learned to take competitive pressures a lot more seriously. This does not mean that you have to slavishly copy everything your competitor does, but at least understand the nature, scale and potential impact of competitive threats.[68] Going back to Michael Porter's Five Forces, competitive threats can be perceived in any of the following ways: [69]

- The *industry* jockeying for positioning among current competitors.
- Bargaining power of *customers.*
- Threat of *substitute products / services.*
- Bargaining power of *suppliers.*
- Threat of new *entrants.*

Given the sudden competitive impact of so-called 'big bang disruptors' - those companies or products obtaining market dominance seemingly out of nowhere - it is plain to see why businesses always need to be on the front foot.[70] Like boxers, we always need to be aware of competitors and try to anticipate their and *our* next move (See fig. 4). Today's businesses are required to excel both at exploiting their

68 "The Relation between Competitive Tension and Strategic Innovation," Ertan Gündüz and Fatih Semerciöz, Procedia - Social and Behavioral Sciences, October 2012, 58, pp. 29-39, https://www.researchgate.net/publication/257717360_The_Relation_between_Competitive_Tension_and_Strategic_Innovation; "Real Competitive Analysis is About Learning to Love Your Competitor," Chris Butler, September 6, 2017, https://medium.com/pminsider/real-competitive-analysis-is-about-learning-to-love-your-competitor-15e45b9ef10a.

69 "How Competitive Forces Shape Strategy," Michael Porter, Harvard Business Review, March 1979, https://hbr.org/1979/03/how-competitive-forces-shape-strategy.

70 "Book Review: Big Bang Disruption," Marc Abraham, As I learn, April 13, 2015, https://marcabraham.com/2015/04/13/book-review-big-bang-disruption/.

existing products to enable incremental improvement and exploring new, emerging opportunities for radical innovation.[71]

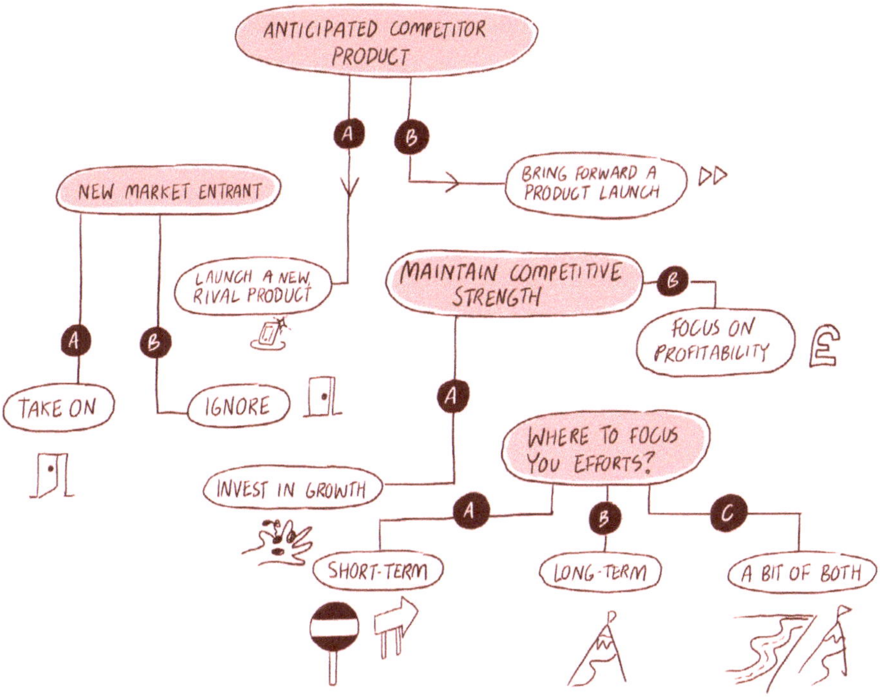

Fig. 4 – What are our competitors doing and how do we respond?

Unless your company holds a strong monopoly, has a first mover advantage or is in an industry with high barriers to entry, you can't afford to simply ignore competitive strains. It is worth taking a leaf out of the book of Hiten Shah, co-founder of analytics company

71 "Managing the Right Tension" Dominic Dodd and Ken Favaro, Harvard Business Review, December 2006, https://hbr.org/2006/12/managing-the-right-tension; "Exploitation Exploration Tensions and Organizational Ambidexterity," Constantine Andriopoulos and Marianne Lewis, Organization Science, August 2009, https://www.researchgate.net/profile/Constantine_Andriopoulos/publication/220520931_Exploitation-Exploration_Tensions_and_Organizational_Ambidexterity_Managing_Paradoxes_of_Innovation/links/55791ea108ae752158703fa4/Exploitation-Exploration-Tensions-and-Organizational-Ambidexterity-Managing-Paradoxes-of-Innovation.pdf

'KISSmetrics' who admitted to having made a 'Billion Dollar Mistake'.[72] Shah explains how at KISSmetrics they ignored competitors 'instead of learning from their moves to evolve our market hypothesis.' As a result, Shah and his co-founder missed out on crucial information because, 'instead of looking at competitors to understand our customers better, we completely ignored them.'[73] By not paying any attention to competitors, KISSmetrics missed out on evolving customer needs and emerging market opportunities. The trick is therefore to find the right balance between a company following its own direction whilst paying a healthy amount of attention to its competitive landscape.

3. THE ' COMPLIANCE TRUMPS EVERYTHING' TENSION

'If you think compliance is expensive - try non-compliance.' **Paul McNulty**

There is another external actor, the regulator, who can place a serious burden on companies. Depending on the remit of the lawmaker, rules or decrees issued are likely to affect business, its people, products and service. Non-compliance with such laws will be severely penalised and herein lies the tension: does any commercial gain outweigh the risk of non-compliance? In purely financial terms: what is the cost of compliance compared to the money generated from violating the law?

Think for instance when all businesses with a presence in the European Union were obliged to comply with General Data Protection Law ('GDPR') which came into effect in May 2018.[74] GDPR presented an external tension for organisations to reckon with: the loss of a

72 "My Billion Dollar Mistake," Hiten Shah, Product Habits Blog, 2019, https://producthabits.com/my-billion-dollar-mistake/.

73 *Ibid 72.*

74 https://gdpr.eu/.

significant number of contactable consumers as well as a hefty fine incurred in the event of a breach of GDPR rules. A recent global survey among 1,100 businesses found that only one third of companies were responding to customer requests regarding their personal data within the mandatory GDPR timeframe.[75]

Consider the challenge of managing products in highly regulated environments like banking, bioscience and pharmaceutics. Products in these industries are tightly governed by detailed regulation and supervisory bodies. The risks in these areas tend to be very high due to the nature of the customer problems their products aim to solve. The simplest mistake made during the process of creating a new drug can affect many human lives, and we don't have to look back that far to see the impact of under-regulated banks.[76]

The pharmaceutical industry forms a clear case in point here; it takes on average at least ten years for a new drug to be launched to market. In the US, clinical drug trials with a select number of volunteers can take a good six to seven years, after which a drug can still fall short at the US Food and Drug Administration review stage.[77] 'See it as an extra constraint to add to the equation', Mat Tylicki explained to me.[78] Tylicki is a product manager at London-based Kheiron Medical and has worked on numerous healthcare products. He mentioned the need for a pre-agreed validation protocol before kicking off a 'full

75 "Businesses struggling with GDPR compliance," Emanuela Hawker, AccountancyAge, November 27, 2018, https://www.accountancyage.com/businesses-struggling-with-gdpr-compliance/.

76 "Risk management in the development of new products in highly regulated industries," Gary Blau, Bharat Mehtra, Shantanu Bose, Joe Pekny, Gavin Sinclair, Kay Keunken and Paul Bunch, Computers & Chemical Engineering, July 15, 2001, Vol. 24, Issues 2-7, pp. 659-664, https://www.sciencedirect.com/science/article/pii/S0098135400003884.

77 "Drug and Biologic Approval and IND Activity Reports," FDA, October 23, 2017, https://www.fda.gov/drugs/how-drugs-are-developed-and-approved/drug-and-biologic-approval-and-ind-activity-reports; "Biopharmaceutical Research & Development: The Process Behind New Medicines," PhRMA, 2015, http://phrma-docs.phrma.org/sites/default/files/pdf/rd_brochure_022307.pdf.

78 Mat Tylicki, *interview by author*, London, July 23, 2019.

blown clinical trial' in order to receive regulatory approval. 'Only then you can start selling your product to customers. It is key to engage regulatory teams early and often in the discovery process. A single feature could increase the regulatory class of your product, adding significant complexity and expanding timelines.'[79]

From talking to Tylicki, it quickly becomes apparent how for him, designing a user interface or conducting product discovery is heavily regulated and has a major impact on ways of working. 'The requirements from the FDA, the International Organisation for Standardisation (ISO) and our own internal quality management system come on top of the day-to-day challenges inherent to product management' Tylicki concluded.[80]

If we take these kinds of regulatory pressure and mix them with the 'Tell Me What to Do' tension inherent in technology as well as the 'Knitting Spaghetti' tensions that humans bring, managing products gets exponentially more complex and filled with friction. This friction becomes even more apparent, when you realise that these complexities have been introduced by regulators or compliance bodies, which makes them unmovable targets for product people.

Internal Tension = (Mind + Matter + Moves) x **Us**

'Push the envelope, don't tear it.' **Rob Minkoff**

Whereas external tensions sit, as we have seen, outside our sphere of influence, internal tensions emanate from within our businesses, teams and our own heads and can have an equally serious effect on our products and their value.

79 *Ibid 78.*
80 *Ibid 78.*

Internal Tension = (Mind + Matter + Moves) x Us

How can **internal tensions** interfere with our products?

1. People become divided over the different challenges, opportunities and trade-offs that a **product life cycle** can pose.
2. When people are assigned to work together but struggle to **collaborate**.
3. **Shareholders** raise their voice with respect to the product.

1. THE 'TUG OF WAR' TENSION

'Good companies manage Engineering. Great companies manage Product.' **Thomas Schranz**

Product life cycles are laddered with internal tension; those strains that manifest themselves within teams, between colleagues and even within individuals. If you think about the stages of the traditional product life cycle from inception to retirement, we can map these states to corresponding self-imposed pressures (See fig. 5):[81]

81 *Ibid 3.*

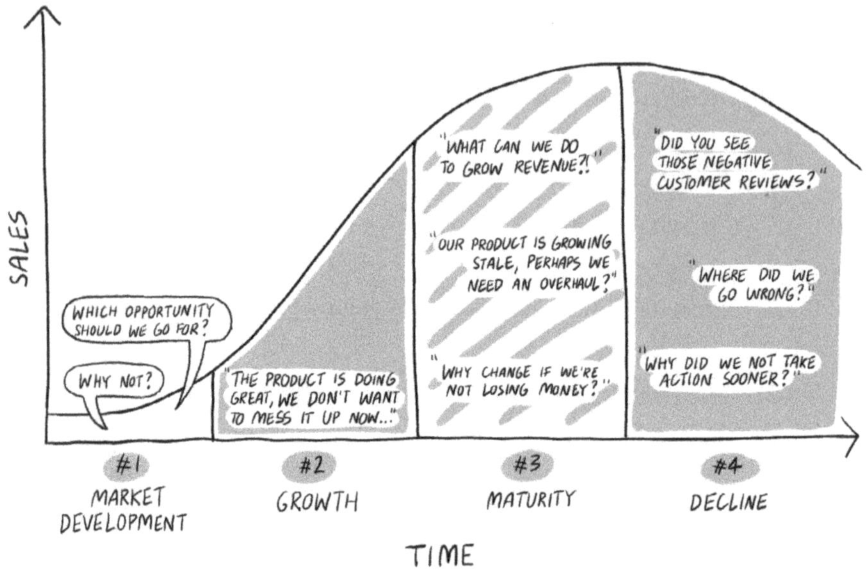

Fig. 5 – Common strains and trade-offs throughout the product life cycle

Market Development - 'Which opportunity should we go for?' 'Why (not)?!' 'My product idea is better than yours!' 'But my product idea will make more money than yours!' 'OK, but your neck is on the block if this product fails ...'

Growth - 'The product is doing great, we don't want to mess it up now' 'I understand why you want to make changes to the product, but the CEO does not want to rock the boat now that we're making money.' 'Yes, I know it feels like a bespoke product for one client, but trust me, it will be worth it ...'

Maturity - 'What can we do to grow revenue?' 'Our product is growing stale, perhaps we need a complete overhaul?' 'Why change things whilst we're not losing money?!' 'There's no alignment about how to move the product forward ...'

Decline - 'Did you see all those negative customer reviews?!' 'Where did we go wrong?' 'Did you see the new feature just launched by [name any competitor here]?' 'Why did we not take action sooner, now it feels like it's too late ...'

The impact of such life cycle tensions is even more intense if your product turns out to be a so-called 'big bang disruption'; an experiment that has gone very well and shown unconstrained, rapid growth (See fig. 6).[82] Whilst scaling a product or an organisation can be exhilarating - as people working at 'hypergrowth' startups can attest - it will also surface a number of internal tensions within a short space of time.[83]

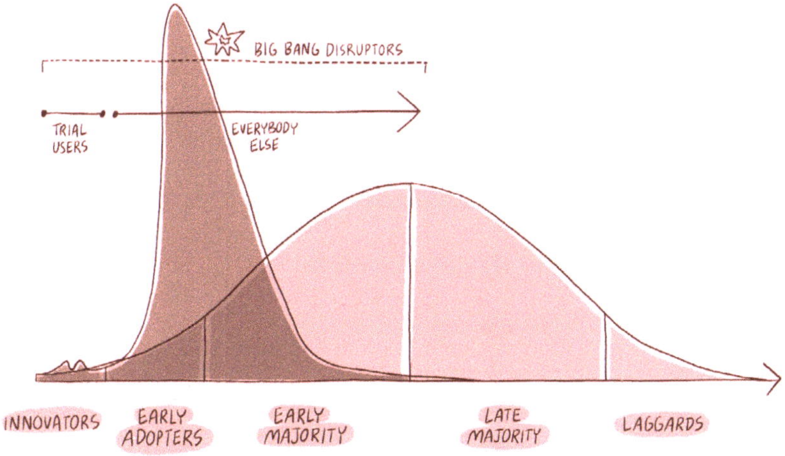

Fig. 6 – Big bang disruptions come (and go) hard and fast

When products turn out to be huge success stories, we rave about them and laud the people who created them. Think back to 2007 when Steve Jobs proudly announced the Apple iPhone to the world and forever changed the way we communicate and interact with digital content.[84]

---

82 Larry Downes and Paul Nunes, *Big Bang Disruption: Strategy in the age of Devastating Innovation* (New York: Portfolio / Penguin, January 2014).

83 See for example: "Managing Hypergrowth," Alexander V. Izosimov, Harvard Business Review, April 2008; https://hbr.org/2008/04/managing-hypergrowth; "When Culture Became a Competitive Advantage at LinkedIn," Steve Cadigan, October 24, 2014, https://www.inc.com/steve-cadigan/when-culture-became-our-competitive-advantage.html; "How I Survived Insane Hypergrowth at Airbnb,"Jonathan Golden, NEA, June 7, 2019, https://www.nea.com/blog/how-i-survived-insane-hypergrowth-at-airbnb.

84 "Apple's six defining products - in pictures," Samuel Gibbs, The Guardian, August 2, 2018, https://www.theguardian.com/technology/gallery/2018/aug/02/apples-six-defining-products-in-pictures.

We, however, tend to turn much less of a spotlight on those products that fail. How about the frustrations, battles or politics involved in those products whose life cycles terminate prematurely or don't get off the starting blocks in the first place? How about 'Ping', for example, launched as a social network for music and an Apple product that lasted for no more than two years, disappearing without so much as a whimper in the social media landscape.[85]

However long or short, the product life cycle is riddled with self-imposed pressures. Growing a product comes with exciting moments, tough tests and everything in between. And that is just the product; how about the burden that collaboration between people introduces?

2. THE 'DYSFUNCTIONAL FAMILY' TENSION

'Alone we can do so little; together we can do so much.' **Helen Keller**

85 "Apple's 12 Biggest Product Flops of All Time," Brad Moon, Kiplinger, February 13, 2019, https://www.kiplinger.com/slideshow/investing/T058-S001-apple-s-12-biggest-flops-of-all-time/index.html.

'Collaboration' and 'cross-functional' are right up there as my favourite words with respect to product management. The dictionary describes collaboration as 'the action of working with someone to produce something.'[86] Organisations will have groups of people working together for a common purpose, achieving a benefit for the business and its customers. At the same time, however, we are now familiar with the 'dysfunctional family' which I mentioned in the first chapter of this book: the tension which raises its head when people struggle to collaborate with each other. While I believe strongly in the value of cross-functional teams, they can also prove to be a recipe for disagreement and discontent ...

Cross-functional teams bundle a range of people and disciplines together. For example, a tight knit unit of software engineers, designers, product and marketing people working together to create a new product or service. If you are a software engineer, collaboration is likely to be your daily bread and butter: 'pairing' is the practice whereby two engineers work off a single computer, or 'mob programming' where a group of engineers will huddle behind a single computer.[87]

In the previous chapter, we have seen some of the benefits of collaboration as well as what happens when teamwork turns sour. When company leaders initiate cross-group initiatives, they often overlook whether the people they require to work together actually get along or work effectively together. People can erect all kinds of barriers to collaboration and sabotage teamwork, purely because they feel threatened.[88]

Collaboration issues aren't merely the result of wilful damage by people who are supposed to work together; often the different characters of the people involved can put a spanner in the works. In fig. 7 I have

86 "Collaboration", *English Oxford Living Dictionaries*, https://www.lexico.com/en/english (accessed June 3, 2019).

87 "What on earth is mob programming?!" Marc Abraham, As I learn, February 5, 2014, https://marcabraham.com/2014/02/05/what-on-earth-is-mob-programming/.

88 *Ibid 14*.

highlighted some of the common barriers to collaboration:[89]

Fig. 7 – Typical barriers to collaboration, their manifestations and ways to overcome them

89 See also: "Michael Schrage and Collaboration," Steve R. Hardin, Bulletin of the American Society for Information Science, August / September 1998, https://onlinelibrary.wiley.com/doi/pdf/10.1002/bult.99; "Boundaries Need Not Be Barriers: Leading Collaboration among Groups in Decentralised Organizations," Heather M. Caruso, Todd Rogers and Max H. Bazerman, 2007; "Are You a Collaborative Leader?" Morten Hansen, August 1, 2011, https://www.mortenhansen.com/are-you-a-collaborative-leader/; https://www.hbs.edu/faculty/Publication%20Files/07-090.pdf; "Overcoming Common Barriers to Collaboration, Part 1," Pabini Gabriel-Petit, , UXmatters, October 9, 2017, https://www.uxmatters.com/mt/archives/2017/10/overcoming-common-barriers-to-collaboration-part-1.php; "Cross-functional collaboration: why we struggle with it and what to do," Jessie Beck, Asana blog, November 17, 2017, https://blog.asana.com/2017/11/cross-functional-collaboration/; "Overcoming Common Barriers to Collaboration, Part 2," Pabini Gabriel-Petit, UXmatters, November 20, 2017, https://www.uxmatters.com/mt/archives/2017/11/overcoming-common-barriers-to-collaboration-part-2.php; "Collaboration Barriers Across Organization Units," Ann Augustine, Lifewire, June 24, 2019, https://www.lifewire.com/collaboration-barriers-across-organization-units-771498.

A lack of respect and trust - 'I feel like my engineers are ganging up on me' is something I have heard fellow product managers say more than once. A (perceived) lack of respect and trust acts like a dam and is a prime catalyst for frustration and anxiety.

My advice is to simply start by sitting together with your engineers or taking part in (virtual) team meetings and ceremonies. This helps to establish both trust and empathy between the people working together. Acknowledge and recognise people's contributions in a genuine manner. Putting an extra spotlight on the team, for instance, when releasing a feature is important for team morale or when it has been a challenge to get something out to market.

People not understanding each other - When assembling cross-functional teams, people with different characters or mindsets might need to go through a period of 'forming–storming–norming–performing' to iron out any misunderstandings or differences of opinion.[90] I have seen teams combining highly creative people, 'creators', with others who are great at making other people's ideas happen, 'editors'. Whilst this combination can be very powerful, it can also create a lot of initial misunderstanding or frustration. 'They just come up with a great idea without considering whether it is even feasible' or 'They are so focused on execution; they shoot every good idea down!' are good examples of this initial frustration.

Involving engineers and stakeholders in product discovery early and often is a great way of dealing with this issue, creating a shared sense of understanding the customer and the problem to solve. 'How might we?' is a powerful question to ask throughout the process of understanding the problem and coming up with solutions. It is important to always tease out underlying assumptions or perceptions, asking respectfully, for instance, why the other doesn't feel that something is their responsibility.

90 "Developmental sequence in small groups," Bruce W. Tuckman, Psychological Bulletin, 1965, 63 (6): 384–399, https://www.ncbi.nlm.nih.gov/pubmed/14314073.

Wanting to 'get one over' someone else - A sense of internal competition that is unhealthy, caused by people wanting to win at all cost, and all the time. Sometimes this competition will be caused by misplaced incentive structures, promotion schemes or the very culture of the organisation. Other times, rivalry comes from responsibilities being ill defined, with different departments or roles overlapping.

Shared goals and results pave the way for shared accountability, followed by collective conversations about roles and responsibilities in view of team goals. Whilst it may seem obvious, a shared mission or set of objectives will reduce internal competition and make it easier to figure out how teams and the individuals within then can best contribute to achieving shared goals.

Working (and communicating) in silos - I used to think that working in silos is a phenomenon exclusive to large companies. Working in startups I then experienced first-hand how the 'not invented here' syndrome can occur just as much in smaller environments. As a result of these silos, knowledge and expertise isn't shared across the organisation, thus hampering effective collaboration.

To try and avoid silos, I highly recommend facilitating regular conversations between team members, ad hoc or more organised. These conversations will help in creating full transparency about e.g. progress, responsibilities and any outstanding issues or blockers.

3. THE 'PAY TO PLAY' TENSION

'Shareholder value is a result, not a strategy ... Your main constituencies are your employees, your customers and your products.' **Jack Welch**

Contributing to board decks or shareholder reports are possibly not the main reason for wanting to become a product person. However, when you join a mature or listed company, you are likely to be exposed to the squeeze put on the company by its board of directors representing the interests of the shareholders. You'll have no choice but to try and manage these strains as best as you can.[91]

No matter its size or previous track record, no company escapes the critical eye of its shareholders, with even Google proving this point recently.[92] Investors will above all want to see the value of their shareholding increase steadily and will come into action as soon as they see a decrease in the value of their stake (See fig. 8). Take the example of Twitter, with its investor Chris Sacca going as far as dishing out free advice on how to best improve the Twitter product, arguing back in 2015 that Twitter would be able to continue its user growth if it could:[93]

1. Make Tweets effortless to enjoy,
2. Make it easier for all to participate, and
3. Make each of us on Twitter feel heard and valuable.

Ultimately, this pressure resulted in Dick Costolo, Twitter's CEO, having to resign.[94] Fast forward to 2020 where current CEO and co-founder Jack Dorsey is under large pressure by activist shareholder Elliott Management who, among other things, have a problem with Dorsey acting as CEO of two publicly listed companies in Twitter and Square respectively.[95] Whereas shareholders and investors might have been more passive in the past, the recent rise of shareholder

91 "A Product Manager's guide to managing upwards," Paul Jackson, Product Management Insider, July 23, 2015, https://medium.com/pminsider/a-product-manager-s-guide-to-managing-upwards-3c3039c5af31.

92 "Shareholders pressure Google executives after scandalous year," Margi Murphy, The Telegraph, June 17, 2019, https://www.telegraph.co.uk/technology/2019/06/17/shareholders-pressure-google-executives-scandalous-year/.

93 "What Twitter Can Be," Chris Sacca, Lowercase Capital, June 3, 2015, https://lowercasecapital.com/2015/06/03/what-twitter-can-be-2/.

94 "Twitter's Costolo Years: An Annal of Missed Opportunities," Robinson Meyer, The Atlantic, June 11, 2015, https://www.theatlantic.com/technology/archive/2015/06/dick-costolo-twitter-ceo-resigns/395705/.

95 "Singer's Elliott Seeks to Replace Twitter CEO Dorsey," Scott Deveau and Ed Hammond, Bloomberg, February 29, 2020, https://www.bloomberg.com/news/articles/2020-02-29/singer-s-elliott-is-said-to-seek-to-replace-twitter-ceo-dorsey; Casey Newton, "Jack Dorsey is in for the fight of his life", The Verge, March 4, 2020, https://www.theverge.com/interface/2020/3/4/21163146/jack-dorsey-activist-investor-paul-singer-elliott-management.

activism has changed that dramatically. Whether it's being vocal at a shareholder meeting or linking with other (influential) stakeholders, company investors are in a strong position to - directly or indirectly - put pressure on all the people in the company and influence its (product) strategy.[96]

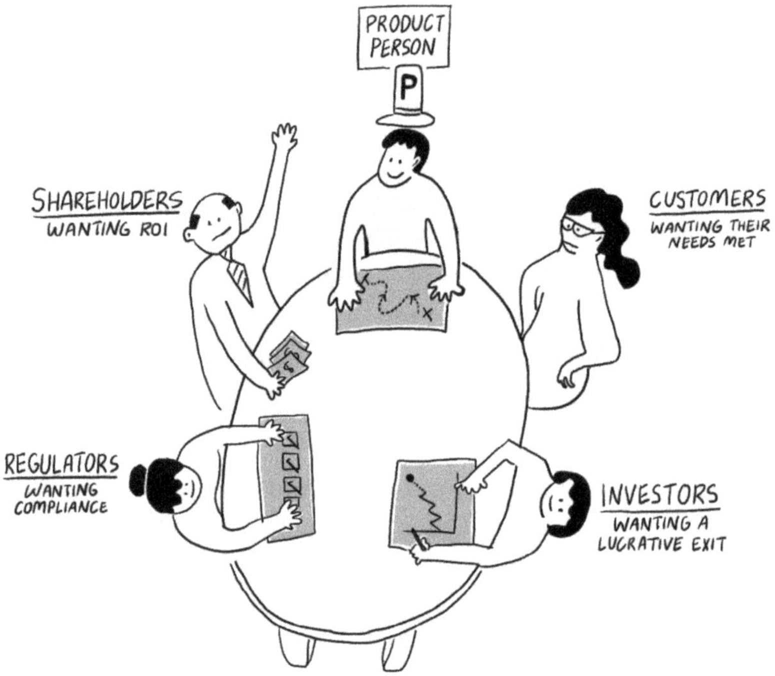

Fig. 8 – The 'Pay to Play' tension in action

96 Jeff Gramm, Dear Chairman: Boardroom Battles and the Rise of Shareholder Activism (HarperCollins, February 2015).

CONCLUSION

Tension is everywhere when managing products. We need to be mindful of the nature of tensions and how they emanate - the pressures that originate externally and those that come from within. Regulators can be a source of external pressure whereas organisational silos can constrain things internally. It is surprising how frequently we make things more difficult for ourselves and our products! Understanding the origin and types of tension will help you gain perspective on the impact of the different tensions, and whether they will strengthen or derail your product. This is something which we will examine closely in the next chapter.

SUMMARY

We encounter two main types of tension when managing products:

- **External tension** - Caused by people or circumstances that we are unable to influence.
- **Internal tension** - Caused by us, with more opportunity for influence.

Pono ultimately succumbed to external tension by the record labels, whilst **Airbnb** continues to battle local regulators. By comparison, **Twitter** CEOs have historically had to contend with vocal and influential shareholders.

Moves made by **others** outside our sphere of influence that cause tension:

- The global outbreak of the Coronavirus is a prime example of an external **circumstance** with significant impact on businesses and their products.
- We can review and learn from their decisions or actions, but we can't control **competitor moves.**
- **Compliance** with rules and regulations trumps everything you want your business or product to do.

Moves made by **us** that cause tension:

- When we get divided over the multiple challenges, opportunities and trade-offs during the **product life cycle.**
- Our product not getting launched or being of a suboptimal quality due to our internal struggles to **collaborate.**
- Battling **shareholders** with strong views on the direction of our business or product.

CHAPTER 3.
THE ROLE AND IMPACT OF TENSION ON MANAGING PRODUCTS

'It ain't about how hard you can hit. It's about how hard you can get hit and keep moving forward.' **Rocky Balboa**

Product Management = Mind + Matter + Moves

In this chapter we will explore:

- The **role and impact** of tension with respect to product management.
- **Compaq vs Apple:** contrasting responses to tension and its impact.
- **Healthy vs unhealthy tension:** the role of tension and how to manage the 'Balancing Act' tension and the 'Walk the Plank' tension.
- **Moves** you can make in response to tension, from 'blocking' to 'leaning in'.

INTRODUCTION

I feel this is the appropriate point in the book to make a confession: I don't like tension. I enjoy being organised, having a sense of control. Tension changes all that. Whether pressure is internal or external, you might feel like you have abandoned the driver's seat, and instead find yourself strapped into a bumper-car, unable to get out. It raises the question about the impact of any form of pressure or ambiguity on product management and how to best engage with such impact.

Whilst I'll take a look at the difference between 'healthy' and 'unhealthy' tension, I believe that as product people we will benefit more from understanding the different ways of dealing with it, and the pros and cons of different responses to the pressures we encounter. We will therefore study five different modes of responding, borrowed from the boxing world, enabling you to pick a stance that works best for you.

GROWTH OR EXTINCTION: HOW DO YOU AND YOUR PRODUCT SURVIVE?

'In the animal kingdom, the rule is, eat or be eaten; in the human kingdom, define or be defined.' **Thomas Szasz**

If we treat tension as an integral part of the product life cycle, the million-dollar question is how best to respond to the inevitable pressures, uncertainty and changes. No matter how successful the company or your product is, you will always have to be on your toes. Think of it as a never-ending boxing match. One round will be against a direct competitor - think Tower Records vs iTunes - or maybe you face multiple rounds against opponents coming from all angles; much as Sony Ericsson did with their mobile phone venture when they found themselves fighting off repeated attacks from Google and Android.[97]

Boxing is a sport which I love dearly, and I enjoy getting in the ring to spar against an opponent. As a boxer, you never know where the blows are going to come from or how they are going to land; your adversary can throw a right hook or kneel slightly to land an uppercut. As we have seen in the previous chapter, it's the same with product tensions. They can come from anywhere, from within or

97 "What You Can Learn From The Demise of Blockbuster, Tower Records and Others," Jeffrey Phillips, Inc., August 17, 2017, https://www.inc.com/jeffrey-phillips/what-you-can-learn-from-the-demise-of-blockbuster-.html; "The rise and fall of Sony Mobile: where next?" Nirave Gondhia, Android Authority, June 18, 2015, https://www.androidauthority.com/where-does-sony-mobile-go-from-here-616815/.

externally. Computer company Compaq comes to mind here: having initially dominated the ring they were suddenly knocked out in the fourth round and left gasping for air.

COMPAQ: THE MOVES THAT DIDN'T PAN OUT

'We are reinventing ourselves as a company. Compaq is taking ownership of its customer relationships and accountability of our customer's needs.' **Eckhard Pfeiffer**

Back in the 1980s and 1990s, Compaq was a powerful force in the world of personal computers. In 1983 Compaq launched its first product, the Compaq Portable (See fig. 9). The Portable was priced at $3,950 and weighed a good 12 kilos! Whilst not exactly portable by today's measures, you could still pack up the computer and move it a lot faster than its then competitor, the IBM PC.[98]

Fig. 9 – Compaq's first product; the Compaq Portable was one of the first personal computers

98 "Compaq Portable Computer," Centre for Computing History, http://www.computinghistory.org.uk/det/1322/Compaq-Portable-Computer/.

Following the initial success of its first personal computer, Compaq continued making desktops, eventually branching out into laptops and palmtops. It launched its final product, the iPAQ H3850, in 2001.[99] Where did things go wrong for Compaq?

External product tensions played a considerable role in the failure of Compaq. Having achieved initial success through computer hardware products, they then found that business was becoming increasingly difficult to such an extent that the survival of the company was threatened.[100] *In response, Compaq decided to transition from a traditional hardware company to focus on providing digital services and software. After all, IBM had successfully undergone a similar transition in the late nineties.*[101]

Unfortunately, Compaq's merger with Digital Equipment Company (DEC), a service company, and its acquisition of Tandem, a mainframe computer maker, did not deliver the desired value.[102] *DEC offered services and products which didn't make for a good match with Compaq.*[103] *The acquisition of Tandem Computers seemed to be a sound business strategy, but unfortunately the integration of Tandem's activities with those of Compaq (and DEC) led to Compaq dropping the ball on its core strength: selling computers to large*

99 "Compaq iPAQ H3850," Centre for Computing History, http://www.computinghistory.org.uk/det/33643/Compaq-iPaq-H3850/.

100 "Four companies that failed spectacularly, and the lessons of their premature demise," David Chancellor, Chartered Management Institute, September 17, 2015, https://www.managers.org.uk/insights/news/2015/september/four-companies-that-failed-spectacularly-and-the-lessons-of-their-premature-demise.

101 "IBM's Transformation - From Survival to Success," Bridget van Kralingen, Forbes, July 7, 2010, https://www.forbes.com/2010/07/07/ibm-transformation-lessons-leadership-managing-change.html.

102 "Compaq: We Learned Our Merger Lesson With DEC," Joseph F. Korver, CRN, March 11, 2002, https://www.crn.com/news/channel-programs/18828094/compaq-we-learned-our-merger-lesson-with-dec.htm; "Why did Compaq fail?" Dave Farquhar, The Silicon Underground, https://dfarq.homeip.net/why-did-compaq-fail/; "Tandem Computers Unplugged: A People's History," Gaye I. Clemson, FastPencil, 2012.

103 "What Happened to Compaq.com?" Brian Stone, PC Guide, April 2019, https://www.pcguide.com/news/what-happened-to-compaq/.

businesses.[104] *Rationalising the product lines and activities between Compaq, DEC and Tandem, caused internal tension which Compaq would never recover from.*

Compaq's demise also provides a case in point with respect to managing external tension. The bursting of the so-called 'Dotcom Bubble' in the early 2000s was not something that Compaq was able to influence.[105] *It was nonetheless seriously affected by this event as the venture capital and IPO backed startups stopped buying large numbers of computers. In addition, as these dotcoms ran out of money, the market became flooded with excess equipment, which in turn meant that Compaq had to compete with its own products re-entering the market.*[106]

After its cash reserve and stock valuation took a number of grave knocks, Compaq merged with Hewlett Packard (HP) in 2002. Interpersonal tensions, mismanagement and underperforming product decisions meant that the merger between Compaq and HP can hardly be regarded as a success, and it merely marked Compaq's ultimate decline.[107]

It is a tale of contrasting fortunes. Whereas Compaq thrived in the nineties but ended up in anonymity, Apple struggled in that period but eventually came up trumps. Articles hailing the return of Steve Jobs to Apple in 1997 and the excitement following the introduction of the Mac G4 in 1999, made me realise how they could easily have

104 "M&A Impact, Tandem and DEC - Still Outsiders at Compaq," Computer Business Review, March 14, 1999, https://www.cbronline.com/news/ma_impact_tandem_and_dec_still_outsiders_at_compaq/; "For Compaq, 1999 was the year that wasn't," Cnet, January 2, 2002, https://www.cnet.com/news/for-compaq-1999-was-the-year-that-wasnt/.

105 "The Dotcom Bubble Crash Explained in a Timeline," John Whitefoot, Lombardi Letter, March 27, 2017, https://www.lombardiletter.com/the-dotcom-bubble-crash-a-timeline/9251/.

106 *Ibid 102.*

107 "Worst tech mergers and acquisitions: HP and Compaq, ZDnet," February 15, 2016, https://www.zdnet.com/article/worst-tech-mergers-and-acquisitions-hp-and-compaq/.

suffered the same fate as Compaq.[108]

APPLE: HOW BEING RUTHLESS PAYS OFF

'The world doesn't need another Dell or Compaq.' **Steve Jobs**

Fig. 10 – The Mac Portable was Apple's attempt to halt Microsoft's dominance

The 90s proved to be a tough time for Apple; Microsoft Windows was the operating system of choice for the lion's share of PCs on the market and Apple struggled to get a foot in the door. Windows put a heap of external product pressure on Apple, which in turn tried desperately to diversify its product portfolio and differentiate from the competition. It led to a number of failures in both product design

108 See: "The Resurgence of Apple Continues," CBS News, September 13, 1999, https://www.cbsnews.com/news/the-resurgence-of-apple-continues/; "Resurgence of an American Icon," Jon Swartz, Forbes, April 14, 2000, https://www.forbes.com/2000/04/14/feat.html#82a647a39b71; "Today in Apple history: Steve Jobs leaves and rejoins Apple," Luke Dormehl, Cult of Mac, September 16, 2018, https://www.cultofmac.com/445723/today-in-apple-history-steve-jobs-leaves-and-rejoins-apple/.

and market performance.[109]

Take the Mac Portable for example (See fig. 10). Launched towards the end of the 1980s, the Mac Portable was a brave attempt by Apple to break the dominance of clunky Windows-based desktops. Unfortunately, the attempt failed: the Mac Portable was heavy, not very portable and expensive - yours for $6,500 on release! To make matters worse, the batteries of the Mac Portable had issues too.[110] *Meanwhile, Apple was engaged in a price war in the PC market, which shaved a cool 30 percent off the average PC price. Consequently, Apple saw its 1993 profits slashed by approximately $400m and its share valuation took a massive beating.*[111]

Apart from unfortunate responses to external pressures, Apple endured numerous internal pressures too. Apple in the nineties was a classic case of people at the top not seeing eye to eye. Following advice by the Apple board that 'adult supervision was needed', Steve Jobs hired the highly experienced John Sculley as Apple CEO.[112] *By his own admission, John Sculley's corporate background never really fitted with Jobs' entrepreneurial and innovative approach.*[113] *Whilst Sculley and Jobs started out as best friends, they fell out over things such as the best pricing strategy to follow and which products to*

---

109 "17 Apple Products From the 90s We Forgot About" Christopher McFadden, Interesting Engineering, May 11, 2018, https://interestingengineering.com/17-apple-products-from-the-90s-we-forgot-about.

110 "The 25 Worst Tech Products of All Time Dan Tynan," PC World, May 26, 2005, https://www.pcworld.com/article/125772/worst_products_ever.html?page=5.

111 "John Sculley Steps Down as Chairman of Apple," Steven Pearlstein, Washington Post, October 16, 1993, http://www.washingtonpost.com/wp-srv/business/longterm/apple/sculley.htm.

112 "Steve Jobs interviewed 20 people to be CEO of Apple and disliked them all - here's the unconventional way John Sculley wowed him and snagged the offer," Alyson Shontell, Business Insider, August 15, 2017, https://www.businessinsider.com/john-sculley-interview-steve-jobs-apple-ceo-podcast-success-how-i-did-it2017-8.

113 "John Sculley admits Steve Jobs never forgave him, and he never repaired their friendship, before Jobs died," Jim Edwards, Business Insider, May 27, 2015, https://www.businessinsider.com/john-sculley-admits-steve-jobs-never-forgave-him-before-jobs-died-2015-5.

offer to customers.[114] It ultimately cost Jobs his job at Apple in 1985.

Desperate times called for drastic measures: Jobs returned to Apple in 1997 and decided to have a clear out. The company had just lost $1.04 billion in the fiscal year of 1997 and sales had nosedived by 30 percent in the final quarter of 1996. Apple's extensive product portfolio was the main victim of Jobs' restructuring exercise and he started with the multiple versions of the Macintosh computer which had been developed purely to satisfy the demands of its various retailers.[115]

'Focus' was at the forefront of Jobs' tactics to deal with tension at Apple. His battle plan concentrated on simplifying Apple's product line and elevating user experience above everything. 'Deciding what not to do is as important as deciding what to do' was Jobs' motto. 'It's true for companies and it is true for products.'[116]

Ironically, Apple got a leg up from competitor Microsoft who were keen to salvage their image due to an antitrust battle over the ways in which it was promoting Internet Explorer in the so-called 'browser wars' with Netscape.[117] It enabled Jobs and Apple to double down on design and innovation, starting with the launch of the iMac in 1998 (See fig. 11), and followed by successful launches of a new operating system - 'Mac OSX' - as well as a revolutionary music player in the form of the 'iPod'.[118] The introduction of the 'iPhone' ten years after Jobs re-joined Apple, further cemented Apple's position as one of the most successful technology companies the world has ever seen.

---

114 "Showdown at Apple: John Sculley vs. Steve Jobs," Christoph Dornbach , Mac History, June 2010, https://www.mac-history.net/showdown-at-apple-john-sculley-vs-steve-jobs.

115 "How Steve Jobs Saved Apple," Jason Fell, Entrepreneur Europe, October 27, 2011, https://www.entrepreneur.com/article/220604.

116 *Ibid 32.*

117 "Aug. 6, 1997: Apple Rescued - By Microsoft," John C. Abell, Wired, August 6, 2009, https://www.wired.com/2009/08/dayintech-0806/.

118 "How Apple became the world's most valuable company," Timothy B. Lee, Vox, September 9, 2015, https://www.vox.com/2014/11/17/18076360/apple.

Fig. 11 – Launching the iMac was evidence of Apple doubling down on design and innovation

Despite declining iPhone sales and strong competition, Apple still recorded $37 billion worth of revenue in 2018 and is slated to reach the $100 billion revenue mark in 2023. In August 2018 Apple's market capitalisation hit $1 trillion for the first time.[119]

HEALTHY VERSUS UNHEALTHY TENSION

'We believe in what we say all the time. "Healthy tension" is a common phrase in industry (...). Don't allow the dialogue. Simply stop saying it and stop if you hear it.' **Kimber Lockhart**

119 "Apple becomes world's first trillion-dollar company," Rob Davies, The Guardian, August 2, 2018, https://www.theguardian.com/technology/2018/aug/02/apple-becomes-worlds-first-trillion-dollar-company.

WHEN THE TENSION IS GETTING TOO MUCH …

I was working at a high-pace digital agency at the time, and my manager - let's call him 'Maurice' - had a loud voice. His voice would typically get even louder if there was an issue with a client or when we were under pressure to deliver against a deadline. Maurice would shout across the office and call people out publicly, telling them in no uncertain terms what they had done wrong. I struggled with Maurice; on a good day, he could be the nicest person but that would all change under pressure.

When I raised Maurice's behaviour with his boss and explained how it made me feel, my boss responded that 'that's just how Maurice is'. My boss added that, having worked closely with Maurice for a good chunk of time, Maurice behaves this way 'just so he can get everyone on the team moving in the same direction.' When my boss then said that 'a bit of healthy tension' was not a bad thing, I knew my days at the agency were numbered. So, when Maurice had a similar outburst a few weeks later, I decided I no longer wanted to work in an environment like this and left the business.

Does tension have to be this way?!

People often talk about 'healthy tension', stating that conflict or pressure are normal if you want to achieve results or unleash creativity. Take Jerry Hirshberg, a former car design leader at Nissan, who introduced the term 'creative abrasion': stimulating the creative process by hiring and pairing people with totally divergent views.[120] Hirshberg would hire experts in their individual fields, pair them and observe the debate that would ensue: 'I'm sorry, I see the project this way. The way you're approaching it is just absurd.' Hirshberg strongly believed in creative abrasion, explaining

120 "Opposites Attract," Katharine Mieszkowski, Fast Company, December 31, 1997, https://www.fastcompany.com/33191/opposites-attract; Jerry Hirshberg, *The Creative Priority* (London: Penguin Books Ltd, July 1999); "How Creative Friction Can Help Your Team," Scott Berkun, May 8, 2018, https://scottberkun.com/2018/how-creative-abrasion-helps-good-ideas/.

'that friction can produce wonderful creative sparks.'[121]

Hirshberg argues that friction is an integral part of creativity. People need to bring their own unique perspective to the table, even if this leads to vehement disagreement. I believe we can take this thinking a step further and look for 'abrasion' when managing businesses and products. 'Tensions around strategic challenges or the business model or scope can be more interesting and even conducive to introducing work', explains Alex Watson, Head of Product at BBC News, with the proviso that this kind of tension works better if 'you have managed to get rid of, or at least seriously reduce, relationship tensions.'[122]

It is vital to have internal debate and friction, especially when companies are under pressure to deliver strong business results or innovate their products. We all deal with friction or ambiguity on a daily basis and will have to accept that living with pressure or uncertainty can be painful at times. However, thinking back to my experiences with Maurice, I believe that tension does not have to lead to bad behaviour or internal rifts, and nor should it. 'Unhealthy tension' includes unwelcome behaviours such as finger pointing, dodging responsibility, bad-mouthing others, dishonesty or downing tools.

Not only is this kind of unhealthy tension petty, childish and undesirable at an interpersonal level, it is also detrimental on a business level. Too much friction can create hurt feelings, an unworkable situation, loss of productivity and ultimately loss of confidence. Economist Albert Hirschman identifies four possible ways in which employees respond to declining businesses or bad organisational culture:[123]

- **Exit** - This includes leaving the company or transferring to another department within the business, trying to get away from an unsatisfactory situation.

121 *Ibid 120.*

122 *Ibid 43.*

123 Albert O. Hirschman, *Exit, Voice, and Loyalty* (Harvard University Press, 1970).

- **Voice** - Trying to change the existing, unsatisfactory situation instead of trying to escape from it.
- **Loyalty** - Passively waiting for conditions of the current situation to improve.
- **Neglect** - Passively allowing for conditions to worsen, e.g. by reducing work efforts, being absent from or late to work.

In other words, when people feel personally hurt by too much tension or a deteriorating company, they will leave, express their discontent, persevere or simply stop caring. None of these options is particularly positive, particularly in an intransigent business culture.

Healthy Tension = Mind = Matter = Moves

How do we achieve **healthy tension**?

1. Managing the **'Balancing Act'** tension, achieving an equilibrium of the upside of opposing poles.
2. Keeping a close eye on the **'Walk the Plank'** tension, making sure that tension doesn't become a permanently destructive fixture.

1. THE 'BALANCING ACT' TENSION

'Creativity comes from a conflict of ideas.' **Donatella Versace**

It is helpful to have different viewpoints on a problem, people adding their unique perspectives to the mix. In 'The Power of Healthy Tension', author Tim Arnold defines polarity as 'a situation in which two ideas, opinions or approaches are completely opposite from each other, yet equally valid and true', resulting in 'a situation in which two opposing

 UNSOLVABLE	THE SITUATION IS NEVER GOING AWAY EG WHEN MANAGING PRODUCTS, WE WILL ALWAYS HAVE A SCARCITY OF BUDGET, PEOPLE, TIME AND WILL THEREFORE HAVE TO MAKE TOUGH TRADE-OFF CALL DECISIONS
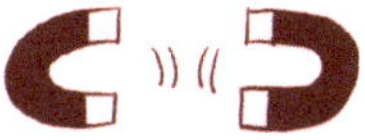 TWO INSEPARABLE POLES	THE TWO POLES OF A POLARITY BECOME INSEPARABLE OVER TIME EG IN PRODUCT INNOVATION, IN ORDER TO BUILD INNOVATIVE PRODUCTS, YOU WILL NEED TO TEST AND LEARN (THE BUILD v LEARN POLARITY)
 A NECESSARY "UPSIDE"	EACH OF THE POLES OFFERS US THINGS THAT ARE NOT ONLY DESIRABLE, BUT ESSENTIAL IN OUR LIVES IF WE LOOK AT THE UPSIDE OF THE LEARNING END OF THE 'BUILD v LEARN' POLE, RISK MITIGATION IS A KEY UPSIDE OF LEARNING AND DOING RESEARCH
 A FEARED "DOWNSIDE"	WHEN WE CHOOSE ONE POLE TO THE NEGLECT OF THE OPPOSITE POLE, WE WILL INEVITABLY END UP LIVING THE DOWNSIDE OF THAT POLE. LOOKING AT THE 'BUILD v LEARN' POLARITY, FORFEITING REVENUE OPPORTUNITIES AND BUILDING THE WRONG PRODUCT ARE THE MAIN DOWNSIDES OF CONCENTRATING SOLELY ON BUILDING PRODUCTS.
 A "HIGHER PURPOSE"	THE HIGHER PURPOSE ANSWERS THE QUESTION, "WHY BOTHER MANAGING THIS TENSION?" MOSTLY, THE CUSTOMER AND BUSINESS WILL BENEFIT FROM POLARITIES BEING WELL MANAGED. EG EG. MANAGING THE TENSION BETWEEN INNOVATION AND KEEPING THE LIGHTS ON CREATES PRODUCTS THAT ARE RELIABLE, VIABLE AND DESIRABLE

Fig. 12 – Different, opposing polarities, their characteristics and impact

ideas exist in seemingly impossible tension'.[124] Irrespective of the specific nature of a polarity, each polarity will have a number of predictable characteristics (See fig. 12).[125]

As we have seen in the previous chapter, tension can be internal or external. Given that there will be two opposing poles when managing products, each with its own up and downside, we need to be careful to not tip the scales in one direction only:

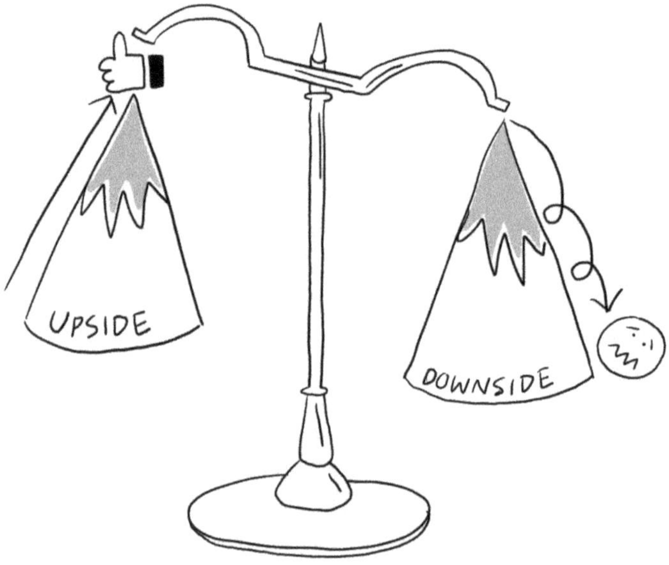

Build vs learn - When managing products there is a continuous balancing act between doing 'just enough' research and building a product.[126] How much do we need to know - about the customer, market conditions, regulations and technology - before we can start

124 Tim Arnold, *The Power of Healthy Tension* (Amherst, MA: HRD Press, October 2017, p. 17).
125 *Ibid 124, pp. 24-26.*
126 Erika Hall, *Just Enough Research* (New York: A Book Apart, 2013); Book review: "Just Enough Research," Marc Abraham, As I learn, July 20, 2017; "The Joys of Polarity Mapping," Stephen P. Anderson, UX Mastery, December 13, 2018, https://uxmastery.com/the-joys-of-polarity-mapping/.

building and shipping the product? For example, at Basecamp, a project management software company we encountered in Chapter 1, they don't ask what customers would pay for something nor do they do any beta testing prior to launch. Instead, they 'rely on the market to tell us the truth.'[127]

Innovation vs 'keeping the lights on' - There is an inherent tension between a business needing to innovate and operating 'business as usual'. Resources are scarce, so all businesses inevitably have to make tough trade-off decisions to make sure they use available people, budget and time as effectively as possible, constantly navigating between short ('what is') and long term ('what could be').

Problem vs solution - Think of the problem space as one pole and the solution space as its opposing pole. 'Don't bring me problems, bring me solutions' is what many a manager will have said. But what if we fully need to understand the problem first before we even get close to finding the right solution?

Group harmony vs distrust - Conformity and distrust are at opposing ends of the spectrum. Teams where its members continuously consent with each other and stop thinking critically can quickly become inert.[128] As Isaac Newton defined gravity, if something or someone isn't moved by an external force, it will continue moving at the same speed or in the same direction.[129] Total

127 Jason Fried and David Heinemeier Hansson, *It Doesn't Have to Be Crazy at Work* (Basecamp, 2018, https://basecamp.com/books/calm); "My product management toolkit (33): launch and learn," Marc Abraham, Medium, November 23, 2018, https://medium.com/@maa1/my-product-management-toolkit-33-launch-and-learn-e1b61bff5026.

128 Tim Harford, *Messy: The Power of Disorder to Transform Our Lives* (New York: Riverhead Books, October 2016, p. 47).

129 Andrew Motte's English translation: Newton, Isaac (1846), *Newton's Principia: the mathematical principles of natural philosophy* (New York: Daniel Adee, p. 72, https://archive.org/details/newtonspmathema00newtrich).

distrust sits at the other end of the spectrum, with team members not being able to agree on anything, operating in a state of suspicion and unproductiveness.

Commercial vs creative - Have you ever been in a situation where a colleague has referred to the marketing team as 'the colouring-in department'? Or perhaps you had a moment of despair caused by those 'number chasers' in the sales team? When managing products, the trick is to maintain a healthy equilibrium between the commercial and creative aspects of a product, respecting the different focus areas of the disciplines that we work with.

Known vs unknown - I like certainty, and therefore really had to learn to adapt to the 'unknown'. Going into unchartered territories and the uncertainty that comes with it is a core part of product management, even if we are working on existing, and more predictable products.[130] I have worked with many engineers, who prefer certainty over unpredictability. I believe this is closely linked to the binary nature of writing software code and the 'Tell Me What to Do' tension this creates (See Chapter 1). Even at a societal level, people will have different levels of tolerance for uncertainty and ambiguity.[131]

Accepting these tensions as unavoidable opposite ends of a pole, means that we have to find a way to best manage these polar opposites. 'Healthy tension' thus reflects a constructive way of managing inevitable polar opposites and perspectives. The toolkit at

130 "How to dance with uncertainty," Todd Henry, Accidental Creative, June 23, 2019, https://accidentalcreative.com/creating/dancing-with-uncertainty/.

131 The 6-D dimensional model of national culture," Geert Hofstede, https://geerthofstede.com/culture-geert-hofstede-gert-jan-hofstede/6d-model-of-national-culture/ (Accessed on September 23, 2019).

the end of this chapter contains a 'Strike the Balance' activity which you can use to both understand and balance the opposing factors that create product tension.

2. THE 'WALK THE PLANK' TENSION

'The best way to complain is to make things.' **James Murphy**

This raises the question about the point at which healthy tension turns unhealthy. The net results of healthy internal debate are creative solutions to complex problems. When internal debate turns sour and creates lasting rivalries within an organisation or a team, it will paralyse innovation or any attempt to move forward.

John Cutler, Product Evangelist at analytics company Amplitude, likens the difference between healthy and unhealthy tension to suffering sports injuries. 'It is the difference between an acute injury and chronic illness,' Cutler explains, 'you could treat healthy tension as an acute stressor which eventually makes you stronger, whereas chronic health issues make you progressively weaker.'[132] This raises the question of whether 'duration' forms the difference between healthy and unhealthy tension. Occasional moments of debate or disagreement are necessary to innovate and solve problems. These moments will help break through groupthink or complacence.

What, however, happens when these debates turn into mudslinging matches, where those who lose the debate feel hurt or deflated?[133] Or when creative disputes are no longer a temporary thing? As we saw at the beginning of this chapter with Maurice, it is easy to see how hurtful and unconstructive behaviours can be disguised as a 'healthy tension'. Whereas healthy tension can help move teams and people forward,

132 John Cutler, *interview by author*, Santa Barbara, September 3, 2019.

133 "The Myth of Healthy Tension," Kimber Lockhart, Medium, May 18, 2016, https://medium.com/@kimber_lockhart/the-myth-of-healthy-tension-1662ca7c669b.

consistently bad behaviours will have an adverse effect on both the people in the organisation and the outcomes that they achieve.

Organisations may well be able to survive these adverse effects in the short term, but endemic bad behaviours aren't sustainable in the long run. Uber, the San Francisco headquartered ride hailing company and Revolut, a London-based Fintech, are both recent examples of high-growth companies that have come to realise that persistent unhealthy tension isn't sustainable. Despite a phenomenal growth trajectory, Uber had been plagued by a whole host of internal scandals, PR disasters and lawsuits, resulting in the stepping down of Travis Kalanick, its co-founder and CEO.[134] Similarly, Revolut was forced to respond publicly to a growing number of claims from former employees who complained about widespread bullying by senior managers, asking job applicants to recruit clients in order to progress through the interview process and a ruthless emphasis on employees meeting their targets.[135] Eventually, Revolut's founding CEO Nikolay Storonsky, publicly acknowledged that 'over the last 18 months, we've spent a lot of time working on our culture.'[136]

Although the complaints aimed at Uber and Revolut are different

---

134 See: "Reflecting On One Very, Very Strange Year at Uber," Susan Fowler, February 19, 2017, https://www.susanjfowler.com/blog/2017/2/19/reflecting-on-one-very-strange-year-at-uber; "Uber's U-turn: How the new CEO is cleaning house after scandals and lawsuits," Dara Kerr, Cnet, April 27, 2018, https://www.cnet.com/news/ubers-u-turn-how-ceo-dara-khosrowshahi-is-cleaning-up-after-scandals-and-lawsuits/; "49 of the biggest scandals in Uber's history," Kate Taylor and Benjamin Goggin, Business Insider, May 10, 2019, https://www.businessinsider.com/uber-company-scandals-and-controversies-2017-11.

135 See: "Digital bank Revolut's sanction's screening issue revealed," James Cook, The Telegraph, February 28, 2019, https://www.telegraph.co.uk/technology/2019/02/28/revolut-failed-block-suspicious-transactions/; "A report describes high turnover and toxic workplace culture at finance startup Revolut," Andrew Liptak, The Verge, March 3, 2019, https://www.theverge.com/2019/3/3/18248826/revolut-workplace-culture-burnout-finance-app-reports; "Revolut says it's cleaning up its act. Evidence suggest otherwise," Emiliano Mellino, Wired, April 29, 2019, https://www.wired.co.uk/article/revolut-compliance-free-work-fintech-application-toxic-storonsky.

136 "Revolut's culture: the past, present and future," Nikolay Storonsky, Revolut Blog, March 4, 2019, https://blog.revolut.com/weve-made-mistakes-but-were-learning/.

in nature, they have two things in common: negative emotions and unconstructive behaviours. Negative emotions are those unpleasant or unhappy emotions that are invoked in individuals to express a negative effect towards an event or person.[137] There are a number of negative emotions and behaviours that come to mind, which - if perpetuated - can evolve into unhealthy tension:

Negative emotions

- **Anxiety** - Anxiety does not have to be treated as a negative emotion per se. The right amount of anxiety can spur us into action.[138] However, too much anxiety can cripple us, leading us to withdraw from certain actions or situations.[139]
- **Aggression** - Aggression is probably the sole negative emotion that is hard to view in a positive light and I am therefore not going to try to frame aggression as something positive.
- **Anger** - Anger doesn't have to be a negative emotion in principle. Anger can be used as a motivating force; when something adds benefits, we want it even more when we are angry. Research has shown that anger can make us push on towards our goals in the face of problems and barriers.[140] Despite this positive aspect of anger, persistent anger or anger bordering on aggression will create unhealthy tension and personal discomfort.

137 "What are Negative Emotions and How to Control Them?" Elaine Maid, Positive Psychology, April 8, 2019, https://positivepsychology.com/negative-emotions./

138 "Embracing uncertainty and anxiety," Robert H. Rosen, Leader to Leader Institute, Executive Forum, September 4, 2008, https://onlinelibrary.wiley.com/doi/abs/10.1002/ltl.304.

139 "Scared Stiff: The Influence of Anxiety on the Perception of Action Capabilities," Meagan M. Craydon, Sally A. Linkenauger, Bethany A. Teachman and Dennis R. Proffitt, Cognitive Emotions 2012, 26 (7), pp. 1301-1315.

140 "The Art of Anger: Reward Context Turns Avoidance Responses to Anger-Related Objects Into Approach," Henk Aarts, Kirsten I. Ruys, Harm Veling, Robert A. Renes, Jasper H.B. de Groot, Anna M. van Nunen and Sarit Geertjes, Psychological Science, September 20, 2010, https://journals.sagepub.com/doi/10.1177/0956797610384152.

- **Frustration** - Similar to anxiety, frustration in itself is not a negative emotion in my view but can trigger other emotions or emotional behaviours. The very fact that things don't always go to plan or our dependency on others can lead to frustration.
- **Sadness** - Change or uncertainty can invoke sadness. As we have seen in the first chapter of this book, product management and ambiguity go hand in hand. Think about the last time you missed a deadline, or your product did not perform as expected. Used constructively, sadness can be a driver for change and continuous improvement. However, unhealthy tension does arise where the sadness feels relentless.

Unconstructive behaviours

- **Conflict** - Conflict can act as a valuable catalyst for solving complex problems and coming up with innovative solutions. Conflict can be cooperative and constructive, when both sides see the benefit of a creative outcome. In contrast, competitive or deconstructive conflict occurs when one party believes that, when helping himself, the other party becomes less powerful.[141]
- **Assigning blame** - I personally don't thrive in a 'blame culture' where people shift blame onto someone or something else. Some will argue that there is a fine line between holding people accountable and finger pointing. Whilst I believe that holding the right people accountable can be effective in learning and improving - on an individual or organisational level - persistent blame shifting will eventually result in unhealthy tension.[142]
- **Raising the bar** - High expectations can act as a great

141 "The Resolution of Conflict: Constructive and Destructive Processes," Morton Deutsch, Yale University Press, 1973; "Workplace Conflict," Muhammad Riaz Khan and Fatima Ali Junaid, SSRN Electronic Journal, April 2013, https://www.researchgate.net/publication/254968171_Workplace_Conflict_Constructive_or_Destructive.

142 "Toxic: Dealing With A Culture Of Blame," Todd Henry, Accidental Creative, https://accidentalcreative.com/teams/toxic-dealing-with-a-culture-of-blame/ (Accessed on September 18, 2019).

> motivator and cause of healthy tension at the same time. People from different backgrounds and with different perspectives can challenge each other to do better or raise the stakes. This becomes problematic as soon as expectations start becoming unrealistic and untenable.[143]

When such negative emotions and behaviours turn from temporary events into a mainstay of the organisation and its individual teams, that is the point where healthy tension becomes unhealthy.

STING LIKE A BEE: DIFFERENT TENSION RESPONSES

'It's the punch you don't see coming that knocks you out.' **Willie Pastrano**

Sting Like A Bee = Moves + Moves + Moves

There are different **moves** you can make in relation to product tension:

- **Blocking:** Focus purely on your defence and keeping your guard up.
- **Dodging:** Ducking away ever so slightly and throwing your own attack.
- **Retreating:** Stepping back, repositioning and coming back stronger.
- **Pivoting:** Shifting your baseline to gain the upper hand.
- **Leaning in:** A risky move, where you leave yourself exposed as you attack.

143 "The human function curve," Peter Nixon, NCBI, 1982, Suppl. 3 (Pt 1):130-3, https://www.ncbi.nlm.nih.gov/pubmed/7183056.

What can we learn from the opposing fates that befell Compaq and Apple at the beginning of this chapter? Both companies faced similar product tensions, internal and external, but whilst one business floundered, the other came out on top. Think of dealing with such tensions as standing in a boxing ring, having to compete against multiple opponents simultaneously. Punches can be coming from all sides, and as a company and an individual you will have to respond to ensure that you don't get knocked out. Learning from this, we can determine four commonplace ways of dealing with tension:

'Blocking'

Blocking shots is probably the most common and 'natural' way of defending against punches. I personally love boxing, but I cringe when I think back to my very first rounds of sparring in the ring: I don't think I landed a single punch, as I was far too busy defending, trying to keep my guard up! Successful blocking starts and ends with keeping your eyes on your opponent. You need to keep your guard up at all times even if your adversary is pounding shots at you relentlessly.

As human beings we are programmed to put our guard up and protect ourselves as soon as we are faced with danger. We often tend to erect a wall when things get tough. I used to get very defensive and locked up in myself when faced with pressure or criticism. My struggle with this evolved into acting in a very (passive) aggressive way as an act of self-defence. Feeling personally slighted by a colleague or from customer feedback, I would get defensive (block) but then lash out verbally to someone else (attack).

Compaq thought it was successfully blocking attempts from IBM and Dell. By continuing to make successful hardware products, Compaq felt it could ward off its opponents. The problem with blocking, however, is that despite the move possibly paying off in the short term, you're nevertheless coming up short in the long run.

'Dodging'

Dodging or 'slipping' from your opponent's punches is probably one of the hardest boxing skills. Instead of blocking a punch, you duck back and move ever so slightly out of the way of a shot. This way of defending sets up you nicely to land a counterpunch and bring your rival out of balance.

Apple used the 'slip' movement masterfully: rather than producing yet another personal computer in a similar vein to Compaq or IBM, it moved sideways - producing a different kind of computer, the iMac. Apple positioned itself perfectly to land some strong blows to the competition; a powerful new operating system and embracing new forms of content through the iPod, iPhone and the iMac.

'Retreating'

I often fight boxers who are much heavier and stronger than me. They force me to be light on my feet and move around a lot ... 'Retreating' or 'backing away' are the boxing terms used frequently to describe moving around to avoid a barrage of blows and regain some energy. Done well, retreating enables you to reposition and create counterpunching opportunities for yourself. Sedat Sag - the owner of the boxing gym where I train – explains: 'Sometimes the best way to throw a punch is to take a step back.' Don't, however, retreat in straight lines, as you will corner yourself, end up against the ropes and will be beaten up!

Apple retreated when Steve Jobs shut down numerous Apple product lines. Whilst Apple retreated in certain areas, it didn't exit the ring altogether as it kept producing personal computers. It retreated only in order to return stronger and forged space to throw some strong counterpunches. In contrast, Compaq retreated in straight lines following its decision to transition from a traditional hardware company to focus on providing services and software.[144]

144 *Ibid 102.*

'Pivoting'

When I am in the boxing ring with someone who is much heavier than me, I will often try pivoting away from their punches. Pivoting is all about footwork. Pivoting to the left means that you push from the right back foot and allow your front foot to spin on its ball. When you pivot to the right, you spin the front foot on the spot and allow your back foot to lift. The outcome of both moves is to shift one's baseline; incredibly helpful, particularly when you are fighting a boxer who is pulling you into a short range battle or one that is literally trying to push you into the ropes and cause a lot of damage once you are against the ropes.[145]

In the past years, the term 'pivoting' has also been coined to describe businesses which have radically changed their strategic direction. The likes of Twitter, PayPal and Starbucks changed their products and value proposition.[146] These companies all made side steps whilst remaining fully focused on their opponents and their own long-term vision. Take Twitter, for example, which started its life as 'Odeo', a network where people could discover and subscribe to

145 "Boxing Footwork - Don't Overlook the Pivot in Boxing!" Fran Sands, My Boxing Coach, May 26, 2010, https://www.myboxingcoach.com/footwork-the-pivot/.

146 "14 Famous Business Pivots," Jason Nazar, Forbes, October 8, 2013, https://www.forbes.com/sites/jasonnazar/2013/10/08/14-famous-business-pivots/.

podcasts. iTunes' gradual domination of the podcast space made Odeo's founders change the focus of the company and concentrate on micro-blogging instead.[147]

ARE YOU BLOCKING, DODGING, RETREATING OR PIVOTING?

I encourage you to reflect on the 'moves' of your business and product by asking yourself the following questions:

Question 1: Reflecting on recent product or feature releases, are these in response to competition or new strategic moves?
If you feel that the majority of new product or feature releases have been in response to the competition, you are probably spending most of your time 'blocking'. This is not a bad thing per se, as it will keep your product up to par with the competition and existing customer expectations, but you remain on the back foot with respect to product innovation and differentiation.

Question 2: When was the last time a product in your company was improved radically?
Wracking your brain in answer to this question is an indication that your company and its products have mostly been blocking, and not taken the risks involved in dramatically changing the product or deciding to kill a product or feature. Attention might well have been solely on 'quick wins' instead of 'big bets', with the business mostly blocking or retreating. In contrast, if you feel that your products have undergone drastic changes, your company is probably adept at 'dodging' and 'pivoting'.

147 "The Real History Of Twitter," Nicholas Carlson, Business Insider, April 13, 2011, https://www.businessinsider.com/how-twitter-was-founded-2011-4.

Question 3: What would you consider the riskiest move you have taken in relation to your product(s) or features?

Failing to terminate underperforming products or features is a sign of not taking enough risk. Not iterating on existing products or experimenting with new ones is another indication. You are probably merely 'blocking' or 'retreating'. The latter move does not have to be bad, as long as you use your backward moves to come back stronger.

'Leaning in'

Most boxing professionals would probably advise against 'leaning in', especially if you have only just started boxing.[148] Leaning in or not punching from an upright position is not without risk. For example, throwing an overhand punch from the rear can generate a lot of power given that your whole-body power is behind it, but you are

148 "Should you really lean into a punch?" Physics Stack Exchange, February 16, 2011, https://physics.stackexchange.com/questions/5243/should-you-really-lean-into-a-punch.

leaving the relatively safe corner of a ring to come out fighting and leaving yourself exposed.[149]

I am thinking of the time I worked for an online marketplace platform and disagreed with some of my colleagues. We had differing opinions about integrating with a third-party financial software product so that we could provide the sellers on our platform with a dashboard showing them their up-to-date financial and sales data. Whilst my colleagues were in favour of integrating with the third party, I believed strongly that regaining control over sensitive seller data was the right thing to do, both by the customer and by our business. I thus went against the grain, but it was worth it: we managed to launch the in-house dashboard far more quickly than we would have been able to do had we gone down the third-party route. It instilled a strong sense of trust among our sellers, knowing that we had not shared their data with another business.

I have found – often to my disadvantage – that leaning in tends to leave you horribly exposed, making it easier for your opponent to hit you hard or throw you off balance. It happened well over ten years ago, but I still remember like it was yesterday; I was fighting another boxer and feeling good about myself. That was until my opponent hit me right in the solar plexus and I went down like a sack of potatoes ... Tony, a veteran heavyweight fighter (RIP Tony) stood at the other side of the ring's ropes and watched it all happening. 'I know it's hurting now, but you will learn from this and will come out stronger' were Tony's words of advice as I lay panting on the floor of the boxing ring.

Going back to the marketplace dashboard product that I was responsible for; I leaned in by making the case for building the dashboard in-house. I stuck my neck out by arguing against using

149 See: "How to throw an overhand," Samuel Ha, Mighty Fighter, http://www.mightyfighter.com/how-to-throw-an-overhand/; "The Art of Body Punching," Johnny N, July 26, 2018, Expert Boxing, https://www.expertboxing.com/the-art-of-body-punching.

third-party dashboard software, a solution that most of my colleagues and stakeholders were in strong favour of. Going against the grain in this way left me exposed and meant that the product needed to work even harder in demonstrating the value of us having built it internally. I leaned in sensibly though; investigating the pros and cons of building the dashboard in-house or using a third-party 'off the shelf' software. Iterating continuously on the product meant that we were still on the front foot and, if necessary, could retreat with our reputation and budget intact. Despite its obvious disadvantages, leaning in can be absolutely necessary at times. You need to take a risk or reach out to create an opening in the fight.

History is littered with companies that failed to lean in and ended up extinct as a result. Leaning in can feel extremely uncomfortable and perilous at times, but imperative if a company wants to innovate and survive. Kodak, once the world's biggest film company, filed for bankruptcy in 2012, after it had missed out on the digital camera opportunity. Don Strickland, a former Kodak director, explained later: 'We developed the world's first consumer digital camera, but we could not get approval to launch or sell it because of fear of the effects on the film market.'[150]

In contrast, Apple did lean in at the most critical of times. When the survival of the company was on the line, it took a chance on obtaining funding from Microsoft, one of its major competitors.[151] The subsequent introduction of the iMac was a gamble, it didn't conform with the types of personal computers dominating the market at the time. Apple took a clear risk, fell victim to a few punches in the process, but came out victorious.

150 "The moment it all went wrong for Kodak," David Usborne, The Independent, January 20, 2012, https://www.independent.co.uk/news/business/analysis-and-features/the-moment-it-all-went-wrong-for-kodak-6292212.html.

151 *Ibid 117.*

CONCLUSION

Whilst leaning in might go against conventional wisdom and will feel counter-intuitive, it is an indispensable skill when dealing with tension or counterforces. The alternatives - blocking, dodging, retreating and pivoting - might work in the short term, but are unlikely to create sustainable advantages for your product or business. In the next part of the book we will further consider leaning into tension when managing products, and how to do so effectively.

SUMMARY

Tension is an integral part of managing products, and our company success is determined by how we respond to the tensions we are faced with.

- **'Balancing Act'** - We get the tensions just right and our businesses and products thrive.
- **'Walk the Plank'** - We are on a tightrope and the tension turns unhealthy, to the detriment of our businesses and products.

Compaq went on the defence, but their strategic moves didn't pan out.
Apple made some hard moves and built their attack around a few new products.

People ultimately influence whether tension remains healthy - leading to constructive outcomes - or turns unhealthy - resulting in consistently negative emotions and bad outcomes. It is a fine balancing act!

The **moves** we can make in response to tension:

- We can **block** the tension, getting defensive and focusing purely on what the opponent causing the tension is doing.
- When **dodging** a tension, you move away slightly from the tension to regain the upper hand over the tension or your competitor.
- While **retreating** involving taking a few steps back, making some hard decisions, in view of a new position for your business or product.
- We **pivot** to shift the baseline of our business or product in response to tension, without losing sight of the overall vision.
- Not without risk, **leaning in** means that we embrace the tension we are faced with and try to optimise it.

TOOLKIT: THE ROLE AND IMPACT OF TENSION ON MANAGING PRODUCTS

1. STRIKING THE RIGHT BALANCE

Outcome: Being able to balance the up and down sides of the different (opposing) poles that create product tension.

With this tool, we will see some examples of the impact of getting the balance right or wrong for each of the aforementioned product management poles. Because each pole has its own upside and downside, the trick is to avoid swinging to one end of the pole only, at the detriment of the other end. I will label each of the different impacts, and share a simple equation which underpins the impact, using one of the following two formats:

- Impact 1 = If we do too little of X, it will negatively impact Y and Z
- Impact 2 = If we do too much of X, it will negatively impact Y and Z

<u>BUILD VS LEARN</u>:

- **'Analysis Paralysis'** = If we do too much learning, it will negatively impact speed to market, team morale and revenue.
- **'Wasted Effort'** = If we do too little learning early and often, it will negatively impact return on investment, brand reputation and team morale.

There is nothing more frustrating than seeing a product or feature flop, after you and your team have invested a lot of money, time and effort into building it. Equally, teams derive satisfaction from 'shipping' stuff; having the product or feature out there and learning from people actually using what has been built. Commercially, the risks of launching too soon or too late can be huge; in the next chapter we will see how a global tyre company and a tech behemoth got burned by launching their respective products to market too late.

Getting this balance right manifests itself in learning early and often, launching products and values that customers value. Not only will revenue increase, customers will derive value from your product and teams will stay motivated to constantly iterate on the product.

INNOVATION VS 'KEEPING THE LIGHTS ON':

- **'Nothing Works Around Here' =** If we do too little on the customer experience or product hygiene, it will negatively impact customer churn, revenue and team morale.
- **'We're from Another Era'** = If we do too much on just product hygiene, it will negatively impact customer acquisition, market share and staff retention.

Maintaining an appropriate balance between innovation and 'business as usual' can be incredibly challenging. How do you prioritise between a future innovation and fixing a product issue right now? In the previous chapter we saw how Apple's market share and revenue surged after it shut down certain products, in favour of doubling down on a select number of innovative products.

Ideally, you want to continuously mix efforts on both 'big bets' and 'quick wins'. Big bets are those products which require a lot of effort in return for a high value. These are typically innovative products, which require more effort because they cover unchartered territory. In contrast, quick wins are typically low effort - low value activities.

I have seen businesses that carved out 6-12 months solely for their development teams to upgrade their technology infrastructure. While this is very valuable from a scalability perspective and the long-term future of the business, the associated opportunity cost might end up being too high, if you miss out on any short-term but high value market opportunities.

PROBLEM VS SOLUTION:

- **'Straight Out the Blocks'** = If we do too little on understanding the problem, this will negatively impact customer adoption, motivation and revenue.
- **'Analysis Paralysis'** = If we do too much problem analysis, it will negatively impact speed to market, team morale and revenue.

It is easy to see how companies go for an all or nothing approach, whereby they either delve fully into testing and building a solution or, adversely, spend a lot of time upfront understanding the problem to solve. It is the responsibility of the product manager to ensure that we don't commit to a single solution without understanding the problem to solve first.

Failure to grasp the problem to address, or not understanding who to provide a solution to, can result in a product that bombs due to a lack of customers and revenue. Similar to the 'building vs learning' pole, too much focus on the problem can result in inertia and a slow release to market.

To get the balance right between problem and solution, the trick is to keep the time required to (1) assess the customer problem and (2) deliver a solution as short as possible. This way you reduce the risk of delivering the wrong product or missing a market opportunity due to analysis paralysis.

GROUP HARMONY VS DISTRUST:

- **'Don't Trust No One'** = If we do too little to trust each other, this will negatively impact progress and collaboration.
- **'Let's Not Rock the Boat'** = If we do too much to create (artificial) harmony, this will negatively impact innovation and risk taking.

As we will see in Chapter 6, trusted relationships are indispensable to effective collaboration and product development. 'Trust' doesn't mean that we all have to like each other, but that we respect each other's opinions and contributions. In a 'don't trust no one' situation, people are either at loggerheads with each other or lack the necessary respect, which leads to a serious lack of productivity and accountability. Even worse, you might end up with a Frankenstein-type product which reflects the organisation's internal communication structures or disagreements.

We want to create an environment where people feel that it's ok to disagree with one another, as long this is done constructively. Disagreements or negative feedback are shared in such a way that there is no adverse impact on trusted relationships.

COMMERCIAL VS CREATIVE:

- **'Someone Forgot the Customer' =** If we do too little challenging commercial considerations, it will negatively impact the customer experience and brand promise.
- **'Show Me the Money'** = If we do too much blue sky thinking, it will negatively impact commercial viability and technical feasibility.

Naturally, all businesses need to make money and one could argue that creating products which don't make any money or create other value, are a hobby, not a business ('show me the money'). The flipside is the creation of a product or experience that is so driven by commercial gain that it creates a bad customer experience or alienates customers. Media companies that constantly face a trade-off between removing all ads from their online articles - which undoubtedly creates a better customer experience - and losing out on a precious revenue from advertising. Or think about products or services that force users to create an account in order to make a purchase.

The obvious sweet spot here is to provide the customer with tangible value for money; coming up with creative and delightful experiences that the customer is willing to pay for. Companies like Netflix and Amazon have proven that it is possible to achieve huge commercial success whilst providing a great customer experience. In contrast, Spotify is the world's number 1 music streaming service but still gets a lot of flak for offering a suboptimal user experience.

KNOWN VS UNKNOWN:

- **'Everything Is Up in The Air'** = If we do too little planning and testing, it will negatively impact our (risk) prioritisation, decision making and team morale.
- **'We Know It All'** = If we do too much planning and research upfront, it will negatively impact our speed to market and ability to be flexible and creative.

In Chapter 1, I introduced the 'I Love It When A Plan Comes Together' tension. It's a tension that arises when we realise that things hardly ever go to plan. We can aim to know it all and set out to mitigate for all circumstances and hope that nothing will catch us off guard. The downside of such an approach is that it's virtually impossible to predict things that might or might not happen, let alone plan for them. Does that mean that we should give up on any form of upfront planning or risk assessments?! No.

Leaving everything up in the air and just firefighting the 'unknowns' as they materialise can harm the ways in which we do business, make us very reactive and negatively influence the morale of those colleagues who prefer certainty over ambiguity. Instead, we can prioritise the riskiest unknowns surrounding a product or things that could go wrong. We are thus retaining a healthy sense of flexibility and direction, whilst being clear on what we (think we) know and what we don't.

CHAPTER 4.
LEANING IN WITH CONFIDENCE

'You may not control all the events that happen to you, but you can decide not to be reduced by them.' **Maya Angelou**

Product Management = Mind + Matter + Moves

In this chapter we will explore:

- How **tension** can be conducive to creating great products.
- **Firestone, The Zune** and **Fat Beats:** unsuccessful moves in the face of tension.
- **Direct Line, Sony** and **National Geographic:** how tension can pave the way for growth.
- **The 'Knitting Spaghetti' tension:** the value of actively seeking out creative tension.
- **Acknowledging, Analysing** and **Springboarding:** three steps to optimising tension in order to create great products.

INTRODUCTION

Now that we have established that tension is inevitable when managing products and have explored different ways of handling such tension, it is worth considering leaning into it. If tension is bound to happen when developing products, why not accept and make the most of it? While I am not ignoring that tension can be difficult or stressful, I will make the case for the benefits of embracing tension.

TENSION CAN BE FRIGHTENING (IF IT ISN'T THEN YOU'RE MISSING THE POINT)

'I spent a lot of years trying to outrun or outsmart vulnerability by making things certain and definite, black and white, good and bad. My inability to lean into the discomfort of vulnerability limited the fullness of those important experiences that are fraught with uncertainty: love, belonging, trust, joy and creativity to name a few.'
Brene Brown

Tension can be dreadful, and there have been plenty of times where I have dreaded tension. As we have seen in Chapter 1, internal and external tensions are bound to occur when building and managing products: *external* tension is typically caused by the market, or regulators, whilst *internal* tension is often generated by us and others on our team or within our company.

WHY I USED TO DREAD TENSION ...

It has taken me a long time to even accept the idea that tension is inherent in living, in being. And that working on products is one of the many areas where tension manifests itself. Grasping the notion that one can embrace tension has been an even bigger leap for me. I welcome structure, certainty and control, which makes the uncertainty and fluidity that come with tension pretty overwhelming at times, and here is why:

- ***I'm not a fan of stepping into the unknown** - Exploring uncharted territory can be pretty nerve wracking. Whereas other people might thoroughly enjoy the unknown because there are no boundaries, I used to struggle with the idea of* *starting from a blank canvas.*[152] *Having little or no constraints to work with can be liberating but can also feel daunting. It is the reason why some people are best at 'creating' whilst others excel at 'editing', i.e. adding to something that already exists.*

- **A love of certainty and control** - *As product people we are often looked upon to upset the status quo and provide clarity in unclear situations. Darlene Miranda, VP of Product Management at Sterling, a company that specialises in background check solutions, points out that 'everyone comes to product managers for answers', and that as product managers 'we are problem solvers, we like having all the answers.'*[153] *In my experience, not being certain or admitting that you don't know can therefore feel incredibly hard.*
- **Being uncomfortable with discomfort** - *It is all well and good me saying that we should seize tension, but the reality is that such tension can often give rise to personal discomfort, be that mental or physical. We product managers frequently find ourselves right at the very centre of that tension. Chris Butler, Product Manager at Facebook, explained to me how, as a product manager you need to excel at receiving feedback since 'you will get it wrong most often.'*[154]
- **A tendency to confirm my biases** - *I like being certain. I have biases, tons of them, and I like seeing those biases confirmed. A cognitive bias is effectively a special brain trick that people use to save time and energy when figuring out what we are*

152 I like how Simon Wardley, specialist in situational awareness and gameplay, distinguishes between "pioneers" and "settlers". Pioneers, Wardley explains, are able to explore never before discovered concepts, the uncharted land. Settlers, in contrast, can turn a half-baked thing into something useful for a larger audience. See: "On Pioneers, Settlers, Town Planners and Theft," Simon Wardley, Bits or pieces? March 13, 2015, https://blog.gardeviance.org/2015/03/on-pioneers-settlers-town-planners-and.html.

153 Darlene Miranda, *interview by author*, New York, February 3, 2020.

154 Chris Butler, *interview by author*, New York, September 27, 2019.

looking at, orienting ourselves around what it means to us, and then deciding what we should do.[155] *As humans we like to think that we are hyper rational, but we are not; we create our own subjective reality.*[156] *I used to get very defensive as soon as I felt that someone was 'attacking' my strongly held beliefs or changing the status quo. Chris Butler argues that 'your past mindset or experience is your biggest adversary.'*[157]

- **It will burst my bubble** - *I remember once presenting some rudimentary prototypes, conveying my ideas around simplifying the process of buying a house (online). The designer and engineers in my team provided some strong feedback about the prototype, and each - well formulated - point of feedback, felt like a blow to my stomach ... I see a risk for product managers becoming (too) attached to the product that they are responsible for; treating the product as your child that can't do any wrong.*
- **Not wanting to cause upset** - *Research shows that when an individual's judgement conflicts with that of a group, the individual will usually conform his judgement to that of the group.*[158] *This behaviour is known as 'social conformity' whereby people will adhere to group opinion in order to 'fit*

155 Buster Benson, *Why Are We Yelling?* (London: Macmillan, 2019, p. 87).

156 See: "The Dominant Logic: Retrospective and Extension," Richard A. Bettis and C.K. Prahalad, , Strategic Management Journal, Volume 16, Issue 1, January 1995, pp. 5-14, http://213.55.83.214:8181/Economics/Economy/00539.pdf; "The curse of expertise: The effects of expertise and debiasing methods on prediction of novice performance," Pamela J. Hinds, Journal of Experimental and Applied Psychology, 1999, Vol. 5, No. 2, pp. 205 – 221; Robert A. Burton, *On Being Certain: Believing You Are Right Even When You're Not* (London: St. Martin's Press, 2009).

157 Chris Butler, *interview by author*, New York, July 9, 2019.

158 "Neurobiological Correlates of Social Conformity and Independence During Mental Rotation," Gregory S. Berns, Jonathan Chappelow, Caroline F. Zink, Giuseppe Pagnoni, Megan E. Martin-Skurksi and Jim Richards, Biological Psychiatry, August 1, 2005, Volume 58, Issue 3, pp. 245 - 253.

in'.[159] It often feels much easier to avoid internal tension and to confirm to the group or ruling social norms instead. We don't want to upset others or rattle the status quo, especially when concerned about professional or personal relationships, and the negativity that comes from not following the majority's opinion. As a result of this desire to conform and fear of causing 'trouble', I initially used to be afraid to speak up or actively seek challenging situations.

The crux of leaning into tension is that it is painful. Especially, if you are risk averse, avoiding tension often feels easier and more comfortable, particularly in the short term. This provides a sense of certainty and stability, leaving negative emotions outside. Yet, the pressure - internal or external - is unlikely to magically disappear. In fact, tension is an integral part of innovation, creativity and moving forward. Managed the right way, tension can pave the way for growth, be it a product, a person, business, team or an industry.

In economic theory, opportunity cost is the benefit an individual, investor or business misses out on when choosing one alternative over another.[160] Whilst avoiding pressures - be they internal or external - can feel like the right thing to do in the short term, companies, products and individuals can miss out on opportunities to advance in the long run. The cost of forfeiting such opportunities can be high. The examples of Firestone, the Zune and an experiences from my own career illustrate how high the price of not embracing tension can be.

159 "To Conform or Not to Conform: Spontaneous Conformity Diminishes the Sensitivity to Monetary Outcomes," Rongjun Yu and Sai Sun, PLOS Cognitive Neuroscience Channel, May 17, 2013, https://journals.plos.org/plosone/article?id=10.1371/journal.pone.0064530.

160 "Opportunity Cost," Will Kenton, Investopedia, June 25, 2019, https://www.investopedia.com/terms/o/opportunitycost.asp.

FIRESTONE TIRE & RUBBER: 'BLOCKING' EXTERNAL TENSION COMING FROM MICHELIN

'Unless one can see and plan for a year or two ahead, one's business will not grow evenly and naturally.' **Harvey S. Firestone**

Firestone Tire & Rubber was a hugely successful tyre manufacturer for about seventy years, very much enjoying a duopoly in the US with its main competitor, Goodyear.[161] The company had become a monument to its own success. Its culture and operations reflected the vision of its founder, Harvey Firestone, Sr., who insisted on treating his customers and employees as part of the 'Firestone family'. Firestone's company culture was therefore one of loyalty and shared values, set against the backdrop of the company's long-standing success.[162]

Until the seventies, that is, when French tyre company Michelin introduced radial tyres to the US market. Radial tyres were proven to be

161 "Why Good Companies Go Bad," Donald Sull, Harvard Business Review, July - August 1999, https://hbr.org/1999/07/why-good-companies-go-bad.

162 "The Dynamics of Standing Still: Firestone Tire & Rubber and the Radial Revolution," Donald Sull, Harvard Business Review, November 27, 2000; "Who is Harvey Firestone? Meet the legend who reinvented the tire," Firestone Blog, May 10, 2018, https://blog.firestonecompleteautocare.com/tires/who-is-harvey-firestone/.

safer and longer lasting than the traditional bias tyres which Firestone produced. Michelin was already a dominant player in Europe, and the writing was on the wall for Firestone.

Despite having ignored early warning signs, Firestone responded as quickly as it could to Michelin's threat and started producing radial tyres. However, the company clung to its existing production processes even though the manufacture of radial tyres required much higher quality standards.[163] *Firestone never recovered from its inadequate response to market pressures, instead suffering the consequences. They doggedly continued to make a product increasingly discarded by customers - the original bias tyre - whilst at the same time attempting to produce a new product, radial tyres, which were inferior in quality to those of its competitors.*

If we reflect back on the ways in which companies can deal with tension as described in the previous chapter, Firestone was trying to *block* shots coming from Michelin. After holding off a response to competitive threats, Firestone eventually started producing radial tyres too. By competing with Michelin in the radial tyre market, Firestone was putting its guard up, defending itself against Michelin, the first mover in this market. Unfortunately, Firestone's defence proved to be inadequate, as it struggled to regain competitive advantage and was ultimately acquired by Bridgestone, a Japanese corporation, in 1988. The former Firestone operations continued to incur losses of up to $1.2 billion over a four-and-a-half-year period, with Firestone's financial haemorrhaging only coming to an end five years after being taken over.[164]

163 *Ibid 161.*

164 "Bridgestone in Deal for Firestone," Jonathan Hicks, The New York Times, March 18, 1988, https://www.nytimes.com/1988/03/18/business/bridgestone-in-deal-for-firestone.html; "Bridgestone took on world with Firestone acquisition," Roger Schreffler, Rubber & Plastics News, September 16, 2013, https://www.rubbernews.com/article/20130916/NEWS/130919964/bridgestone-took-on-world-with-firestone-acquisition.

THE ZUNE: A BUSINESS THAT FAILED TO PIVOT ENOUGH TO OVERTAKE THE IPOD

'We're working on the specific areas of video, music, gaming and mobile, and also trying to work to make all those things come together in a coherent, logical way.' **Robbie Bach**

The Zune was supposed to be Microsoft's answer to Apple's iPod. But it wasn't. Similar to the Pono, which we studied in Chapter 2, the Zune was a portable music device launched by Microsoft in 2006 as a great alternative to the iPod.[165] Despite Microsoft's great ambitions with the Zune, it only lasted a few years before they discontinued the product in 2012. At the time of its launch, the Zune was already on the back foot and lagging behind the breakthrough success of Apple's iPod which had been released five years prior.[166]

165 "Biggest product flops from the world's biggest companies," Ben Gilbert, Business Insider, October 17, 2019, https://www.businessinsider.com/biggest-product-flops-in-history-2016-12.

166 "The Flop That Saved Microsoft," Farhad Manjoo, Slate, October 26, 2012, https://slate.com/technology/2012/10/microsoft-zune-how-one-of-the-biggest-flops-in-tech-history-helped-revive-a-great-american-tech-company.html.

This didn't stop Microsoft from placing a lot of its chips on the Zune becoming a mainstream success.[167] *Zunes came with preloaded content - audio and video - and the product had its own marketplace where purchases could be made using 'Microsoft Points', with users prepaying $5 for a block of 400 songs (paying up to 79 points per song).*[168] *In this respect, Microsoft offered a subscription service long before the likes of Spotify and Netflix.*[169] *Zune users could even 'squirt' songs to each other; the device would alert users to the presence of another Zune within 30 feet and users could send a song, photo or podcast to any nearby fellow Zune user. The potential recipient of the content would get a message asking whether he or she wanted to accept it. If yes, the squirting would start and take 10-15 seconds to share the content.*[170]

Based on all these unique features, you might be inclined to think that the Zune should have knocked Apple's iPod off its perch or at least posed a serious threat. It didn't. So how did Microsoft get it so wrong?

- **They were on the back foot** - Instead of being on its toes, the Zune was simply too far behind the iPod. Despite being late to the party, that in itself need not have been a showstopper. But the Microsoft Zune's failure to provide a compelling point of differentiation proved to be the nail in its coffin. Robbie Bach, then Microsoft's executive responsible for the Zune,

167 "Gone too Zune: We reflect on Microsoft's failed music project," Terrence O'Brien, Engadget, September 17, 2015, https://www.engadget.com/2015/09/17/gone-too-zune/.

168 "Zune," Fandom, Microsoft Wiki, https://microsoft.fandom.com/wiki/Zune (Accessed on October 29, 2019).

169 "Zune Brings Powerful New Entertainment Features To Every Zune Portable Media Player With Software Release," Ben Ryon, Microsoft, September 16, 2008, https://news.microsoft.com/2008/09/16/zune-brings-powerful-new-entertainment-features-to-every-zune-portable-media-player-with-software-release/.

170 "Zune Should Go Beyond 'Squirting'" Steven Levy, Newsweek, October 26, 2011, https://www.newsweek.com/zune-should-go-beyond-squirting-107255.

later admitted as much: 'The portable music market is gone, and it was already leaving when we started. We just weren't brave enough, honestly, and we ended up chasing Apple with a product that actually wasn't a bad product, but it was still a chasing product, and there wasn't a reason for somebody to say, oh, I have to go out and get that thing.'[171]

- **Their marketing was too narrow** - When talking about the Zune, Bach later also conceded that 'I think our marketing message was very confused...We did some really artsy ads that appealed to a very small segment of the music space, and we didn't captivate the broad segment of music listeners.'[172] That statement ties in with the aforementioned lack of internal clarity about the Zune's positioning and differentiation. Were the makers of the Zune clear enough about the customer problem their product was looking to solve?[173] And if so, how well was that intention reflected in the product (design) choices Microsoft made?[174]

With the Zune, Microsoft tried to *pivot* in its ongoing fight with Apple, but the device didn't sidestep far enough from the iPod. The new features Microsoft introduced as part of the Zune were neither sufficiently different from the iPod nor compelling for customers. Bach's retrospective admission that 'we just weren't brave enough' feels very apt in this respect.[175]

---

171 "Zune hardware was a mistake, admits former Microsoft exec Robbie Bach," Tom Warren, The Verge, May 14, 2012, https://www.theverge.com/2012/5/14/3019100/zune-hardware-mistake-robbie-bach.

172 *Ibid 171.*

173 "Robbie Bach Explains Why The Zune Flopped," Matt Rosoff, Business Insider, May 11, 2012, https://www.businessinsider.com/robbie-bach-explains-why-the-zune-flopped-2012-5.

174 "Five Reasons the Microsoft Zune is Dead," Nick Mokey, Digital Trends, May 17, 2009, https://www.digitaltrends.com/mobile/five-reasons-the-microsoft-zune-is-dead/.

175 *Ibid 171.*

MY 'RETREAT' FROM FAT BEATS

'At the beginning, I was together with the rest. But not anymore. I mean, I'm close to 50 years old. I don't want to be that guy anymore who decides what's worth releasing and what's not.' **Joseph 'DJ Jab' Abajian**

Finally, as we will see in the remainder of this book, I have my own ways of dealing with tension. The period in which I completed my MBA resulted in a great deal of tension, both internal and external. From working in teams of people with different perspectives and professional backgrounds to the pressure of getting a job post-MBA, I found it to be a life changing but challenging experience. This feeling is probably best embodied by my experience of wanting to start a Hip Hop company in the UK ...

For my MBA thesis, I concentrated on market entry and positioning strategies, taking my favourite Hip Hop record label and retailer Fat

Beats as the focal point of my research.[176] *The central question of my thesis was whether it would make sense for Fat Beats to enter the UK market, both as a retailer and distributor of Hip Hop music. Applying theory about market segmentation and niches, I researched the UK landscape for music and artists alike, assessing the different strategic opportunities available to Fat Beats.*

The deeper I got into my thesis the more I started pondering whether I should start getting Fat Beats off the ground in the UK after my MBA, putting my learnings and recommendations to the test. Considering both the opportunity and complexity involved in starting a business, and after spending time with Fat Beats' founder / CEO Joseph 'DJ Jab' Abajian, I was torn. Should I go for it and dedicate a period of my life to raising capital to make it happen? Or was it all too risky a venture in a saturated and uncertain market? How would I handle the pressures of being an entrepreneur, running a business?

After long deliberation, I decided not to pursue the Fat Beats UK dream and I still look back on that decision with a tinge of regret. I carefully contemplated the pros and cons of the Fat Beats opportunity and the pressures I envisaged. I retreated, I backed too far away from the opportunity, and failed to come up with an approach to make the opportunity work and make it happen.

The experience made me realise that I am probably more of an 'editor' than a 'creator'; more suited to taking an existing project or venture forward instead of starting a new venture from scratch. It also made me reflect on my appetite for risk; understanding my 'risk profile' helped me avoid making a decision that felt beyond the level of discomfort that I was comfortable with. Conversely, I was comfortably uncomfortable

176 Fat Beats was founded in 1994 by Joseph Abajian, starting with a vinyl record shop in Manhattan's Lower East Side, subsequently opening up new stores in Amsterdam, Tokyo, Los Angeles, and Atlanta. The company has evolved over the past 25 years and in its current guise Fat Beats specialises in distribution of vinyl and specialty item records. See: https://www.fatbeats.com/pages/about-us (Accessed on November 2, 2019).

with my decisions to make a career switch from law to marketing and, eventually, a career in digital technology.[177]

Hindsight and life experience are two beautiful things, and I sometimes wish I could go back to my MBA days to come up with new ways to perhaps *retreat* first in the face of pressure and uncertainty, and see if I could take on the opportunity, *leaning in* on all the uncertainties and challenges. I particularly like how Brandon Chu, VP Product & GM of Platform at Shopify, explains the shift from 'nervous to infectious energy' and how we need to change our perception and mindset to enable this. Chu shared the example of public speaking where one might feel nervous beforehand, but as soon as you step on the stage, you're fine.[178]

Author Robert Fritz talks along similar lines in his bestselling book 'The Path of Least Resistance', where he analyses the creative tension inherent in the discrepancy between what you want and what you have.[179] In the next section, we will delve into the relation between tension and creativity, aiming to better understand how we as product people can optimise this.

---

177 I talk about my journey from law into product management: "Marc Abraham about his role as Product Ownership Practice Lead at ASOS," Tim Herbig, Digitale Leute podcast, December 18, 2019, https://www.digitale-leute.de/interview/episode-24-marc-abraham-product-ownership-practice-lead-at-asos-com/; "Can a Product Career be Planned? By Marc Abraham," Andres Phillips, Mind the Product, January 20, 2020, https://www.mindtheproduct.com/can-a-product-career-be-planned-by-marc-abraham/.

178 Brandon Chu, *interview by author*, Toronto, August 29, 2019.

179 *Ibid 6, p. 116.*

Leaning into Tension = Mind + Matter + Moves

When leaning into tension, it is important to be mindful of **the 'Knitting Spaghetti' tension**: the creative tension between the existing and the new. Your product will benefit from you deliberately seeking this tension, bridging the gap between existing and desired outcomes.

Three main steps to start **leaning into tension**:

- Acknowledge tension; instead of ignoring tension, **'pause'** to take it in.
- Analyse tension; create a **moment of choice** and study your options.
- Use tension as a springboard; **reframing** tension in such a way that tension paves the way for growth.

THE 'KNITTING SPAGHETTI' TENSION

'Instead of thinking outside the box, get rid of the box.' **Deepak Chopra**

Managing products requires creativity. Whether you are inventing something new or are iterating on an existing invention, creating typically comes down to your ability to adjust or correct what you have done so far.[180] It means that when building products, we often need to find the right balance between the comfort derived from the familiar and our desire to explore new things. In 'The Creative Curve',

180 *Ibid 6, p. 53.*

Allen Gannett examines the optimal tension between people craving the familiar - to protect us from the unknown - and seeking the novel - to get satisfaction and rewards from surprises and unusual things (See fig. 13).[181]

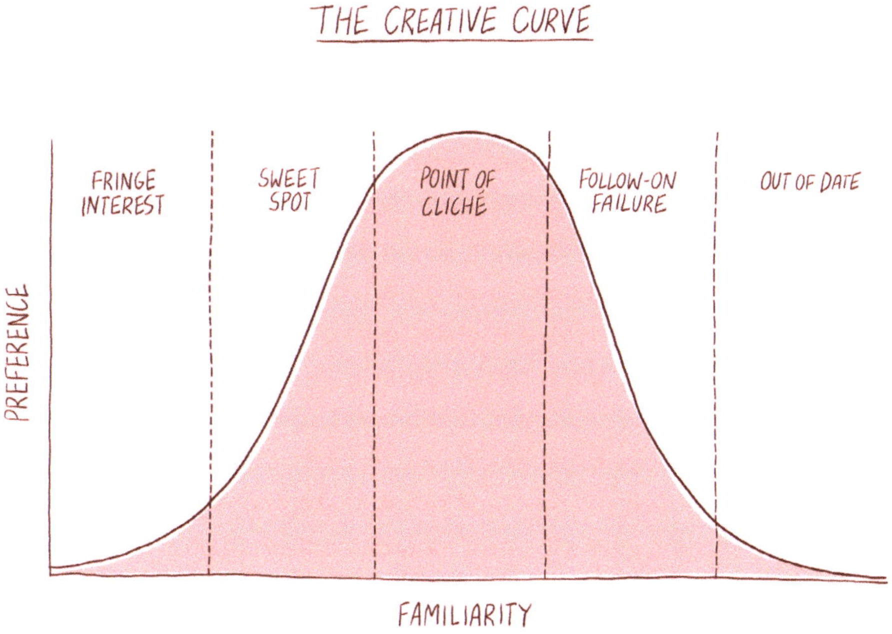

Fig. 13 – Allen Gannett's Creative Curve; tension between craving familiarity and seeking novelty

Actively seeking this creative tension is a deliberate process. Product managers generally set out to achieve specific results, for their customers and the businesses that they work for. For example, reducing the amount of time and effort involved in consumers getting a mortgage is a concrete result that product people can help deliver. If this outcome is successfully achieved for customers, the mortgage

181 *Ibid 16, pp. 17-18.*

business should see positive business results at the same time.[182]

Contrary to popular belief, creativity is more often than not the result of an intentional pursuit. In the words of the painter Georgia O'Keeffe: 'I don't start until I'm almost entirely clear. It is a waste of time and paint if I don't.' When we are being creative, we are looking to generate specific results, aiming to bridge the discrepancy between the current state of affairs and the desired result.

Product management is all about bridging the gap between the existing and the desired outcome and handling the tension that arises when overcoming this gap. 'Product people are ambiguity eaters' is how the aforementioned Chris Butler explained it to me. 'This is because we have to absorb and digest much of the uncertainty that the team has to deal with. We are not keeping it away from everyone but helping them find certainty in the uncertainty.'[183] At the intersection of the customer, technology and the business, where product managers operate, uncertainty is at its highest.

If we define creativity as the act of invention - as opposed to convention - most product managers will have front row seats to the act of creation. And if we treat creativity as a process rather than a fluke, we need to acknowledge the pressure inherent in creating the unprecedented and managing the creative process. Professor Mihaly Csikszentmihalyi in his work on the state of 'flow' distinguishes three components of creativity:[184]

- **A culture that contains symbolic rules** - The domain within which people create the subject matter which guides innovations. In other words, the environment *where* the creativity is.

182 See: Joshua Seiden, *Outcomes Over Output: Why Customer Behaviour Is The Key Metric For Business Success* (Sense & Respond Press, 2019); "Book review: Outcomes Over Output by Joshua Seiden," June 27, 2019, Medium, https://medium.com/@maa1/book-review-outcomes-over-output-by-joshua-seiden-eac32ace928a.

183 *Ibid 157.*

184 Mihaly Csikszentmihalyi, *Flow: The Psychology of Optimal Experience* (Harper & Row, 1993).

- **A field of experts who recognise and validate the innovation** - The field in which certain people are responsible for deciding what is creative and has value, and what does not. These people, who don't have to be subject matter experts, decide about which inventions or products to keep and which to discard. Think, for example, about consumers providing product feedback or literary critics reviewing the latest novels. In other words, the *who* which judges the creativity.
- **A person who brings novelty into the symbolic domain** - The individual that possesses the necessary combination of technical talent and practical attributes to engage with the existing culture and the field of experts. In other words, this is the person who introduces original ideas into existing domains or fields.

It is easy to see how these three elements of creativity can cause friction. Think about a scenario where a product idea is explored. One that goes beyond prevailing convention, ignores prevailing perceptions or upsets entrenched views held by individuals within the organisation. Let's say you work for a company that is looking to make its first move in the field of voice technology. Conventional wisdom among your colleagues doubts the value this will add. Added to that, due to lack of familiarity with the capabilities of voice technology, team members have had heated debates about how to best apply voice technology and come up with wildly different suggestions. This kind of debate is 'healthy', the team is leaning into the pressure of implementing a technology, new to the company and its customers. This situation qualifies as a 'task conflict', where people have a difference of opinion about the task or challenge at hand.

For example, Shaheena Attarwala, Design Manager at Microsoft, tends to be deliberate about highlighting different perspectives among the members of her team: 'From time to time I make my team aware of each other's differences and their purpose as a design crew.'[185] Attarwala uses the same approach when any tensions arise between her team members and other teams. She explains that 'this helps team members from within the design team and cross-functional teams recognise that others have different views and ultimately people anticipate dissimilarities and disagreements in work and team members as a part of a healthy working relationship.'[186]

In contrast, 'relationship conflict' centres around personal friction, for example when team members are not getting along or people are simply being jerks.[187] I might for example feel strongly about a one-step customer onboarding process, whereas my colleague Keji is of the view that customers need to go through multiple onboarding steps. Conflicts like these, about the task of creating an onboarding flow, are easier to manage than situations which occur as a result of differences of personal style.

I see task conflict as a key ingredient of creativity and - consequently - of developing products and creating value. Regardless of your role within the product management process, you are bound to be engaged in task conflict at some point or another. You might have a totally opposing view to a fellow engineer about how to best build a product or feature. You might disagree on how to best achieve value for your customers.

Or you think you might have come up with a great idea for a new product, only for the rest of the team to vehemently dismiss the premise of your great idea ... As digital product leader Ken Chin says,

---

185 Shaheena Attarwala, *email to author,* January 15, 2020.

186 *Ibid 185.*

187 "Teaming: How Organizations Learn, Innovate, and Compete in the Knowledge Economy," Amy C. Edmondson (San Francisco: Jossey-Bass, 2010, pp. 70 – 71); "Book review: The No Asshole Rule," Marc Abraham, As I learn, March 12, 2018, https://marcabraham.com/2018/03/12/book-review-the-no-asshole-rule/; "Atlassian ditches 'brilliant jerks' in performance review overhaul," Frank Chung, news.com.au, July 19, 2019, https://www.news.com.au/finance/work/at-work/atlassian-ditches-brilliant-jerks-in-performance-review-overhaul/news-story/82a5e2abba1939f51d68ae81db8f05bd#.Im5rv.

'expect tension as a normal part of a high-performing team. If not, you're not being innovative enough.' High performance teams are able to work through conflict and use it as a source of creativity and innovation. Chin stresses that conflict does exist in less mature teams too but 'they just haven't figured out how to get past it.'[188] Creativity can thus be a risky business where we leave ourselves open to criticism from others and venture beyond our comfort zone.[189]

My point is that albeit indispensable, creative tension does not have to be antagonistic or insufferable. According to acclaimed author and entrepreneur Shane Snow, the 'zone of optimal tension' is where 'the rubber band is stretched tight, but we don't want to turn it on each other and shoot each other with it.'[190] Add to that the reality of constraints within products; budget, technology, people, expertise and time which can all work to restrict creativity. There is nothing more frustrating than coming up with exciting product ideas, only to find out that there isn't the budget or expertise to implement them. Or when innovation is being held-up by legacy systems or 'technical debt', the latter usually the result of technical or design decisions made to yield short-term benefits.[191] However, as we will see later in this book, it can be beneficial to look for things that are wrong with your idea or to acknowledge flaws that could hinder success.[192]

---

188 Ken Chin, *interview by author*, London, November 11, 2019.

189 See: "Creative Thinking is Product Management," Jon Kolko, This Is Product Management podcast, January 2018, https://www.thisisproductmanagement.com/episodes/creative-thinking/; "Why Criticism Is Good for Creativity," Don Norman, LinkedIn, July 22, 2019, https://www.linkedin.com/pulse/why-criticism-good-creativity-don-norman/.

190 Shane Snow, *Dream Teams: Working Together Without Falling Apart* (New York: Portfolio, June, 2018); "Discovering the Secrets of "Dream Teams"," Shane Snow on Evernote podcast, July 2, 2018, https://medium.com/taking-note/discovering-the-secrets-of-dream-teams-1b4de086bf0a.

191 Technical Debt Quadrant," Martin Fowler, ThoughtWorks, October 14, 2009, reposted on November 19, 2014, https://martinfowler.com/bliki/TechnicalDebtQuadrant.html.

192 "Strategy Needs Creativity," Adam Brandenburger, Harvard Business Review, March - April 2019, https://hbr.org/2019/03/strategy-needs-creativity.

HOW TENSION CAN PAVE THE WAY FOR GROWTH

'The road is always better than the inn.' **Cervantes**

Like it or not, tension isn't going to go away when you are managing products. Yes, there will be times where you and your product team are riding a wave of success or the product is clearly on top, but tension is always close by. This is why we have to lean into tension and embrace the pressures or challenges that come our way. There are three steps to doing so effectively: (1) acknowledge the tension (2) analyse tension and (3) use tension as a springboard. Instead of trying to block out the inevitable strains that occur when managing a product, these three steps will help your product, your team, business or you individually grow through tension. Let me break down the approach to leaning in and apply these to the different actors involved in building and managing products.

Step 1 - Acknowledge tension

The first thing to do when tension arises is to acknowledge it. Let's pause here, as acknowledging tension sounds much easier than it is. On a personal level, when I am conscious of tension, it will always 'hit' me initially, no matter how big or small or where it is coming from. I will often have a physical reaction when I sense any form of tension, even if I am not involved directly. 'So how can you still advocate the need to acknowledge tension?!' you might be wondering, and the answer is simple: the alternative, *ignoring* tension and simply carrying on, didn't work for me. Pretending that the tension wasn't there left some of the daily pressures of being a product person unresolved.

Even though ignoring the rumblings of pressure might have helped me in the short term, in the long term the tension would still continue to bubble up. Take a bleak weekday night three years ago where I completely lost my cool with the engineers in my team. In our conversation it became apparent that a piece of work we had committed to doing had not been done. I asked my colleagues why we hadn't done the work that day, they said that 'the business analyst hadn't written the user stories'. When the engineers noticed my slightly puzzled face, one of them explained 'Marc, you know how it works. If there are no user stories, we are not going to do the work...' On hearing that statement, I completely lost it: I shouted, cursed and stormed out of the room, leaving my colleagues understandably shaken and upset by my outburst. Soon after, I pulled my colleagues into a room and apologised profusely, explaining my reaction without trying to justify it. Trust me, I wasn't proud of my behaviour that night ...

When I reflected on the incident afterwards, I realised that I had not acknowledged the pressures I was feeling. Suppressing a lingering unhappiness with our way of working, my concerns about not meeting expectations and a lack of shared ownership ultimately resulted in me losing my composure and the trust of the team in the process. Psychologists Janet Metcalfe and Walter Mischel qualify my response as coming from the 'go' or 'hot system', i.e. the system designated for quick emotional processing and responding immediately to certain triggers. In contrast, Metcalfe and Mischel's 'cool' system is designated for reflection and thought.[193] Acknowledging tension does not mean that you should not feel affected or just laugh pressures away. Instead, you accept things for what they are and stop fighting reality.[194]

This requires self-awareness to see what is happening and the different (emotional) responses available to you. Internationally renowned psychologist Daniel Goleman is the leading scholar

193 "A Hot/Cool-System Analysis of Delay of Gratification: Dynamics of Willpower," Janet Metcalfe and Walter Mischel, Psychological Review 1999, Vol. 106, No. 1, pp. 3-19, http://www.columbia.edu/cu/psychology/metcalfe/PDFs/Metcalfe%20Mischel%201999.pdf.

194 Tara Brach, *Radical Acceptance* (New York: Bantam Dell, December 2004); "4 Lessons from Radical Acceptance by Tara Brach," Keith E. Edwards, August 3, 2006, https://www.keithedwards.com/2016/08/03/4-lessons-from-radical-acceptance-by-tara-brach/; "My Product Management Toolkit (32): managing your frustrations," Marc Abraham, Medium, November 5, 2018, https://medium.com/@maa1/my-product-management-toolkit-32-managing-your-frustrations-bd022779923a.

on emotional intelligence, which he explains as operating at the intersection between one's emotions and rational thoughts.[195] As we have seen throughout this book so far, pressure is an integral part of life, work, being. We might as well accept this tension, starting with a full awareness of how we perceive tension and how others around us view our perceptions and behaviours.[196]

Building in a *pause* helps you to become fully aware of what your head is thinking and your heart is feeling, and avoids what Goleman refers to as 'emotional hijacking'.[197] Pausing for a moment helps you to acknowledge what is happening and how you feel about this, and prevent a so-called fight or flight response; an innate, physiological reaction that occurs in response to a perceived harmful event, attack or existential threat.[198] In my earlier example, I felt threatened by the words and behaviours of my engineering colleagues, and I responded 'in the moment', almost literally coming out fighting. Had I instead acknowledged the rising tensions early on, I would have been able to 'pause' and *analyse* these tensions first.

Step 2 - Analyse tension

Pausing creates a moment of choice. And we do have a choice when faced with tension. As William Ury writes in 'Getting to Yes with Yourself', when we react straight away, we typically fall into what Ury calls the '3A trap': we attack, we accommodate or we avoid altogether.[199] Ury goes on to say that we don't have to react, and that we can instead observe ourselves by what he refers to as 'going to the

195 Daniel Goleman, *Emotional Intelligence: Why it Can Matter More Than IQ* (New York: Bantam Dell, September 2006).

196 "Rethinking What We Think About How to Change," Prof. Scott Babson, TEDx Talk, May 3, 2019, https://www.youtube.com/watch?v=FClv1h4L1H8; "How self-awareness can make you a better leader," Laura Montgomery, The Economist, https://execed.economist.com/blog/career-hacks/how-self-awareness-can-make-you-better-leader (Accessed on November 19, 2019).

197 *Ibid* 195.

198 Walter Cannon, *Wisdom of the Body* (W.W. Norton & Company, 1932).

199 William Ury, *Getting to Yes with Yourself* (HarperOne, 2015, p. 20).

balcony'.[200] These are some questions I recommend asking yourself when you are going to the balcony:

- **Stop!** What is the bigger picture here?
- **Self:** What does this situation mean to me?
- **Others:** What does this situation look like to others involved? (e.g. the team, the company, etc.)
- **Outsider:** How does this appear to someone outside this situation?
- **Wise mind:** What would be the best thing to do in this situation? For me, for others, for this situation?

Going to the balcony or taking a helicopter view effectively means that we are retaking control of our emotions or pressures that we might be feeling in the moment. I like how Malia Lazu, culture creator at Berkshire Bank, views self-reflection as 'one of the biggest smallest things you can do' whilst Kazuo Inamori, founder of Kyocera, the electronics and ceramics manufacturer, advocates 'paying our best attention, regardless of the situation or environment'.[201]

Failing to create a moment of choice, means that we are more likely to fall off the balcony or miss the helicopter taking off. In other words, pausing creates the mental space to *analyse*, both the tension that we are observing and the different options available to us with

200 *Ibid 199, p. 21.*

201 "Dangerous unselfishness is what inclusion looks like when it's an action," Malia Lazu, Creative Mornings Boston, April 26, 2019, https://creativemornings.com/talks/malia-lazu/; "Essential Leadership Qualities: Paying Voluntary Attention Sharpens Judgment," Kazuo Inamori, Official Website of Kazuo Inamori, https://global.kyocera.com/inamori/philosophy/philosophy47.html.

regard to responding to tension.[202] Like most things, 'doing nothing' is always an option. You might analyse the tension and come to the conclusion that there is nothing that you can do about the situation, deciding to accept things for what they are.[203] We all know the age-old adage about 'picking your battles', which in my view does not mean that you simply succumb to tension, but understand what is happening and why, and make a conscious call to let it rest. You can ask yourself 'what can I influence?' and work on those things that you can do something about.[204]

I strongly believe that simply acknowledging and analysing tension can be hugely beneficial to you, your team, product or company. Having full *awareness* of a challenging situation should at least give you a grip on what is happening and why, even if you decide not to act or try to resolve the situation.

Step 3 - Use tension as a springboard

Naturally, the list of choices open to us will depend largely on the situation at hand, but *reframing* is the first option that often arises once you start analysing tension. Shedding a different light on the circumstance helps you to use tension as a springboard:

- **Tension as a source of information** - Try treating tension as a source of information, an opportunity to learn about things that don't work, or challenges not encountered before. Can

202 See: "How to Practice Emotional Intelligence: 10 Expert Tips for Expanding Choice," Michael Miller, Six Seconds, https://www.6seconds.org/2018/03/28/emotional-intelligence-tips-choice/; "The Six Seconds Model of EQ," Joshua Freedman, Six Seconds, https://www.6seconds.org/2010/01/27/the-six-seconds-eq-model/; "This 1 Practice Will Dramatically Increase Your Emotional Intelligence," Justin Bariso, Inc., March 10, 2016, https://www.inc.com/justin-bariso/emotional-intelligence-101-practicing-this-one-thing-will-dramatically-increase-.html; "4 Habits You Should Pick Up if You Want to Be Well-Liked at Work," Aja Frost, The Muse, https://www.themuse.com/advice/4-habits-you-should-pick-up-if-you-want-to-be-wellliked-at-work.

203 *Ibid 194*.

204 Stephen R. Covey, *The 7 Habits of Highly Effective People* (Simon & Schuster: Second Edition, 2004, pp. 81-83).

you treat tension as an opportunity to *learn* and develop?[205]

- **Tension as an opportunity to react differently** - I like the well-known quote by NBA basketball coach Greg Popovich; 'The measure of who we are is how we react to something that does not go our way.' Have a go at flipping tension into an opportunity to respond in a way that might feel different or unnatural.
- **Tension as an opportunity to restate a problem** - Can you restate the tension, using different language or perspectives, in order to gain a different perspective on what is happening and explore different avenues to managing or resolving the tension?[206]
- **Tension as a source of strength** - Tension often unsettles individuals, organisations or societies. Neither our instincts nor our environments are geared towards using tension as a power. Doubt, for example, is often seen as a sign of weakness; that you are lacking the confidence to commit fully. Damian Bradfield, co-founder of file sharing platform WeTransfer, refreshingly views doubt as a strength and integral to learning. 'When we harness doubt, use it to test ideas, ask questions of ourselves, investigate and appraise before blindly stumbling forwards,' Bradfield argues, 'then we have fully utilised the power of doubt.'[207]

I would be lying if I claimed to have fully mastered the ability to deal with tension in any given circumstance. In contrast, I try to remind myself almost every day to pause whenever I feel tense or anxious. Time and practice – lots of it – have helped me to acknowledge

205 "Skilled Incompetence," Chris Argyris, Harvard Business Review, September 1986, https://hbr.org/1986/09/skilled-incompetence.

206 Morgan D. Jones, *The Thinker's Toolkit: 14 Powerful Techniques for Problem Solving* (Crown Business, June 1998); "11 Ways To Restate Problems to Get Better Solutions," Paul Williams, Idea Sandbox, https://idea-sandbox.com/blog/11-ways-to-restate-problems-to-get-better-solutions/.

207 "Embracing doubt," Damian Bradfield, Mission.org, Medium, January 4, 2017, https://medium.com/the-mission/embracing-doubt-fd86989b2ad3.

and analyse tension and enabled me to grow as a person. Instead of becoming resistant to pressure or developing a Teflon skin, I have learned to take pressure and uncertainty in my stride. And I would like to think that this has also rubbed off on the teams I have been part of and the products I have been working on.

If you recall the battle between Compaq and Apple described in the previous chapter, no one is immune from tension. Sooner or later, products, teams and whole businesses will be exposed to pressure. Some products and teams won't recover, whilst others will come out stronger and prosper after a tough period. Surges in fortunes are typically the result of organisations and their people reframing tensions and turning them into opportunities for positive change.

DIRECT LINE: SEIZING A DISRUPTIVE SITUATION

Started in 1985, Direct Line became the first UK insurance company to use the phone as its main communication channel. Instead of having a physical presence, Direct Line used the phone to acquire and support customers.[208] *The company were eventually acquired*

208 "Our Story," Direct Line Group, https://www.directlinegroup.co.uk/en/who-we-are/our-story.html, (Accessed on November 25, 2019).

by Royal Bank of Scotland ('RBS') which had to return Direct Line into a standalone business, following the 2008 financial crisis. This could have been a disruptive and risky exercise for Direct Line and its business, especially when there was no plan B.

Then Direct Line's CEO Paul Geddes led an 18-month operation to separate the Direct Line business out from RBS, doing so as rapidly and efficiently as possible. As soon as the company had been separated, the focus shifted to turning Direct Line into a business that could stand on its own two feet, healthy financially and with its own strong brand.[209] *Direct Line has proven to be a good example of a company reframing its challenging situation into a positive one, as illustrated by Geddes: 'Anyone leading a change programme will have to repeat the key messages over and over, and to multiple audiences. (...) Respect the past, be honest about the present, and be optimistic about the future.'*[210]

SONY: RESPONDING TO THE INVENTION OF THE TRANSISTOR

SONY

The invention of the transistor in the 1950 and 1960s posed a serious threat to incumbent TV manufacturers like LG, Samsung and Sony. Up to that point, TVs were designed based on vacuum tubes. These tubes contained electron guns and a phosphorescent screen to display

209 "The 5 greatest examples of change management in business history," Paul Arnold, Chartered Management Institute, July 20, 2015, https://www.managers.org.uk/insights/news/2015/july/the-5-greatest-examples-of-change-management-in-business-history.

210 "Ten years at the top: the change manager changes ... himself," Matthew Rock, Chartered Management Institute, May 10, 2019, https://www.managers.org.uk/insights/news/2019/may/ten-years-at-the-top-the-change-manager-changes-himself.

images.[211] *Some players in the TV industry decided to ignore or restate the external tension posed by the introduction of the transistor. A notable example is RCA, a dominant electronics company at the time, who were slow to apply new technologies to their TV line.*[212]

Sony, LG and Samsung, in contrast, actively drove the growth of flat panel TVs, effectively cannibalising their existing cathode ray tube products. They adopted LCD technologies, which they in time replaced by LED in order to create the slimmest TV sets possible.[213] *The eventual outcome feels as tragic as it was inevitable: RCA no longer exists, whilst Sony, LG and Samsung are battling it out on the market for flat screen TVs.*

NATIONAL GEOGRAPHIC: STAYING RELEVANT IN THE DIGITAL AGE

211 "Television History and the Cathode Ray Tube," Mary Bellis, ThoughtCo., April 6, 2017, https://www.thoughtco.com/television-history-cathode-ray-tube-1991459.

212 "First-Hand: Apple, RCA and the Visionaries," Michael Ettenberg, Engineering and Technology History Wiki, January 12, 2015, https://ethw.org/First-Hand:Apple,_RCA_and_the_Visionaries; "Avoiding technology risk and the demise of big businesses Henry Kressel," Asia Times, November 18, 2018, https://www.asiatimes.com/2018/11/article/avoiding-technology-risk-and-the-demise-of-businesses/.

213 "R.I.P. Cathode ray tube monitor," BBC News, July 27, 2001, http://news.bbc.co.uk/1/hi/uk/1459817.stm; "The evolution of TV - from black and white to HDR," Currys, January 26, 2016, https://techtalk.currys.co.uk/tv-gaming/tv/the-evolution-of-tv-from-black-and-white-to-hdr/.

The yellow-bordered National Geographic magazine is a true institution, and has been that for over 130 years.[214] *The magazine has been feeling the pressure though as a result of the rapid rise of digital content; National Geographic subscriber revenue had dropped from $289 million in 1999 to $211 million in 2009 and it was clear that some drastic action was needed.*[215] *Whilst National Geographic was slow in responding to a changing environment, it is now treating the significant threats to its original business model as an opportunity to innovate.*

Apart from agreeing a substantial cable programming deal with media company Fox in 2012, National Geographic has been diversifying its media platforms, and widening its reach as a result. In addition to its physical magazine and cable, you can now find National Geographic content using a variety of digital channels including Instagram and YouTube. This isn't just repurposed content, but often content tailored to the relevant channel and users of that channel.[216] *Its social media strategy, for example, has given National Geographic a huge audience on platforms such as Instagram and Facebook, which it almost certainly would not have gained had it just remained a physical product. Whereas other well-known magazines like Gourmet and Loaded have disappeared altogether, National Geographic has opened up new channels and audiences, beyond*

---

214 "January 27, 1888: National Geographic Society Founded" History.com, January 23, 2020, https://www.nationalgeographic.org/thisday/jan13/national-geographic-society-founded/.

215 "5 Companies who Evolved with New Tech," Krisha Maclang, Glia, June 28, 2016, https://blog.glia.com/5-companies-evolved-embracing-new-tech/.

216 "Reinventing the National Geographic Society," Sean Silverthorne, Harvard Business Review, April 4, 2011, https://hbswk.hbs.edu/item/reinventing-the-national-geographic-society; "How National Geographic is innovating its brand with purpose," Nadia Cameron, CMOAustralia, March 23, 2017, https://www.cmo.com.au/article/616491/how-national-geographic-building-brand-purpose-led-future/; "In Focus: National Geographic on Bringing a Legacy Brand to New Platforms," The Telly Awards, https://www.tellyawards.com/in-focus/in-focus-national-geographic-on-bringing-a-legacy-brand-to-new-digital-platforms/.

their print publication and expanding its value propositions.[217] *In 2019, ownership of National Geographic changed from Fox to Walt Disney, as part of their $71 billion acquisition of 21st Century Fox.*[218]

All three examples illustrate the power of reframing a difficult situation and using it as a springboard instead. Both in the case of tension created as a result of internal organisational problems (Direct Line) or external threats (Sony and National Geographic), all three companies utilised tension as a launch pad for growth and innovation.

CONCLUSION

There is no doubt that most people don't necessarily welcome tension, particularly when growing businesses or managing products. Due to the creativity and ambiguity involved in managing products, it is hard to circumvent tension. A wide array of failed products has shown that ignoring tension is counterproductive in the long term. Businesses and products that have faced difficulty but came out stronger, all accepted and analysed their predicament, using it as a springboard. This is what 'leaning into tension' is all about, and in the next chapter we will examine more ways in which we can lean in effectively.

217 "6 Social Media Lessons from National Geographic's Huge Instagram Following," Liz McBrayer, Clickdimensions Blog, July 9, 2019, http://blog.clickdimensions.com/6-social-media-lessons-from-national-geographics-huge-instagram-following/.

218 "It's official: Disney now owns Fox," Michael Grothaus, Fast Company, March 20, 2019, https://www.fastcompany.com/90322666/its-official-disney-now-owns-fox; "Where Next for National Geographic?" Chris Harvey, Financial Times, April 11, 2019, https://www.ft.com/content/bbf5bcce-579e-11e9-8b71-f5b0066105fe.

SUMMARY

- **Leaning into tension** doesn't have to be daunting; in fact, done sensibly, embracing tension will be advantageous to your company and product.
- The **'Knitting Spaghetti' tension** is largely created by people, navigating between the familiarity of the existing and the surprise of the novel.
- **Firestone, the Zune** and **I** demonstrate how ignoring tension, or retreating from it, can backfire from a growth point of view.
- In contrast, **Direct Line**, **Sony** and **National Geographic** all optimised the tension that came with their business and product being disrupted.

When faced with tension, there are three steps to take and start leaning in:

- **Acknowledge** - Take the time to pause and simply allow the tension.
- **Analyse** - Utilise the moment of choice to understand what is happening and outline your options in terms of responding to the tension.
- **Springboard** - Reframe the tension and use it as a growth opportunity.

CHAPTER 5.
LEANING INTO TENSION EFFECTIVELY

'Failing to engage in conflict is a terrible decision, one that puts our temporary comfort and the avoidance of discomfort ahead of the ultimate goal of our organisation.' **Patrick Lencioni**

Product Management = Mind + Matter + Moves

In this chapter we will explore ways to **lean into product tension** effectively:

- **Start with yourself** and understand your appetite for tension, before actively seeking or embracing it.
- **Optimising 'Product Tension'** using techniques that help you zoom in on your product and its competitors.
- **Being OK with 'Individual Tension':** what are the ways in which you personally can be (more) comfortable with tension.
- **Tools and techniques**: each aspect covered in this chapter will have related tools and techniques for you to apply. You will find these in the toolkit section at the end of the chapter.

INTRODUCTION

Think of the last time you felt that creeping tension while managing a product. I imagine that it wasn't a nice feeling; the strain of working on something that lagged behind its competitors or the mounting frustrations in your product team when you missed a critical deadline. The previous chapter outlined how tension can pave the way for growth, as an individual, a team or as a product. In this chapter we will explore some critical tools and techniques to use if you wish to look for tension proactively or embrace existing pressures or frustrations in an effective manner. Before we explore some tools, we will start with the self and your own appetite for tension.

START WITH YOURSELF

'I think self-awareness is probably the most important thing towards being a champion.' **Billie Jean King**

The product that you and your team built is not doing half as well as you expected. You are struggling to raise funds for your startup. Or the priorities set by senior leadership at the large corporate organisation you work at don't align with your customer needs. There is a rift within the product development team about how to best solve a critical customer problem through your product. And then there is me encouraging you to lean into the tension!

Yes. Scenarios like the ones above can act as the perfect launch pad for growth and learning. And in fact, when tension is absent, you or your product team might be doing something wrong. As Ken Chin, an experienced digital product leader, explained to me, 'I always mention to my teams to expect tension as a normal part of a high-performing team. If not, you are probably not being innovative enough.'[219]

Adding to Chin's words, I expect product managers and product teams to pursue tension actively - both internally and externally. Actively seeking tension and conflict is a daunting prospect for most of us and I am no exception. Not a day goes by without me feeling some sense of anxiety or tension – self-induced or external - or just the classic imposter syndrome. It has made me realise that I need to start with myself when it comes to leaning into tension.

219 *Ibid 188.*

'Who am I?'

How self-aware are you?! To be able to embrace tension or conflict, it is important that you are aware of how you see yourself and how you see others. Equally, consider how others perceive you. For instance, do you know when you feel most vulnerable as a product manager or what your colleagues think of you? I know that I often picture myself as a fraud or imposter, which will at times shine through in my behaviour. Equally, I am aware that colleagues of mine sometimes wish I would be less direct and opinionated.

'What sets me off?'

As we covered in Chapter 1, emotional triggers are those people, words, opinions or situations that provoke a strong emotional reaction within us. Such reactions are typically based on a narrative built up in our brains since birth, this system interprets all the 'inputs' we receive against our pre-existing narrative and we respond accordingly.[220] There are common 'life scripts' that come into play and we tell ourselves things like 'everyone else is better than me'; 'I'm not good enough' or 'failure is for wimps'.[221] Anger, sadness and fear are often triggered as a result. When working in cross-functional teams, I used to feel both anger and sadness when I imagined the team were pointing the finger at me for a product underperforming or for not being clear about priorities.

'How do I react?'

What is your go-to behaviour in difficult or uncertain situations? How do others behave when the heat is on, and why? My first response in tense situations is often to take things personally, getting very defensive or passive aggressive as a result. Awareness of these

220 *Ibid 26.*
221 "What is your life script and are you happy with it?" Mel Johnson, Bestselfology, March 21, 2017, http://bestselfology.com/life-scripts/.

tendencies and behaviours is critical if we want to manage tension or conflict constructively. Tools such as the iMA test or the Meyers-Briggs Type Indicator provide valuable insights into your personality and preferences.[222]

When I took the iMA test - a quick behavioural survey designed to gain insight into your performance and collaboration style - the outcome was that I am 'cool, independent and competitive' and that I 'need to be in control of my situation and also need tangible evidence of progress.' I am aware of how anxious or irritated I can get when things are not going to plan, making me more likely to behave impulsively. Knowing these things about myself doesn't mean that I will never display those behaviours again, but it does help in pre-empting certain situations or triggers.

'Creator or editor: What am I?'

Creators are more likely to dive headfirst into tension, actively looking for uncertainty and learning and happy to start from a blank page. As a creator, you will find yourself more often than not in a situation where people will give you direct feedback. As Reid Hoffman - serial entrepreneur and venture capitalist - suggests 'you might even be actively asking others to point out what is wrong with your idea or creation.'[223] In contrast, when you are *editing* someone else's idea or product, there is less of a need to fly in the face of uncertainty or embrace tension. Most of the strong product people I have come across are creators, and very aware of the tension this mindset brings.

'How does uncertainty impact me?'

When we talk about dealing with tension, it is critical that we consider

222 iMA questionnaire, http://imahigh.com/ and The Meyers-Briggs Type Indicator, https://www.myersbriggs.org/my-mbti-personality-type/mbti-basics/home.htm?bhcp=1.

223 "The Power of Conflict with Ray Dalio," Masters of Scale podcast with Reid Hoffman, Episode No. 52, November 2019, https://mastersofscale.com/ray-dalio-the-power-of-conflict/.

our appetite for uncertainty. Some people appear to thrive on ambiguity, whereas others - myself included - have a natural tendency towards certainty. In Chapter 3, we looked at the tension between *known* and *unknown* as innate to product management; we will need to understand how comfortable we are 'dancing with uncertainty' as Jonathan Fields, founder of the Good Life Project, puts it.[224]

Managing products requires the understanding and acceptance of doubt. If we want to get our teams, colleagues and customers to lean into tension, we will first need to harness the power of doubt and uncertainty. The fact is, most product people will have to go through the so-called 'valley of doubt'; given all of the uncertainty involved in bringing an innovation to life and to market, it is reasonable to feel anxious about the journey (See fig. 14). The valley of doubt describes the points during the product journey where people across the organisation will need to take leaps of faith, and product people will typically encourage others to take these leaps.[225]

224 "Jonathan Fields' interview with Todd Henry," Accidental Creative Podcast by Todd Henry, Episode No. 215, 2019, https://accidental.wpengine.com/podcasts/ac/ac-podcast-215-jonathan-fields/.

225 Larry Keeley, Ryan Pikkel, Brian Quinn and Helen Walters, *Ten Types of Innovation: The Discipline of Building Breakthroughs* (Hoboken NJ: Wiley, 2013, p. 224).

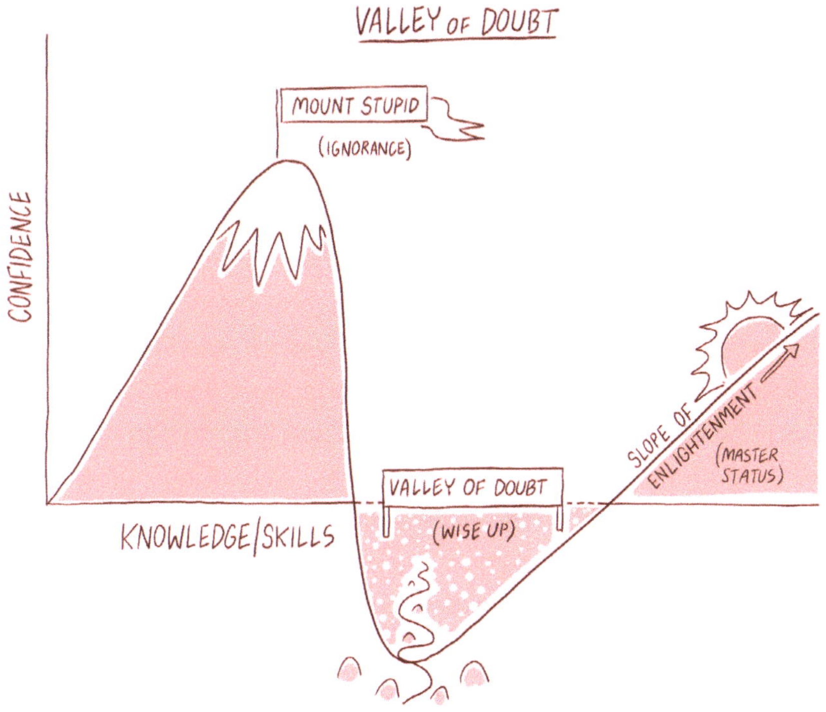

Fig. 14 – The Valley of Doubt and how we go from high confidence to a rude awakening

Rik Higham is a Product Lead at Deliveroo and highly experienced in product management and experimentation.[226] When I interviewed him for this book, it quickly became apparent that as much as product managers might dislike unknowns, part of us will actively be looking for it. Higham explained that as a product manager 'you are in a position where you hear a lot of noise, but at the same time you need to actively go out looking for the most valuable noise.'[227] When you actively decide to step into the unknown or a pressure cooker, you will need to accept the friction and 'messiness' that comes with it.

226 I highly recommend Rik's site on all things product experimentation: http://www.experimentationhub.com/hypothesis-kit.html.

227 Rik Higham, *interview by author*, Edinburgh, November 12, 2019.

'Which battles am I willing to fight?'

Given the tension seeking nature of product management, you will face lots of challenges and battles. Lots of them! While you can't always remove them, you have the power of choice. Do I react to the tension or do I let it be (for now)? You don't have to react; you have a choice and you can learn to observe yourself instead.

'God grant me the serenity to accept the things I cannot change; courage to change the things I can; and wisdom to know the difference' goes the 'Serenity Prayer' which was widely used by theologian Reinhold Niebuhr and subsequently adopted by Alcoholics Anonymous.[228] It is a helpful approach, see it as taking a helicopter view or 'going to the balcony', effectively detaching ourselves from the tense situation.[229] Techniques like Suzy Welch's 10/10/10 Rule are also great in taking a step back or picking your battles: how will I feel about this 10 minutes from now, how about 10 months from now, and how about 10 years from now?[230]

Deep knowledge of your perceptions, triggers and behaviours isn't just critical in view of tension. I believe this kind of understanding is also indispensable for successful collaboration due to the need for empathy when interacting with others, i.e. the ability to assume and understand other people's viewpoints.[231] In order to truly empathise with others, we need to understand and empathise with ourselves first. We will cover this more deeply in the next chapter.

228 Wikipedia, *Serenity Prayer*, https://en.wikipedia.org/wiki/Serenity_Prayer (Accessed on April 11, 2020).

229 *Ibid 212.*

230 Suzy Welch, 10-10-10: *A Life Transforming Idea* (Scribner, April 2009); "The 10/10/10 Rule For Tough Decisions," Chip and Dan Heath, Fast Company, January 1, 2013, https://www.fastcompany.com/3007613/10-10-10-rule-tough-decisions.

231 "Great Leaders Can Think Like Each Member of Their Team," Brian Uzzi, Harvard Business Review, July 8, 2015, https://hbr.org/2015/07/great-leaders-can-think-like-each-member-of-their-team.

TENSION TRACKER

We have arrived at a point in the book where I would encourage you to reflect on which of the tensions covered applies to your product, company, team or you individually. Which tensions are relevant to your situation, and why? What is your appetite for actively managing these tensions, even going as far as leaning into them? Understanding the impact of these tensions as well as your team or business' current response and identifying appropriate ways to best manage tensions and pressures when managing products.

Understand the tension profile of your product, your team or you individually by answering the following questions. Take a moment to reflect on the triggers, emotions and behaviours in the face of pressure or ambiguity. Ask your teammates to complete the Tension Tracker, after which you can use the tension profiles of your team members as a discussion starter. Are there any significant discrepancies between the different scores, and if so, why? Where are we in agreement, and why?

Even if your colleagues don't complete the Tension Tracker, use its questions as a conversation starter about the appetite for tension within the team. You can then use the outcomes from this to pick and mix from the different tension management tools and techniques that we will be covering in the next section.

TENSION TRACKER: WHERE DO YOU FEEL THE TENSION?

Product Tension

1. My product suffers from a lack of differentiation compared to our competitors:

- ***Not true:*** *my product is highly differentiated (1 point)*
- ***Somewhat true:*** *my product could differentiate more (2 points)*
- ***Very true:*** *my product is almost the same as other products in the market (3 points)*

2. Choose one of the following statements which best explains the lack of differentiation in your product:

- *My product was the first mover in the market, and we could do more to keep innovating (1 point)*
- *The market is highly saturated, and it is becoming increasingly hard to stand out (2 points)*
- *There is a lot of internal pressure to keep up with the competition by simply copying competitor features or propositions (3 points)*

3. Which of the following best describes the competitive power of your product?

- ***Customer experience:*** *customers find my product easy to use (1 point)*
- ***Speed to market:*** *we gain a lot of early traction with customers by being quick to market (2 points)*
- ***Pricing:*** *my product is priced competitively; customers rate its value for money (3 points)*

Team Tension

4. At my company there is strategic alignment between business goals and day-to-day priorities.

- ***True:*** *our product team executes against a well-defined business strategy (1 point)*
- ***Somewhat true:*** *we do have clear strategic goals but there is room to work on ad hoc initiatives or to iterate on products (2 points)*
- ***Not true:*** *did someone say strategy?! (3 points)*

5. Which of the following best describes your working relationship with your direct stakeholders:

- *Fully aligned and collaborative (1 point)*
- *OK, but we could be more aligned (2 points)*

- *Conflicted as we come from opposing perspectives (3 points)*

6. The product development team that I am part of is highly collaborative and aligned:

- ***Very true:*** *our days of 'norming and storming' are well behind us and we deliver value constantly against a shared mission (1 point)*
- ***Somewhat true:*** *we could do with more discussion within the team to make sure we build the right product, and in the right way (2 points)*
- ***Not true:*** *things are not going well in the team; we argue a lot and struggle to achieve our objectives (3 points)*

Individual Tension

7. Select one of the following statements that best describes your approach to ambiguity:

- *'I eat uncertainty for breakfast, and remain unfazed in ambiguous situations' (1 point)*
- *I don't mind a few unknowns, but do need some level of certainty to hang onto' (2 points)*
- *'I hate ambiguity, and like to feel that I am in control' (3 points)*

8. Select one of the following statements that best captures your approach to conflict:

- *'I thrive on conflict as it leads to the best outcomes in the long run' (1 point)*
- *'As long as the conflict remains healthy, I'm good' (2 points)*
- *'I absolutely hate conflict; it makes me feel anxious and unproductive' (3 points)*

Your Tension Profile

Now add up the number of points based on your responses in the Tension Tracker. Your 'score' should give you an indication of your tension profile; your exposure to tension and ambiguity:

Low Tension: < 10 points

Your exposure to tension - internal and / or external - is probably quite low. This doesn't necessarily have to be a good thing, as it might hint at a lack of product innovation or cognitive diversity within your organisation.

Medium Tension: 10 - 17 points

You experience tension on a regular basis, either in relation to the product that you manage or the people that you work with, or both. There is, however, room to build on this tension and use it constructively, to progress the product or improve your individual or team performance.

High Tension: > 18 points

You are probably exposed to tension on a continuous basis, and not all of it healthy tension. Some of this tension is caused by a lack of internal alignment, e.g. with respect to product positioning or strategic direction of the organisation. It would be good to both optimise those tensions worth leaning to and identify any 'unhealthy' tensions which could be used constructively for the good of the product and the *people involved in developing it.*

Naturally, the indicative profiles generated through the above Tension Tracker are meant to be just that: indicative. If I had to score myself, I'd probably fall somewhere between medium and high tension, and this might even depend on which day you ask me!

Irrespective of your score, I believe there is value in reflecting regularly on your appetite for tension, and that of your environment.

If anything, these reflections will provide food for thought on how to best optimise your situation - embracing tensions for the growth of your product, your team or your personal development.

WAYS OF EMBRACING TENSION

'Relax, let go and listen.' **David Allen**

The good news about tension is that there is a wide variety of practical tools and techniques out there to help pre-empt and manage it. We want to use tension for good, allowing it to make our products, our teams or us as individuals stronger. Tools like active listening and harm reduction work best if we not only apply them in real-life situations but also *reflect* on their effectiveness and learnings afterwards.

In this section, we will deep dive into different tactics and approaches available to manage the tension inherent in developing products. We will apply the lenses of both the product and the individual to manage tension, outlining how and when each individual tool can help pre-empt or mitigate tension.

OPTIMISING 'PRODUCT TENSION'

'If you always do what you did, you'll always get what you got.' **Marian Diamond**

Thus far we have mostly looked at the tensions we encounter on a personal level. How about the pressures or unknowns that impact our products? In Chapter 2 we encountered some of the internal and external tensions that a product is likely to face throughout its life cycle. Factors such as competitive threats or customer bargaining power can make life hard for a product manager. In this section we will look at a number of useful tools and techniques you can use to mitigate the impact of such tensions on your product or decide whether to not pick up the battle. From competitor analysis to lean product development, there are a number of ways to successfully optimise product tension.

Optimising 'Product Tension' = Mind + Matter + Moves

What are the tensions that your product is or will be facing? How can you best **seize these tensions** for the good of your product or business?

- **Competitor analysis:** using tools such as SWOT analysis, OODA loop, Kano model, Lean Canvas and direct customer feedback to understand competitive pressures and identify market opportunities for your product.
- **Managing risks and unknowns:** identifying your riskiest assumptions - about the product and the customer - and creating experiments around these assumptions. Running a pre-mortem creates a shared understanding of key risks or unknowns to test. Formulate a hypothesis to determine a measurable outcome.
- **Apply constraints:** you can apply deliberate constraints to your product, or a constraint is imposed through an external factor. Irrespective, it is worth actively exercising constraints as a way to reduce complexity and tension.

1. COMPETITOR ANALYSIS

'If all you're trying to do is essentially the same thing as your rivals, then it's unlikely you'll be very successful.' **Michael Porter**

'Obsess over customers, not over competitors' is a well-known quote by Amazon CEO Jeff Bezos from one of his annual shareholder letters.[232] While I agree that there is little point in agonising constantly over your competitors' every move, I do believe there is value in studying the market in which your product operates and the direct and indirect competitors within it. Conducting competitor analysis will not remove external pressures but will help in identifying early where the tension is coming from and its (potential) impact on your product.

Chris Butler, Product Manager at Facebook, talks about real competitive analysis being about learning to love your competitor, using it to inform how to best take on the opportunities and challenges ahead. 'Competitive analysis is essentially how your strategy works in comparison to your competitor's strategies in today's world.'[233] Before delving into ways in which we can analyse competitors, let's first look at the 'what' and 'why' of it:[234]

- **Understand where your product fits** - Reviewing competitors helps you to understand where your product sits within the market and its main point of differentiation, analysing and comparing aspects such as features, pricing,

232 "Bezos shareholder letter: Don't let the world push you into becoming a 'Day 2' company," Anita Balakrishnan, CNBC, April 12, 2017, https://www.cnbc.com/2017/04/12/amazon-jeff-bezos-2017-shareholder-letter.html.

233 "Real Competitive Analysis is About Learning to Love Your Competitor," Chris Butler, Medium, September 6, 2017, https://medium.com/pminsider/real-competitive-analysis-is-about-learning-to-love-your-competitor-15e45b9ef10a.

234 "My product management toolkit (29): analysing competitors," Marc Abraham, Medium, May 28, 2018, https://medium.com/@maa1/my-product-management-toolkit-29-analysing-competitors-6db60f787fe6.

and perceived customer benefits.

- **There is no need to look at ALL competitors** - It is impossible to keep up with all of your competitors, all the time. When you narrow things down, you are likely to find that only a small percentage of companies in the market either scoop up most of the revenue or offer direct competition within your specific market segment.
- **Treat competitor analysis for what it is; valuable guidance** - Instead of becoming obsessed with your competitors, get obsessed with your customers and their needs! As Chinese general Sun Tzu outlines in 'The Art of War': 'If you know the enemy and know yourself, you need not fear the result of a hundred battles.' It can be very helpful to understand the competitive landscape and the position of your product or business within it, without becoming completely distracted by the features a competitor product does or doesn't offer. You should avoid allowing the competitive landscape to dictate which features should or should not be included in order to avoid what I call the resulting 'featuritis'![235] Instead of actively fighting your competitors, concentrate on finding a way of bypassing your competition altogether. This comes back to creating 'the moment of choice', akin to deciding which battles to pick, as covered in the previous section.
- **Find the perfect niche for your product** - The likelihood is for most of us that your product will be targeting the same customers that other companies and their product are already serving. Your product needs to be exceptional and differentiated enough for customers to consider switching.

235 "My product management toolkit (10): jobs-to-be-done," Marc Abraham, Medium, June 2, 2016, https://medium.com/@maa1/my-product-management-toolkit-10-jobs-to-be-done-f0468f569f88.

> Look at the market and ask yourself: 'are we solving the same problem, but differently?' or 'are we tackling a different customer problem altogether?'

In the toolkit section at the end of this chapter you will find some common tools you can use to analyse your competition: the SWOT analysis, the OODA loop, the Kano analysis, the Lean Canvas and direct customer feedback.

2. MANAGING RISKS AND UNKNOWNS

'Of all the words of mice and men, the saddest are, 'It might have been.' **Kurt Vonnegut**

Identifying and testing riskiest assumptions

Tension becomes immediately apparent the moment you understand you are making decisions based on assumptions. Consciously or unconsciously we create assumptions, and before we know it, we treat them as ironclad truths and certainties. We all have biases and make unconscious assumptions. When developing products, the trick is to both identify and qualify our biases and assumptions early and often. Not all assumptions or biases need challenging, but it is critical to identify and test those assumptions that are instrumental to the success or failure of your product:

'We believe customers will pay for this product.'

'We believe we can build this new feature, using this new technology, within the given timeframe.'

'We believe that customers will find this improved feature easier to use.'

The first few times I heard assumptions like the ones mentioned above I assumed they were true - mostly based on the experience level of the person uttering them. But then I learned to convert these assumptions into questions or bets by simply adding a question mark or adding the words 'I bet':

- 'We believe customers will pay for this product?'
- 'I *bet* that customers will pay for this product.'

Do we know which customers will use our product? Why would they pay for our product? How big is the gamble that we are taking on this product?

- 'We believe we can build this new feature, using this new technology, within the given timeframe?'
- 'I *bet* we can build this new feature, using this new technology, within the given timeframe.'

How do we know we can successfully utilise a new technology? Why do we think we can deliver within a given timeframe? What if things don't go to plan?

- 'We believe that customers will find this improved feature easier to use?'
- 'I *bet* customers will find this improved feature easier to use.'

Why do we think we will improve ease of use for the customer? Why are we certain?

Converting assumptions in measurable hypotheses

With all these examples, 'how do we know?' is the principal question. As soon as we phrase strongly held beliefs and assumptions as questions or bets, the underlying equation shifts from certainty to uncertainty. This uncertainty comes from information hidden within these assumptions.[236] For instance: we don't *know* whether customers will use our product, let alone pay for it. Or that the technology that we are banking on can be implemented effectively. By embracing uncertainty, we unlock valuable learning and risk management through customer research and experimentation.[237]

To learn the right things from customer research, experiments or even product launches we need to formulate a hypothesis. A hypothesis is a more granular version of the original assumption and is formulated in such a way that it is easy to test and measure specific desired outcomes:[238]

We believe that ***[doing this]*** *for* ***[these people]*** *will achieve* ***[this outcome].***

We will know this is true when we see ***[this market feedback].***

For example:
We believe that ***by introducing a free trial feature*** *for* ***people new to 10 pin bowling*** *they will spend more time* ***honing their virtual 10 pin bowling skills.***

We know this is true when we see ***5,000 people signing up for a free trial within three months of releasing the free trial feature*****.**

236 See: Annie Duke, *Thinking in Bets: Making Smarter Decision When You Don't Have All the Facts* (Portfolio -Penguin: February 2018); Annie Duke, *Thinking in Bets*, Talks at Google, June 21, 2018, https://www.youtube.com/watch?v=uYNsSeYjkp4.

237 "My product management toolkit (5): assumptions and hypotheses," Marc Abraham, Medium, February 18, 2016, https://medium.com/@maa1/my-product-management-toolkit-5-assumptions-and-hypotheses-828314511dc0.

238 " Lean UX + UX STRAT," Josh Seiden, Talk at UX Strat 2013, September 10, 2013, https://www.slideshare.net/UXSTRAT/ux-strat-2013-josh-seiden-lean-ux-ux-strat.

Once you have formulated a hypothesis, you can use it to test a specific product area, feature or workflow. A focus on behavioural outcomes or changes is a key aspect of hypotheses. In other words, does the product succeed in the user showing more or less of a certain behaviour? Let's say that you are building a money saving app and you want to test whether the app is indeed helping its users to save more. The core premise here that you want to test is whether the product is successful in motivating users to save more. A simple 'before and after' test, where we compare individual saving behaviours with and without the app, should prove or disprove our main hypothesis.

Moreover, if your goal is to mitigate product risk, it makes sense to test your riskiest assumptions first. You can use simple prototypes to test risky assumptions such as 'this feature will definitely solve our customer problem' or 'customers will pay for this new feature' before committing lots of time, money and effort to solving a problem. I will include an example of how to take an assumption and convert it into a hypothesis in the toolkit section at the end of this chapter.

Conducting a pre-mortem

As helpful as 'post-mortem' sessions can be, how often do you find yourself wondering 'if I'd only thought about that beforehand!' or pondering what could have been. In a medical environment, a post-mortem offers the opportunity for health professionals and the family to establish a patient's exact cause of death.[239] With digital products, a post-mortem typically happens at the end of a project, after a big product release or a major system failure. The goal of these sessions is to reflect on areas for improvement and identify related actions for future projects and releases.[240]

239 "What happens during a post-mortem," Royal College of Pathologists, 2020, https://www.rcpath.org/discover-pathology/what-is-pathology/information-about-post-mortems-for-friends-and-relatives-/what-happens-during-a-post-mortem.html (Access on March 5, 2020).

240 "How to Run a Seriously Productive Project Post-Mortem," Karla Cook, Hubspot, October 7, 2019, https://blog.hubspot.com/marketing/productive-project-post-mortem.

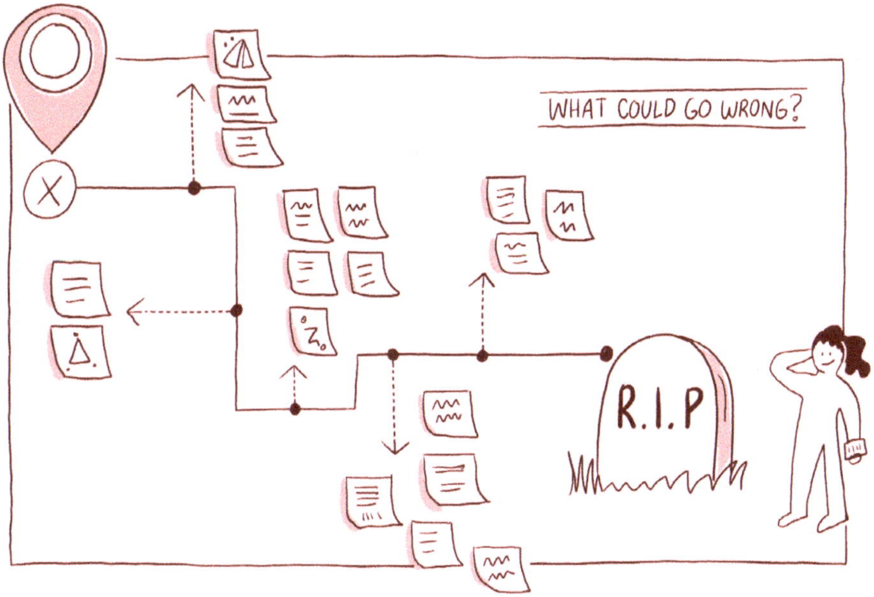

Fig. 15 – Use a pre-mortem to think about all the things that could go wrong

The problem, however, with most post-mortem sessions is that often the patient has already died, or the project has failed. Any learning or actions for improvement can only be of real value to future projects or iterations. In contrast, a *pre*-mortem gives you a chance to think about a project or a piece of work and its associated risks **before** you commence (See fig. 15). A pre-mortem can be done either individually or as a group, with someone explaining the product or project, followed by participants imagining the product or project to have failed.[241] For example:

241 See: "Performing a Project Premortem," Gary Klein, Harvard Business Review, September 2007, https://hbr.org/2007/09/performing-a-project-premortem; "Pre-Mortem," Dave Gray, Gamestorming, January 27, 2011, https://gamestorming.com/pre-mortem/; "13 Questions to Ask in a Product Pre-Mortem," Heather McCloskey, UserVoice, March 15, 2016, https://community.uservoice.com/blog/pre-mortem-analysis/; "The Product Pre-Mortem," Ross Mayfield, Product Coalition, November 7, 2019, https://productcoalition.com/the-product-pre-mortem-d466237f6b7a.

- *'This product has failed because nobody wanted to pay for it'*
- *'The technology didn't work'*
- *'The product was never released in the end because the regulator refused to approve the product and its underlying business model'*
- *'The product has failed because many of its users complained about its poor user experience'*
- *'The product failed because the design and build project had to be rushed in the end to get it over the line'*

A pre-mortem enables you to start by working backwards, looking at the individual factors that could lead to failure as well as the actions to take in order to avoid certain risks from materialising in the first place. Once you have identified these factors, you can start thinking about how to best avoid or mitigate these risks from occurring. Naturally, it will be up to you and your team to figure out how to structure your pre-mortem, but the toolkit at the end of this chapter has some helpful pointers.

3. APPLY CONSTRAINTS

'The absence of limitations is the enemy of art.' **Orson Welles**

Applying constraints can be done in two different ways with respect to welcoming and managing tension. Firstly, you can deliberately apply constraints to reduce the scope of problems to solve opportunities to venture into. As Brandon Chu, VP Product & GM of Platform at Shopify, explains, 'when you are dealing with infinitely complex problems, it helps to put boundaries in place through constraints.'[242]

Let's not, however, forget that constraints are often imposed externally - think for example of the 'Iron Triangle' and its constraints in terms of time, cost, scope and quality which we examined

242 *Ibid 178.*

in Chapter 1. 'Don't let constraints curtail creativity, reframe constraints as a moment to be effective, for the team to reach full potential' advises Chu.[243]

It is what Carol Dweck, Psychology Professor at Stanford University, describes as the difference between a 'fixed' and a 'growth' mindset.[244] In a fixed mindset, people believe their qualities are fixed traits and therefore cannot change. The same mindset applies to constraints, where people believe that their circumstances or limitations are fixed and cannot be amended or influenced. I often see this mindset rear its head when people complain about not having enough resources. They view a lack of people as an immutable constraint, whereas there are often creative ways to maximise customer value with the people that they have. Similarly, we could look at more ruthless prioritisation to ensure we focus on the right things with the people, budget and time that we have at our disposal.

Secondly, constraints are likely to evolve, often hand in hand with a product, organisation or individual(s). 'Constraints are not immutable, they change based on creative exploration,' explains Jon Kolko, Partner at Modernist Studio.[245] Kolko and his team conduct qualitative research and based on people's actual behaviours and real word views, constraints often emerge.

JON KOLKO AND LEARNING ABOUT PEOPLE' S ACTUAL BEHAVIOURS ...

Kolko's team recently conducted research within the financial space and spent time with customers of a large bank. 'We spent 2-3 hours in their homes and had them show us how they think about and organize their finances. Some people showed us paperwork in file folders and

243 *Ibid 178.*

244 Carol S. Dweck, Mindset: *The New Psychology of Success* (Random House, February 2006).

245 Jon Kolko, *email to author*, December 10, 2019.

walked through the materials. Others showed us digital tools that they use to manage their overall mental model of money. And some showed us nothing - they had no way of organizing and no method for reflecting. One participant showed us money she kept in jars around her house, rather than in a savings account. Her explanation was that the money was out of sight, so she wouldn't spend it. Even though it was literally in her field of vision, she didn't see the money when she checked her bank balance on her phone, so she ignored it.'

Out of their exploration a theme became apparent to Kolko and his team: that people have developed strategies for managing their money, often based on a loose understanding of complex financial terms. That loose understanding is typically established through word-of-mouth recommendations from trusted sources, passed down from family behaviour, or based on illogical introspection. A constraint for any new product or service that the bank creates should therefore take into account this theme, and lead to a set of design constraints. Kolko explains that a 'good' solution supports the illogical and vague understanding people have about money. 'The constraints have become vetting criteria for the quality of new ideas. These constraints challenge more logical approaches to money and begin to challenge even the most basic assumptions we make about customers - they may not even know what a savings account or checking account is.'

BEING OK WITH ' INDIVIDUAL TENSION'

'You've always been what you are. That's not new. What you'll get used to is knowing it.' **Cassandra Clare**

START WITH THE SELF

Now that we have looked at ways to manage tension at a product level, the question arises as to how we handle tension as product people. We have already established that feeling tension is inescapable, so

I recommend having an extensive toolkit to use whenever you are facing or feeling pressured or frustrated. Managing tension on an individual level will ultimately feed into your product as well as the team and organisation that you are part of. In other words, starting with the self will have a positive impact on the things that you work on and the people that you work with.

Being OK with 'Individual Tension' = Mind + Moves

How do we best handle tension as **individual product people**? These are some tools and techniques you can use to manage any personal tension:

1. **Do a self-check:** take time out to check your behaviours or thoughts.
2. **Listen actively:** listen out to fully grasp where the other person is coming from.
3. **Manage conflict:** we need to actively understand and manage conflict if we want to welcome tension.
4. **Accept radically:** accept situations or feelings for what they are, instead of constantly fighting battles.
5. **Say 'I don't know':** explore the liberating and educational effects of admitting that you don't know.
6. **Just ask:** find ways to ask questions, especially when you are dependent on the other person.
7. **Give and receive feedback:** care personally but challenge directly when giving feedback, whilst listening to understand when receiving feedback.
8. **Disagree and commit:** get comfortable with disagreement, but still getting to a decision and commit to the decision made.

1. DO A SELF-CHECK

'You better check yo self before you wreck yo self.' **Ice Cube**

To stimulate self-awareness, I highly recommend checking in with yourself on a regular basis. Irrespective of whether you do this daily, weekly, monthly or yearly, taking time out to do a self-check will help you to observe and critique your own tendencies. You can hone in on certain behaviours, approaches or thought patterns that you have observed or that others have raised with you.
For example:
'Why did I respond rudely to the colleague that challenged my idea in the meeting?'

'How can I avoid taking things less personally next time I get feedback?'

'I have noticed how incredibly nervous I get each time people start asking questions during a product demo. Why is that? What can I do about my nervousness?'

Provided you take this exercise seriously and are honest with yourself, you can gain valuable insights and learnings. Not only will a self-check help you grow as an individual, it will also contribute to successful collaboration with others.[246] We will cover this in more detail when we look at 'reflection' in Chapter 7.

246 "Cracking the Code of Sustained Collaboration," Francesca Gino, Harvard Business Review, November - December 2019, https://hbr.org/2019/11/cracking-the-code-of-sustained-collaboration.

2. LISTEN ACTIVELY

'When you talk, you are only repeating what you already know. But if you listen, you may learn something new.' **Dalai Lama**

If you think about your 'tension toolkit' containing actual tools, then active listening would be the wrench. Listening actively helps you to open things up, prying things apart when you are listening to others. In 'The Art of Active Listening' Josh Gibson and Fynn Walker describe active listening as the art of listening for meaning; active listening requires you to understand, interpret, and evaluate what you're being told.[247]

So, next time you feel an inner urge to say something, to respond, try to stop this urge and instead concentrate on what's actually being said. Here is what sometimes happens when I think I am listening but not doing so actively:

Speaker: *'So we decided to do X. This felt like the best approach, because of Y.'*
Me: *'Why did they decide to do X, that doesn't make sense!'(completely ignoring the 'Y' part of the speaker's statement.)*

Or:

Speaker: *'The difficulty is that I don't know how to best design this feature.'*
Me [thinking: 'Whatever!']: *'We should never have designed this feature in the first place!'*

247 Josh Gibson and Fynn Walker, *The Art of Active Listening: How to double your communication skills in 30 days* (September 2011); "Book review: "The Art of Active Listening"," Marc Abraham, April 13, 2017, https://marcabraham.com/2017/04/13/book-review-the-art-of-active-listening/.

It is easy to see from this example how people like me run the risk of missing critical bits of a conversation, due to my urge to respond before listening actively. Listening actively is a major manifestation of empathy since it allows you to truly hear what the other person is saying; switching perspectives with the person speaking and thereby grasping their intentions.

As Rik Higham says, there can be a significant amount of noise in creating products, coming from the people we are working with.[248] I would go a step further and suggest that you apply your active listening skills to the things that you are saying - to yourself and your others - too. While active listening might not help remove tension it is an important tool with respect to the initial understanding of tension, listening out for its meaning and potential impact.

3. MANAGE CONFLICT

'When you have a conflict, that means that there are truths that have to be addressed on each side of the conflict. And when you have a conflict, then it's an educational process to try to resolve the conflict. And to resolve that, you have to get people on both sides of the conflict involved so that they can dialogue.' **Dolores Huerta**

Being able to avoid or manage conflict is an important skill if you are looking to welcome tension when managing products. In the previous chapter we saw that there are two conflict types to consider here: task conflict and relationship conflict. Task conflict occurs where people have a difference of opinion about the task or challenge at hand, whereas relationship conflict centres around personal friction.[249] To manage disputes effectively we need to apply another useful distinction; that between tolerable conflict and structural conflict. Tolerable conflict

248 *Ibid 240.*
249 *Ibid 199.*

only occurs against the backdrop of trying to achieve what is realistic and least risky.[250] Given the limited extent to which conflict is tolerated, I believe that this level of conflict is insufficient in fully embracing tension and creating successful products. At the other end of the spectrum, structural conflict hints at a situation that is almost beyond resolve, since there is a persistent gap between potential solutions which can't be bridged. In other words: structural conflict is not resolvable, and therefore not helpful when leaning into tension.[251]

Tension needs some form of resolution, especially when the tension is affecting people. When comparing tolerable and structural conflict, the question that arises is how we can determine whether conflict is truly structural or actually tolerable, but negatively affecting risk-averse people. Learning about the exact nature of conflict helps us better understand whether the conflict is structural or not. What is the source of the conflict and why is it considered an issue? Do people see opportunities to resolve the conflict? How constructive are our conflicts, and why (not)? Are people looking at a way out of the conflict together? How do the people involved in the conflict feel? Do they all feel the same?

Instead of avoiding or blowing up conflict between people, I suggest using conflict for good. Non-structural task conflict is desirable when developing products. It is often very healthy and constructive to have a difference of opinion within a group of people about the task or challenge at hand. Ross McNairn, Chief Product Officer at Travelperk, uses friction to help people get out of their comfort zone and to challenge. He explained to me how this approach is not aimed at the person, but rather a style.[252] McNairn's approach to conflict feels close to that of 'Conflict Manipulation', a concept introduced by Robert Fritz. Conflict manipulation consists of two steps:[253]

---

250 Ibid 6, p. 92.

251 *Ibid 6, p. 87.*

252 Ross McNairn, *interview by author*, Barcelona, December 4, 2019.

253 *Ibid 6, p. 93.*

1. **Intensify the conflict** - Usually by presenting a 'negative vision' or unwanted consequences if action isn't taken.
2. **Take action to reduce the pressure** - Actions designed to reduce pressure, usually by preventing any unwanted consequences from happening.

Granted, conflict manipulation can sometimes feel more reactive than proactive, but it does offer a measured and constructive approach to managing conflict. If you are in a situation where you want to create conflict proactively, then I would recommend applying the Ritual Dissent approach or acting as your own adversary (see the toolkit at the end of this chapter).

4. RADICAL ACCEPTANCE

'What would it be like if I could accept life - accept this moment - exactly as it is?' **Tara Brach**

If you are anything like me, and you experience regular tension when managing products, you could benefit significantly from accepting radically. With the tensions I have experienced - both externally and internally - I sometimes wish I could rewind and just accept these situations for what they are. I first learned about radical acceptance from reading the book by Tara Brach, where she explains that Radical Acceptance is 'the willingness to experience ourselves and our lives as it is.'[254]

I have come to interpret and apply radical acceptance to stop the urge to fight reality, and instead accept things for what they are. This means that when we experience tension, instead of combating it we can use radical acceptance as a tool to lean into it. Accepting things for what they are doesn't mean that we have to either just give

254 *Ibid 206.*

in to the situation or simply feel sorry for ourselves. It also doesn't mean that you can't feel frustrated or anxious when tension hits. But instead of trying to suppress feelings of discomfort, we accept the emotion for what it is and don't try to ignore it.[255] Start by taking some hypothetical but common product challenges:

- We haven't shipped anything for a while ...
- Why has this feature been deprioritised and why now, given that we have already been working on it for months ...
- We need more people to deliver all the things we committed to ...
- Why is our Chief Marketing Officer telling us what product and features to create, even fancying himself as a bit of a designer!?
- I know that I will be hung out to dry at our executive meeting since our main product is clearly underperforming ...
- What do I know about solving this customer problem? This is a completely new area to me, and I feel like an imposter ...
- This feedback from the engineers about how I messed up prioritisation last quarter hit me hard ...
- I so wish we had a clearly defined business strategy and objectives, as it would make it so much easier to prioritise and make tricky trade-off decisions ...
- Why does my Chief Technology Officer never seem to be listening to me!?

Accepting some of these challenges or feelings will not make them go away or make them feel any less challenging, but I have experienced first-hand how this acceptance can help in keeping your emotions

255 See: "Should we be treating temperament instead of anxiety and depression?" David H. Barlow, Talk at Anxiety and Depression Association of America, April 2015, https://adaa.org/sites/default/files/Barlow_Ross%20Lecture.pdf; "The Past and Future of Anxiety: An Interview with Dr. Barlow," Arash Emamzadeh, Psychology Today, March 1, 2018, https://www.psychologytoday.com/gb/blog/finding-new-home/201803/the-past-and-future-anxiety-interview-dr-barlow.

under control in the moment, being more 'emotionally controlled', as Dr Carole Pemberton who specialises in resilience, refers to it.[256]

Up until a few years ago, obstacles or backward steps of any kind used to frustrate me immensely. Anything that didn't go to plan when developing products would throw me; any feedback about me or my product would feel like a punch in the gut. Accepting things for what they are, does at least allow me not to lose it in the moment and remain realistically optimistic. You can find some suggestions for how you can practice radical acceptance in the toolkit at the end of this chapter.

5. SAYING 'I DON'T KNOW'

'Life is about not knowing, having to change, taking the moment and making the best of it, without knowing what's going to happen next.'
Gilda Radner

Being honest and saying that you don't know enables you to welcome the uncertainty and seize the opportunity to explore. It seems so simple, three words, and yet it can be one of the hardest things for us to say. I bet that the following hypothetical scenario will ring true to a large proportion of readers of this book:

CEO/CPO/CTO/CFO/CMO/COO (or any other impressive sounding job title you can think of):

'Do you think it will be hard to build this new feature that isn't on the roadmap?'
Me (on the back foot, thrown by this question posed by my larger than life executive):
'Uhm, no, should be fine.'

256 "Measure Your Resilience," Dr Carole Pemberton, July 5, 2014, https://carolepemberton.co.uk/measure-your-resilience/.

I have found that scenario not only plays out when facing a superior but also between peers or when managing direct reports. We don't want to be seen as 'weak' or lacking expertise. Instead, we like to be perceived as all-knowing and confident. Which makes the climb down when we have to confess that we didn't know, and that we didn't have all the answers, all the harder.

In situations where there is ambiguity, because we are doing something that has not been done before or it is likely that things will change, it can be dangerous *not* to admit that you don't know. If we give off the impression that we do know or that the situation is in hand, we are adding significant risk of future tension.

Junior Product Manager:
'Have you got experience with doing X? I am unsure how to best go about it.'

Me:
(scratching my head, stroking my chin, as I don't have a clue)
'Do Y, that's the best thing.'

Alternatively ...

Junior Product Manager:
'Have you got experience with doing X? I am unsure how to best go about it.'

Me:
'I don't unfortunately, but let's figure it out.'

I find it interesting that some places seem to have a culture where you are not expected to have questions after your initial honeymoon period at the company, or where it is frowned upon when you say that you don't know and have to look into things. This approach doesn't fly in scenarios where there are lots of unknowns or where there is tension that is worth embracing, since this tension by its very nature will provoke questioning and a need to discover and learn continuously. There is simply no expiry date on uncertainty or new opportunities.

It is therefore ok to say that you don't know and that you will find out or learn. It doesn't matter whether you are a junior product manager or a highly experienced product veteran. As Julie Zhuo, VP of Product Design and author of 'The Making of a Manager' states, it is ok to say, 'I don't know but let's figure it out together.'[257] Don't pretend that you know what you are doing or that you have all the answers.

Justus Fokker, a freelance product manager, says, 'If you didn't feel like an imposter, you would probably not appreciate what you don't know.'[258] As Fokker explained to me, we can only make other people feel comfortable saying that they don't know if their leaders are honest about not knowing themselves.[259] When leaders admit that *they* don't know, they allow the team to admit that they don't know. In fact, I believe that being open about not knowing opens the door for yourself and others to learn continuously.

6. JUST ASK

'The first and simplest emotion which we discover in the human mind,

---

257 "Interview with Julie Zhuo," Gretchen Rubin, March 19, 2019, https://gretchenrubin.com/2019/03/julie-zhuo-interview/. See also: Julie Zhuo, *The Making of a Manager: What To Do When Everyone Looks to You* (Portfolio, March 2019); "Book review: The Making of a Manager," Marc Abraham, Medium, March 26, 2019, https://medium.com/@maa1/book-review-the-making-of-a-manager-by-julie-zhuo-c6ac21886dc4.

258 "The Big Secret - Nobody Knows What They're Doing," Justus Fokker, UX Collective, December 9, 2019, https://uxdesign.cc/the-big-secret-nobody-knows-what-theyre-doing-3fac5994cd93.

259 Justus Fokker, *interview by author*, Amsterdam, January 3, 2020.

is curiosity.' **Edmund Burke**

In the previous section we looked at the scenario where someone asks you a question. How about a situation where you ask the questions as a way to navigate through tension or uncertainty? What if the situation is new and you are keen to learn and find answers? In this section, we will go through a number of techniques you can use to ask questions and learn.

5 Whys

I presume a lot of you will already be familiar with the '5 Whys' technique where you ask 'Why' five times to get to the bottom of an issue (see toolkit at the end of this chapter).[260] Originally developed by Sakichi Toyoda and used within car manufacturer Toyota, the primary goal is to figure out the root cause of a defect or problem. By simply repeating the question 'Why?' five times, each answer forms the basis of the next question. The 'five' in the name derives from an anecdotal observation on the number of iterations needed to resolve the problem. A hypothetical problem could be the problem of the coffee I ordered at the coffee shop that was delivered cold. This is what the analysis could look like when we apply the 5 Whys:

1. ***Why?*** – The coffee machine did not work properly. (First why)
2. ***Why?*** – There was not enough hot water in the machine. (Second why)
3. ***Why?*** – The hot water indicator did not indicate an issue. (Third why)
4. ***Why?*** – The hot water indicator had not been checked recently. (Fourth why)
5. ***Why?*** – The barista did not know to check the hot water indicator on a regular basis. (Fifth why, a root cause)

260 "Five whys," Wikipedia, https://en.wikipedia.org/wiki/Five_whys (Accessed on January 9, 2020).

Asking 'Why?' five times can be particularly helpful when dealing with unknowns or complex situations, collaboratively working through the questions to get to the underlying issue at hand.

Humble Inquiry

Sometimes we ask questions or even the 5 Whys whilst already knowing the answer. This is because we are keen to verify whether we have got the right answer or because we see value in the other person getting to the answer.[261] It can be equally valuable asking those questions when you don't already know the answer. Or where you feel reluctant to say, 'I don't know'. Think about that very complex problem that you and your team are looking to solve or a domain of expertise that you are unfamiliar with.

Edgar Schein, a former MIT professor specialised in organisational culture, refers to this kind of questioning as 'Humble Inquiry': asking questions to which you don't already know the answer, based on an attitude of curiosity, interest or wanting to learn something about the other person. When inquiring humbly you are asking as opposed to telling or assuming; you are humble because you are dependent on the other person because he or she knows or can do something that helps you achieve your task or goal.[262] Over the years I have developed my own set of go-to questions that I typically ask when I am curious or want to learn about the other person:

- What did you do / decide?
- Why did you do / decide that?

261 "My product management toolkit (19): Socratic questioning," Marc Abraham, Medium, March 8, 2017, https://medium.com/@maa1/my-product-management-toolkit-19-socratic-questioning-ae1f54ee7e8f.

262 Edgar Schein, Humble Inquiry: *The Gentle Art of Asking Instead of Telling* (Oakland, CA: Berrett-Koehler Publishers, 1st edition, January 2013, p. 12); "Edgar Schein on Humble Inquiry," YouTube, January 14, 2015, https://www.youtube.com/watch?v=BOwOIDrKvuw; "Humble Inquiry - by Edgar Schein," Marcella Bremer, Leadership & Change, November 29, 2016, https://www.leadershipandchangemagazine.com/humble-inquiry-by-edgar-schein/.

- What is the difference? Why?
- Just for my learning, can you please explain.
- What are the pros and cons?
- What kinds of risks most concern you, why?
- How do you know that?
- How did this become a problem in the first place?
- I'm not sure I understand you, could you please talk me through that.

This is not a finite set of questions, but humility is the one aspect that all these questions have in common. The questions are open-ended, rather than closed or leading questions. You are listening *actively* to what the other person has to say in response to your question as well as the person speaking to you.

7. GIVE AND RECEIVE FEEDBACK

'Saying 'your work is shit' is way better than saying 'you are shit', but it is still totally obnoxious.' **Kim Scott**

When you feel like the walls are coming down on you or when the temperature is rising, feedback becomes even more critical. Both giving and receiving feedback is an important skill for all people, but I have found that as a product manager you are especially exposed to feedback. Given that we work with so many different people at any given time, it can feel like the feedback can come from anywhere. There is no doubt that we need to listen to feedback while also being prepared to give it.

What if you feel that the work of a teammate is below par? Or you are missing a shared sense of urgency among your team? What if you have just delivered a product with plenty of bugs? In the book 'Radical Candor', Kim Scott examines the factors that underpin an environment where people don't shy away from difficult conversations.[263] Scott explains how trusting relationships are key to being fully honest and open with each other. Once a relationship of trust has been established between people, it becomes so much easier to practice 'radical candour' on a daily basis. Unfortunately, there is no set formula for developing trust. Scott, however, has identified two dimensions that help people move in the right direction: 'care personally' and 'challenge directly':

- **Care personally** – Scott slashes the idea of people having two radically different personas – with people's work persona being radically different from their private persona. Instead, she suggests you need to be your whole self to ensure strong relationships. Scott also talks about genuinely caring for the people who work for you as a critical prerequisite for a strong relationship.
- **Challenge directly (1)** – 'Challenge directly' involves telling people that their work is not good enough. I have found this the hardest part to implement as there is a fine line between challenging directly and coming across as overly critical. Scott argues that challenging people 'is often the best way to show them that you care'. As counter-intuitive as it may sound, challenging people directly can be a great way to establish a relationship.
- **Challenge directly (2)** – Challenging people, in a clear but constructive way, is often appreciated – despite it feeling hard initially (for both the giver and the receiver of the challenge). It shows (1) you care enough to point out both the things that are going well and the things that aren't and (2) that you are willing to admit when you are wrong and that

263 Kim Scott, *Radical Candor: How to Get What You Want by Saying What You Mean* (New York: St. Martin's Press, March 2017); "Book review: "Radical Candor", Marc Abraham, As I learn, August 17, 2017, https://marcabraham.com/2017/08/17/book-review-radical-candor/.

you're committed to fixing mistakes that you or others have made. At the end of the day, it is all about fixing a problem or, as Anthony Casalena, Founder / CEO of Squarespace says, 'if you don't listen, you create this seismic shift whenever something breaks.'[264]

- **'Operationalising' good guidance** – In 'Radical Candor', Scott introduces a helpful matrix, which has four quadrants to consider in light of how to best care personally and challenge directly: 'ruinous empathy'; 'manipulative insincerity'; 'obnoxious aggression' and – the desired one – 'radical candour', where you challenge directly without being discouraging.
- **How to criticise without discouraging?** – Be humble, both when receiving and giving feedback. Be helpful and specific when giving feedback, offer guidance in person and immediately, criticise in private, and don't personalise. Make it clear that the problem is not due to some inflexible personality flaw and share stories when you have been criticised for something similar.[265]

Scott helpfully offers practical tips if you are actively looking for feedback or guidance, which I have included in the toolkit at the end of this chapter. Similarly, American psychologist Marshall Rosenberg has written extensively about non-violent communications that are founded on language and communication skills that strengthen our ability to remain human, even under trying circumstances.[266] Rosenberg's non-violent communication framework ('NVC') consists of four elements: observation, feeling, needs and request:[267]

264 "Interview with Anthony Casalena," Guy Raz, NPR "How I Built This" podcast, March 4, 2019, https://www.npr.org/2019/02/28/699096835/squarespace-anthony-casalena?t=1578847940546.

265 "How to Communicate Dissent at Work," John T. Garner, Harvard Business Review, February 4, 2013, https://hbr.org/2013/02/how-to-communicate-dissent-at.

266 Marshall Rosenberg, *Nonviolent Communication: A Language of Life* (Puddle Dancer Press, 2nd Edition, 2005, p. 3).

267 *Ibid 266, pp. 6-7.*

- The concrete actions we are *observing* that affect our wellbeing;
- How we *feel* in relation to what we are observing;
- The *needs*, values, desires, etc. that are creating our feelings;
- The concrete actions we *request* in order to enrich our lives.

NVC works both ways: giving honest feedback through the four aforementioned components and receiving feedback empathically through the same components. In design critiques, people provide feedback to the designer about his or her work. As the aforementioned Jon Kolko outlines in his book 'Creative Clarity', a good design critique feels like a dialogue, governed by a layer of trust and solely focusing on the work. This means that the designer is receptive to criticism but also has a chance to explain and justify creative decisions in a way that isn't defensive. Consequently, the relationship between the designer and the participants of the design critique isn't combative.[268] Bob Iger, CEO of Walt Disney, offers similar guidance: 'Don't start negatively, and don't start small. People will often focus on little details as a way of masking a lack of any clear, coherent thoughts: If you start petty, you seem petty.'[269]

8. DISAGREE AND COMMIT

'If you have conviction in a particular direction even though there is no consensus, it is helpful to say, "Look, I know we disagree on this, but will you gamble with me on it? Disagree and commit?' **Jeff Bezos**

The risk when leaning into tension too much is that we never get a chance to step away, and the tension gets the better of us as a result. The risk with group discussion is that we can get stuck in a

268 Jon Kolko, *Creative Clarity* (Brown Bear LLC, 15 September 2017, pp. 121-122).

269 Bob Iger, *The Ride of a Lifetime: Lessons Learned from 15 Years as CEO of The Walt Disney Company* (Random House, September 2019, p. 43).

rut, endlessly trying to reach consensus. 'Humans are often natural conflict avoiders,' says Duncan Barrigan. Barrigan is the Chief Product Officer at GoCardless, and very experienced with team processes. 'People need to have the confidence to disagree and then commit,' he explains.[270]

The 'disagree and commit' principle has two ultimate objectives. Firstly, to encourage the team to disagree when making an important decision. It needs to be understood that it is ok to disagree with one another. For instance, a few years ago, I saw a yellow sign on one of the walls at the Government Digital Service in London, stating among others that it is ok 'to challenge things you're not comfortable with'.[271] This is a good example of creating an environment where it is ok to disagree.

Secondly, disagree and commit aims to unite the team in committing to a decision once it has been made.[272] 'Whilst it is good to have disagreement, it will eventually have to be closed off by a decision,' Barrigan mentioned when we talked about the potential downsides of dissent.[273] Jeff Bezos wrote in his now famous 1997 Amazon shareholder letter that disagree and commit doesn't mean thinking that your team is wrong or missing the point; 'it's a genuine disagreement of opinion, a candid expression of my view, a chance for the team to weigh my view, and a quick, sincere commitment to go their way.'[274] 'Do no harm' is the only thing that I want to add

270 Duncan Barrigan, *interview by author*, London, November 22, 2019.

271 "It's ok to say what's ok," Giles Turnbull, Government Digital Service, May 25, 2016, https://gds.blog.gov.uk/2016/05/25/its-ok-to-say-whats-ok/.

272 "Disagree and Commit: The Importance of disagreement in decision making," Simón Muñoz, Hackernoon, January 17, 2019, https://hackernoon.com/disagree-and-commit-the-importance-of-disagreement-in-decision-making-b31d1b5f1bdc.

273 *Ibid 270.*

274 Jeffrey P. Bezos, Shareholder Letter, Amazon, 1997, https://www.sec.gov/Archives/edgar/data/1018724/000119312517120198/d373368dex991.htm; "In Just 3 Words, Amazon's Jeff Bezos Taught a Brilliant Lesson in Leadership," Justin Bariso, Inc., April 13, 2017, https://www.inc.com/justin-bariso/it-took-jeff-bezos-only-three-words-to-drop-the-best-advice-youll-hear-today.html.

here: making a decision to commit to even if there is disagreement, provided the decision doesn't harm your customer or your product.

CONCLUSION

To successfully identify and manage the tensions specific to your product or feature, it is important to develop a thorough understanding of both your product and you as an individual. Understanding your product, its customers and its competitors enables you to be more proactive in terms of pre-empting or diffusing any tensions that your product might be facing, now and in the future. Once you have identified any risks or unknowns, it pays to learn early and often whether these risks and unknowns hold true or not.

I believe it is just as important to understand *you*. Being aware of how you manage tension, listen to others and your appetite for dissent as well as learning to pick your battles. These aspects aren't just beneficial to you as an individual but also, as we will see in the next chapter, when collaborating within a team to develop great products.

SUMMARY

Product Management = Mind + Matter + Moves

To lean into tension sensibly and productively, it is important to focus on both our products and ourselves.

Start with yourself first to understand your appetite for tension and become aware of the tensions you are experiencing. Ask yourself questions like:

- What sets me off?
- How do I react?
- Am I a Creator or an Editor?
- How does uncertainty impact me?
- Which battles am I willing to fight?

There are two main ways to embrace tension: optimising **'Product Tension'** and being ok with **'Individual Tension'**.

Optimising product tension means that that you make the most of the tensions that are affecting your product or business.

- **Analyse the market and your competitors** to pre-empt competitive pressures, as well as defining the position and points of differentiation for your product. You can use tools such as SWOT analysis, OODA loop, Kano model, Lean Canvas and direct customer feedback in this respect.
- **Manage risks and unknowns** and make sure to learn early and often about risks, to your business - bottom line, operations or reputation - or your product - customer experience, scalability or performance.

- **Apply constraints:** accept the inevitability of constraints - financial, regulatory, technical or operational - and use constraints as a way to reduce complexity and tension.

Managing your personal tension is as important as managing the tension affecting your product. There are a number of things you can do to both be aware of tension and to address it:

- Doing a regular **self-check** to zero in on your feelings, thoughts or behaviours.
- **Listen actively** to fully understand what is happening or where the other person is coming from, to gain a better perspective on the tension and how to manage it.
- Conflict can be conducive to your personal growth and development, provided you **manage conflict**, understanding the nature of the conflict and steering it towards a resolution.
- **Accepting radically** doesn't mean that you resign yourself to the situation or throw in the towel. Instead, you accept things for what they are (and aren't).
- It is ok to **say, 'I don't know'**, admitting that you don't have the answer or need to look into the matter.
- If you are ever in doubt about whether to ask a question, **just ask** and concentrate both on what you want to know and how to ask the question.
- Be direct and specific when **giving feedback**, focusing on the task or behaviour and not on the person. Listen to understand and not to respond when **receiving feedback**.
- To avoid tension due to indecisiveness, follow an approach where you and your team **disagree and commit**, being clear about the point where a decision needs to be reached and committed to.

TOOLKIT: LEANING INTO TENSION EFFECTIVELY

1. SWOT ANALYSIS

Outcome: Identify the strengths, weaknesses, opportunities and threats for your company or product.

The SWOT analysis, devised by Albert Humphrey from Stanford University's Research University Lab, is probably one of the more traditional ways of studying and comparing competitors.[275] It might be an older method, but SWOT still holds true and is a tried and tested way of understanding your competitors:

- **Strengths** - Specific characteristics and attributes which offer a company a competitive advantage. For example, one could argue that design, brand, a loyal customer base and innovation are key strengths of Apple.
- **Weaknesses** - Specific characteristics and attributes which reduce the competitive strength of a business. For example, major debts and inadequate online presence hinder lots of today's retailers in trying to compete effectively with Amazon.
- **Opportunities** - Advantageous situations or circumstances that can create new competitive powers for businesses. Think, for example, of entering new geographic markets, new customer segments or new product opportunities.
- **Threats** - Disadvantageous situations or circumstances which can hamper companies in their ability to compete. For instance, the high cost of labour can hinder companies to compete effectively with those competitors that operate in countries where labour is cheap.

275 "History of SWOT analysis," Tim Friesner, marketingteacher.com, September 3, 2008, https://www.marketingteacher.com/history-of-swot-analysis/.

2. OODA LOOP

Outcome: Using the observe, orient, decide and act stages to make decisions.

The OODA loop was introduced by military strategist John Boyd, who developed the so-called OODA loop based on his experiences as a fighter pilot and later as an instructor, as a way to constantly adapt to changing circumstances.[276] The 'loop' consists of a set of interacting loops, originally designed to be kept in continuous operation during a combat situation. These days, the OODA loop is often used as a decision-making framework, helping people make tough decisions. The model consists of four distinct stages: Observe, Orient, Decide and Act:

- **Observe** - Our observations are the raw information which we base our decisions and actions on. Taking a 'helicopter view' or, as author William Ury calls it, 'going to the balcony', we can detach ourselves from the situation and understand quickly what is going on.[277] Which companies are competing with your product? Do they form direct or indirect competition? What is the impact of their competition on your business or product? These are some sample questions that act as 'source material' for the subsequent stages of the OODA loop.
- **Orient** - At this stage you are very likely to know what needs to be done, understanding both your position and the options available to you. John Boyd states that we tend to filter

---

276 "A Briefing on Metrics and Risks for Autonomous Decision Making in Aerospace Applications," Susan A. Frost, Kai Goebel and Jose Celaya, American Institute of Aeronautics and Astronautics, June 2012, https://www.researchgate.net/publication/266557385_A_Briefing_on_Metrics_and_Risks_for_Autonomous_Decision-making_in_Aerospace_Applications; "OODA Loop," Patty Mulder, Toolshero, https://www.toolshero.com/decision-making/ooda-loop/ (Accessed on December 22, 2019).

277 *Ibid 199.*

information and action, based on our culture, genetics, our ability to analyse and previous experience. In order to win, Boyd argues, we need to get inside of the OODA loop of our adversary.[278]

- **Decide** - Based on your current mental perspective, you will make a decision and determine what actions you need to take.
- **Act** - You now act on the decision made; implementing the action or approach that you decided on during the previous 'Decide' stage.

If you apply the OODA loop in a competitive context, the trick is to go through the OODA at a much quicker pace than a competitor when managing products that you will continuously need to innovate and improve on. Whilst there is no need to become obsessed with your competitors, the OODA loop does show the importance of understanding your competitor's context and what their logical next move might be.

3. KANO ANALYSIS

Outcome: Understand your product's hygiene factors and 'delighters' and compare against competitors, all considered from a customer satisfaction perspective.

Developed by Noriaki Kano in the early eighties, the Kano analysis provides a theory for customer satisfaction (See fig. 16). The model classifies customer preferences into five categories:[279]

278 "The Essence of Winning and Losing," John R. Boyd, June 28, 1995, https://web.archive.org/web/20110324054054/http://www.danford.net/boyd/essence.htm; Frans Osinga, Science, Strategy and War: The Strategic Theory of John Boyd, p. 208, http://www.projectwhitehorse.com/pdfs/ScienceStrategyWar_Osinga.pdf.

279 "Attractive Quality and Must-Be Quality, Journal of the Japanese Society for Quality Control (in Japanese)," Noriaki Kano, Nobuhiko Seraku, Shin-ichi Tsuji and Fumio Takahashi, April 1984, https://ci.nii.ac.jp/naid/110003158895/en/.

- **Must-be quality:** These are the requirements that customers expect and consider normal. For example, when customers shop with an ecommerce site, they expect to be able to pay online. An online payment feature is therefore considered as basic *hygiene* for any ecommerce site.
- **One-dimensional quality:** These product attributes result in customer satisfaction when fulfilled and customer dissatisfaction when not fulfilled. An example of this would be when a company promises 24-hour delivery. The customer will be satisfied when a product is indeed delivered within 24 hours but will be dissatisfied if it is delivered outside of the promised timeframe.
- **Attractive quality:** These are the so-called *delighters*; those product attributes which will cause unexpected satisfaction when satisfied. Thinking back, for example, to when I used white goods site ao.com a few years ago; when I copied the name and type of a certain washing machine to compare prices online, the site automatically showed a notification letting me know that I could call ao.com and they would try to match any price I would find online.[280]
- **Indifferent quality:** These product attributes refer to aspects that are neither good nor bad, and they do not result in customer satisfaction or customer dissatisfaction. Whether a banking app has got pictures of happy customers is not going to make any difference to the users of the app, as long as they can carry out their banking transactions.
- **Reverse quality:** These product reviews refer to a high degree of achievement resulting in dissatisfaction and to the fact that not all customers and their needs are the same. For example, some of your customers might be very tech savvy

280 "Site review: ao.com," Marc Abraham, As I learn, April 7, 2015, https://marcabraham.com/2015/04/07/site-review-ao-com/.

and therefore prefer high-tech products rich with features, whilst others might opt for a more basic version of the product instead.

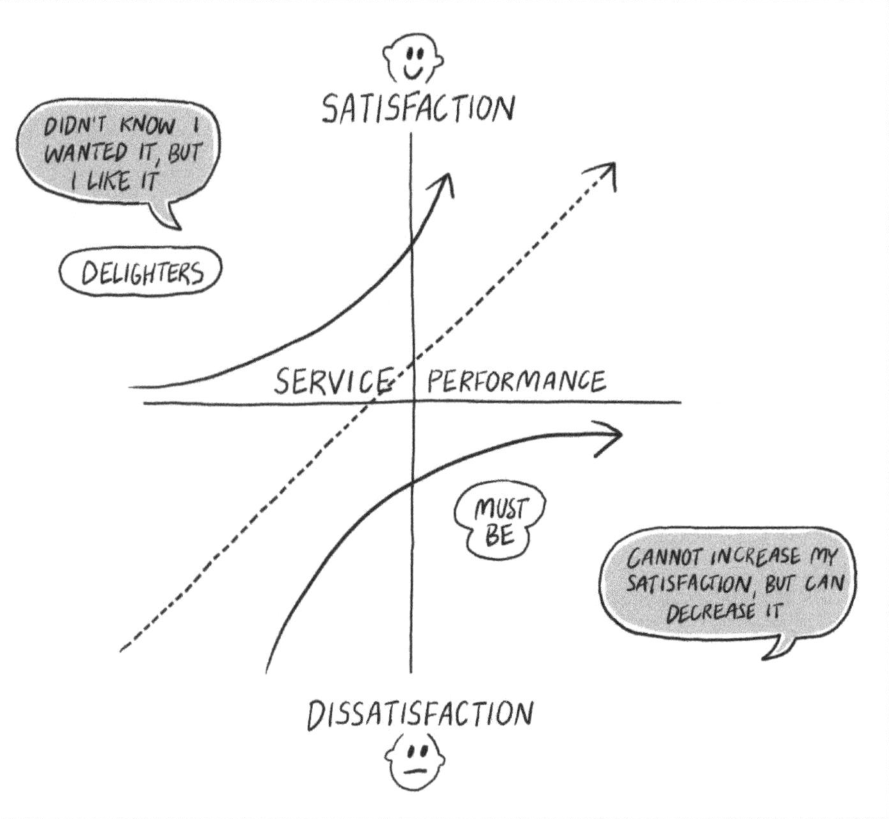

Fig. 16 – Understanding hygiene and delighters from a customer's perspective

I find the Kano analysis very helpful when looking at the competition from a customer point of view, as well as gaining a better understanding of the marketplace and the position of the relevant competitors in it. Understanding what the 'basic needs' and 'delighters' are in your market will help you understand:

- **The position of your product** - Understanding where a product sits vis-a- vis customer expectation.

- **Which battles (not) to pick** - Where do you want your product to play and what will you be playing for? Are you happy to just focus on so-called 'hygiene' factors or do you want to focus on more uncharted territory?
- **Potential product opportunities** - Where are the opportunities for either improved or totally new products, and why? Identify potential *niches* i.e. a subset of the market which a product could focus on.

4. LEAN CANVAS

Outcome: Investigate the components that make up the business model for your business or product.

Ash Maurya's 'Lean Canvas' is a great framework for better understanding your product and market, as well as comparing and contrasting competitors (See fig. 17):[281]

- **Problem** - List the top 3 problems that a competitor product is trying to solve. Are these the same problems your product is looking to solve?
- **Solution** - What are considered the top 3 features of a competitor product? Why?
- **Key metrics** - How does your competitor measure success? Can their product's success be quantified? If so, how does this compare to what your product has achieved thus far?
- **Unique value proposition** - What is the unique benefit of a competitor product? One can assess this either from the vantage point of the customer or from a company's positioning of the product. What makes the product stand

281 Ash Maurya, *Running Lean: Iterate from Plan A to a Plan That Works* (O'Reilly, First Edition, January 2012); "Book review: "Running Lean," Marc Abraham, As I learn, February 25, 2013, https://marcabraham.com/2013/02/25/book-review-running-lean/.

out or get customers to switch from an incumbent product?

- **Unfair advantage** - An aspect of the product that can't be easily copied or bought. Think for example of the breadth of online content that the likes of Spotify and Netflix have amassed over the years. Do their catalogues form a barrier to entry for your product or service?
- **Channels** - Which paths to customers are your competitors using? Consider whether competitors have both an offline and an online presence? How successful are they in their routes to market, and why (not)?
- **Customer segments** - Which customer segment(s) are your competitors targeting? What are the specific characteristics of these customers and are they different from the customers that you and your product are going after?
- **Cost structure** - Just as it is critical to understand your own company's business model, it is important to understand the business model of your competitors. Think for example about the cost to acquire customers, people, content, etc.
- **Revenue streams** - Do you have a rough idea what the revenue streams of your competitors look like? How do they generate gross margins on their products or transactions?[282]

282 "My product management toolkit (25): understanding the unit economics of your product," Marc Abraham, Medium, December 28, 2017, https://medium.com/@maa1/my-product-management-toolkit-25-understanding-the-unit-economics-of-your-product-69aedff237ed.

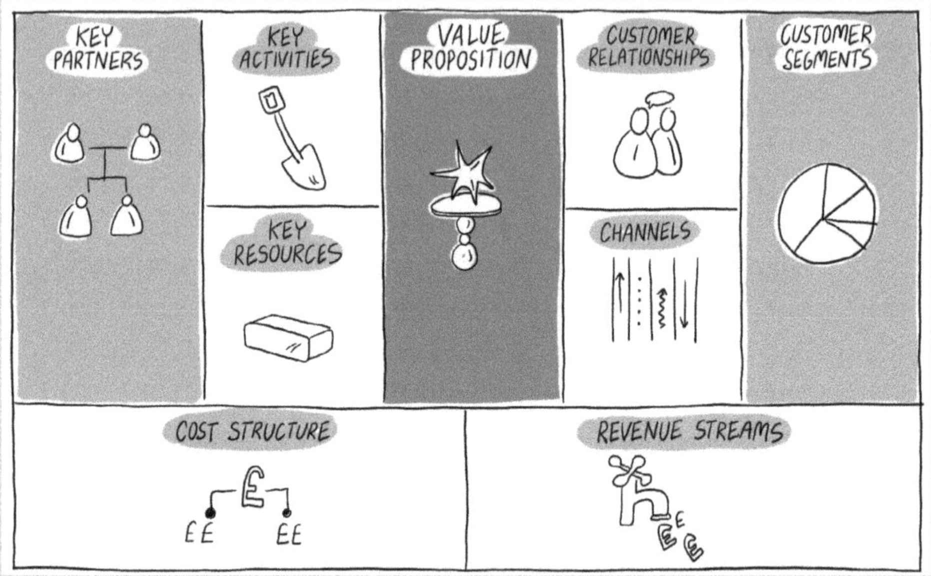

Fig. 17 – Ash Maurya's 'Lean Canvas' zooms in on our business or product

5. DIRECT CUSTOMER FEEDBACK

Outcome: Learn about competitor products directly through the customer.

My favourite way of analysing competitors is hearing directly from customers. For example, when I worked at a digital music service, I ran sessions simply observing people using Spotify, Rdio (which died a few years ago) and Soundcloud. This way, my colleagues and I could learn first-hand about how people felt about our product in comparison to the competition.

With digital products and services, it is harder to do a traditional 'blind product test' - where people don't know which products or brands they are using[283] - but you can still observe and listen to people testing different products which are all trying to solve a similar

283 "Blind Testing," Ipsos Encyclopaedia, June 4, 2016, https://www.ipsos.com/en/ipsos-encyclopedia-blind-testing (Accessed on April 10, 2020).

problem. People will happily tell you why they think product A is better than product B, especially when you make it clear that you don't have an allegiance with any of the tested products.

At the same time, you want to avoid getting too hung up on the product vantage point. 'You can't only look at customer problems through the lens of our product,' says Darlene Miranda, 'because this feels myopic'. Miranda, VP of Product Management at Sterling, suggests that we instead ask the following: look at *how* customers do things currently and *why* they do things in a certain way?'[284]

Products will naturally be surrounded by a healthy level of tension. Even if a product is a first of its kind in the market, there will be a need to stay ahead of any new entrants. Understanding the competitive positioning of your product helps to understand how to best differentiate your product and drive future innovation. While I strongly believe one should worry more about customers than competitors, it is important to fully understand how your product and underlying business model compares to competitors, enabling you to stay ahead of the competition.

6. RED TEAMING

Outcome: Simulate the moves you expect competitors to make and how you would respond.

If you truly want to understand about your competitors and their products, or want to pre-empt their next move, then red teaming might just be the exercise for you. Equally, if you want to let in the tension surrounding a new product or innovation, you can use red teams to work through the things that could go wrong, anticipate potential competitor moves and identify countermeasures.

Just like the OODA loop, red teaming hails from the military world and helps businesses think differently, combat deeply ingrained

284 *Ibid* 153.

assumptions or challenge groupthink.[285] As we have seen, groupthink or complacency can be devastating when developing great products. Having someone who plays or *is* a devil's advocate and challenges prevalent thinking is often a welcome aspect of the product management process.[286] Instead of just analysing the competition, you could have dedicated teams acting as competitors.

These so-called 'red teams' take playing devil's advocate to the next level; the mission of such teams is to force businesses and people to think differently. Red teams will push businesses to consider alternative points of view or contemplate worst case scenarios. Red teaming thus makes us aware of our assumptions and cognitive biases and offers us a means of overcoming them. Red teaming exercises are applied in a wide range of contexts:

- **Cybersecurity** - Companies hiring specialised red teams to attack their technology and exploit security vulnerabilities. Going beyond standard penetration tests, red teams will act as aggressively and unrestricted as any hacker would.
- **Intelligence** - Whether it's NATO, the CIA or the Israeli army, they all have teams dedicated to doing 'alternative analysis', set up explicitly to challenge prevalent assumptions within intelligence bodies.
- **Business** - When developing a business strategy, companies often consider a best-case scenario, assuming that everything will go to plan. Red teaming exercises can help in laying bare any strategic gaps or flaws, helping companies scan the business environment for both threats and opportunities.

---

285 Bryce G. Hoffman, Red Teaming: *How Your Business Can Conquer the Competition by Challenging Everything* (Crown Publishing Group, May 2017); "Book Review: "Red Teaming" by Bryce Hoffman," Marc Abraham, Medium, September 10, 2019, https://medium.com/@maa1/book-review-red-teaming-by-bryce-hoffman-5f060e82f551.

286 "My product management toolkit (9): playing devil's advocate," Marc Abraham, Medium, May 7, 2016, https://medium.com/@maa1/my-product-management-toolkit-9-playing-devils-advocate-400656f719a6.

Irrespective of context, red teaming is all about rigorous questioning and thinking unconventionally. Red teams often consist of people who have proven to be contrarian thinkers. These are the three phases of a typical red teaming exercise:

1. Using **analytical tools** to question the arguments and assumptions that too often go unquestioned during the regular planning process.
2. Using **imaginative techniques** to figure out what could go wrong - and what could go right - with the plan in order to expose hidden threats and missed opportunities.
3. Applying **contrarian thinking** to challenge the plan and force the organisation to consider alternative perspectives.

Red teaming offers a great opportunity to figure out and mitigate anything that could go wrong with your product or imagine the kinds of products your competitors might be developing. It's also kind of fun and great for team building exercises!

7. TURNING AN ASSUMPTION INTO A HYPOTHESIS

Outcome: Prioritise the riskiest assumption and turn it into hypotheses that can be tested and measured.

Assumption:
'We believe customers will pay for this product.'

Hypothesis:
We believe that by introducing a new 'daily genre-based recommendations' feature for our subscribers only, we expect more of our customers to sign up for a subscription.

We know this is true when 1,000 customers sign up for a subscription after having received free daily recommendations for a 5-day period.

How you subsequently test a hypothesis is the relatively easy part, as there are numerous ways to test, varying from simply launching the product to doing a painted door test. At Basecamp, the company which we first encountered in Chapter 1, new products or features don't get Beta-tested. Instead, the belief at Basecamp is that 'the market will tell us the truth.'[287] In a painted door test, you use the suggestion of a feature or a solution to learn how many people actually use it. When a customer clicks on the call to action of the dummy feature, a message will appear that says something like 'Thanks. This feature isn't live yet, as we're thinking about building it. Could a product manager reach out to you to learn more about your interest in this feature?'[288]

The main prerequisite for any successful test - i.e. proving or disproving your hypothesis - is being clear about what you are trying to learn and why. How can we quickly test the riskiest assumption which will determine product success or failure? Once we have proven this hypothesis, what is the next riskiest assumption worth testing? The tension inherent in managing products is thus brought forward and kept under control.

8. CONDUCTING A PRE-MORTEM

Outcome: Assess any things that could go wrong and how to mitigate these risks from materialising.

A pre-mortem enables you to start working backwards and look at the individual factors that could lead to failure as well as the actions to take in order to pre-empt certain risks from materialising. Once

287 Jason Fried and David Heinemeier Hansson, *It Doesn't Have to Be Crazy at Work* (Harper Business, October 2018); "My Product Management Toolkit (33): launch and learn," Marc Abraham, Medium, November 23, 2018, https://medium.com/@maa1/my-product-management-toolkit-33-launch-and-learn-e1b61bff5026.

288 "How do you Implement Effective Product Experimentation?" Jon Noronha, Mind the Product, October 16, 2018, https://www.mindtheproduct.com/how-do-you-implement-effective-product-experimentation/.

you have identified these factors, you can start thinking about how to best avoid or mitigate these risks from occurring. Naturally, it will be up to you and your team to figure out how to best structure your pre-mortem, but these are some proposed aspects and scenarios worth considering when running one.

The product has bombed - Rather than considering the possible failure of a product or project, in the pre-mortem the product is assumed to have failed. Similarly, if you are doing a pre-mortem at the start of a new project, it is really helpful if all pre-mortem participants think of any reason why the project could fail dramatically.

Does this mean that nothing will go wrong? - Of course, even with the most detailed pre-mortem exercise and follow-up, things will not go according to plan and the unexpected will still happen. However, right from the get-go, you are creating an environment that allows people to think and continuously talk about risk. You are effectively creating an environment where people can speak freely about potential risk scenarios, without fear of being seen as impolite or difficult.

Identify threats and risks - There are a number of ways to elicit risks and threats from the pre-mortem. You could do a simple 'brain dump' or try a more structured approach whereby people need to come up with risks within certain areas (see 'Categorise failures' below).

Analyse likelihood - Once you have collated threats and risks, you can use a simple scale ranging from 'highly unlikely' to 'highly likely' to assess the likelihood of a specific risk or threat materialising. I have found that the activity of placing risks against the aforementioned scale, helps create a shared understanding of the biggest risks. It also focuses the mind on the actions that need to be taken or things that need to be in place to mitigate risk.

Are the right people in the room? - When running a pre-mortem session with a number of people, it is important to make sure you have got the right people in the room. For example, if you are looking to work on a digital product, it's important to have developers and designers present. Similarly, if you're working in a highly regulated industry, having a compliance person brainstorming upfront about potential risks will work in your favour.

Brainstorm and assess preventative actions - Once you have collectively established your highest risks, you can start thinking about ways to mitigate these risks. Realistically, you might not be able to stop all risks from happening (think about a garden party being impacted by a sudden rain downpour ...). In these scenarios, you can still figure out how to best reduce the *impact* of a risk happening and come up with a 'plan B'. For example, if the heavens open during your garden party, people could always seek shelter in the tent that you put up 'just in case'.

Not a one-off exercise! - The risks and actions that you identify during your pre-mortem are something that you can use as ongoing reference points. 'How are we doing against risk X?' or 'We can see risk Y materialising soon, how can we best pre-empt things?'

Categorise failures - When getting people to think about the reasons for failure, I always find it helpful to think about failures in specific areas, dependent on your product, market or organisation:

- **Marketing**- Think upfront about what could go wrong with your product's go-to-market strategy and the marketing channels that you're looking to use. For example, what would be the impact if product messaging fails to resonate with your target audience?
- **Customer** - What if customers don't want to pay for our product? What if we're addressing the wrong customer

segment? What if we've got customer needs wrong?

- **Technology** - The chosen technology implementation doesn't work, what do we do? The technology isn't scalable!? At this stage, it's very valuable to explore the complexities or unknowns related to the technical implementation. As a group, you might agree on running discovery sprints to test certain technologies or non-happy path scenarios to deal with some of the 'unknown unknowns' being discovered early on.
- **Stakeholders** - Many people like stakeholder mapping, but the pre-mortem can also help in figuring out who the relevant stakeholders are upfront and how best to communicate with them. It can also be helpful to identify which stakeholders have the most knowledge in a particular domain.
- **Cost** - What if our budget gets slashed halfway through the project? What if costs spiral because we failed to budget properly? What if the technology we've chosen turns out to be far too expensive or complex to implement?
- **Compliance** - Compliance and regulation can sometimes be easy to forget at the start of a project. However, compliance can have a massive impact on a product or a project. I was once involved in a project where we only found out halfway through that launching in China would be very tricky from an internal compliance and external regulation point of view. This proved to be a major stumbling block and it would have been far better if we had identified this as a major project risk beforehand.
- **Competition** - What if your direct competitor launched the same product as yours, but just a bit quicker? Or we imagine a situation where the product has failed because the competitor lowered its product price. Do we need a plan B for when this scenario happens? If so, what should this plan look like?

9. LISTEN ACTIVELY

Outcome: Not just hearing what the other person is saying, but truly understanding where they are coming from.

Fully understanding what is being said and where the other person is coming from helps us reduce noise and filter out the key aspects to know or act on. In order to listen actively, the onus is on the listener to actively develop and apply a number of components:[289]

- **Acceptance** – Acceptance is about respecting the person that you are talking to; irrespective of what the other person has to say but purely because you are talking to another human being. Accepting means trying to avoid expressing agreement or disagreement with what the other person is saying, at least initially. I have often made this mistake; being too keen to express my views and causing the speaker to feel disrespected.
- **Honesty** – Honesty comes down to being open about your reactions to what you have heard. Similar to the acceptance component, honest reactions given too soon can easily stifle further explanation on the part of the speaker. This also means that we need to set aside any previously formed opinions about the speaker or your views on the subject of the conversation.
- **Empathy** – Empathy is about your ability to understand the speaker's situation on an emotional level. Centring your understanding on your own view instead of on a sense of what should be felt, creates empathy instead of sympathy. Empathy can also be defined as your desire to feel the speaker's emotions, regardless of your own experience.[290]
- **Specifics** – Specifics refers to the need to deal in

289 *Ibid 247.*

290 Indi Young, *Practical Empathy* (Brooklyn, NY: Rosenfeld Media, 2015, pp. 49 – 67).

detail rather than generalities. The point here is that for communication to be worthwhile, you should ask the speaker to be more specific, encouraging the speaker to open up more or 'own' the problem that they are trying to raise.

Practically speaking, the four components of active listening mean that you will spend more time listening than talking, restating or clarifying what you have heard and deciphering the feelings behind the words. For example:

- **Speaker:** *The difficulty is that I don't know how to best design this feature.*
- **Me [Thinking empathetically and accepting the speaker]:** *I hear what you are saying, and I can imagine it must be difficult to design a new feature from scratch.*
- **Me [Listening for specifics and asking]:** *What is it about the new feature that you aren't sure about? Would it help if we did some sketches together, just to get going?*

Apart from these four components of active listening, Gibson and Walker suggest a number of tips to help improve our listening skills:[291]

1. Minimise external distractions
2. Face the speaker
3. Maintain eye contact
4. Focus on the speaker
5. Be open-minded
6. Be sincerely interested
7. Have sympathy, feel empathy
8. Assess the emotion, not just the words
9. Respond appropriately
10. Minimise internal distractions
11. Avoid 'me' stories

291 *Ibid 247.*

12. Don't be scared of silence
13. Take notes
14. Practice emotional intelligence
15. Check your understanding

10. RITUAL DISSENT

Outcome: being able to facilitate sessions where people can share their challenges, doubts or ideas in return for constructive feedback.

When I first heard the term 'Ritual Dissent' I imagined a state of constant disagreement, with people dissenting as a matter of course. Almost as if the conversations that people have around the watercooler or behind closed doors are out in the open all the time.

In fact, ritual dissent is a workshop method designed for people to air their challenges, doubts and suggestions and receive constructive feedback in return. The main idea behind ritual dissent is that ideas are reviewed and criticised without facing the presenter of the idea. This technique helps to de-personalise the feedback and create a safe environment for the group to attack the idea vigorously (dissent) or suggest a better idea or improvement instead (assent).[292] Listening and constructivism are two key ingredients of ritual dissent:

- **Listening** - While the presenter is outlining her idea or a series of ideas, the group presented isn't allowed to talk or ask questions; they have to listen in silence. Once the presenter has finished her presentation, she turns around with her back facing the group, after which the group will start discussing the idea. The presenter isn't allowed to interact with the group and can only take notes while she listens intently to the group discussion (See fig. 18).

292 "Ritual Dissent," Dave Snowden, Cognitive Edge, https://cognitive-edge.com/methods/ritual-dissent/ (Accessed on January 5, 2020).

- **Attacking** - Participants in ritual dissent should be made aware that the idea is not to be fair, reasonable or support but to attack the idea (and not the presenter) or to provide a better alternative. The goal is to learn from others through complete openness and to end up with the best, stress-tested ideas.

Ritual dissent has been designed to avoid people making decisions by groupthink or easily reaching consensus. The lack of eye contact and the obligation to listen in silence create an environment where people can truly listen, and focus exclusively on what a person is saying, not who is saying it. With others going through exactly the same process, feedback is less likely to be perceived as a personal attack, but supportive and par for the course.

Fig. 18 – Using Ritual Dissent to actively listen to what someone is saying

11. BE YOUR OWN ADVERSARY

Outcome: act as your own 'devil's advocate' and challenge your own assumptions or ideas.

Ritual dissent is a good way for people to disagree and challenge in an open and constructive setting. It is like saying 'it's ok to knock out my idea, as long as you don't knock me out at the same time ...' The same applies to red teaming, where a group of people will take on the adversary's mindset.

However, you don't need a workshop setting or a dedicated 'red team' to disagree or throw spanners into the works. Anyone can play 'devil's advocate' at any given time, and you can even play this back internally. Chris Butler, who has done a lot of work around adversarial thinking, encourages us to be 'adversarial to ourselves, at random moments'.[293] You could take an outsider perspective and answer the following questions:

- What holes are there in the evidence or assumptions that underpin my idea or decision?
- Are you being honest with yourself?
- What biases have you applied and how can you refute them?

12. RADICAL ACCEPTANCE

Outcome: accepting things for what they are, understanding what is really happening and why.

- **Acknowledge your inner narrative** - What is happening here? versus what am I telling myself? What is the evidence?

- **Write it down** - I often use a 'Thought Diary', which is an idea that comes from Aaron Beck's Cognitive Behavioural Therapy ('CBT'), and involves writing down the difficult situation that you feel you are in, your thoughts about the situation, the evidence for and against your thoughts, and any alternative thoughts to help reframe things (See fig. 19).[294]

293 *Ibid 157.*

294 "The key principles of cognitive behavioural therapy," Kristina Fenn, , Royal College of General Practitioners, Volume: 6 issue: 9, pp. 579-585, September 6, 2013, https://journals.sagepub.com/doi/full/10.1177/1755738012471029.

- **Determine what you can influence** - Radical acceptance is a key step to picking your battles; what are the things that you can realistically influence and which things you can't?

- **Recognise that you will make mistakes** - Instead of beating yourself up when you feel pressure or things don't go according to plan, you accept mistakes that you have made. This doesn't mean that the mistake will go away or lose its severity; you can change the way you perceive your mistake, making sure you learn from it and avoid making the same mistake twice.

- **Recognise when you are wrong** - For all the times that we might share an idea or thought that turns out to be wrong, we are likely to be wrong much more often. Rather than not sharing our ideas or thoughts, I suggest *accepting* that we will be wrong and learning from those experiences.

Radical acceptance is an important step towards both accepting, and - where appropriate - fully embracing certain tensions.

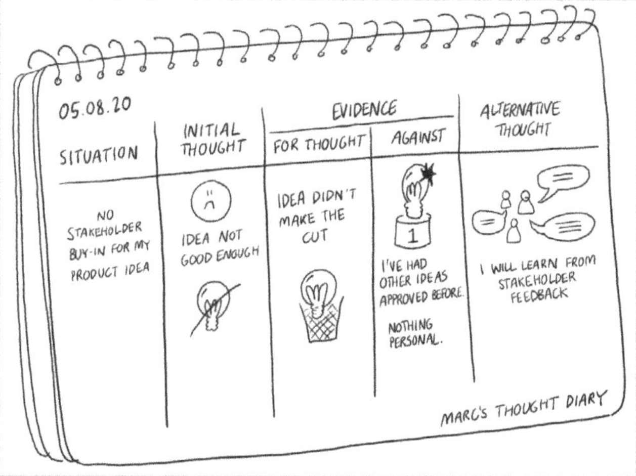

Fig. 19 – Write it down in your Thought Diary

13. ASK ' 5 WHYS'

Outcome: asking 'why' to try and get to the bottom of things.

If you don't do anything else, just ask 'why'. Such a simple word, but oh so powerful:

- Why are we doing this?
- Why are we not doing this?
- Why are you saying that?
- Why is that your preference?
- Why did we make that decision?

14. RADICAL CANDOUR

Outcome: being comfortable seeking and processing impromptu guidance.

In her book 'Radical Candor', Kim Scott offers valuable tips on how to best ask for and process guidance from others:[295]

- **Have a go-to question:** In order to make it easier and less awkward to ask your direct reports for performance feedback or guidance, Scott suggests using a go-to question. She learned this technique from Fred Kofman, who used to be her coach at Google and is the author of 'Conscious Business'.[296] 'Is there anything I could do or stop doing that would make it easier to work with me?' This sample go-to question will get the conversation flowing and remove any feelings of awkwardness.
- **Embrace the discomfort:** In the event your go-to question fails to have the desired effect, and the other person answers that everything is fine or struggles to come up with

295 *Ibid 263, pp. 130-136.*

296 Fred Kofman, *Conscious Business: How to Build Value Through Values* (Sounds True: 1st Edition, July 2005).

something - remain quiet. It can be tempting to say, 'Well, that's great' or 'fine, let's move on' but that is not going to help. Leaving some silence or suggesting a follow up can help in getting your direct reports over any awkwardness?

- **Listen with the intent to understand, not to respond:** If you're anything like me, i.e. not super comfortable with asking people for feedback, your initial response might well be to act defensively and respond to the criticism. Scott urges us not to do that; don't start criticising the criticism! Instead, she suggests saying something like 'So what I hear you saying is ...'
- **Reward criticism to get more of it:** If you received feedback, the next important thing is to follow up and show that you genuinely welcomed it. If you agree with what was said, you should make a change as soon as possible. If the necessary change will take time, do something visible to show you're trying.
- **Gauge the guidance you get:** I love Scott's suggestion to try and keep a tally of the number of times people reporting to you have criticised you. Equally, measure how often they praise you. Scott mentions that you should be wary if it's all praise and no criticism! It means that you'll have to work harder to get people to criticise you.

CHAPTER 6.
SO. YOU WANT TO LEAN INTO TENSION *COLLABORATIVELY?!*

'Humble people are better at bringing others together to solve tough problems.' **Laszlo Bock**

Product Management = Mind + Matter + Moves

In this chapter we will explore:

- Working with your team to **manage tension collaboratively** when developing products.
- The basic tenets for **effective collaboration**.
- How to encourage **constructive dissent** within teams.
- Ways we can help to create **psychologically safe** environments.

INTRODUCTION

Much like managing products, leaning into tension is not something that should be restricted to a solo effort. No one should carry all the stress, frustration and sometimes downright panic inherent in creating products on their own shoulders. In other words: product management is a team sport and so is managing tension.

In the first chapter of this book, I outlined why things are often not as simple as putting a team together and automatically expecting that team to develop successful products. In this chapter we will have a closer look at how to encourage effective collaboration, and how we can best incorporate the tension that is inherent when creating products collaboratively.

OVERCOMING COMMON BARRIERS TO EFFECTIVE COLLABORATION

'No matter how brilliant your mind or strategy, if you're playing a solo game, you'll always lose out to a team.' **Reid Hoffman**

Leaning into tension if you are facing an opponent in the boxing ring is one thing, but what if you are trying to fight multiple opponents at the same time?! 'I feel like the engineers in my team are all ganging up on me' and 'we constantly argue about even the smallest of things in our team' are complaints frequently voiced by some of my product management peers and something I used to utter too! As you may recall from Chapter 1, there are a number of common barriers to adequate teamwork:

- Lack of respect for diverse opinions or viewpoints.
- Trust missing within a team or between certain team members.
- Failure to address perceived threats.
- Lack of shared information or a single source of truth.
- Weak or bad relationships between (non) team members.
- Managing emotional triggers.
- Misalignment on purpose or goals.

Naturally, if any of these barriers remain in place, leaning into tension will be very difficult, if not impossible. If, for example, the team is lacking a shared sense of direction or goals, challenging each other about how best to achieve certain outcomes becomes unattainable. Similarly, if the product manager does not trust the engineers, and vice versa, any form of collaboration will be nigh on impossible.

I believe that the product manager often finds him or herself in an interesting position; while none of the people that you work closely with are your direct reports, you are in a good position to help foster inter- and cross-team collaboration.

PRODUCT MANAGEMENT IS A TEAM EFFORT

'So, I came up with this word "scenius" – and scenius is the intelligence of a whole... operation or group of people. And I think that's a more useful way to think about culture, actually. I think that – let's forget the idea of "genius" for a little while, let's think about the whole ecology of ideas that give rise to good new thoughts and good new work.' **Brian Eno**

The role of the product manager is that of a facilitator bringing people together on a journey rather than a mini CEO. When I started my career in product management, I thought that I needed to come up with all the great product ideas. I had this perception of great product inventors like Stephanie Kwolek at DuPont, Steve Jobs at Apple or Tony Fadell at Nest, single-handedly driving a product end to end; from discovering a problem to solve all the way through to coming up with a solution to bring the product to market. The reality of building products couldn't be further removed from my initial understanding. As a product manager I am nowhere without the trust and collaboration of a whole host of people, from discovery to execution.

No matter whether you are managing a new, greenfield product or evolving an existing one, I often compare a product to a jigsaw puzzle. Most products that we work on consist of a hundred or more 'pieces'; with people in operations, technology, design, customer success, supply chain, finance or sales either holding these pieces, or being in the best position to come up with them and fit them together.

'There is never a shortage of ideas - from stakeholders across the organisation, competitors, customer research and feedback from the team' says Jo Wickremasinghe, Product Director at Zoopla, when I asked her about teamwork. Wickremasinghe believes that 'the best product managers are those who are able to facilitate all the different groups and inputs to get alignment on a set of ideas or hypotheses that everyone believes are the best bets. This means that taking inputs from the product development team is critically important.'[297]

To enable successful collaboration, acknowledging that team success trumps individual accomplishments is vital if you want to create successful products. 'The star of the team is the team', argues basketball coach John Wooden in his book on leadership, insisting that team members share the 'ball' - information, ideas and more.[298] Product managers can only be successful if the teams they are part of, or work with, are successful. If a team is performing well, the greater the likelihood of the product performing well. The complicating factor here is that product people hardly ever have any authority, formal at least, over the people and teams that we work with.

'Product is about getting the job done right, and creating value for users and the business, and you are just not going to be able to do that if you are fighting with colleagues or alienating parts of the business' explains Alex Watson, Head of Product at BBC News. 'It doesn't mean you have to be loved by all, or even to work in a way that is about being popular - but you do need to hold yourself and your team to high standards.'[299] To be able to create and uphold such standards, product managers can contribute in two significant ways: establishing trusted relationships and encouraging constructive dissent within our teams.

297 *Ibid 51.*

298 John Wooden, *Wooden on Leadership* (McGraw-Hill Education, April 2005, pp. 130 – 131).

299 *Ibid 43.*

Establishing Trusted Relationships = Mind + Moves

Three elements are critical if you want to build and maintain **trusted relationships:**

- Empathise to use the right currencies and **influence without authority.**
- Work towards a **shared goal** or set of outcomes.
- Be **fully transparent**, treat collaborators as partners, making it ok to share openly and constantly.
- Foster a **psychologically safe** environment that allows people to take risks and display vulnerability.

1. ESTABLISHING TRUSTED RELATIONSHIPS

'So, what is trust? We could say that a person or organization trusts another when both sides have reason to expect that neither will take advantage of the other, and, whenever possible, will even do things that advance the other's interests.' **Brigitte Jordan**

Brigitte 'Gitti" Jordan, Principal Scientist at Xerox, has spent a lifetime sharing valuable insights about the concept of trust. Jordan argues that trust can't be designed; it has to be built, little by little.[300] She makes clear that trust is not the same as being liked. It is a relationship where the other person's brain is rewarding another person for the engagement, for acting in a way that depends on another.[301]

300 "Notes on Trust and why it matters in corporations," Brigitte Jordan, September 11, 2011, https://www.lifescapes.org/Papers/notes_on_trust.htm.

301 See: Robin Dreeke, *The Code of Trust* (St. Martin's Press, August 2017); "An FBI Agent Reveals 5 Steps To Gaining Anyone's Trust. Shane Parrish," Farnam Street, January 2014, https://fs.blog/2014/01/robin-dreeke-interview-no-5/.

She also suggests that there is a clear link between levels of trust and communication. When trust is low, then the level of communication is likely to be defensive, often characterised by formal language. In contrast, when trust is high, communication is more likely to be 'synergistic', meaning that people will communicate openly to create better, creative solutions.[302]

Despite the obvious importance of trust, we often forget about trust and relationships. Instead, we spend most of our time on organisational reorganisations, team structures or large transformation programmes. I am not saying that these things don't have any value; companies need to evolve and adapt. Effective collaboration, however, doesn't come from creating teams on paper. Working together effectively *and* managing product tension together comes from relationships built on trust.

As we will see in the remainder of this chapter, trusted relationships don't mean that we all have to be best friends and be careful to not upset each other. Trusted relationships are those between people with shared goals and values and based on a reciprocal give and take. 'And by *giving* others our respect, we have already, in a sense, adopted an attitude of giving' argues William Ury, highlighting 'giving' as a key building block of trusted relationships.[303]

This raises the question of how one goes about building relationships, especially in highly pressured or uncertain environments. To add some more complexity to this question; as product people we also need to reckon with the fact that we more often than not work closely with people that we don't have any formal authority over. Rather than dwelling over our lack of authority, I believe that product managers are possibly in the best imaginable position to build and manage trusted relationships.

Provided it is genuine, 'influence without authority' is a very natural

302 Pat MacMillan, *The Performance Factor: Unlocking the Secrets of Teamwork* (Nashville: B&H Publishing Group, 2001, pp. 165-170).

303 *Ibid 199, p. 146.*

but powerful part of building relationships. Giving and taking sits at the very heart of influencing without authority, understanding the things that matter to the other person and to yourself.

Influence without authority

We will need to invest time and effort in understanding what makes the other person tick. To do so, we can use so-called 'currencies' which we can exchange to create a situation based on mutual trust. The concept of currencies is derived from the 'Influence Without Authority Model' by Allan R. Cohen and David L. Bradford.[304] This model is based on exchange and reciprocity – making trades for what you desire in return for what the other person desires (See fig. 20). There are a number of potential currencies that one can use to trade: inspiration, task, position and personal currencies:

- **Inspiration-related currencies** - These currencies reflect inspirational goals which provide relevance and meaning to the work that a person does.
- **Task-related currencies** - These currencies are all about getting the job done and relate directly to the satisfaction a person derives from completing a task.
- **Position-related currencies** - These currencies enhance a person's position in the organisation and, thereby, indirectly aid the person's ability to accomplish or advance a career.
- **Relationship-related currencies** - These currencies cover building or strengthening the relationship with someone.
- **Personal currencies** - These currencies could form

304 Allan R. Cohen and David L. Bradford, *Influence Without Authority* (Wiley, 2nd Edition, March 2005); "Book review: Influence Without Authority," Marc Abraham, As I learn, April 25, 2017, https://marcabraham.com/2017/04/25/book-review-influence-without-authority/.

an infinite list of idiosyncratic needs. They are valued because they enhance the individual's sense of self. They may be derived from task or interpersonal activity.

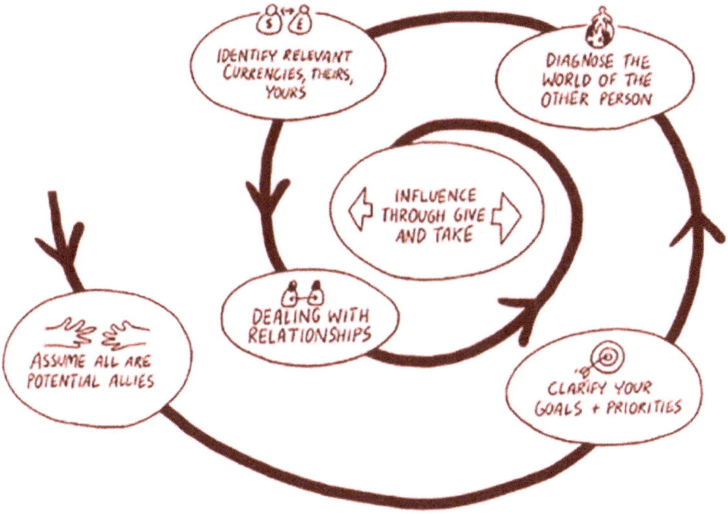

Fig. 20 – Exchange relevant currencies to establish trusted relationships

For example, some people that I have worked with put a lot of value on doing work that has value and meaning and where I successfully used 'inspiration-related currencies' to build and maintain trusted relationships. Other people, by contrast, cared less about meaningful work, rather they got much more satisfaction from getting the job done. With the latter group, 'task-related currencies' proved to be highly effective.

Both inspiration and task-related currencies are positive ones, and can be used to build genuine, trusted relationships. In contrast, 'negative currencies' are those things that people don't tend to value and wish to avoid. Negative currencies can lead to bad or non-existent relationships and I have included both the positive and negative currencies in the toolkit section at the end of this chapter.

Being aware of your own currencies and those of the other person is an important starting point for building trusted relationships.

If we want to influence successfully without authority, we will need to devote time and effort to understanding the other person, what they value and how we can accommodate these values through the relevant currencies. Exchanging currencies, if done with genuine intentions, forms the heart of any trusted relationship.

Shared goals

Earlier in this book we learned about 'constructive conflict' deriving its productive nature from a shared objective. Trusted relationships emanate from exactly the same source: a shared goal or set of outcomes. 'Teams who dream together, achieve together' is how Canva co-founder Melanie Perkins frames the importance of having a shared goal. Canva is an eight-year-old online design company valued at $1bn which places a lot of significance on having the company driving towards a larger, shared vision: 'the bigger the vision, the easier it is to have a goal-driven culture, as each "goal" is simply a step towards that bigger mission' according to Perkins.[305]

To be clear, team members might still disagree about *how* to best achieve a goal or vision, but such disagreement is a lot less likely to act as a showstopper with respect to product success if team members have all 'enrolled' in the same outcome.[306] As long as we all trust each other to be acting in the interest of the same end result, we can have healthy disagreements on how best to get there. Shared goals play just as important a role on an interpersonal level. You don't have to be best friends, or even like each other, to work collaboratively towards shared outcomes. At Atlassian, a global maker of software and collaboration tools, they measure shared understanding amongst the

305 "Creating a goal-driven culture at Canva," Melanie Perkins, Canva, March 3, 2019, https://product.canva.com/creating-a-goal-driven-culture-at-canva/.

306 "In search of enrollment," Seth Godin, Seth's Blog, July 16, 2017, https://seths.blog/2017/07/in-search-of-enrollment/.

members of their product teams by asking three simple questions, each question accompanied by a 1-5 scale for people to indicate their agreement.[307] 'I understand how my work fits into the bigger picture (our vision and strategy)' is one of the questions that Atlassian asks its team members. I will include Atlassian's questions in the toolkit section at the end of this chapter for you to consider. Again, positive answers to such questions is by no means a foolproof guarantee against disagreement or distrust within teams, but it does create a shared foundation for any difficult conversations in the future.

OVERCOMING INITIAL DISTRUST OF MY TEAMMATES ...

Not long ago I worked on improving the user experience for new visitors arriving on our site. My colleagues in the marketing team had historically put a lot of effort into creating a compelling experience, continuously improving the site's homepage on the web and mobile apps, working directly with the company's engineers and designers. When I got involved as a product manager, I could clearly sense a feeling of distrust. My colleagues were fully professional and perfectly nice, but it was plain to see that they were unclear why I was joining the conversation, unsure about my 'angle'.

Before we got to a point where we started working closely together, we spent some time clarifying the bigger, shared goal that we all had in common: improving the experience of new customers. Once we had established this, it became much easier to talk about our respective roles and responsibilities with respect to this goal, reassuring each other that 'we are all in it together'.

---

307 "Is your product management team doing a good job?" Sherif Mansour, Medium, January 30, 2017, https://medium.com/@sherifmansour/is-your-product-management-team-doing-a-good-job-4a211d327deb.

When I asked Kristina Walcker-Mayer, Product Lead at N26, about her views on having shared goals when building products, she explained: 'From my experience, the most successful outcomes have been created by a deep understanding of the WHY from a business and customer perspective and communication of change and iterations during the process.' Even daily, more tactical product conversations such as 'which content to show first?' or 'should we optimise on improving our personalisation or drive direct sales' benefit from a shared set of goals, says Walcker-Mayer. 'In these cases, it helps to have a common understanding on a company level of the initiatives that we want to invest in the long term and how much time we give ourselves in order to evaluate the success of those initiatives.'[308] From this point of alignment we can start building trusted relationships and allow each other to be open and vulnerable with one another.

Transparency

I bet that when you are reading this, you are thinking 'I am 100% transparent, always open and clear with everyone.' More often than not, we find ourselves dealing with situations where we have not been as fully transparent as we might think, or someone else has not been fully open or clear with us. The more frequently this happens the more likely we are to start feeling a sense of distrust. Why wasn't I aware of this information? Was it a simple oversight or am I not trusted with this knowledge?

When companies grow, it becomes even harder to keep everybody within the organisation informed or to continue to be fully open with people outside your business. Personally, I find it much easier to be open with everyone instead of having to constantly remember who I have told what ... Moreover, the benefits of transparency affect both the organisation and the individuals within it:

- **Decision making** - We can make better decisions if we are aware of all relevant decision factors. I am pretty sure

308 Kristina Walcker-Mayer, *email to author*, January 23, 2020.

we have all been in meetings that felt 'asymmetric', purely because the participants didn't have the same pieces of information. These kinds of meetings always feel like they go on for ages because we first need to make sure we all tackle a problem from the same perspective, considering the same data points. If we want to delegate decisions to teams or individuals, we need to ensure we supply them with all the information needed to make decisions.

- **Collaboration** - Not only does the speed of collaboration improve if we are transparent with each other, sharing knowledge and data with each other contributes to a shared sense that 'we are in this together'. Transparency signifies that we trust each other with all knowledge - sensitive or not - and that we need to use this shared understanding to work together effectively.
- **Trust** - Transparency is an important instrument in setting up and maintaining trusted relationships. Employees are more likely to feel a true part of the organisation if they are fully aware of what is happening within the business and the rationale for its actions. Equally, today's customers increasingly appreciate brands being open with them about cost, origin of the materials used, etc. For instance, take Everlane - a mostly online fashion company with a couple of US stores - which shares all the costs of its production process with its customers as well as the names and locations of its factories.[309] Through this level of transparency, Everlane sets out to instil trust among its customers with respect to the origin of its products, and its manufacturing conditions.
- **Morale** - I once worked at a company where a number of

309 "How Everlane Your Wardrobe," Lizzie Widdicombe, The New Yorker, September 25, 2017, https://www.newyorker.com/culture/on-and-off-the-avenue/how-everlane-hacked-your-wardrobe; "About Everlane," https://www.everlane.com/about (Accessed on June 1, 2020)

people worked on a new product which carried the code name 'Project Trojan'. Initially, this concerned a small group of employees who all had to sign a separate non-disclosure agreement to be able to work on the product. As the number of people involved with the product grew, the count of uncomfortable meetings or conversations between people who were 'in the know' and those who weren't grew exponentially. Those people not privy to the sensitive information, increasingly started feeling that they were less important to the business or that their contributions weren't valued properly. I thus experienced first-hand how a lack of transparency can directly influence employee morale.

'Transparent by default' is the motto of UK challenger bank Monzo. This means that Monzo have created policies and practices to bring information out into the open, wherever possible - 'sharing information in the right place, with the right people'. Monzo believes that 'transparency builds trust' both internally with its employees and externally with its customers, as well as playing a vital role in a number of other areas.[310]

WHY MONZO IS ' TRANSPARENT BY DEFAULT'

This is the take of Jonas Huckestein, co-founder of Monzo, on the aims behind ensuring Monzo is as transparent as possible:[311]

- ***Independent decision making by teams*** - *'We believe the key to a successful business is to hire people that are smarter*

310 "Transparent By Default," Jonas Huckestein, Monzo, March 10, 2017, https://monzo.com/blog/2017/03/10/transparent-by-default; "How Monzo uses radical transparency to build a bank for the people," Chief Digital Officer, October 8, 2018, https://channels.theinnovationenterprise.com/articles/how-monzo-used-radical-transparency-to-build-a-bank-for-the-people.

311 *Ibid 310.*

than you and then let them get on with their jobs. We expect our teams to make decisions independently that help them to achieve their goals, while being aware of the overall goals and direction for the company and following relevant policies and procedures. This is only possible if we supply all the information required to make such decisions.'

- **Remote workers being fully up to speed** - *'While most of our team work on-site in London, we do have 10 fully remote workers and more join every month. Sharing meeting notes, team updates, and documents by default helps them stay up to speed with what is happening in the office and ensures they don't miss out.'*
- **Easier onboarding of new teammates** - *'Together with formalised joining processes, new joiners find the ability to read through old documents, meeting notes, and conversations invaluable to help get up to speed and get an instant feel for how we work.'*
- **Supporting personal development** - *'Transparency helps personal development. We've brought together people from a wide variety of backgrounds, including some who haven't worked in banks before. By sharing everything internally, people can get an unfiltered view of what building an innovative and trustworthy company involves — both the good and the bad! I hope that this gives them valuable experience and context for the future when they eventually move on to work somewhere new, start their own business, or otherwise follow their ambitions.'*
- **Build and maintain customer trust** - *'Externally, transparency also builds our customers' trust. We need this trust if we want to ask people to deposit their money with us - a key part of our aim of building a safe, reliable and trustworthy bank.'*

At Monzo, each email sent is copied into an email list that everyone within the organisation can see. Meetings are open for every employee to join, as well as the outputs from meetings being made available to everyone at Monzo. There are Slack channels for every product initiative, and it is standard practice at Monzo to request for comment before an initiative or project starts. Such requests for input are open to the entire company. Monzo's customers can see about any banking issues and their impact as soon as they arise on @MonzoStatus on Twitter. I can imagine that sharing of emails across the entire company might not be feasible or even desirable for every company out there but being transparent by default means that you will at least question yourself or others as to why you can't disclose something.

Similar to Monzo's approach, Darlene Miranda, VP of Product Management at Sterling, talked to me about the importance of 'visibility'. 'Being visible about your decision-making process, team values, stories etc ...' she explains how this transparency helps to remove a feeling of 'us versus them', reducing friction between people or even teams of people within the same organisation. 'As soon as you make things visible, people start becoming partners' Miranda argues.[312] It is easy to see how transparency generates trust, and how this in turn contributes to embracing tension. Having faith in the goodwill of the people that we collaborate with is a vital stepping stone to accepting and managing the tension inherent in human relations and teamwork.[313]

312 *Ibid 153.*

313 See: "Trust and Law's Facilitating Role," T.L. Fort, American Business Law Journal, 1996, Vol. 34 (2), pp. 205-215; "Should we trust in trust?" D. Koehn, American Business Law Journal, 1996, Vol. 34 (2), pp. 183-203; "Measuring the relationship between organizational transparency and employee trust," Brad R. Rawlins, Public Relations Journal, 2008, Vol. 2 (2), pp. 1-21.

Creating a psychologically safe environment

The words 'effective collaboration' are much easier said than done. In Chapter 2 we saw why collaboration can easily turn sour. Bringing a wide range of perspectives and backgrounds together is a good ingredient for teamwork and innovation; however, just throwing a bunch of cognitively diverse people together is no guarantee of success. In 'No Hard Feelings', Liz Fosslien and Mollie West Duffy argue that psychological safety matters when it comes to building diverse teams: 'there is an unambiguous and meaningful benefit to having people from different backgrounds on your team only when psychological safety exists.'[314] This claim by Fosslien and West Duffy raises the question about what psychological safety is and how it relates to embracing tension.

I initially thought that psychological safety referred to a personality trait, or a skill that one can master individually. Psychological safety is none of those things; it is a feature of the workplace that is created collectively, enabling people to take risks and display vulnerability in front of each other.[315] Amy Edmondson, a renowned management professor at Harvard Business School and specialist in psychological safety, defines it as 'a shared belief held by members of a team that the team is safe for interpersonal risk taking.'[316] Thinking that psychological safety equals an environment where anyone can get away with anything is easily done, but this assumption is far from correct. Edmondson describes all the things that psychological safety is *not*:[317]

---

314 Liz Fosslien and Mollie West Duffy, *No Hard Feelings: The Secret Power of Emotions at Work* (Penguin - Portfolio, February 2019, p. 110).

315 See: "Building a psychologically safe workplace," Amy C. Edmondson, TEDx, May 4, 2014, https://youtu.be/LhoLuui9gX8; "Project Aristotle," Google, re: Work, 2015, https://rework.withgoogle.com/print/guides/5721312655835136/.

316 "Psychological Safety and Learning Behavior in Work Teams," Amy C. Edmondson, Administrative Science Quarterly, Vol. 44, No. 2, June 1999, pp. 350-383.

317 Amy C. Edmondson, The Fearless Organization: Creating Psychological Safety in the Workplace for Learning, Innovation and Growth (Hoboken, NJ: Wiley, November 2018, pp. 15 -19).

- **Psychological safety is not about being nice** - Working in a psychologically safe environment doesn't mean that people always agree with one another for the sake of being nice. It also doesn't mean that people offer unequivocal praise or unconditional support for everything you have to say. Psychological safety is about candour, about making it possible for productive disagreement and free exchange of ideas. Conflict inevitably arises in any workplace. Psychological safety enables people on different sides of a conflict to speak candidly about what's bothering them, without the disagreement feeling highly personal.[318]
- **Psychological safety is not a personality factor** - Some have interpreted psychological safety as a synonym for extroversion. They might have previously concluded that people don't speak up at work because they're shy or lack confidence, or simply keep to themselves. Psychological safety, however, refers to the work climate, and climate affects people with different personality traits in roughly similar ways. In a psychologically safe climate, people will offer ideas and voice their concerns regardless of whether they tend toward introversion or extroversion.
- **Psychological safety is not just another word for trust** - Although trust and psychological safety have much in common, they aren't interchangeable concepts. A key difference is that psychological safety is experienced at a group level.
- **Psychological safety is not about lowering performance standards** - Psychological safety is not an 'anything goes' environment where people aren't expected to adhere to high standards or meet deadlines. It is not about becoming

318 "Managing Confrontation in Multicultural Teams," Erin Meyer, Harvard Business Review, April 6, 2012, https://hbr.org/2012/04/how-to-manage-confrontation-in.

'comfortable' at work or allowing people to 'coast'. Psychological safety enables candour and openness and, as such, thrives in an environment of mutual respect.

Instead, a psychologically safe environment or team is characterised by continuous learning.[319] Whilst accountability for achieving certain performance outcomes is very high, it is safe for people to take risks, collaborate and learn. In other words, if a team takes a calculated risk with a particular product or feature and the risk does not pay off, the team and its individual members are not at risk of being punished. This means that whenever a team or an individual encounters tension when developing products, it will be ok to acknowledge it, taking risks and learning as part of working through the tension. Edmondson provides seven survey items to assess whether your organisation or team is psychologically safe, and she uses a seven-point Likert scale (from strongly agree to strongly disagree) to obtain responses. Four of the seven items are expressed positively, such that agreement indicates greater psychological safety, and three are expressed negatively (represented with an 'R' for reverse):[320]

1. If you make a mistake on this team, it is often held against you. (R)
2. Members of this team are able to bring up problems and tough issues.
3. People on this team sometimes reject others for being different. (R)
4. It is safe to take a risk on this team.
5. It is difficult to ask other members of this team for help. (R)
6. No one on this team would deliberately act in a way that undermines my efforts.

319 "The Imperative of Learning," Amy C. Edmondson, , Harvard Business Review, July - August 2008, https://hbr.org/2008/07/the-competitive-imperative-of-learning.

320 *Ibid 317, p. 20.*

7. Working with members of this team, my unique skills and talents are valued and utilised.

For collaboration to be effective, people need to feel safe when it comes to taking risks or making mistakes. This extends to people feeling comfortable in suggesting what others might perceive as outlandish ideas. 'In every brainstorming session, you will find a move towards average, almost like a Bell curve' according to Mukesh Gupta, Director of Customer Advocacy at SAP. He therefore encourages his colleagues 'to go for extremes', arguing that it is easier for a remarkable idea to become practical yet remain remarkable, whilst it is much harder to make an average or practical idea turn remarkable. Teams that collaborate effectively, Gupta explains, have a shared understanding of the idea that it is ok to poke holes in the idea, but not in people.[321] Unfortunately, a lot of us will most likely have found ourselves in one of the following two scenarios at some point in our career: personal attack and toxic disagreement:

- **'Personal attack'** - Instead of suggesting that your idea has flaws and targeting the idea in question, the feedback is directed at you as a person; people claiming that the other person has a lack of experience or doesn't know what they are doing.
- **The 'toxic disagreement'** - Personal attacks spread like wildfire and before you know it, the team is massively divided, and effective collaboration has been reduced to nothing but a pipe dream. Every time there is a disagreement, tensions rise, and the overall atmosphere becomes one of argument and discontent.

These scenarios raise the question of how we can build psychological safety. One important way is to stimulate dissent that is constructive, does not hamper collaboration and embraces tension.

321 Mukesh Gupta, *interview by author*, Singapore, December 6, 2019.

2. ENCOURAGE CONSTRUCTIVE DISSENT WITHIN OUR TEAMS

'Managing dissent is about recognising the value of disagreement, discord and difference.' **Noreena Hertz**

Constructive dissent is the second important ingredient of effective collaboration. If we want to truly collaborate when developing products, we need to recognise dissent and allow it to play out, all for the greater good of our collective intelligence; 'none of us is as smart as all of us' as the quote by Ken Blanchard, author of numerous management and leadership books, goes. We saw in the previous chapter how techniques like Ritual Dissent help to enable and depersonalise dissent within teams. It is, however, not always possible to keep dissent and the subsequent discussions anonymous. This in turn introduces a fear of conflict, team members preferring to keep their (dissenting) opinions or ideas to themselves.[322] How do we therefore keep such disagreement constructive? How do we avoid a team becoming fragmented due to differences of opinion or approach?

One of Amazon's principles for its leaders is that they 'Are Right, A Lot'. This means that people at Amazon should 'seek diverse perspectives and work to disconfirm their beliefs'.[323] Or take German energy giant RWE, which kicked off an organisation-wide cultural transformation programme to effectively create an obligation for people to dissent, making them comfortable with a certain degree of conflict and calling out each other's biases.[324] The main thing is to make sure that any dissent is voiced and perceived constructively,

322 *Ibid 9.*

323 "Amazon Leadership Principles," Amazon Jobs, https://www.amazon.jobs/en/principles (Accessed on February 9, 2020).

324 "A case study in combating bias: Interview with Bernhard Günther," Sven Heiligtag and Allen Webb, McKinsey Quarterly, May 2017, https://www.mckinsey.com/business-functions/organization/our-insights/a-case-study-in-combating-bias.

meaning that team members are challenging ideas and not attacking personalities. Sounds like a daunting task?! It should not be, especially since there are a number of principles and techniques that we can use to stimulate constructive dissent within our teams.

Encouraging Constructive Dissent = Mind + Moves

There are a number of ways to stimulate **disagreement** within teams, and to do so constructively:

- **Liberating conversation structures** that encourage free-flowing thoughts and interactions.
- **Wicked questions** get people to think about the double-sided nature of corporate challenges or personal behaviours.
- **Agreement / certainty matrix** helps people collectively assess the complexity of a problem or project and evaluate potential approaches together.
- **Plussing** means that every criticism must come with a plus, with a better idea attached.

Liberating conversation structures

The point of liberating conversation structures is that they encourage free-flowing thoughts and interactions. When was the last time you were in a dull presentation where someone took you through 15,000 PowerPoint slides, only allowing you to ask one or two questions at the end? Or imagine being in a 100-member symphony orchestra, where you can only play your specific part of the sheet music in front of you ... Compare this to playing jazz with a number of other musicians; everybody can leap in and there are no recriminations when someone messes up.[325] We can apply the same free-flowing mindset to encouraging constructive dissent, starting with methods that shift interactions and encourage structured critique:[326]

- **Stories versus PowerPoint** - Enable people to tell and share real world stories, focusing the conversation on experiences and examples instead of careful PowerPoint designs.
- **Big questions** - Centring the interaction on a key question, or problem to solve, creates a background against which people can explore ideas and disagree.
- **Diversity of formats** - Instead of always having large team meetings, consider breaking down discussions into pairs or small groups which are typically better suited to debate and constructive dissent.
- **Inviting participation, minimising status differences** - Whether you are the CEO or a junior product manager, everybody can voice their opinion and disagreement.
- **Social elements, mixing participants** - There is a wealth of liberating conversation structures out there which can be used to enable people to interact with each other, sharing ideas and opinions with others that they might not normally engage with.
- **Movement, fun** – Hugely underrated in my view, but interactions that incorporate movement, fun and improvisation are a great way to empower constructive

325 See: Frank J. Barrett, *Yes to the Mess: Surprising Leadership Lessons from Jazz* (Harvard Business Review Press, July 2012); "Product Managers: Please Make Yourself Uncomfortable," Ken Norton, Mind the Product conference San Francisco 2016, 18 May 2016, https://www.mindtheproduct.com/product-managers-please-make-uncomfortable/; "Book review: Yes To The Mess," Marc Abraham, As I learn, March 5, 2017, https://marcabraham.com/2017/03/05/book-review-yes-to-the-mess/.

326 Adapted from "Liberating Structures: Innovating by Including and Unleashing Everyone," Henri Lipmanowicz and Keith McCandless, E&Y Performance, 2010, Vol. 2(4), pp. 6-19.

dissent. It becomes a lot easier to disagree if this is done against the backdrop of a game or role play, for instance.

When we successfully shift our interactions to be more inclusive and engaging, it becomes a lot easier for people to disagree constructively. Henri Lipmanowicz and Keith McCandless are the leading voices on liberating conversation structures and have introduced an ever growing variety of formats and techniques that you can use to tease out constructive dissent.[327] In addition to liberating conversation structures, there are a number of techniques you could apply in order to stimulate disagreement. I will cover three of them below, but in the toolkit section at the end of this chapter you can find practical detail about the others.

Wicked questions

The idea behind the concept of asking 'wicked questions' is to get people to think about the double-sided nature of challenges or personal behaviours, revealing inherent nuances or contradictions that might not always be obvious.

At a corporate level you could ask questions like: 'How is it that we are always and never the same; an organisation with a singular global identity and we are uniquely adapted to each local setting?' 'How is it that we are integrated and autonomous?' On a more personal level you could ask a question such as: 'How is it that you are simultaneously dedicated to your work and fully present for your family?'[328]

Agreement / certainty matrix

This exercise is designed to help participants solve a problem with

327 Henri Lipmanowicz and Keith McCandless, *The Surprising Power of Liberating Structures* (Liberating Structures Press, February 2014).

328 "Wicked Questions," Henri Lipmanowicz and Keith McCandless, http://www.liberating-structures.com/4-wicked-questions/.

the right methods. Non-constructive dissent frequently arises due to teams not being on the same wavelength with respect to the best approach to tackling a problem (See fig. 21). Start the exercise by asking participants to categorise their current challenges as simple, complicated, complex, or chaotic.

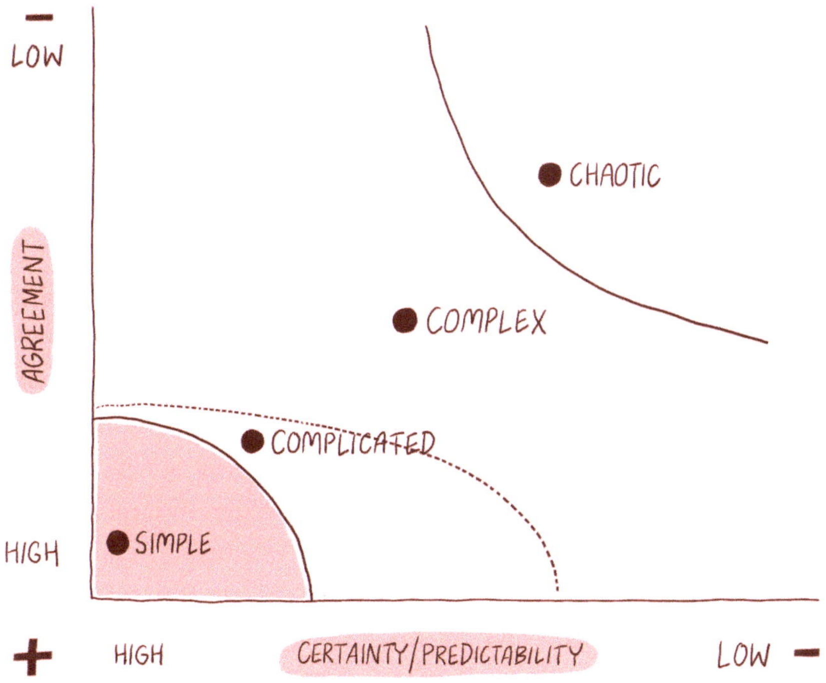

Fig. 21 – How certain are we about the challenge? Do we know how to address the challenge?

Participants then place every challenge in the matrix based on their answers to two questions: To what extent do the participants agree on the challenge and the best way to address it? How much certainty and predictability are you likely to generate from the solutions proposed for addressing the challenge?

A problem is *simple* when you can solve it reliably with well-known or previously used practices that are easy to duplicate. It is *complicated* when you require a sophisticated solution. A problem is *complex* when there are several valid ways to proceed but no visible correlation between cause and effect. *Chaotic* describes a context that is too turbulent for you to identify a logical path forward to a solution.

By getting participants to reflect on the approaches they are using, or to consider how best to address each challenge, any mismatches and best ways forward will become apparent very quickly.[329]

Plussing

When it comes to constructive dissent, Alfred P. Sloan, long-time General Motors leader, is probably the textbook example of someone actively looking for dissent. Sloan famously interjected during an important meeting, asking: 'Gentlemen, I take it we are all in complete agreement on the decision here?' When the meeting participants all nodded agreeingly in response, Sloan then continued 'Then, I propose we postpone further discussion of this matter until our next meeting to give ourselves time to develop disagreement and perhaps gain some understanding of what the decision is about.'[330]

Sloan realised that his team would be better equipped to solve tough problems if he allowed for and actively encouraged disagreement. Fast forward to more recent times, where the teams at Pixar Animation Studios rely on criticism to strengthen their creative work. When making animation films, the teams apply a concept called 'plussing' - anytime someone comments on another person's work, that comment must contain a 'plus' - a way to improve or build

329 "Agreement & Certainty Matrix," Henri Lipmanowicz and Keith McCandless, , http://www.liberatingstructures.com/27-agreement-certainty-matrix/; "Ralph Stacey's Agreement & Certainty Matrix," Brenda Zimmerman, Schulich School of Business, 2001, https://www.betterevaluation.org/en/resources/guide/ralph_staceys_agreement_and_certainty_matrix.

330 David Burkus, *The Myths of Creativity: The Truth About How Innovative Companies and People Generate Great Ideas* (San Francisco: Jossey-Bass, October 2013, p. 151).

on the work.[331] During production meetings at Pixar, instead of simply dismissing ideas, every criticism must come with a plus, with a better idea or suggestion attached. This 'yes and' way of critiquing helps to reduce the negative perceptions surrounding criticism, focusing instead on how to best improve the quality of the work, as best demonstrated in this example:[332]

'Consider the situation where a director is working with an animator on a scene. The director may not like much about the entire sequence. However, she will identify one aspect of the scene she does like (perhaps the movement of the main character) and then say, "I like how Huck's body twists as he swings the bat and what if he were to smile as he does that?" Now the animator has some feedback to build on. Notice that "and" does not imply judgement as the word "but" would have. Rather, "and" opens up the possibilities for discussing ideas and thoughts.'

Plussing is ultimately about optimising for collective intelligence, acknowledging the wisdom of the crowds and allowing for disagreement in a way that it leads to constructive solutions.

CONCLUSION

Just as managing products isn't a solo effort, managing tension is a highly collaborative activity. If you want to lean into tension, it is vital that the team that you are part of or are working with is fully on board with this. Only when the entire team buys into the value of tension and embraces the related uncertainty, will your product and organisation benefit fully.

Even if the people that you collaborate with are happy with the concept of leaning into tension, you will still have a key role to play when it comes to facilitating it and encouraging constructive dissent.

331 "How Criticism Creates Innovative Teams," David Burkus, Harvard Business Review, July 22, 2013, https://hbr.org/2013/07/how-criticism-creates-innovati.

332 "Pixar and Plussing," Jim Dunbar, infoGumshoe, November 17, 2011, http://www.infogumshoe.com/2011/11/17/pixar-and-plussing/.

The good news is that there are a whole host of approaches and techniques which help create a psychologically safe atmosphere where people feel comfortable being uncomfortable and know that it is ok to challenge or disagree.

SUMMARY

Things can get more challenging if we collectively lean into tension, but having teams leaning into tension is a prerequisite for creating great products.

Successful products come from healthy, collaborative teams. To collaborate successfully, you should (1) establish trusted relationships and (2) encourage constructive dissent.

Establishing trusted relationships is pivotal, particularly for product managers as we rely on many stakeholders. These four components underpin trusted relationships:

- **Influence without authority** - Invest in relationships, based on 'give and take' with the other person, provided this is based on genuine empathy.
- **Be fully transparent** - Be open by default when engaging with people and avoid hidden information or gotchas.
- **Share goals** - You don't have to be friends with all your co-workers, nor do they need to like you, but a shared mission and outcomes form a keystone to effective collaboration.
- **Create a psychologically safe environment** - This means that it is ok for people to take risks or make mistakes and be vulnerable in front of each other.

Encouraging constructive dissent implies healthy disagreement about ideas or opinions. The goal is to ensure that any dissent is voiced and perceived constructively. There are a number of methods to encourage constructive dissent:

- **Liberating conversation structures** that use stories, elicit big questions or encourage free-flowing thoughts and interactions, thus making it ok for people to explore and challenge.
- **Wicked questions** get people to think about the double-sided nature of challenges or personal behaviours, and spend time understanding nuances and different perspectives.
- **Agreement / certainty matrix** helps people collectively assess the complexity of a problem or project and evaluate potential approaches together. The main benefit of this approach is that it helps people agree on the problem to solve, before identifying the best way to tackle it.
- **Plussing** means that every criticism must come with a plus, with a better idea attached. It is the 'yes *and*' approach that reduces the negative perceptions surrounding criticism and optimizes the wisdom of the crowds.

TOOLKIT: SO, YOU WANT TO LEAN INTO TENSION COLLABORATIVELY?!

1. CURRENCIES TO INFLUENCE WITHOUT AUTHORITY

Positive currencies:

- **Inspiration-related currencies** - Inspiration-related currencies reflect inspirational goals that provide meaning to the work that a person or a team does. 'Vision' is a good example of an inspiration-related currency; overcoming personal objections and inconvenience can inspire the potential ally to see the larger significance of your request. Similarly, 'excellence' is another important inspiration-related currency; the opportunity to do something really well and pride in having the chance to accomplish important work with genuine excellence can be highly motivating.
- **Task-related currencies** - Task-related currencies are directly related to getting the job done. They relate to a person's ability to perform his or her assigned tasks or to the satisfactions that arise from accomplishment. 'Challenge' - the chance to work at tasks that provide a challenge or stretch - is one of the most widely valued currencies in modern organisational life. When tension is high, 'assistance' gains significance, i.e. the opportunity to get support in getting tasks completed or shed.
- **Position-related currencies** - Position-related currencies enhance a person's position in the organisation and thereby, indirectly aid the person's ability to accomplish tasks or advance a career. 'Recognition' is a widely accepted and used position-related currency; many people will extend themselves for a project when they believe their contributions will be recognised. Or think of those things that can help

enhance a person's 'reputation'. A good reputation can pave the way for lots of opportunities while a bad one can quickly shut the person out and make it difficult to perform.

- **Relationship-related currencies** - Relationship-related currencies are more connected to strengthening the relationship with someone than directly accomplishing the organisation's tasks. Organisational goals might be met indirectly, but the immediate focus is on currencies such as 'personal support' or 'understanding'. For some people, at particular times, having the support of others is the currency they value most. When a colleague is feeling stressed, upset, vulnerable, or needy, he or she will doubly appreciate – and remember – a thoughtful gesture.
- **Personal currencies** - These currencies could form an infinite list of idiosyncratic needs which are valued because they enhance the individual's sense of self. They may be derived from task or interpersonal activity. Think of currencies such as 'gratitude', which doesn't necessarily need to be job - related but can instead be valued highly by some people who make a point of being helpful to others. For their efforts, some people want appreciation from the receiver, expressed in thanks or deference.

Negative currencies:

'Withholding payments'

- Not giving recognition
- Not offering support
- Not providing challenge
- Threatening to quit the situation

'Directly undesirable'

- Raising voice, yelling

- Refusing to cooperate when asked
- Escalating issue upwards to common boss
- Going public with issue, making lack of cooperation visible
- Attacking a person's reputation or integrity

2. ATLASSIAN' S QUESTIONS TO MEASURE SHARED UNDERSTANDING

At Atlassian, a global maker of software and collaboration tools, they measure shared understanding amongst the members of their product teams by asking the following questions, each question accompanied by a 1-5 scale for people to indicate their agreement:[333]

- **The who:** 'I have enough customer context and feedback on what I am working on'
- **The what:** 'I understand the customer problem I'm working on'
- **The why:** 'I understand how my work fits into the bigger picture' (our vision and strategy)

3. 1-2-4 ALL

This exercise follows a set sequence: reflect on something (a question, a topic, an idea) for 1 minute individually in silence, then discuss it in pairs for 2 minutes, then in fours for 4 minutes, and then come together as a whole group and pick some highlights from each four rounds, then share with the entire group.[334]

4. WHAT. SO WHAT. NOW WHAT DEBRIEF

It is possible to reflect on a shared experience while allowing every voice in the group to be heard, by progressing through the experience in stages. This debrief activity starts with collecting facts about 'what happened', followed by making sense of these facts through

333 *Ibid 307.*

334 "1-2-4-All," Henri Lipmanowicz and Keith McCandless, http://www.liberatingstructures.com/1-1-2-4-all/.

the 'so what' stage. Finally, the group looks at the next steps in the 'now what' stage. The shared progression eliminates most of the misunderstandings that otherwise fuel disagreements or confusion about what to do.[335]

5. FISHBOWL

With the fishbowl exercise, a subset of people with relevant experience in a specific area are surrounded by a larger outside circle of participants. The inside group is formed with people who have made concrete progress on a challenge or opportunity of interest to those people in the outside circle.

The fishbowl design makes it easier for people in the inside circle to share experiences, learnings and challenges. It is a great structure for stimulating constructive dissent, breaking down communication barriers between the two groups, and facilitating viewpoints, questions and answers flowing back and forth.[336]

6. BRAINWRITING

In the previous chapter we looked at the Ritual Dissent technique, whereby ideas are reviewed and criticised without facing the presenter of the idea. Brainwriting offers another way of depersonalising the voicing and criticising of ideas. Instead of stating ideas out loud, team members are asked to write their ideas down on cards. These cards are then posted on a wall for the rest of the team to vote on.[337] The 'out loud' part of coming up with new ideas is the problem that the brainwriting technique aims to solve. If you think about brainstorming sessions and their focus on generating as many ideas as possible, there is,

335 "What, So What, No What?' Henri Lipmanowicz and Keith McCandless, http://www.liberatingstructures.com/9-what-so-what-now-what-w/.

336 "User Experience Fishbowl," Henri Lipmanowicz and Keith McCandless, , http://www.liberatingstructures.com/18-users-experience-fishbowl/.

337 Matthew Syed, *Rebel Ideas: The Power of Diverse Thinking* (London: John Murray, September 2019, p. 118).

paradoxically, the risk of actually stifling idea generation and dissent. Leigh Thompson and Loran Nordgren, both management professors at Kellogg School of Management, talk about the risk of 'anchoring' with respect to traditional brainstorming: the person expressing their ideas early in the brainstorming session unwittingly sets the tone for the rest of the session, influencing any subsequent ideas.[338]

Brainwriting ideas are written down quietly by each participant individually, thus giving all participants a chance to contribute, sharing their ideas and views. For brainwriting to work fully, Thompson argues, one rule should be followed: nobody is allowed to identify themselves with their written contributions. This rule makes sure that the idea is being separated from the status of the person who came up with it.[339] Brainwriting can thus act as a great tool to allow equal contribution as well as facilitate healthy discussion about ideas, without having to worry about the hierarchical status of the person who came up with the idea.

7. CRAZY 8' S

Crazy 8's is a sketching exercise that is designed to help people come up with ideas quickly (See fig. 22). You sketch eight distinct ideas in eight minutes, simply using an A4 sheet of paper folded into eight sections. It is a very easy and cheap way to consider a whole range of product ideas before turning a specific idea into a prototype.[340]

338 "Brainstorming Doesn't Work; Try This Technique Instead," Rebecca Greenfield, Fast Company, 29 July 29, 2014, https://www.fastcompany.com/3033567/brainstorming-doesnt-work-try-this-technique-instead.

339 *Ibid 338.*

340 See: "Crazy 8's," Google Design Sprint, https://designsprintkit.withgoogle.com/methodology/phase3-sketch/crazy-eights (Accessed on February 14, 2020); "Honing Crazy Eights with Randomness," Chris Butler, UX Collective, January 27, 2017, https://uxdesign.cc/honing-crazy-eights-with-randomness-1c8100b94824; "How to run a Crazy eights workshop," Hana Stevenson, Prototypr.io, July 21, 2019, https://blog.prototypr.io/how-to-run-a-crazy-eights-workshop-60d0a67b29a.

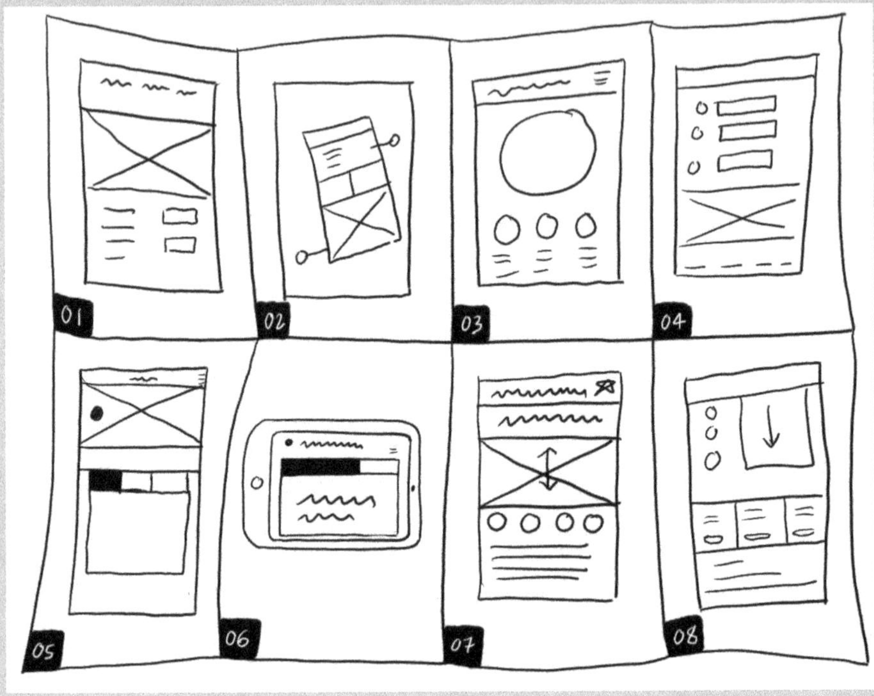

Fig. 22 – Sketch eight ideas – good or bad – in eight minutes

Not only does the Crazy 8 exercise work well in generating potentially great ideas fast, I have also found it to be a great tool to tease out bad ideas. To that end, you could explicitly ask people doing the exercise to come with eight really bad ideas. This can feel counter-intuitive to some people, but actively considering bad product ideas creates an environment where all ideas are being considered, and where it is safe to disagree on proposed solutions.

CHAPTER 7.
MANAGING PRODUCT = MANAGING RESILIENCE AND GROWTH

'Let your curiosity be greater than your fear.' **Pema Chodron**

Product Management = Mind + Matter + Moves

In this chapter we will explore:

- Ideas and tools that help us manage the **resilience and growth** required to build great products and be strong product managers.
- Continuous learning about the performance of your product, making sure that you are offering **the right product** to your customers.
- The importance of **curiosity** and **asking for help** with respect to becoming a product manager that is comfortable leaning into tension.
- The moves that you can make to nurture your **personal resilience and growth** which you can utilise when being faced with product tensions.

INTRODUCTION

'Managing tension is not just for Christmas' was the original working title for this final chapter. I was keen to reiterate the point that tension is omnipresent, especially when managing products. As I thought more about this, it dawned on me that having the groundwork in place to manage tension is a great place to end the book, and for you to start. In this final chapter, our focus will be on resilience and growth, both with respect to you as an individual and your product.

KEEPING ON TOP OF YOUR PRODUCT

'A problem well stated is a problem half solved.' **Charles Kettering**

If you do nothing else after finishing this book, just keep on top of your product. What I mean by this is that you continuously monitor the performance of your product and the feedback from customers using it. Given the length and variation in the product life cycle, we as product people need to learn constantly about our product and its users. The insights we generate help us deal with the inevitable tensions - internal and external - that we will be faced with.

Product Management = Mind + Matter + Moves

How you can **keep on top of your product**:

1. **Product Principles** are great for keeping you, your team and stakeholders honest about the direction of your product and help in making trade-offs.
2. Having regular **Product Retrospectives** is the easiest way to keep on top of your product collectively, monitoring performance stats or qualitative customer feedback.

1. PRODUCT PRINCIPLES

'Change your opinions, keep to your principles; change your leaves, keep intact your roots.' **Victor Hugo**

'Values' - every organisation has them. Whether these values have been stated explicitly or are more implicit, strong company values support everything a company does and doesn't do. 'Serve Our Users', for example, is a core value articulated in Google's Code of Conduct: 'Our users value Google not only because we deliver great products and services, but because we hold ourselves to a higher standard in how we treat users and operate more generally.'[341] Compare that to Amazon's Leadership Principles which, among others, stipulate that leaders 'Invent and Simplify': 'Leaders expect and require innovation and invention from their teams and always find ways to simplify.'[342] Such company values permeate company culture and daily working practices. Although linked in spirit to company values, product principles are typically specific to an individual product or a portfolio of products.

When managing products we use product principles as a way of connecting company values with the outcomes our product is trying to achieve.[343] Product principles are a clear set of standards and goals that we can use to inform overall product strategy; apply on a daily basis to prioritise work, make product decisions and generally ensure that what we are doing fits with overarching company values. A good example is the product principles of ecommerce platform Shopify, which link closely to Shopify's business vision and values whilst being concrete enough to act upon.

341 "Google Code of Conduct," Alphabet Investor Relations, https://abc.xyz/investor/other/google-code-of-conduct/ (Accessed on March 9, 2020).

342 *Ibid 323.*

343 "My product management toolkit (34): Product Principles, "Marc Abraham, Medium, January 11, 2019, https://medium.com/@maa1/my-product-management-toolkit-34-product-principles-7f48424358ce.

SHOPIFY'S PRODUCT PRINCIPLES

At ecommerce platform Shopify the mission is to: 'help people achieve independence by making it easier to start, run, and grow a business. We believe the future of commerce has more voices, not fewer, so we are reducing the barriers to business ownership to make commerce better for everyone.' From this mission statement, Shopify has derived its Product Principles:[344]

Considerate - *Above all else, we show care for the people who use our tools and products. We're here to make their day-to-day and long-term work better — no matter who they are, where they are, or what platform they're using.*

- *Build experiences that work on every screen, on every platform, in every language, and in every country.*
- *Take time to understand where we can build for a general audience, and where we should offer different paths for different needs.*
- *Respect the reality of this work – don't assume the perfect situation, preparation, or usage.*

Empowering - *We want people to feel like they can accomplish whatever they're trying to do. Our experiences should give people confidence that they're capable of achieving their goals, no matter their level of experience.*

- *Help users complete their tasks, without taking away decisions or independence.*

344 See: "Shopify's Lynsey Thornton talks mission-driven decisions at Traction '19," Isabelle Kirkwood, Betakit, August 13, 2019, https://betakit.com/shopifys-lynsey-thornton-talks-mission-driven-decisions-at-traction-2019/; "About us," Shopify, https://www.shopify.co.uk/about (Accessed on March 9, 2020); "Shopify experience values," Shopify, https://polaris.shopify.com/foundations/experience-values (Accessed on March 9, 2020).

- *Optimise for the most important tasks without blocking people from doing the rest.*
- *Hide complexity where you can, but give people access to more sophistication if they need it.*

Crafted - *Shopify experiences should feel like they were created with the highest level of craftsmanship. Through thoughtful details and small touches, we combine the power of professional tools with the simplicity of consumer products.*

- *Work to understand the complex problems users face, then find clear and approachable solutions to those problems.*
- *Delight people with how powerful and effective an experience is, not with extra decoration or flair.*
- *Look for meaningful ways to make experiences more natural, friendly, and thoughtful.*

Efficient - *Shopify experiences should help people achieve their goals quickly, accurately, and with less effort. We value speed and simplicity, but we value productivity even more.*

- *Break complex tasks down into simple steps and remove repetitive tasks whenever you can.*
- *Use friction to highlight important decisions, then let users get back to work.*
- *Give users the ability to reduce and optimize their workloads through automation and bulk actions.*

Trustworthy - *We constantly work to recharge our users' trust batteries. We sweat the details. We're genuine and transparent to show users that we're always acting in their best interest.*

- *Fix the small mistakes and inconsistencies that erode trust.*
- *Be transparent about what a feature or tool can do and what it can't.*

- *Make safe and positive actions frictionless. If they're risky, give clear instructions and greater control. Make it easy to recover from mistakes.*

Familiar - *We want people to feel comfortable using our products, whether it's their first time using them or their hundredth. Our experiences should embody the same principles, act the same way, and fit together seamlessly.*

- *Think bigger than any individual task or product. Understand the context users are working in.*
- *Use familiar patterns to make experiences intuitive and recognizable.*
- *Evolve experiences seamlessly. They should keep getting better with time and information.*

Product principles are incredibly handy if you wish to keep on top of your product throughout the different stages of the product life cycle. In my experience, product principles ultimately help with decision making. Questions such as 'should we add feature A or B?'; 'Is this the kind of experience we want to give our customers?' and 'Which channels should we use for this product?' can all be determined with the guidance of product principles.

2. PRODUCT RETROSPECTIVE

'Life can only be understood backwards; but it must be lived forwards.'
Søren Kierkegaard

Any self-respecting software engineer or product person is likely to participate in regular team retrospectives. A retrospective is a ceremony which is held at the end of an iteration in the Agile software development life cycle. Typically, at the end of a one- or two-week period, the team comes together to reflect on what happened in the iteration - from a people and ways of working perspective - and identify what can be improved going forward.[345]

However, I have found *product* retrospectives to be a lot less common. When I talk about 'product retrospectives', I am referring to a regular opportunity for a team to reflect on their product or service. A product retrospective is meant to zoom in on the product and not on team or process improvements.[346] You can, for instance, use each retrospective to mull over how your product is performing (or not) and what your users are saying or doing. I have added more detail about questions to cover in a product retrospective and how to structure the session accordingly in the toolkit at the end of this chapter.

KEEPING ON TOP OF YOURSELF

'It does not matter how slowly you go so long as you do not stop.'
Confucius

Plenty of books have been written on the subject of personal resilience and growth; the foundations worth having in place in order to live a fulfilled life or to be more resilient. There are four aspects to personal growth and resilience which I believe are particularly relevant to managing product tension: continuous learning, curiosity, self-awareness and asking for help.

---

345 See: "Agile Retrospective Resource Wiki," Rob Bowley, December 12, 2016, http://retrospectivewiki.org/index.php?title=Agile_Retrospective_Resource_Wiki; Esther Derby and Diana Larsen, *Agile Retrospectives: Making Good Teams Great* (Pragmatic Bookshelf, July 2006).

346 "Why we need a PRODUCT retrospective," Marc Abraham, As I learn, June 4, 2015, https://marcabraham.com/2015/06/04/why-we-need-a-product-retrospective/.

Product Management = Mind + Matter + Moves

How you can **keep on top of yourself:**

1. Continuous **learning** is essential to developing personal resilience and growth; learning as tensions arise.
2. **Curiosity** is a key trait of any self-respecting product manager, and you can start with simply asking 'why'.
3. Build in time to **reflect;** even 1 hour per week goes a long way in looking back and learning.
4. **Awareness** of self and your circumstances helps in better understanding and managing tensions.
5. Feeling comfortable **asking for help** is crucial in any profession, but particularly so for product managers.

1. BECOMING A LEARNING MACHINE

'Product people are learning beings.' **Stephanie Hannon**

Learning is a vital life skill, one that I believe is essential regardless of your age, profession or position in society. Managing products is not a static activity or one that happens in isolation. As we have seen, the dynamic and uncertain aspects of product management are the very things that cause tension in the first place. Learning in itself is not a guarantee for product or business success, but the pace and frequency of learning can play a key part in how we manage tension and accomplish things:

- **Learning early and often** - The faster you can learn, the better. Whether you are learning about your company, your product, a new technology, even about your own business I believe that the pace and frequency of learning will determine your ability to detect tension early and often. The risks of *not* learning early and often are too big to ignore.
- **Delivering value in order to learn** - You must be smart about the things that you want to learn. The best opportunity to learn comes when you are confident about the *value* that you're delivering to the customer. Naturally, people might not buy or use your product despite the value it is intended to deliver, but that is a valuable learning in itself.
- **Don't build or release without knowing what you want to learn!** - Whether you do or don't engage with target customers before building and launching a product or a feature, be clear about why you are building in the first place. What does product success look like? What are you looking to learn? The users of your product can be external or internal, it doesn't matter, it is important to be clear upfront about the specific things that you want to learn both before build and post-release.[347]
- **Does the release contain enough for you to get desired learnings? -** Once you have established why you are building a product in the first place, being clear about what you are looking to learn from a subsequent release is paramount. Are you releasing enough value and functionality to obtain meaningful customer and market insights? Naturally, we all want our products to do incredibly well

347 Amy Edmondson, *Teaming: How Organizations Learn, Innovate, and Compete in the Knowledge Economy*, (San Francisco: Jossey-Bass, April 2012, p. 241); "My product management toolkit (33): launch and learn," Marc Abraham, Medium, November 23, 2018, https://medium.com/@maa1/my-product-management-toolkit-33-launch-and-learn-e1b61bff5026.

and generate lots of revenue and profit. But there are so many more data points that will help to inform the ongoing development of your product. Take for instance simple but powerful questions like 'How are people using our product?' 'What do the performance stats tell us?' 'Are there any features people particularly like or dislike, and why?' Insights into some of these questions will only come if you are actively looking for them or at the very least open to them. It is easy to lose a learning mindset; it is in my experience much harder to acquire and maintain one.

2. CURIOSITY

'The important thing is to not stop questioning. Curiosity has its own reason for existing.' **Albert Einstein**

Curiosity is one of the main ingredients in instilling and nurturing a learning mindset. It is one of the things I love about kids; their innate curiosity, not feeling burdened by the concept of 'dumb questions'. It is easy to see how this curiosity starts eroding as we get older or our professional careers progress. The 'curse of knowledge' is a cognitive bias that occurs when an individual, communicating with other people, assumes that the others have the knowledge required to understand.[348] The side effect of this curse of knowledge is that it will in turn stop people from being curious or asking questions, as they feel that they should know the background and have all the answers ...

In a world where there is so much uncertainty, and where there is no set formula for building products, it is important to stay curious and ask questions, lots of them ... When hiring and working with

348 Jane Kennedy, Debiasing the Curse of Knowledge, The Accounting Review, Vol. 70, No. 2, April 1995, pp. 249 - 273.

people, we traditionally zoom in on people's IQ or their experience; we tend to look a lot less at what author Thomas Friedman dubs 'the curiosity quotient'. Friedman states that when curiosity is combined with passion in the exploration of a subject, an individual may be able to acquire an amount of knowledge comparable to that of a person who is exceptionally intelligent, due to the vast amount of information resources accessible through the internet.[349] Research by Francesca Gino, behavioural scientist at Harvard Business School, has found some of the key benefits of curiosity:[350]

- **Fewer decision-making errors:** Gino found in her research that when our curiosity is triggered, we are less likely to fall prey to confirmation bias. We saw in Chapter 1 how we all have the tendency to cling to deeply-held biases (the 'Not Seeing the Wood for the Trees' tension). Curiosity, Gino found, has a positive impact on confirmation biases, because it leads us to generate alternative thoughts and ideas.
- **More innovation and positive changes in creative and non-creative jobs:** When we are curious, we view tough situations and challenges more creatively. Studies have found that curiosity is associated with less defensive reactions to stress and less aggressive reactions to provocation.[351]
- **Reduced group conflict:** From her research, Gino found that curiosity encourages group members to put themselves

349 Thomas L. Friedman, *The World is Flat: A Brief History of the Twenty-first Century* (Farrar, Straus and Giroux, January 2005); "It's the P.Q. and C.Q. as Much as I.Q.," Thomas L. Friedman, The New York Times, January 29, 2013, https://www.nytimes.com/2013/01/30/opinion/friedman-its-pq-and-cq-as-much-as-iq.html.

350 "The Business Case for Curiosity," Francesca Gino, Harvard Business Review, September - October 2018, https://hbr.org/2018/09/curiosity#the-business-case-for-curiosity.

351 "Curiosity made the cat more creative: Specific curiosity as a driver of curiosity," Lydia Paine Hagtvedt, Karyn Dossinger, Spencer H Harrison and Li Huang, Organizational Behavior and Human Decision Processes, Academic Press, January 1, 2019, Vol. 50, pp. 1-13.

> in one another's shoes, taking an interest in another's ideas and perspectives. This increased empathy in turn causes them to work together more effectively and smoothly, thus reducing group conflict.

You can apply curiosity in a variety of ways, but there is one simple method to developing and satisfying your curiosity: asking questions. Listening with curiosity and asking the right questions, at the right time and in the right way, can unlock valuable answers. The appendix at the end of this chapter contains a number of suggested questions worth asking as well as *when* to consider asking them.[352]

3. REFLECTION

'We cannot change what we are not aware of, and once we are aware, we cannot help but change.' **Sheryl Sandberg**

Reflection and self-awareness are vital hygiene factors for any individual, irrespective of whether you are impacted by product tension. I strongly believe that, especially in our uncertain and rapidly changing world, it is important to take a step back at times and reflect. Much like building in a 'pause' during an interaction with someone else, reflecting is nothing more than looking back, projecting ahead or looking inward (self-reflection):

- What have I achieved?

352 See: Hal Gregersen, *Questions Are the Answer: A Breakthrough Approach to Your Most Vexing Problems at Work and in Life* (New York: Harper Collins, November 2018); "Hal Gregersen," Disrupt Yourself Podcast with Whitney Johnson, August 20, 2019, https://whitneyjohnson.com/hal-gregersen/; "How to Ask Your Team the Right Questions," Dave Bailey, Medium, September 24, 2019, https://medium.dave-bailey.com/how-to-ask-your-team-the-right-questions-19b83eab017f; "Leadership is Language with L. David Marquet," Todd Henry, Accidental Creative podcast, February 12, 2020, https://accidentalcreative.com/podcasts/ac/leadership-is-language-with-l-david-marquet/; "What is a Beautiful Question?" Warren Berger, https://amorebeautifulquestion.com/what-is-a-beautiful-question/.

- What has my team achieved?
- What have I learned?
- What has been a highlight?
- What has been a lowlight?
- What has been my biggest mistake or lesson learned?
- What would I do differently next time, and why?
- What is happening __ in my job, my company, with my product, in the market, with my team, etc.?
- What are my strengths and weaknesses?

Reflection doesn't have to be onerous or time consuming. I have taken inspiration from George Schultz, former US Secretary of State under President Reagan. Each week, without fail, Schultz would schedule in one hour to reflect in solitude. He would use this weekly hour for daydreaming and thinking about the strategic aspects of his role. He felt that failing to carve out this hour of reflection would tie him into moment-to-moment tactical issues, instead of being able to focus on larger questions of national interest. During this hour Schultz instructed his secretary to only interrupt him if his wife or the president called. In addition, Schultz always kept a pen and paper nearby, so that he could jot down his thoughts.[353] Regular reflection slots are a great way of forcing yourself to learn early and often, using any insights that you gain to strengthen specific areas or to do things differently in future. On the rare occasion that I miss my weekly hour for reflection, I will at a minimum ask myself - and write down the answers to - the following questions:

- **Highlights** - What were this week's highlights; why? For instance: we solved a critical bug in our checkout experience,

353 "You're Too Busy. You Need a 'Schultz Hour'," David Leonhardt, The New York Times, April 18, 2017, https://www.nytimes.com/2017/04/18/opinion/youre-too-busy-you-need-a-shultz-hour.html.

which makes it easier for customers to complete their purchase and will drive down the number of abandoned baskets.

- **Lowlights** - What were this week's lowlights or disappointments; why? For instance: failing to reach agreement with my executive sponsor about the best way forward for our product, given the consistent dip in performance in our key market.
- **Learnings** - What were my biggest learnings this week; why? For instance: when I spoke with my executive sponsor about options to improve product performance, I realised that I just provided her with a bunch of options. Because I didn't provide a clear recommendation or a concrete action plan, we left the conversation without a clear outcome or agreed next steps. Next time, I will make sure to present options, followed by recommendation for concrete next steps - underpinned by clear rationale and expected benefits.

Whether you manage to carve out an hour a week or just a few minutes, the practice of reflection is a valuable tool for understanding and managing the tensions and ambiguity that surrounds us.

4. SELF-AWARENESS

'Self-awareness involves deep personal honesty. It comes from asking and answering hard questions.' **Stephen Covey**

If you are keen to keep developing as a person, self-awareness is key. As I always try reminding my two young sons when they get cross about their friends or the football referee (don't ask!), you can't change the other person's behaviour, you can only influence your own. The same applies in a professional context; we ultimately only have control over ourselves, what we think or how we behave.

Self-awareness is a lifelong pursuit. I love how Scott Belsky, Chief Product Officer at Adobe, thinks about it in his latest book, 'The Messy

Middle'. In his book, Belsky eradicates any illusions about the process of creation being painless - be that in business or with a product; the journey between start and finish is messy, a collection of ups and downs.

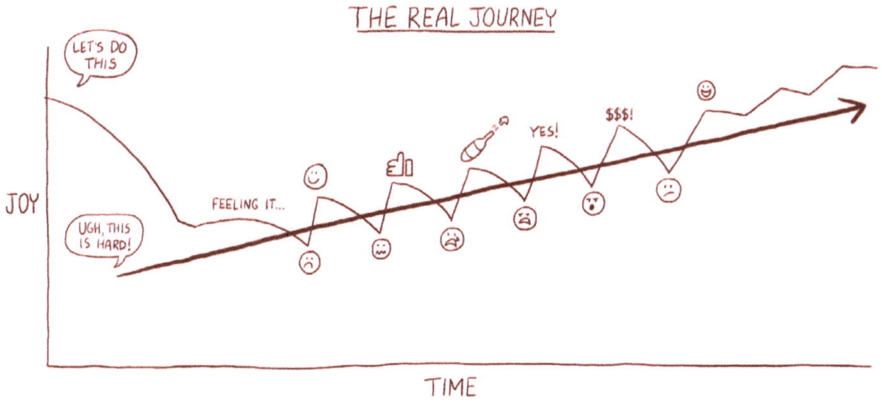

Fig. 23 – The process of creation is a messy one; a true collection of ups and downs

During this journey, Belsky argues, it is important to be self-aware, both when you are feeling low or high (See fig. 23):[354]

- Self-awareness starts with the realisation that when you are at a peak or in a valley, you are not your greatest self.
- Self-awareness means understanding your own feelings enough to recognise what bothers you.
- Self-awareness means being permeable.
- Self-awareness comes from chronicling your patterns.
- Self-awareness means dispelling your sense of superiority and the myths that people believe about you.

If you are struggling to visualise how you would look inward and have self-aware moments, think about the last time you acknowledged a feeling of stress or sadness. Or when someone gave you performance feedback that you didn't see coming. These experiences trigger us to

354 Scott Belsky, *The Messy Middle* (Portfolio / Penguin, 2018, pp. 54 – 56).

reflect on what has happened and how we are feeling. Alternatively, if you wish to be more 'proactive' about self-awareness, I would highly recommend one of the world's oldest skills: writing. Especially, when you are in a moment or extended period of tension, writing down your thoughts or feelings can help take the sting out of the situation and help you gain a different perspective. In the appendix to this chapter I elaborate on these benefits of writing and share a simple writing technique to get started.

5. DON' T BE AFRAID TO JUST ASK

'Don't be afraid to ask questions. Don't be afraid to ask for help when you need it. I do that every day. Asking for help isn't a sign of weakness, it's a sign of strength. It shows you have the courage to admit when you don't know something, and to learn something new.'
Barack Obama

It is vital to admit that you don't know. It is impossible to have all the answers - let alone all the questions! I believe it is just as vital to ask for help, particularly when you feel that pressures are mounting or when you feel you need a 'safety net', i.e. a trusted relationship with someone that you can confide in. A mentor or a coach, for example, can act as a safety net, and I will elaborate on these respective roles in this chapter. We all talk about having to step outside our comfort zones, without necessarily acknowledging the need to ask questions or call in help. Let us first acknowledge that it is not always easy to ask for help. I see three reasons why product managers might at times struggle with this. Firstly, they just don't feel it is ok to ask for help. Secondly, they don't know *where* to ask for help. Thirdly, they don't know *how* to ask for help.

It's ok to ask for help

'Your job is not to know it all,' says Tanja Lau, Founder of Product Academy. She mentions the liberating effect of both accepting that you don't need to have all the skills related to managing the product and admitting that you don't know something. 'As long as you're aware of your blind spots, you can mitigate those with your team.'[355] Or as Tim Nunn, Digital Product Practice Lead at Kiwibank said to me: 'I just wish I had reached out earlier in my career, realising that people can and are even very happy to help.'[356] You could argue that the free nature of asking for help is not limited to product people, but there are a number of reasons why the very nature of managing products makes asking for help even more pressing:

- **Dealing with unknowns** - As we have seen earlier, products are often surrounded by unknowns and product managers find themselves in the front line in having to deal with this uncertainty. 'We need help with making unknowns known', explains Zara Hegemann, Product Owner at Digitec Galaxus.[357]
- **No one right answer** - Product management is a highly fluid discipline, and there isn't a blueprint or a single right answer. 'There is often no "right answer" and it is therefore important we ask for different perspectives,' Hegemann explains.[358]
- **Multiple perspectives** - Given the multifaceted nature of products and the 'mind-matter-moves' involved, we cannot achieve our objective without getting input from relevant people. Asking for help from a wide range of people, each bringing their own unique perspective, can thus be invaluable when faced with unknowns or complexity. Nunn is clear about the value of asking for help and gaining different perspectives, 'even from people who aren't in the product space, psychologists and data scientists.'[359]

355 Tanja Lau, *interview by author*, Zurich, April 10, 2020.
356 Tim Nunn, *interview by author*, Wellington, April 7, 2020.
357 Zara Hegemann, *interview by author*, Zurich, April 11, 2020.
358 *Ibid 357.*
359 *Ibid 356.*

- **Bottleneck risk** - Ultimately, product people risk becoming a bottleneck if they don't ask for help. Given the time-constrained nature of product management, I believe that we simply can't afford *not* to ask for help early and often!

Where to ask for help (and the value of a safety net)

Tom Comerford, Group Product Manager at Walmart eCommerce, emphasises that though it is incredibly useful having a safety net, it isn't always possible to provide one. Referring to his own team, Comerford says that 'when we are under pressure to deliver an impactful new feature or product, I often take a heavier hand in leading my product managers to a solution that my experience tells me is more likely to be successful. When we have moments where there is less business pressure, I give my team more latitude to experiment and make mistakes as a means for their continued growth. It's a very delicate balance.'[360]

360 Tom Comerford, *email to author*, March 27, 2020.

Product managers are not unique in this respect, but their role can feel quite isolated at times. As my friend Martin Eriksson, co-founder of Mind the Product, says: 'Product management can be a pretty lonely job. If you are lucky you might have 7 engineers and a couple of designers for every PM in your org. In most startups this means you are the sole PM, but even in larger organisations it can be hard to gather a critical mass of product managers.'[361]

For me, providing a safety net comes down to one word: trust. The person providing the safety net must trust that the other person will act in a rational and a considered way. The relationship can be with a line manager, a colleague, a mentor or coach, it doesn't matter; trust forms the foundation of the relationship. As the person looking for a safety net, you should expect to be listened to without being judged. As a serial entrepreneur and Product Manager at Facebook, Jason Shen sees two main scenarios where it can be beneficial to have a safety net. Firstly, when you want to check whether you are on the right track: 'a trusted relationship with someone that you can confide in.' Shen explains that the trust here allows people to share in confidence things like 'I'm not sure about this _____' or 'I have a challenge with ____'. Secondly, Shen says, you can have a safety net that you can fall back upon 'when you're not sure what to do with a product.' You can use the other person as a sparring partner for any product-related issues or questions that you are facing. He stresses that this doesn't always have to be about new products or fancy integrations, but rather a sounding board about any product bugs or performance issues to resolve.[362]

I recall one specific example of a time when I was able to offer a safety net to a member of my team. In this particular case, the subject matter expert with whom my team member was working had built

361 "Product managers, you're not alone," Martin Eriksson, Inside Intercom, April 22, 2016, https://www.intercom.com/blog/product-managers-youre-not-alone/.

362 Jason Shen, *interview by author*, New York, April 8, 2020.

up extensive knowledge of a specific area, and my product manager needed to build up her own understanding of the same area. By giving my product manager the space and time to make mistakes and learn through the product development process, I was rewarded with a highly effective employee in the medium-term. After she ramped all the way up on the domain knowledge, my product manager became a top performer and quickly delivered value that exceeded the 'cost' of providing her with an early safety net.

The lonely nature of the product management role makes it even more essential that product managers are able to ask for help. Sabrina Rzepka, Lead Product Manager at BMW and co-founder of Product Professionals highlights the link between asking for help and self-reflection: 'reflect on what you can and can't do. What do you lack?' Becoming aware of these things and being open about them is something that requires strength.[363] In her career, Rzepka has both benefited from and helped others through what she refers to as a 'Co-Pilot'.

SABRINA RZEPKA AND LOOKING FOR YOUR CO-PILOT:

What do you do when you need to get up to speed quickly? Or are you dealing with an ambiguous situation? Sabrina Rzepka, Lead Product Manager at BMW and co-founder at Product Professionals, advocates the use of a 'co-pilot'. 'As product managers we are generalists in a world of specialists', she explains.[364] A co-pilot is typically someone who has been in the organisation for a while or has done a specific task or project before and will therefore know about the history of the product or problem, knows the relevant people in the company, valuable 'tricks & tweaks' and any oddities to take into account.[365] In addition, a co-pilot can help you with any of the following:

- *Finding important shortcuts that help you get to desired*

---

363 Sabrina Rzepka, *interview by author*, Munich, March 27, 2020.

364 *Ibid 363.*

365 "How to keep pace in an over 100-year old organisation," Sabrina Rzepka, Talk at JAM London, December 2, 2019, https://www.youtube.com/watch?v=K4gElErGcRl.

learnings or outcomes quickly, especially if you are new to an organisation or product.
- *Gaining speed fast, getting to grips with a problem or organisation quickly.*
- *Focus on the right aspects to ask and learn about; it is impossible for you to try and figure out everything for yourself.*

A co-pilot can start entering the picture as soon as you ask for help. Rzepka realises that asking for help requires courage as she feels that many product managers think that they are expected to have all the answers and need to be seen to be in charge. 'People have this idea that because they were hired for a reason or put on a product for a reason, they need to have all the answers. It therefore takes courage to admit that you don't know all the answers or aren't 100% sure,' she explains.[366] *Apart from having co-pilots within BMW, Rzepka has established a team of coaches as part of Product Professionals. These coaches act as co-pilots, being able to support product managers with their challenges and opportunities.*

How to ask for help

Asking for help is a reciprocal activity; you need to have the confidence to ask for help and then hope the other person agrees. It can be hugely disappointing, though, if your ask falls on deaf ears Here are six practical suggestions which should help lead to a positive outcome:[367]

- **Make it specific** - Instead of simply stating that you need help or that you would like to pick someone else's brains, it pays to be specific about your ask. What specifically would you like help with? Why do you want the help? For instance: 'I would

366 *Ibid 363.*

367 Adapted from: "How to ask for help - and get a "yes"," Heidi Grant, TED Salon, June 2019, https://www.strategyzer.com/blog/psychological-safety-in-the-workplace-a-pre-requisite-for-high-performing-teams.

appreciate it if we could work through this product prioritisation problem together, as there are some trade-off decisions to make and I'm not sure how to best go about things.'

- **Be prepared** - It helps to do your homework beforehand. Zara Hegemann says, 'I find it helps if I at least bring my own suggestion, a clear indication of my own thought process.'[368] Also, 'be prepared to understand the needs of the person that you are asking for help,' adds Adriana Landaverde, Chief Product Officer at Clim8. She explains that the person you are going to for help, might not be immediately inclined to grant help. If this is the case, Landaverde suggests finding a common ground with the other person as well as being ready to provide more context about why you are asking, e.g. by mentioning your goals or constraints.[369]
- **Accept rejection** - Naturally, you need to be prepared for the other person to turn down your request for mentoring. The person that you would like to be your mentor might not have the bandwidth or feel that he or she wouldn't be the best person to mentor you. If this is the case, graciously accept the rejection, thank them for at least considering your question and perhaps ask whether they might know someone within their network who could be a suitable alternative.
- **Avoid incentives or disclaimers** - Both asking and giving help come from having a relationship with someone. It can therefore become awkward if you start incentivising the person you are asking for help, and it will shift the dynamics from a relationship to a transaction. Equally, apologising profusely when you ask for help also isn't advisable: saying 'I really hate asking you for help' or 'Normally I would do this

368 *Ibid 357.*

369 Adriana Landaverde, *interview by author*, London, April 15, 2020.

myself __' does diminish the other person's satisfaction of being asked for help.[370] Naturally, this doesn't mean that you can't give a present to show your appreciation or buy the other person a nice coffee!

- **Ask in person** - It is worth asking a person for help face to face, instead of over email, text or messenger if at all possible. It makes it easier to get the 'what' and 'why' of your ask across (see 'Make it specific' above). If you do ask for help remotely, you might have to spend more time upfront to get to know each other and provide context to what you are asking for. The aforementioned Tim Nunn stresses the importance of trust if you want to really help and be helped. Whether you connect in person or virtually, it is vital to invest in establishing this trust. Even if you don't know what kind of help you are looking for, having a trusted relationship with another person will make it easier and safer to figure out together what support you need.[371]
- **No 'spray and pray'** - It is more often than not effective to ask a specific person for help rather than posing the question to a large group, hoping that one person will help you. When you ask a large group, there is a large chance of 'diffusion of responsibility' kicking in. This is a socio psychological phenomenon whereby a person is less likely to take responsibility for action or inaction when others are present. In other words; if I get an email where a large group of people are being asked a specific question, I expect that 'someone else' will respond.[372]

370 "A social psychologist explains why we should ask for help more often," Angela Chen, The Verge, June 22, 2018, https://www.theverge.com/2018/6/22/17475134/heidi-grant-reinforcements-help-social-psychology.

371 *Ibid 356.*

372 Saul M. Kassin, Steven Fein and Hazel Rose Markus, *Social Psychology* (Houghton Mifflin: Seventh Edition, January 2007).

- **Follow up on the help received** - If you have been introduced by someone to an expert within your field, do ensure that you go back to the person who made the intro and tell him or her about the conversation you had with the expert. Not only will this make the experience more rewarding for the person providing help, it will also increase the likelihood that they will help you or someone else again in future.

Finally, don't assume that people will know or sense that you need help, and that you therefore won't need to explicitly ask for it. This cognitive bias is referred to as the 'illusion of transparency', a tendency for people to think that their emotions and thoughts are more apparent to others than is actually the case.[373] If you feel a need for help, be explicit and ask for it!

A mentor or a coach can act as a great safety net. Mentors and coaches are typically highly experienced practitioners who you can build a trusted relationship with, and who can help you achieve change - either in your career or your behaviours. Before you start thinking about engaging with a coach or a mentor, it is important to figure out what you need, at what stage and why. You can engage with coaches to work on specific skills or improvement areas without the coach needing to come from the same field. He or she doesn't have to have any experience in product management to be helpful. 'A coach will typically help you find your own answers,' says Adriana Landaverde.[374] A coaching relationship is typically more short-term and performance focused. In the past, I have engaged coaches because I wanted to get better at communicating with difficult stakeholders or because I was keen

373 "The Illusion of Transparency: Why You're Not as Obvious as You Think You Are," Itamar Schatz, Effectiviology, https://effectiviology.com/illusion-of-transparency/ (Accessed on March 23, 2020).

374 *Ibid 369.*

to become more resilient.

By comparison, a mentoring relationship is often long-term and career focused. Mentors usually operate in the same field as their mentees and will likely have more experience than you or have achieved the specific things that a mentee is hoping to achieve. If, for example, you are looking to lead a product in a high-growth environment, you will no doubt do well out of engaging with a product leader who has successfully grown a product and customer base in a scaleup environment. Zara Hegemann mentions that a mentor can bring an outside perspective, even if they are from another team within the same organisation. 'Mentors in another team might be more challenging, or give more critical feedback, than your direct colleagues would.'[375]

In reality, most of the product people that I have spoken to don't worry too much about the differences between coaches and mentors and focus on their specific needs and career aspirations instead. Tanja Lau, for example, talks about how she has established her own 'board of directors', a group of trusted people that she consults with as and when needed.[376] To help you find the support that best serves your needs, I have added two common support scenarios in the toolkit section at the end of this chapter. For each scenario, I outline the value of a mentor or a coach and provide some pointers on how to best establish a relationship.

CONCLUSION

We have seen how products and the people working in them inevitably face all kinds of tension. It might be hard - impossible if you ask me! - to fully eradicate these tensions; however, there is a lot that can be done to build resilience and drive the growth of your product and the individuals working on it. It all starts with curiosity, not being afraid

375 *Ibid 357.*
376 *Ibid 355.*

to pause or ask questions. You will find that this to be an ongoing process, especially if you are managing products!

SUMMARY

Product Management = Mind + Matter + Moves

Managing products successfully means committing to resilience and growth - both of your product and you as an individual.

Keeping on top of your **product** means continuous learning and improvement, with a relentless focus bettering your ways of working:

- Use **Product Principles** to guide the overall direction of your product as well as day-to-day product decisions.
- Running regular **Product Retrospectives** offers a great way to reflect on product performance collectively and determine areas for improvement or innovation.

Keeping on top of **yourself** means trying to develop yourself continuously, reflecting, learning and growing as a result:

- Become a **learning machine**, mastering the tensions you encounter.
- Nurture your **curiosity** by simply asking 'why'.
- **Reflect** regularly to look back or understand what has or might happen.
- Remember that the impact of being **self-aware** is huge; on yourself, your product, your team and the relationships you build.
- Don't be afraid to **ask for help**! From saying 'I don't know' to engaging with a coach or mentor. The nature of product management is such that it is critical you feel comfortable asking for help, early and often.

There are two main ways to embrace tension: optimising **'Product Tension'** and being ok with **'Individual Tension'. Optimising product tension** means that you make the most of the tensions that are affecting your product or business.

- **Analyse the market and your competitors** to pre-empt competitive pressures, as well as defining the position and points of differentiation for your product. You can use tools such as SWOT analysis, OODA loop, Kano model, Lean Canvas and direct customer feedback.
- **Manage risks and unknowns** and make sure to learn early and often about risks, to your business (bottom line, operations or reputation) or your product (customer experience, scalability or performance).
- **Apply constraints:** accept the inevitability of constraints - financial, regulatory, technical or operational - and use constraints as a way to reduce complexity and tension.

Managing your individual tension is as important as managing the tension affecting your product. There are a number of things you can do to both be aware of tension and to address it:

- Doing a regular **self-check** to zero in on your feelings, thoughts or behaviours.
- **Listen actively** to fully understand what is happening or where the other person is coming from, to gain a better perspective on the tension and how to manage it.
- Conflict can be conducive to your personal growth and development, provided you **manage conflict**, understanding the nature of the conflict and steering it towards a resolution.
- **Accepting radically** doesn't mean that you resign yourself to the situation or throw in the towel. Instead, you accept things for what they are (and aren't).

- It is ok to **say, 'I don't know'**, admitting that you don't have the answer or might need to explore something more before committing.
- If you are ever in doubt about whether to ask a question, **just ask** and concentrate both on what you want to know and how to ask the question.
- Be direct and specific when **giving feedback**, focusing on the task or behaviour and not on the person. Listen to understand and not to respond when **receiving feedback**.
- To avoid tension due to indecisiveness, follow an approach where you and your team **disagree and commit**, being clear about the point where a decision needs to be reached and committed to.

TOOLKIT: MANAGING PRODUCT = MANAGING RESILIENCE AND GROWTH

1. FACILITATING A PRODUCT RETROSPECTIVE

Outcome: Shared understanding of product performance and agreement on next steps.

Here are some typical questions that might be used for a product retrospective:

- **How is our product performing (or not)?** – I appreciate that many of us will monitor product performance on a daily or even hourly basis. However, there might be people in your business who don't keep track of recent product releases or performance or have simply moved on to concentrate on the next project. What are the key stats telling us? How has the product or feature been performing against key performance indicators ('KPIs') around usage or revenue? They might also not be familiar with the assumptions – business and user – which underpin a particular product feature or improvement. Product retrospectives provide a great forum to reflect collectively on the data, discuss learnings and identify actions for improvement.
- **How are we doing against our roadmap and business objectives?** – This is an opportunity to look at the bigger picture and review progress against key roadmap milestones and success factors. What have we been doing (and why)? What's coming up and what's the impact that we are expecting?
- **What are our users saying?** – If you're getting user feedback on a regular basis, I find product retrospectives a great time to share user learnings and insights. This can be as simple as sharing excerpts or quotes from user feedback

sessions or a video of users testing your product remotely.

- **What is happening in the market?** – To avoid looking at a product or proposition in isolation, I always try to look at competitors as part of a product retrospective. What are our competitors doing? Why? Similarly, I also like broadening perspectives by learning from businesses in different sectors or markets.
- **What product ideas do you have?** – Facilitating a product retrospective isn't a one-way street. It's also an opportunity for the people in the session to provide their suggestions based on the data and learnings that you discuss with them.

This is how you could structure your product retrospectives in a similar way to regular Agile retrospectives:

1. **Set the stage** – Outline the goal for the retrospective, identifying both the desired outcomes of the session as well as what you expect to cover. Explain how you will use the product retrospective to further shape the product roadmap and that some concrete product objectives are a desired retrospective outcome.
2. **Gather data** – To create a shared picture of what's happened or is happening, start off by presenting hard facts around releases, roadmap progress, business objectives and key results. Use these facts as a starting point for discussion, facilitating a conversation around data, underlying assumptions and problems to address.
3. **Generate insights** – This part of the product retrospective is about asking 'why' and thinking about what could be done differently. At this stage, talk about qualitative user feedback and discuss the 'why' behind the insights.
4. **Decide what to do** – At this point in the product retrospective, the audience is likely to have some product

ideas or suggestions worthy of further exploration. From experience I've learned that the format of a product retrospective does not lend itself particularly well to a lengthy discussion about the merits of a product idea. However, it's a great opportunity to gather thoughts and to prioritise ideas for further discovery.

5. **Close the retrospective** – Recap the main insights and actions discussed during the retrospective swiftly. Ask if there are any specific items that the audience would like to see covered in the next product retrospective.

2. QUESTIONS WORTH ASKING

Outcome: Having a wide range of questions available for different things you want to learn.

Simple questions

Simple clarifying questions such as 'Why?', 'So what?' or 'Wait, what?' are often the most challenging to answer. Equally, these simple questions can lead to other, more complex questions. Equally, these simple questions can lead to other, more complex questions. 'You suggested *A*, but also took into account *B* and *C*, and I wondered about the trade-offs that you made when considering A, B and C' is a complex and convoluted way of asking 'What is your biggest priority?'

Open questions

Open questions empower the person answering in any way they choose. A closed question, in contrast, only allows the recipient to answer with a simple 'yes' or 'no'. Think about questions that start with 'do you _' or 'are you _' which don't leave much room for an open answer; think about asking someone 'are you ok?' (closed) versus 'how are you feeling?' (open).

Curious questions

In a similar vein to open questions, curious questioning gives the person answering more of an opportunity to express themselves, showing their thought process. For example, by asking 'what challenges do you see here?' or 'which options do you feel we have?' you phrase the question in such a way that it could elicit a thoughtful answer. Other good examples are questions such as 'What are we missing?' or 'How might this go wrong?'[377]

Keystone questions

In his excellent book 'Questions Are the Answer', Hal Gregersen - Senior Lecturer at MIT - describes keystone questions as 'the deeply established questions we ask of ourselves in the attempt to be our best selves.' These are fundamental questions that help us to make tough decisions and are designed in such a way for us to figure out what truly matters to us. Gregersen himself tries to live by the question – 'How can I make a positive difference in this person's life right now?'[378] I personally have a similar keystone question where I ask myself 'where can I have some positive impact?'

Catalytic questions

Catalytic questions challenge fundamental assumptions or perceived ways of thinking. Not only will these questions challenge but also generate energy and focus on action. In the memorable commencement speech that Harvard Dean, James Ryan gave in 2016, he started with: 'I wonder _' as an important catalytic question. You could start with 'I wonder *why*' with the word 'why' indicating your curiosity or challenging popular belief, followed by 'I wonder *if*' to express action, potential improvement.[379]

377 L. David Marquet, *Leadership is Language* (Portfolio Penguin, 2020, p. 63).

378 Hal Gregersen, *Questions are the Answer* (New York: Harper Business, 2018, p. 273).

379 "5 Essential Questions In Life," Dean James Ryan, Harvard Graduate School of Education, May 29, 2016, https://www.youtube.com/watch?v=bW0NguMGIbE.

Reflective questions

The main purpose of asking a reflective question is not to gather information. Instead, reflective questions like 'What did you observe?' or 'If you could do this project again, what would you do differently?' are more for the benefit of the person answering the question, than the person asking. These questions are designed to get the respondent to think about their experience or insights gained and you can use this method to ask about four broad categories:[380]

- **Knowledge / understanding (what you know)** - 'How does that compare to what you know about __?' or 'How do you plan to learn more about __?'
- **Practice (what you did)** - 'When did you first notice this?' or 'What would you need to do personally in order to __?'
- **Outcomes (what was the result)** - 'How did you know that you needed to do something else?' or 'What might make it work even better next time?'
- **Evaluation (what about the process)** - 'What support was the most helpful?' or 'How was that consistent with what you expected?'

3. WRITE IT DOWN

Taking a minute to step out of whatever is happening in the moment helps to take the sting out of a situation. I often find myself in situations that feel overwhelming or that send me into a spiral of negative thinking. I have seen people stepping out of a meeting, going for a walk or simply taking a moment to breathe deeply. Writing things down has the same impact; it prevents me from lashing out at other people or thinking that the world is going to come to an end ...

380 See for more examples: Dathan D. Rush and M'Lisa L. Shelden, *The Early Childhood Coaching Handbook* (Baltimore: Brookes Publishing, 2001); "8 Reflective Questions To Help Any Student Think About Their Learning," Terry Heick, TeachThought, March 21, 2018, https://www.teachthought.com/learning/use-twitter-exit-slip-teaching/.

Writing down your thoughts or feelings can also help with gaining an alternative perspective. In the moment you might feel that the tension is insurmountable - that everything is doom and gloom.

Writing, however, enables you to shape your thoughts and ponder what you observe or feel. It forms a cornerstone of Cognitive Behaviour Therapy ('CBT'), a present-oriented psychotherapy that helps people be cognizant of how they perceive a situation. People's perception of a situation is often more closely connected to their reaction than the situation itself.[381] The simplest thing to do is to grab a pen and paper in the moment and write down your thoughts:

- **Date:** 21 March 2020
- **Situation:** Company trading has declined due to growing concern about the Coronavirus pandemic.
- **Initial thought:** The world will never be the same, and my company will go out of business.
- **Evidence for initial thought:** A growing number of people are dying as a result of the virus and we are seeing a sharp decline in trading activity.
- **Evidence against initial thought:** While there is a lot of uncertainty, China is slowly coming back from the virus, with factories opening again and trading resuming.
- **Alternative thinking:** This is tough and unsettling, but there is still great value in helping our current customers and providing them with the best product and experience.

If you wish to keep track of your thoughts, evidence for and against as well as your alternative thoughts, you can start keeping a so-called 'Thought Diary'; this is a journal of all your time-sensitive thought

381 "What is Cognitive Behavior Therapy (CBT)," Beck Institute for Cognitive Behavior Therapy, 2019, https://beckinstitute.org/get-informed/what-is-cognitive-therapy/.

records.[382] Taking a moment to reflect or write things down will benefit both your self-awareness and your *situational* awareness.

- **'Perception'** is the first level of situational awareness; how do you perceive the elements that make up the current situation?
- **'Comprehension'** forms the second level; forming a joined-up picture of the different elements that you perceive. Both perception and comprehension are typically more tactical and short term, effectively assessing the situation at hand.
- In contrast, **'projection'**, the third and highest level of situational awareness, involves us processing the information collated in the previous two levels - perception and comprehension - to understand how it will affect future states of a business or operational environment.[383]

4.GETTING SUPPORT FROM A COACH OR A MENTOR

These are two common scenarios where we can benefit from reaching out to a coach or a mentor:

Scenario 1

'I keep bumping into the same issues with my stakeholders at work, trying to come to an agreement with them about our product priorities. Despite me trying to align them around business goals and KPIs, we end up committing to the wishes and desires of the most senior person in the room. I know that we have to compromise at times, but we always end up building products that show our compromises, even to the customer!

382 See: Aaron T. Beck, A. John Rush, Brian E. Shaw and Gary Emery, *Cognitive Therapy of Depression* (Guildford: The Guilford Press, February 1987, First published 1979); "CBT Basics and Beyond Worksheets," Beck Institute for Cognitive Behavior Therapy, 2020, https://beckinstitute.org/get-informed/tools-and-resources/professionals/cbt-basics-and-beyond-patient-worksheets/.

383 "Toward a Theory of Situation Awareness in Dynamic Systems," Mica R. Endsley, Human Factors Journal, 1995, Vol. 37(1), pp. 32 - 64.

I would like to work through some of these challenges and work on the best approach to stakeholder management.'

Scenario 2

'I want to progress my career as a product manager. Up to this point I have only worked on B2B products and I would like to manage a B2C product instead. It has been difficult to get interviews for B2C product management roles, and my CV seems to be the biggest stumbling block. I am looking for help with how to best position myself and perhaps some intros to businesses that make customer-facing products.'

Coaching or mentoring? - Scenario 1

Scenario 1 is best geared to engaging with a coach or someone who will ask you coaching type questions. Coaches are typically engaged on a time-sensitive basis, e.g. to help on a specific project or help people develop specific skills. In this specific scenario, the coach is likely to ask you specific questions. Coaches will not give you the answer or advice on a plate; they will help you work through the problem and help you arrive at the best solution or approach yourself.[384] These are some of the questions someone coaching you might ask in this particular scenario:[385]

384 See: "The similarities and differences between coaching and therapy," Peter Bluckert, Industrial and Commercial Training, 2005, Vol. 97, Issue 2, pp. 91 - 96; "Mentoring Vs Coaching," iMentoring, https://mentoringgroup.com/mentor-vs-coach-differences.html (Accessed on March 25, 2020); "Coaching and Mentoring - the difference," Richard Winfield, https://richardwinfield.com/coaching-3/coaching-and-mentoring/ (Accessed on March 25, 2020).

385 See: Sir John Whitmore, *Coaching For Performance: The principles and practice of coaching and leadership* (Boston: Nicholas Brealey Publishing, 5th Edition, 2017); "Coaching 101: Ask Powerful Questions," Stephanie Soler, Medium, November 21, 2014, https://medium.com/@StephanieLSoler/to-be-a-great-coach-ask-powerful-questions-d6b18614fffb; Richard Boyatzis, Melvin L. Smith and Ellen Van Oosten, *Helping People Change: Coaching with Compassion for Lifelong Learning and Growth* (Harvard Business Review Press, August 2019).

Build understanding [gaining context and identifying what is important]:

- What are you trying to achieve?
- What challenges are you facing?
- What is your goal related to this challenge?
- What actions have you taken so far?
- How has that been going?
- What else?

Set direction [start exploring what is possible]:

- What is the best possible outcome here?
- How will you know if you have succeeded?
- When are you looking to achieve it?
- What will it be like when you achieve your goal?

Explore options [generating ideas and opportunities]:

- What alternative options do you have to achieve your goal?
- What else could you do?
- How feasible is each option?
- What would you have to believe for this option to be right?

Define next steps [clarifying what happens next]:

- What data / information / support do you need to make a decision?
- Which options will you choose to act on?
- What can you do now?
- What are you taking away from this conversation?
- How can I help?

Coaching or mentoring? - Scenario 2

Scenario 2 lends itself well to a mentoring relationship, ideally with someone who has experience in the same line of work as you. Mentoring relationships tend to be longer term and more informal than coaching. For instance, my mentoring relationships are pretty ad hoc and spread out over a longer period of time; I turn to a selected group of trusted people when I need advice, support or an introduction. When I act as a mentor to others, my mentees reach out if they need some guidance on a particular challenge or are considering new opportunities. Mentors are experienced colleagues - inside or outside your organisation - who are happy to give you their time and share their expertise to help you develop your career. Their engagement can range from guidance on key skills to making connections for you within their network.[386]

When I asked Tom Comerford, Group Product Manager at Walmart eCommerce, about the role of mentoring, he mentioned that 'mentorship gives the opportunity for the mentor and the mentee to learn and grow symbiotically.' In this sort of relationship, the topics can vary from tactical issues to broader strategic career discussions, or in some cases, even personal life topics.'[387] In the above scenario, you could engage with a mentor for guidance on how to best put together your CV, making sure it fits with the career opportunities that you want to pursue. A mentor might further have valuable contacts within your space and might be able to introduce you to them for a call or coffee.[388]

386 See: Lois J. Zachary, *The Mentor's Guide: Facilitating Effective Learning Relationships* (San Francisco: Jossey-Bass, January 2000); Ellen Ensher, *Power Mentoring: How Successful Mentors and Proteges Get the Most Out of Their Relationships*, (San Francisco: Jossey-Bass, January 2005); Lois J. Zachary and Lory A. Fischler, *The Mentee's Guide: Making Mentoring Work for You* (San Francisco: Jossey-Bass, June 2009).

387 *Ibid 360*; "How Do You Mentor a Product Manager?" Tom Comerford, Medium, September 9, 2019, https://medium.com/everyone-is-a-product-expert/how-do-you-mentor-a-product-manager-387e14e1dc22

388 It is worth reiterating that a mentor can be a colleague or a manager within your company. I like the concept of the "connector-manager", introduced by Jaime Roca and Sari Wilde. This is a manager type that drives performance by driving peer-to-peer coaching or filling skill gaps by connecting you to relevant people in or outside the organisation; Jaime Roca and Sari Wilde, *The Connector Manager: Why Some Leaders Build Exceptional Talent - and Others Don't* (London: Virgin Books, 2019, Chapter 3).

CONCLUSION

'We sail within a vast sphere, ever drifting in uncertainty, driven from end to end.' **Blaise Pascal**

As the writing of this book drew to a conclusion, I started to reflect on the process of producing it and all the things that had happened throughout this period. It couldn't have been more timely. Just as I was writing about tension and uncertainty, a global pandemic broke out. Millions of us have been affected; people have become ill and many have lost their lives, businesses have struggled and thousands of employees have been furloughed or have lost their jobs. Some products have been sunset or shut down completely whilst others have grown beyond imagination. Things that were already uncertain have been amplified, and I have spoken to many of my friends and peers who are facing difficult times - both on a personal and a professional level.

If I think about what drove me to write this book, the feelings of frustration and lack of control have by no means abated over the past year and a half. Product priorities have changed and in some cases, a step forward has been followed by two steps back. At the same time, writing this book has reinforced a sense that as product managers we are in a great position to make the most of the pressures and challenges that come our way. Through our work with a wide range of people, we are exposed to a variety of learning opportunities as well as testing situations. As difficult as it can sometimes feel, the very nature of product management allows us to bring people together and to work through problems collectively.

My hope is that this book will give you a good insight into the nature of product management and offer you tangible ways to make the most of the tensions that this amazing discipline offers. Whether you focus on your own approach to leaning into tension or getting others comfortable with unknowns or pressure, I believe that product people can really help make the most of those situations or feelings that might typically create fear or uncertainty. Embracing tension is not easy, but it is absolutely worth it!

ACKNOWLEDGEMENTS

This book would not have been possible without the help from a great number of people. I am hugely grateful for the contributions of some amazing product colleagues: Adriana Landaverde, Alex Watson, Brandon Chu, Chris Butler, Craig Strong, Darlene Miranda, Duncan Barrigan, Hope Gurion, Jason Shen, Jo Wickremasinghe, John Cutler, Jon Kolko, Justus Fokker, Ken Chin, Kristina Walcker-Mayer, Mat Tylicki, Mukesh Gupta, Rik Higham, Ross McNairn, Sabrina Rzepka, Shaheena Attarwala, Tanja Lau, Tim Nunn, Tom Comerford, Wayne Greene and Zara Hegemann.

I would also like to thank the following people for reviewing the work in progress, providing valuable feedback on structure and content as well as spotting many grammatical errors! Andy Ayim, Asha Haji, Craig Strong, Jonathan Norman, Lindsey Keighley, Lonnie Rosenbaum, Louise Mantin, Mark Wickstead, Roman Pichler, Simon Whatley, Tony Llewellyn, Toon Gerbrands and Victoria Dalrymple.

Once again, Rachel Smith has been fantastic in grasping what I was trying to achieve with 'Managing Product = Managing Tension' and has translated this into a series of awesome illustrations.

My biggest thanks go out to my wife, Tracy Abraham. Not only did she painstakingly go through every sentence in this book, Tracy acted - yet again - as an invaluable sounding board throughout the writing process. Thank you!

ABOUT THE AUTHOR

Marc Abraham is an experienced product management practitioner who has worked for a large number of successful digital organisations, from high-growth startups to well-known established brands. He is also part of the team behind Mind the Product, an international community for and by product people, consisting of more than 100k members globally. Having begun his professional career as a corporate lawyer in Amsterdam, Marc took up blogging at marcabraham.com as a way of discovering more about the digital ecosystem and ultimately as a way of breaking into it. In 2018 he wrote 'My Product Management Toolkit' and continues to write and speak about his lessons learned, encouraging product managers to retain curiosity and pursue a journey of continuous learning.

Marc lives in London with his wife Tracy and two children, Oscar and Zac.

Defenc
SUSSEX BEACHES 1940 - 42

From Selsey Bill to the Kent Border

John Goodwin

MP Middleton Press

Front Cover
Colour Photograph: The Seven Sisters cliffs, East Sussex.
Black and White Photograph: The Pier and beach at Worthing during the 1940s.

Back Cover
Top Photograph: A Humber armoured car squadron ready to move off.
Lower Photograph: A 4 inch (QF) Quick Firing gun, fires from Brighton sea front.

To Jean

with my love and affection
for our many happy years together

Also by John Goodwin

Eastbourne Redoubt, 1976 (Worthing Library)

The Military Defence of West Sussex
ISBN 0 906520 23 1
Middleton Press, 1985

Fortifications of the South Coast -
The Pevensey, Eastbourne and Newhaven Defences
ISBN 0 9524158 0 1
published by the author, 1994

Military Signals from the South Coast,
ISBN 1 901706 54 0
Middleton Press, 2000

Published June 2010
First reprint September 2010

ISBN 978 1 906008 79 6

Design Deborah Esher

Published by
Middleton Press
Easebourne Lane
Midhurst
West Sussex
GU29 9AZ
Tel: 01730 813169
Fax: 01730 812601
Email: info@middletonpress.co.uk
www.middletonpress.co.uk

Printed in the United Kingdom by I.J. Graphics, Guildford. GU2 9XW

CONTENTS

Chapter		Page
1	Invasion Threatens and Plans Change	4
2	German Intelligence about the Sussex Coast Defences	11
3	The Infantry behind the Beaches	15
4	Armoured Divisions and Tank Brigades	24
5	Artillery, Rail Guns, and Armoured Trains	29
6	Deployment of an Infantry Division: Selsey Bill to Newhaven	38
7	The Rush to build Obstacles	46
8	Fortification of a Sussex Sea Front	54
9	The Emergency Coast Defence Batteries: Selsey Bill to Dungeness	62
10	Old Newhaven Fort and its Role in the 1940s	76
11	HMS Forward. An Underground Headquarters	83
12	Military Signals between London and the South Coast	88
13	Nets, Fire Booms and Minefields	91
14	The Army Coast Watching Radar and the Beachy Head Rotor Bunker	100
	Index	106
	Further Reading	108
	Principal sources consulted	109

ACKNOWLEDGEMENTS

The Second World War began seventy years ago, but the two years 1940-42, when the country came seriously close to being invaded, left its mark on those who remembered what those times were like. This book is about how the military took over the beaches and the countryside of Sussex to ensure that no invasion would succeed. To do this I am grateful for information and illustrations from the National Archives, the War Office, the Imperial War Museum, the National Army Museum, the National Railway Museum, and East and West Sussex Record Offices. Eastbourne, Brighton, Hove and Worthing Libraries (Walter Gardiner Photography Collection) were at all times helpful. I am also indebted to Terry Gander for his generous loan of contemporary pictures, to the late Peter Cobb and fellow members of the Fortress Study Group. Peter Longstaff-Tyrell of the Sussex Military History Society, and Ron Martin of the Sussex Industrial Archaeological Society contributed little known facts about Sussex defences. There are many others who have been very helpful in providing evidence of military activity during those years and to all those I give my thanks.

Chapter 1

INVASION THREATENS AND PLANS CHANGE

When war broke out on 3rd September 1939 the great fear was that railways, towns and ports, would be bombed and destroyed from the air leaving the population to flee for safety. London was most at risk and the first priority was to evacuate schools to safer areas. Many children came to Sussex coastal towns and villages. All available resources were put to digging air raid trenches, sandbagging public buildings and making arrangements for life to continue if the bombers destroyed local services. There was little military presence in Sussex at this time apart from the requisitioning of commercial vehicles, the army being short of transport.

It was not many months before the Sussex coast became a danger area and the children were sent off to safer places. The fear of widespread death by bombing was replaced in 1940 by the greater danger of invasion. It was fortunate that Winston Churchill's challenging spirit of defiance rallied and inspired the nation to rise and fight even though the man in the street was not aware of the deplorable state of the British forces. Understandably, there was little taste for war after the horrors of 1914-18 and this had led to Parliament being reluctant to spend money on modernising the army, and bringing its equipment and training up to date.

The British Expeditionary Force which had been sent to France was not only under strength in manpower, but also under equipped in tanks, anti-tank guns and Bofors guns. A secret report on the armament situation dated June 1940 outlined the deficiencies in fighting material following the Dunkirk evacuation. It estimated that it would take from one to five months to replace the artillery, tanks, anti-aircraft guns, Bren guns and transport lost in Europe. Ironically ammunition stocks were satisfactory because of the reduction in the number of guns available to fire them. One result of the losses was to postpone the equipping of extra divisions until existing ones were brought up to their full war establishment.

Changes in Defence Strategy 1939 - 1940

Within a year the army had three Chiefs of Staff, each with a different view as to how the defence of the country should be organised.

In September 1939, General Kirke, the Commander-in-Chief of the army, was told that the threat of invasion was not serious. His advisors reckoned that any raids on the coast supported by airborne troops could be isolated and defeated by the home army with the help of the navy and airforce.

Eight months later at very short notice Kirke was replaced by General Ironside. The threat of a serious invasion had changed from possible to very likely. Hampered by a scarcity of transport, armour and artillery, much of it obsolete, Ironside had little choice but to plan for lines of fixed defences. Thus orders were given for a network of pill boxes and road blocks to be built. These were to be armed with machine guns and anti-tank weapons, where these were available. Thus a defence in depth for the field army to fall back on was intended to avoid the situation in France where, when the German army broke through the front line, there was little in their way to stop them.

Ironside's strategy also turned towns, villages and road junctions into defended localities called Nodal Points and intended to delay an enemy advance inland until reinforcements could be sent. Pill boxes, dug outs, sand bagged posts, road blocks, loop holed walls, ditches and barbed wire were all part of the defensive perimeter put in place around road junctions, towns and villages.

A yellow booklet, "Nodal Points - Operation, Information and Instructions for the Civil Authorities" was issued in June 1941 throughout Sussex. Nodal Points were to be garrisoned by the Home Guard and any other troops in the vicinity. To assist the defence a 200-500 yard (185-450 metres) perimeter around the Nodal Points was evacuated and cleared to allow the defenders to do their job. This caused some confusion locally. The Police wanted small communities, (ie outside Arundel) to be moved inside the perimeter. The army wanted them to "stay put." The matter was never satisfactorily resolved.

A few of the Sussex Nodal Point defence plans have survived from 1940 and are shown at the end of this chapter. Although crudely drawn and short on detail, they reflect the urgency of the times and show the streets around which the slit trenches, loop holed walls and pill boxes would have been sited. The construction of Nodal Points continued until 1942 when work ceased due to the lessening of the invasion threat and materials and manpower being required elsewhere for the war effort.

By the end of 1940-41 a lot of hard work had gone into creating a web of strongly defended areas throughout Sussex, even though many had not been completed. Fixed defences take time to build, some were poorly sited and some planned were never even started. The Home Guard took many over as guards and served a useful purpose in releasing the field army for more important tasks.

In July 1940, Ironside was replaced by General Alanbrooke who disagreed with the building of fixed defensive lines and the bunker mentality it encouraged. He and his generals, notably Montgomery and Padget, preferred light (and expendable) forces on the coast to delay an invasion, and aggressive tactics by highly mobile reserve forces of infantry and armour to attack the landing places and prevent a beachhead being established. He did not rule out using mustard gas if the coast could not be held and Churchill had already sanctioned setting fire to the sea around troops being landed on the shoreline. Because they existed the strategy of making use of fixed defended localities continued for some time until eventually Alanbrooke acquired the resources not available to his predecessor, and was able to train and build up the strong reserves he wanted to implement his more flexible plans for defeating an invasion.

German Plans for a Landing in Sussex

Shortly after the end of the war British and American intelligence officers found a collection of documents headed "Minutes of the Fuehrer Conferences on Naval Affairs" in archives stored in the forests of Tambach Dietharz in North West Germany. The papers consisted of minutes of meetings between Hitler and commanders of the German armed forces relating to Operation Sealion and other matters.

There were many changes in the plans for the invasion of England. After translation into English the documents were edited with the inclusion of information from other German sources and admiralty records.

The following extract of decisions taken relate directly to Sussex:-

The Fuehrer and Supreme Commander has decided that a landing in England is possible, providing air superiority can be attained and certain other necessary conditions fulfilled. The date of commencement is still undecided. All preparations are to begin immediately.
(Order from Field Marshall Keitel. Chief of Staff at the Supreme Command Fuehrer's Headquarters 2nd July 1940). ***Page 61***

The landing operation must be a surprise crossing on a broad front extending approximately from Ramsgate to a point west of the Isle of Wight. The invasion will be referred to by the code name Sealion.
(Directive No 16 from the Fuehrer and Supreme Commander of the Wehrmacht dated 16th July 1940 and signed Hitler and initialled by Keitel and Jodl). ***Page 67***

The Commander in Chief Navy, having reported on 31st July that the necessary preparations for Sealion could not be completed before September 15th the Fuehrer has ordered that preparations are to be continued, and must be completed by the Army and Air Force by that day.

In spite of the Navy's warning that they can only guarantee the defence of a narrow strip of coast (as far west as Eastbourne) preparations are to be continued for the attack on a broad basis as originally planned.
(Supreme Command, Fuehrer's Headquarters dated 1st August 1940. Signed Keitel) **Page 81**

The General Staff, Army, has asked for a simultaneous strong landing in the Brighton area, consolidated with sufficient speed. The success of such an undertaking cannot be guaranteed, however. The naval staff comment as follows on the various conclusions of the General Staff:- simultaneous landing operations near Brighton in the west and Deal in the east cannot be carried out.
(Views of the Naval staff on the memorandum of the C. in C. Army. Sachniewind, (Chief of Naval Staff) 14th August 1940) **Page 84**

On August 15th the following decision was made by the Fuehrer: Preparation for Sealion to take place on September 15th 1940 are to be continued. Dispositions should be made in such a matter as not to exclude the possibility of an attack on a narrow front; should this be ordered at the last minute and to leave open the possibility of a single landing in the Brighton area.
(Supreme Command. Fuehrer's Headquarters, Signed Keitel 16th August 1940).

A further directive followed stating: the main crossing to be on a narrow front with simultaneous landing of 4-5,000 troops at Brighton by motor boats.

In the end it was decided that four divisions would be landed at Brighton in the first instance, and additional troops would follow if the situation permitted.

On August 27th final decisions were made. Landings were to take place in four main areas: *Folkestone to Dungeness; Dungeness to Cliff End (Hastings); Bexhill to Beachy Head; Brighton to Selsey Bill.*

The first operational objective of the army was a line drawn from Southampton to the mouth of the Thames embracing all of Kent and Sussex. **Page 85**

The Fuehrer has decided that from now until the Spring of 1941 preparations for Sealion shall be continued solely for the purpose of maintaining political and military pressure on England.
(Fuehrer's headquarters. Keitel. 12th October 1940). **Page 103**

An acknowledgement of the Sussex Defences

The time and effort put into converting beaches, towns and villages into strongly defended areas and resistance points was not entirely wasted and may have helped to make the German High Command pause before starting an invasion. Their intelligence services sent a report to the Naval staff in September 1940 and included a warning about the Sussex coast: the area Tunbridge Wells to Beachy Head, especially the small town of Rye and also St Leonards is distinguished by a special labyrinth of defences. These are so well camouflaged that a superficial observer would not discover anything extraordinary. This area is extremely well guarded. In Hastings most of the defences can be recognised quite plainly. In the town the presence of troops and light and heavy tanks is most striking. Numerous armoured cars are also seen in St Leonards. It is probable that at this date the strength of defences were over stated, but it gave everyone much needed time and within a few months the chances of successfully resisting an invasion were stronger.

The accompanying illustrations include some of the very early, and often obsolete, armoured vehicles seen in Sussex at the start of the emergency and surviving plans of Nodal points ordered by General Ironside.

History

By the Spring of 1941 Hitler and his staff were deeply involved in preparations for the invasion of Russia. Sealion was shelved indefinitely.

Hitler died in his bunker in Berlin. Both Field Marshall Keitel, (Chief of the German High Command) and General Jodl, (Chief of Operations) were found guilty of war crimes at the Nuremberg Tribunal and hanged.

1.1 A standard Beaverette armoured car. It was named after Lord Beaverbrook and produced in 1940. It was armed with one machine gun. There were many similar versions manufactured

1.2. An armoured car stationed at a rather pathetic road block

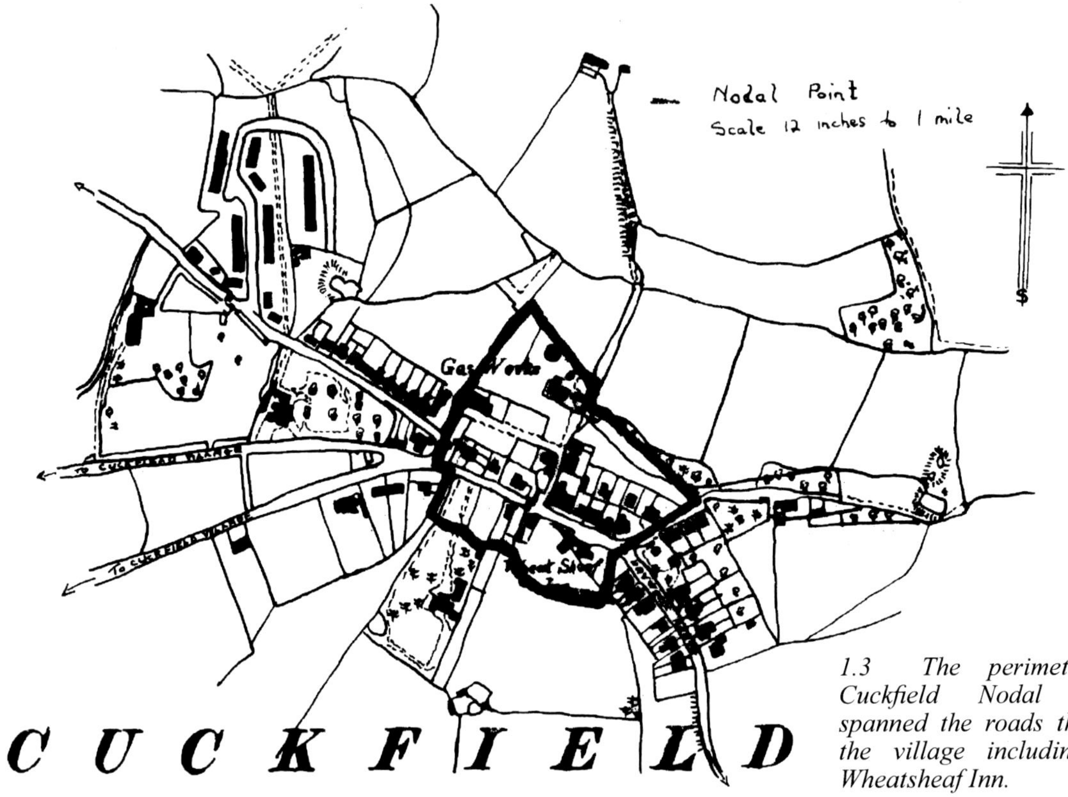

1.3 The perimeter of Cuckfield Nodal Point spanned the roads through the village including the Wheatsheaf Inn.

1.4 Littlehampton Nodal Point had four sectors (A-D). Slit trenches and other strong points were grouped in self supporting patterns.

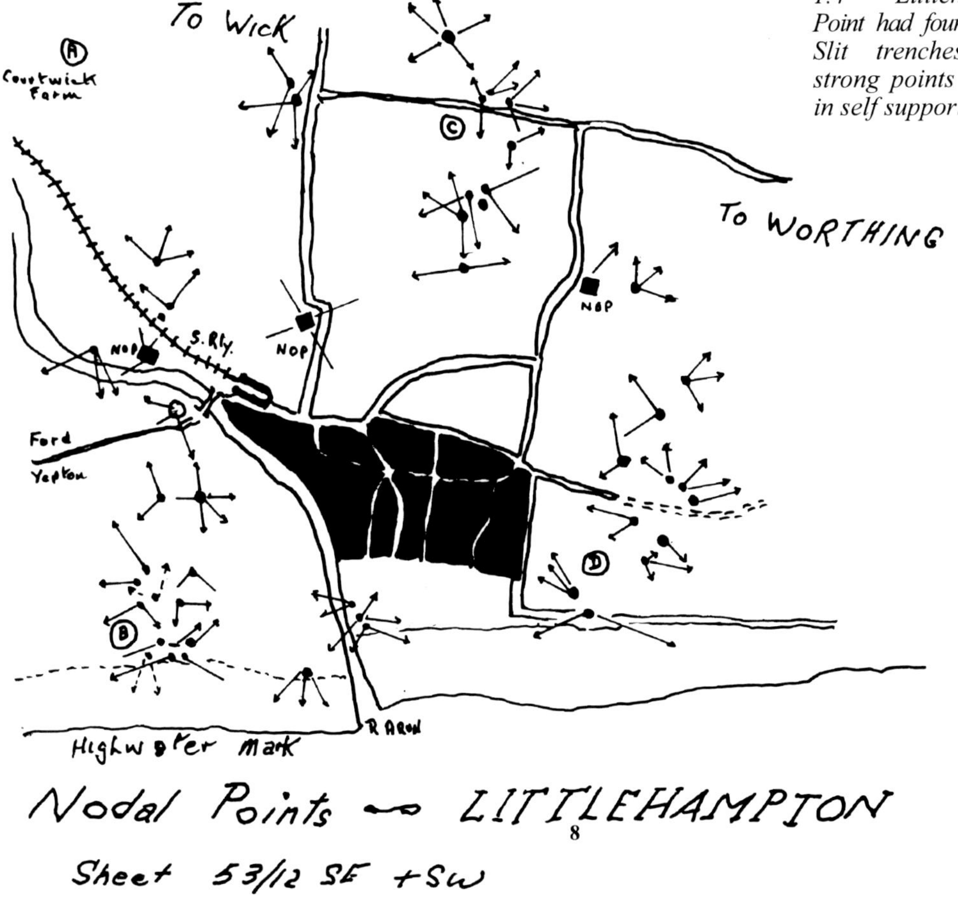

1.5 The commander of a later version of the 1920 Rolls Royce Mark I armoured car with a single .303 Vickers machine gun seeks directions on a country road.

1.6 Infantry of 5th Kings Regiment in machine gun positions inside the ruins of Pevensey castle in 1941.

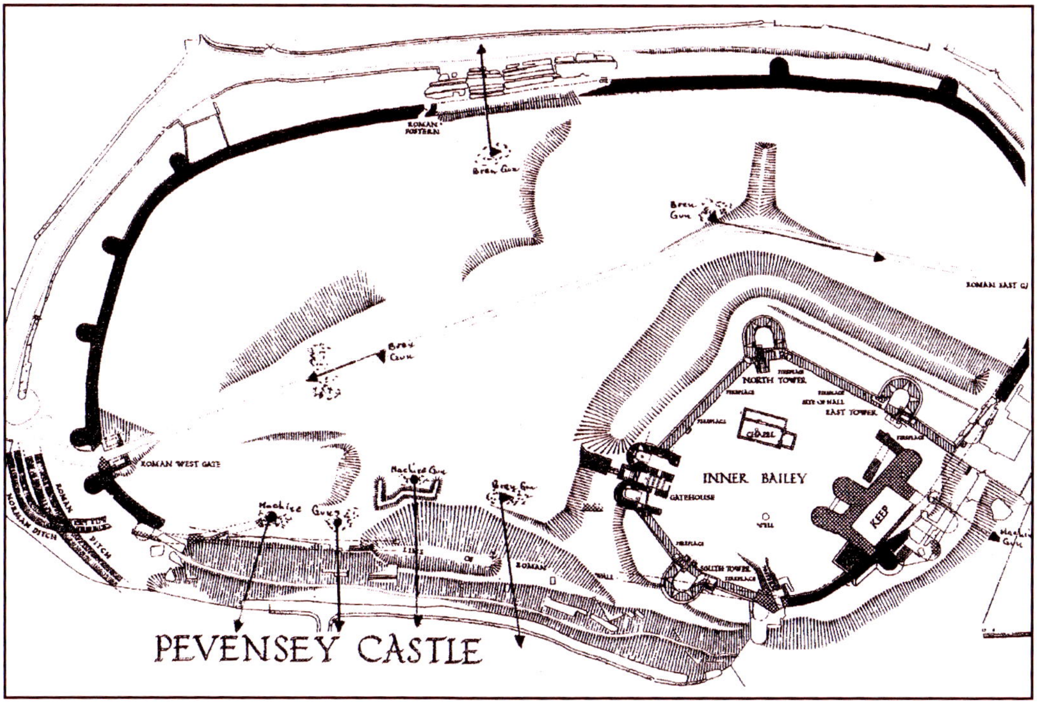

1.7 The long black slits in the walls of Pevensey Castle are for machine guns and rifles

1.8 A mobile Vickers machine gun on a carriage carrying 8,000 rounds of ammunition. Designed in Sussex by Major Furber of the Home Guard.

Chapter 2

GERMAN INTELLIGENCE ABOUT THE SUSSEX COAST DEFENCES

In preparation for 'Sealion', code name for the invasion of Britain, the planning staff issued many documents to army commanders. One such document was Copy No 005730 issued by the German High Command, General Staff, Division West, entitled, "Specification and Technical Data of the English Fortifications and Defences". Dated 30th August 1940 it is marked 'Secret' (Geheim) and its purpose was to give army commanders some idea of the defences that would await them on landing on the South Coast. The text includes brief details of British tanks, their armament, infantry, transport and the guns used in beach defences. There are also fifty-five photographs taken either at ground level or from the air. Unfortunately these are of such poor quality that with their annotations they are unsuitable for reproduction here. The words show obstacles; road blocks, anti-tank ditches, and machine gun positions and in some instances are probably guesses by the interpreters. There are also drawings of coast batteries, pill boxes, anti-aircraft positions and searchlights. Even the Martello Towers in East Sussex are mentioned although these are referred to as old works.

Twelve of the pictures are of Sussex and Dungeness, all taken from the air.

On Dungeness suspected minefields and batteries are marked as are barbed wire fences and machine gun posts along the old military canal which exits at Cliff End in the Pett marshes. North of Rye tanks are identified although comments were made that they may have been silhouettes to deceive.

At St John's Cross, north of Hastings, anti-tank ditches and blocks were spotted to turn the road junction into a securely defended area.

A photograph of Eastbourne pier shows it cut in half to prevent it being used for landing infantry and lines of blocks along the sea front are marked. Views of nearby East Dean show similar defence works. The valley behind Cuckmere Haven shows up clearly as ploughed land although curious Z shaped furrows or tracks defy explanation. The fields and high ground behind the port of Newhaven are described as unsuitable for gliders because of obstructions.

The quality of the intelligence given in this document is not high and there are no reports that commando units visited Sussex to examine the strength of the defences, the tides and the suitability of the landing areas. If they had they might have been surprised by gaps in the preparedness of the army and defences. What they did not under estimate was the difficulties of crossing the English Channel and the uncertainty of sea and weather. This made the German navy very cautious about the undertaking without complete air superiority, which was promised to Hitler by Reichsmarschall Goring but never achieved.

To familiarize British infantry on the coast with German assault troops the War Office issued pictures of the enemy and some of those are reproduced here.

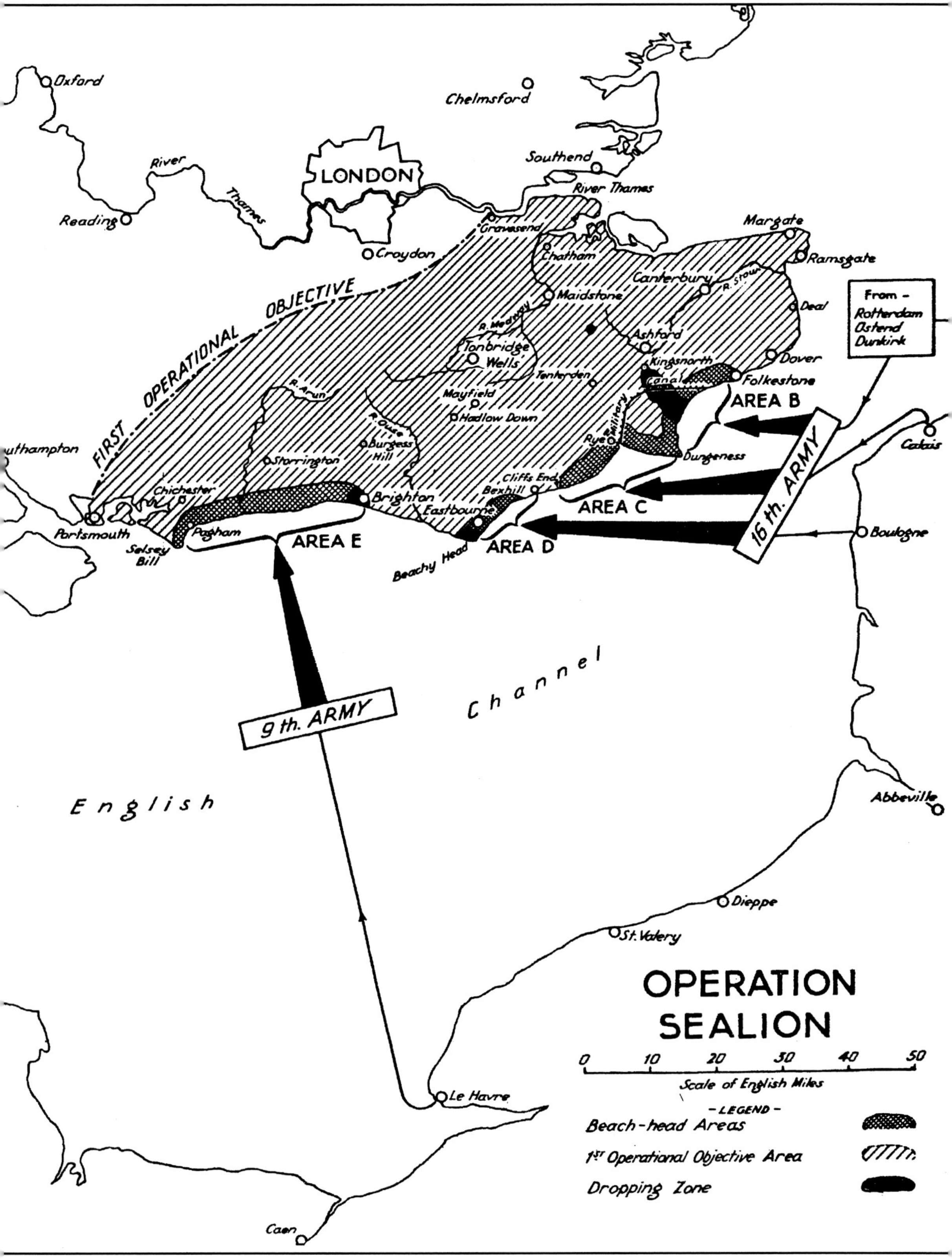
OPERATION SEALION
Oxford
Chelmsford
Southend
River Thames
LONDON
River Thames
Reading
Gravesend
Croydon
Chatham
Margate
Ramsgate
Canterbury
R. Stour
Maidstone
Deal
FIRST OPERATIONAL OBJECTIVE
R. Medway
Ashford
Tonbridge Wells
Dover
Kingsnorth
Tenterden
Canal
Folkestone
R. Arun
Mayfield
Military
Hadlow Down
AREA B
From - Rotterdam Ostend Dunkirk
R. Ouse
Burgess Hill
Rye
Dungeness
Calais
Southampton
Storrington
Cliffs End
Chichester
Bexhill
Brighton
Eastbourne
16 th. ARMY
AREA C
Portsmouth
Pagham
Selsey Bill
AREA E
AREA D
Boulogne
Beachy Head
Channel
9 th. ARMY
English
Abbeville
Dieppe
St. Valery
0 10 20 30 40 50
Scale of English Miles
- LEGEND -
Beach-head Areas
1st Operational Objective Area
Dropping Zone
Le Havre
Caen

← 2.1 Operation Sealion planned for the landing of two complete German armies along on the Sussex coast between Selsey Bill and Dungeness.

2.2 A corporal of the German 15th Infantry Regiment in Field Service uniform and wearing a ribbon of the Iron Cross Class 2 in his button hole.

2.3 This is a heavy (15cm) close support gun for German infantry. It is recognizable by its old fashioned appearance and is often mistaken for divisional artillery.

2.4 This portable flame thrower was operated by two men and had a range of 5-25 yards. It was used to attack loop holes in pill boxes, in 12 second bursts

2.5 A group of German parachute troops in full kit but without parachutes. They were armed with automatic pistols for the jump

Chapter 3

THE INFANTRY BEHIND THE BEACHES

In the years leading up to WW 2 the British mainland was split for military command purposes into six geographical areas. Sussex was part of Eastern Command which curiously stretched from the Wash in Norfolk to Portsmouth in Hampshire. The decision to include the South Coast in such a large and unwieldy area was probably due to economy in military budgets and the absence of any serious threat of invasion for over one hundred years.

Following the fall of France in May 1940 the forces in Eastern Command were separated as follows, the most likely vulnerable invasion coast of Kent and Sussex being less well protected with fewer troops.

On the East Coast (about 69,000 men)

Four infantry and one armoured divisions.

South of the River Thames (about 45,000 men)

Chatham and Maidstone to Rye about 14,000 men (1st London Division)

Rye to Thorney Island about 14,000 men (45th Infantry Division)

In Hampshire about 17,000 men (52nd Division) were held in reserve.

General Alanbrooke, who became Chief of the General Staff in the critical summer of 1940, did not like the tactical problems this separation of Eastern Command into two parts caused. The River Thames split the area making the movement of troops to any threatened part of the coast too difficult and slow. He was also doubtful about the fighting leadership of General Charles Williams whose background was entirely as an engineer and who he thought was too set on building lines of concrete defences which locked up troops they did not have. Alanbrooke split Eastern Command in two by creating a separate South Eastern Command for Kent and Sussex, and he put General Padget in whom he had more confidence in charge.

A year later the British Army re-equiped and undergoing extensive retraining under new commanders, one of whom was General Montgomery, was in a much stronger position to resist an invasion. The infantry and armoured divisions in and around Sussex were;-

38th Welsh Infantry Division, (about 17,000 men)

55th (West Lancashire) Infantry Division, (about 17,000 men)

29th Independent Infantry Brigade, (about 3,000 men)

1st Canadian Division, (about 17,000 men)

2nd Canadian Division, (about 17,000 men)

1st Armoured Division, (about 11,000 men)

1st Army Tank Brigade, (about 600 men)

25th Army Tank Brigade, (about 600 men)

31st Army Tank Brigade, (about 600 men)

Thus the number of fighting troops, tank crews, artillery men, drivers and personnel of the other support services in Sussex at this time totalled well over 100,000 men. It goes without saying that a single division occupied many square miles of countryside and all vacant buildings, private and public were taken over for army use.

War Office policy had an authorised War Establishment of the men and equipment needed by each army formation to do its job. Although actual numbers fell short from time to time for various reasons some idea of the amount of warlike equipment concentrated in Sussex for its defence is given below.

The Infantry Division

The 38th Welsh Infantry Division was one of three divisions spread across West Sussex in

1941. There were 17,000 men in nine battalions. Each battalion had three brigades. The division was responsible for the defence of the county stretching from Selsey Bill to Newhaven between the South Downs and the sea. Its artillery included three field regiments with seventy-two 25 pounder guns, forty-eight 2 pounder anti-tank guns and forty-eight 40 millimetre mobile anti-aircraft guns.

The troops were armed with 13,000 rifles and carbines, 2,000 pistols, and 819 Bren and Vickers machine guns. There were 218 two and three inch mortars which were carried by patrols.

Divisional transport included 1,064 motor cycles for despatch riders and 554 cars, reconnaissance vehicles, carriers and ambulances. For the transportation of ammunition, food and stores there was a fleet of 2,000 lorries and trucks; 3-ton lorries and 15-cwt trucks being the most numerous. Also within the divisional area were six light aid detachments, command and control headquarters, ordnance workshops, mobile bath units, field hygiene sections ambulances and a postal unit.

All over Sussex the men were accommodated in hastily built tented or hutted camps. Empty properties, hotels and houses of which there were many in the coastal region were requisitioned. Billets were arranged in private houses; residents with spare rooms being required to take one or two soldiers for which standard rent allowances were paid. Many British and Canadian soldiers slept at night in houses in Worthing, Brighton and Hastings, but went out to army messes where army cooks prepared meals. Church halls and large houses were taken over for unit headquarters staff, medical and signal centres.

Canadian Army Forces

The first Canadian troops arrived in Britain in January 1940 and were quartered around Aldershot. By Christmas the 2nd Canadian Infantry Division had arrived in stages and the 3rd Canadian Infantry Division and the 1st Army Tank Brigade followed in 1941. There was subsequently some reorganisation of corps and commands. Three battalions of the 2nd Canadian Infantry Division took over responsibility for the defence of the East Sussex beaches from the British 55th Division in September 1940. By the end of the following year Canadian battalions had moved into most areas of both East and West Sussex. The 1st Canadian Infantry Division was to remain in Sussex until 1943, when they went overseas to take part in the Eight Army assault on Sicily.

The Home Guard

An appeal from the Government for all men between the ages of 17 and 65 to volunteer for military training in a new force the Local Defence Volunteers, later renamed the Home Guard, was made in May 1940. The Germans had made great use of a Fifth Column - persons to spread rumour and fear and disrupt communications - when they had over run Holland and Belgium. Paratroops and gliders had landed before the advancing troops to capture key points such as bridges and airfields. The purpose of the Home Guard was to mobilise all males not in the armed services and to give them weapons and training so that they could support the army and fight as necessary under the direction of the field army commanders. As they knew their own locality well their task was to relieve the army of protecting vulnerable points against sabotage, and to help out in watching the coast and to patrol the countryside. The Home Guard was organised into battalions of about 1600 men broken down into companies, platoons and sections. The battalion strength varied over time according to the numbers of men fit and available in the district. Home Guard soldiers had to fit their training and guard duties in with their day jobs (often involving war work, travel and overtime) which meant that attendance was sometimes patchy. In December 1941 all fit males between 18 and 51 not otherwise engaged on war duties were compelled to register for the Home Guard and this substantially increased their numbers. There were eleven general service battalions of Home Guard (potentially nearly 18,000 men) whose boundaries included the Sussex coast. Twice this number of battalions served in and around inland towns in the county manning road blocks and patrolling the countryside.

The Home Guard kept their uniforms, weapons and ammunition at home, and since few had telephones they were called out by local alarm arrangements or by the ringing of church bells, although this was looked upon as unreliable because of the danger of false alarms through human error. Not surprisingly given the general apprehension of the times false alarms and mistakes made commanders very jittery. My own experience illustrates this point. As a youth of 17 I was on guard duty at the main post office and at 2 am it became necessary to unlock the gates to let in the night mail van. Unfortunately I pressed the bell for an invasion alarm and a lot of sleepy and irate postmen had to rise from their beds in the guardroom. The guard commander was not pleased.

Although full of enthusiasm for their role the Home Guard was poorly equipped, untrained and probably ineffective in its very early days. Had an invasion happened those units on the coast would have been expendable. By the time proper weapons and training were provided the threat of invasion had greatly diminished. They gradually undertook more specialised tasks and from August 1942 were manning some of the six inch gun batteries on the Sussex coast.

No reliable published figures exist of the number of Home Guard recruited in Sussex, or involved in the defence of the coastal strip. The number changed over time as men were called up for the army, or discharged on health or age grounds, although there was an increase after December 1941 when a form of compulsory direction was introduced. However, in Sussex there were 26 battalions with a potential enlistment of about 40,000 men and even if there were fewer on the ground it was a useful manpower addition. Home Guard commanders worked closely with the field army in their area and came under their orders in an emergency.

Training for Battle

Training the infantry to fight whether regular soldiers, conscripted civilians or Home Guard has always been done by the issue of instructional pamphlets and manuals approved by the Army Council and issued by the War Office. Many thousands of these were issued during WW 2 covering every aspect of weapons equipment and warfare. Only by the issue of these publications could those in charge ensure that fighting and killing the enemy was done effectively. As the introduction to one manual put it, "It is better to know instinctively some orthodox line of action than to be paralysed by the uncertainty of what to do."

Were the forces in Sussex sufficient to resist an invasion?

General Alanbrooke who took charge from General Ironside wanted many more infantry and tank divisions than he had to ensure that no German invasion force could land and establish a bridgehead on the coast. He was not to get them. Discussions over this issue by the Chiefs-of-Staff continued throughout 1941-42. In the end defence needs overseas took priority and new intelligence assessments led to a reduction in the possibility of an invasion threat.

The photographs which follow show some aspects of the army and Home Guard presence in Sussex during the expected invasion years.

3.1 Infantry and Worthing Home Guard in an anti invasion exercise near the Pier in August 1941.

3.2 Southwick Home Guard with their Northover projector, which fires hand grenades.

3.3 An example of a defended locality around a wood with trenches, wire and machine gun positions.

3.4 A brick pill box for infantry built into the banks of Broad Rife near Selsey Bill.

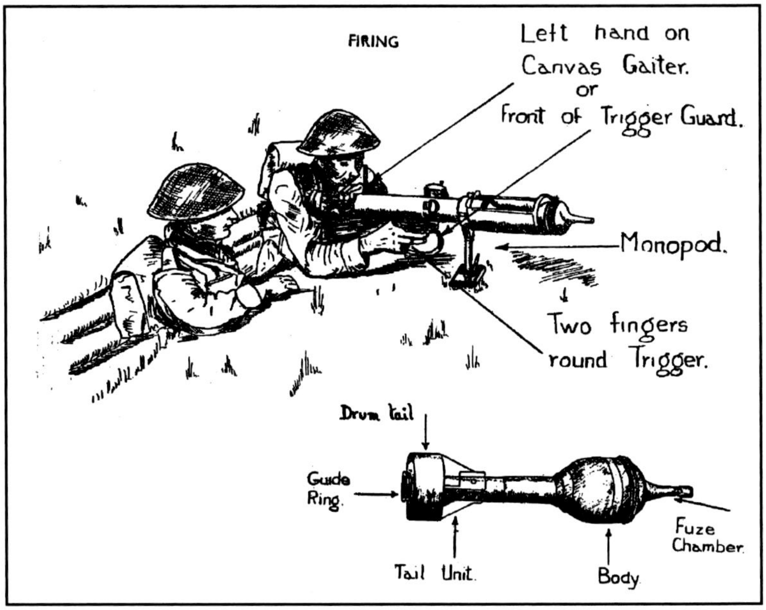

3.5 A PIAT gun. An effective anti-tank weapon carried by one man. The bomb weighed one kilo and had a range of 350 yards (320 metres).

3.6 An infantryman armed with a Bren gun and the load he was expected to carry into action.

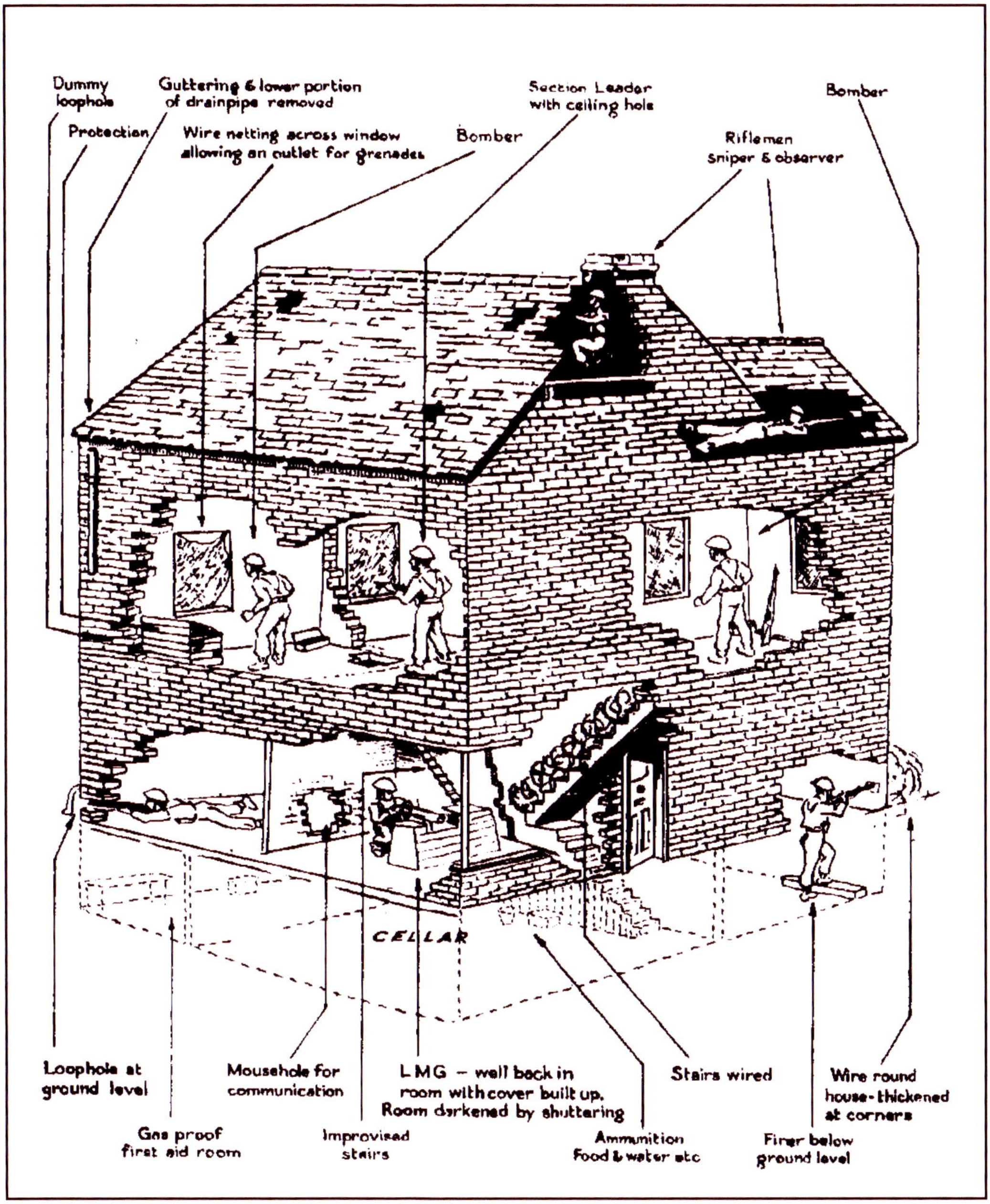

3.7 Fieldcraft. Buildings can be made into strong points and defended by infantry with rifles and machine guns.

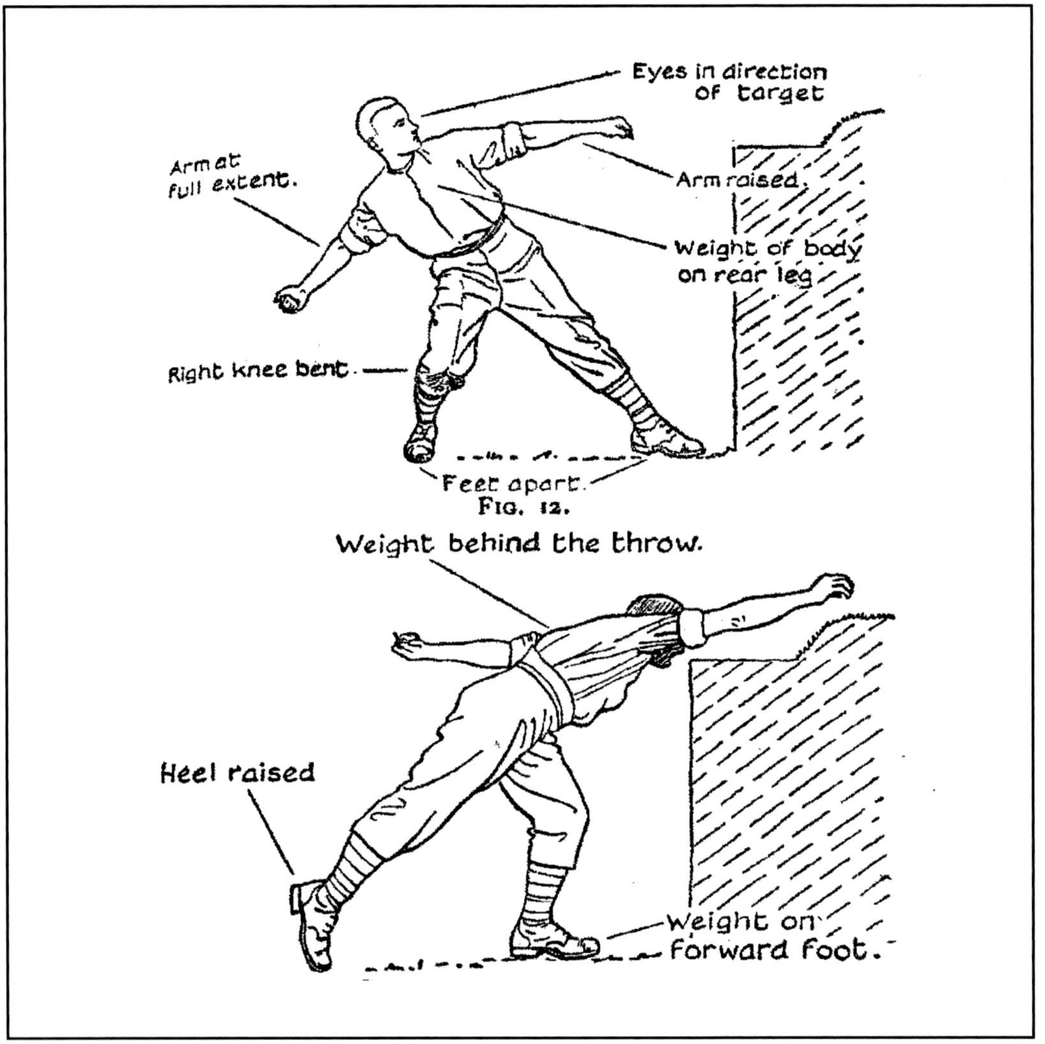

3.8 The soldier pulls out the safety pin and lobs the hand grenade at the target. The striker lever flies off when the grenade leaves his hand and fragments within 7 seconds. A quick thinking enemy might just have time to throw it back

3.9 Troops from the 5th Worthing (Post Office) Home Guard during a Sunday morning exercise.

3.10 Soldiers with rifles and a Bren gun on sentry duty on the cliffs at Birling Gap.

Chapter 4

ARMOURED DIVISIONS AND TANK BRIGADES

In June 1940 an assessment of the availability of armoured units to repulse an invasion force moving inland from the beaches was not good. About one third of the total strength of 600 cruiser and infantry tanks had been lost or left in France. There was a shortage of trained tank crews. It was calculated that it would not be until September that the factories could make good the loss. Training up the crews with battle experience would take longer. What was left in the meantime were 110 infantry tanks, 103 Cruiser tanks and 600 light tanks of doubtful value. There were also 132 older tanks which were obsolete or of doubtful reliability.

The Armoured Division

Deployed across the Sussex and Hampshire borders the 1st Armoured Division settled down to regroup ready to move closer to the coast. Within the Division were two armoured brigades, six armoured regiments and six light aid detachments. In support were anti-aircraft and anti-tank regiments and some motorised infantry and artillery units. The Light Aid Detachments attached to both infantry and armoured divisions were small mobile workshops capable of making minor repairs and recovering vehicles from the battlefield.

The fighting strength of an armoured division in 1940 was supposed to be 13,000 men if manned up to its full War Establishment complement. There were 342 Cruiser and close support tanks which were either Crusader, Valentine or Matildas mostly armed with 2-pounder guns. In addition there were 88 Universal (Bren gun) Carriers and 125 reconnaissance cars and light tanks of various obsolete types. The Divisional artillery, when at full strength, amounted to sixteen 25-pounder guns; 328 2-pounder anti-tank guns, thirty- six three inch howitzers and their associated trailers, limbers and quads, (gun towing vehicles).

Army Tank Brigades

The 1st (Regular Army) 25th (Territorial) and 31st (new) Army Tank Brigades served in South Eastern Command during 1941. The 31st Tank Brigade was stationed at Eastbourne, the others elsewhere across Sussex and Hampshire. All took part in large scale training exercises throughout the region. Units, including those of the Canadian Army were moved in and out of the county at the direction of their respective army commanders.

A tank brigade had a War Establishment of about 600 men and 178-202 tanks armed usually with two pounder guns. Infantry or (I) tanks were heavily armoured for attacking defended positions in close co-operation with infantry, speed being sacrificed for armoured protection.

The photographs supporting this chapter show the tanks and armoured vehicles encountered in the lanes and fields of Sussex during the 1940s. Many of these photographs were taken on exercises in South Eastern Command and have a censor's stamp and comments on the back. Because of war time security locations were not always clearly identified.

Particular attention was given to conceal tanks and lorries from air attack and and most vehicles carried heavy bundles of camouflage nets into which were sewn fluttering strips of material which helped to hide their shape. Dispersal of units and their transport over a wide area was necessary to avoid destruction from air attacks. Trees, hedgerows, public parks and woodlands were favourite places of concealment. Even today cracked and chipped kerb stones in towns and villages are a reminder of where tanks manoeuvred through narrow streets, seventy years ago.

Most of the tank manoeuvres in wartime Sussex were carried out on the South Downs. The cliff tops in East Sussex were particularly suitable for firing exercises as misdirected shots would land in the sea. Many concrete roads found on downland today were built to move tanks to exercise areas. Hard standing platforms hidden in woods were used for the same purpose or as a base for Nissen huts for tank crews.

4.1 Mark II (I) tanks of 44 Battalion, Royal Tank Regiment, perched on the cliff top at Seaford Head. The cliffs of the Severn sisters form a backdrop.

4.2 A squadron of cruiser B tanks crossing a hillside at the back of Seaford in 1941.

4.3 Sussex folk were used to seeing their village green and narrow lanes chock a block with Matilda tanks, Bren gun carriers and army lorries. This scene in October 1941 was commonplace. Probably the convoy had lost its way?

4.4 A Medium tank Mark II with the driver's hatch open parked on a country road somewhere outside Lewes in the Ouse valley.

4.5 A Cruiser tank on a bend, possibly at Houghton, West Sussex in February 1941. An armoured reconnaissance vehicle and staff car are parked in the background.

4.6 A squadron of I tanks (for infantry support) move rapidly along a rough track towards Cissbury Ring on the South Downs in the summer of 1940.

4.7 A Matilda MK2 tank with others awaiting orders to move out from the edge of a wood.

Chapter 5

ARTILLERY, RAIL GUNS, AND ARMOURED TRAINS

Until the early part of 1940, there were no guns on or behind the Sussex coast except for those in Newhaven Fort. Moreover those artillery regiments which later struggled back from Dunkirk with or without their guns were in a weakened state.

At that time there was widespread fear, even panic by both generals and public, of enemy parachute divisions landing inland behind the coast. This leap frogging tactic had been extremely successful in the German advance across Europe. In Sussex this led to the creation of infantry stop lines, and artillery being positioned to cover places where gliders or parachutists might come down. To fill the gaps between the newly formed six inch gun batteries on the coast field guns were sited in a static anti-tank role while mobile anti-tank guns were locked up in pill boxes .

By July 1940 with determined new army commanders, (Alanbrooke and Montgomery), and the regiments having begun to sort themselves out after Dunkirk, the army's overall fighting organisation and capacity to fight had improved. The Chief of the General Staff issued Artillery Instruction No 3, part cautionary, part advisory, but with the intent of moving artillery priorities from a standing defensive role to a mobile offensive one. In other words to back up infantry counter attacks. The new advice to commands was that where local circumstances permitted, field and medium artillery were to make full use of their range, shell power and mobility to support infantry engaged in throwing any invading force back into the sea. Heavy artillery was to be kept inland several miles from the beaches to give defensive fire to support to an area under attack. Anti-tank guns were to be put on beaches to replace mobile guns which were be used instead to defend communication centres or junctions on roads leading inland from the coast. Mobile anti-tank guns were not expected to be used in a static role, but were to form a mobile reserve with positions reconnoitred and prepared in rear areas.

As to the type of artillery immediately available for the defence of Kent and Sussex, many of the guns were survivors from the 1914-18 war. They included, 18 pounders, old 18 pounders converted to 25 pounders, and a small number of new 25 pounder guns. Additionally there were some French 75 mm field guns brought back from France. There were also 4.5 howitzers which although due for replacement had been repaired. Medium artillery consisted of old 60 pounders which had been refurbished.

Each infantry division in the coastal areas had a fire plan. When the 38th Welsh Division moved into West and part of East Sussex early in 1941 they took over from 47th Division and adopted their fire plan, which had already been worked out and which complied with Artillery Instruction No 3 for the more effective use of artillery.

From east to west, the guns were kept back from the coast in front of the South Downs, or on their lower slopes. Their task was to support infantry engaging the enemy especially any who had landed behind the coast and penetrated inland. In many cases it was not practical for them to bring down effective fire onto the beaches, but where enemy armour had advanced and were in sight they were under orders to stop them by direct fire over open sights. Along the coast, were some 4 inch, 3 inch, and 6 pounder guns also manned by field artillery gunners and their role was to engage any vessels, barges and tanks approaching the beach. These guns fired at ranges up to 1000 yards and needed supporting infantry to prevent them being over run.

The chart at the end of this chapter shows the fire power of the artillery of the 47th Infantry Division in February 1941 in three sectors of West Sussex. It shows their numbered battle positions and the area upon which accurate fire could be brought down. Their battle positions are further explained below.

Eastern Sector: Brighton to Lewes

Units in this sector: 138 Field Regiment, RA (four batteries)

21 Brighton Golf course: four 4.5 howitzers

22 On the Downs around Devil's Dyke Hotel: four 75 mm guns
23 Whitehawk: four 75 mm guns
24 Kingston near Lewes: four 4.5 howitzers

Centre Sector: Littlehampton to Shoreham-by-Sea

Units in this sector: 114 Field Regiment, RA (four batteries)
11 Cross Bush near Arundel: two 75 mm guns
12 Ecclesden Common near Patching: four 75 mm guns
13 Cissbury, north of Worthing: four 4.5 howitzers: two 75 mm guns
14 Annington Hill, near Lancing: four 4.5 howitzers
15 Lancing Hill: four 75 mm guns

Western Sector: Selsey Bill to Bognor

Units in this sector: 117 Field Regiment, RA (four batteries)
1 Earnley Grange: four 4.5 howitzers
2 Vicinity of Pagham harbour: four 75 mm guns
3 Brambles Farm. Sidlesham: four 75 mm guns
4 Near North End Yapton: four 4.5 howitzers

Reserve Batteries

Batteries of 75 mm guns were sited at Chilgrove and Henfield with four 4.5 howitzers behind the South Downs at Storrington.

The 47th Infantry Division and its artillery moved out of the area in April 1941 and the 38th Infantry Division replaced it and although they kept to the fire plan, the units and their armament changed.

Heavy Artillery

Further back from the sea, batteries of super heavy artillery were ranged on vital places on the coast. In West Sussex 14th Super Heavy battery arrived from Wareham (Dorset) and was encamped in Oaklands Park, Chichester where the Festival Theatre now stands. Its purpose was to neutralise the airfield on Thorney Island nine miles away if it was captured by troop carrying gliders. In late 1941 these guns were replaced by two 12 inch railway guns on sleighs at Chichester railway station. Railway guns were not armoured, they were put on special low railway mountings with several pairs of bogies. The Chichester train, consisting of engine, accommodation and ammunition wagons, stood on specially built spur lines. Three firing positions were on the north side of the main line, slightly west of the station. Two new sidings were built, one close to the station and the other on the south side near Terminus Road. This latter one seems to have followed the line of the Selsey tramway which ceased to function in 1935.

Rail guns also travelled along the now disused line from Chichester to Midhurst where they had practise firings just north of Singleton station.

On the hills at the back of Arundel were two 9 inch howitzers ranged on Littlehampton harbour, its beaches, and Ford airfield about six miles distant.

In East Sussex there were more railway guns. 18th and 19th Super Heavy batteries of 12 inch howitzers had prepared firing positions at Hailsham, Hellingly, and Glynde, near Lewes. The guns were able to move around the railway system to bring down fire on the Ouse valley, Newhaven, Cuckmere Haven and the open landing beaches between Pevensey and Bexhill, all within a ten mile range. In addition heavy batteries of guns were sited on the hills behind Alfriston and ranged on the river mouth at Cuckmere Haven. Further east in Sussex on higher ground at Peasmarsh three miles inland from Rye town two 12 inch howitzers were sited to destroy enemy forces attempting to land on the low flat coastline between Fairlight at Hastings, Rye Bay and Dungeness.

Armoured Trains

Soon after the war began the War Office thought that an armoured steam train would be useful for patrolling in possible invasion areas and one was allocated to the lines on the South Coast.

An armoured train was usually made up of a tank engine, water tender and trucks, one or more each side of the engine. There was a truck at each end of the train with a pedestal mounting for a six pounder Hotchkiss Mark 2 gun with a shield to protect the gunners. The gun had a limited traverse over the cut down back of the truck. Engine, tender and trucks were protected by steel plating which was bolted on over the vital parts at the Ashford Railway works. The train also carried Bren guns which could fire through ports in the armour plating for defence against infantry attacks.

Because of the needs of normal rail traffic, the patrol limit was 30 miles and was limited by the availability of watering points. The train which first patrolled in Sussex was train F of No 2 Armoured Train Group. The steam engine which pulled it was built in 1909. Breakdowns were said to be frequent. It was manned with Royal Engineers as drivers, and men from the Royal Tank Corps as gunners. On mobilisation at Ashford Kent in 1940 its task was to support 45th Infantry Division by patrolling at night along the route, Ashford to Lewes, with a detour at Appledore down to Dungeness and back. The journey took four hours each way. After train F had made this journey six times it was transferred to Devon and replaced by train E which worked out of Tonbridge and had a wider patrol area summarised rather vaguely as "East, North East, or South East as required".

Although a hangover from its usefulness in the 1914-18 war there was some support from the military for more armoured trains, but the War Office lost interest, and decided that scarce resources could be better used elsewhere. It cancelled all outstanding orders and no more trains were built.

It might be judged that the armoured train had had its day and become military history.

The photographs illustrate some of the guns which were seen in Sussex in the 1940s. The Field Regiments of Artillery spaced out on or near the South Downs in their battle positions were ready to fire in support of troops defending the low lying beaches. The rail guns and armoured trains had more a more specialised role, but their fire power would have been useful as long as their lack of mobility did not cause them to be over run by the enemy.

5.1 A 25 pounder field gun in action. It had proved to be a good anti-tank gun in France. Superior to German guns it could fire as well as the French 75. Sjt Davies gives the order to fire.

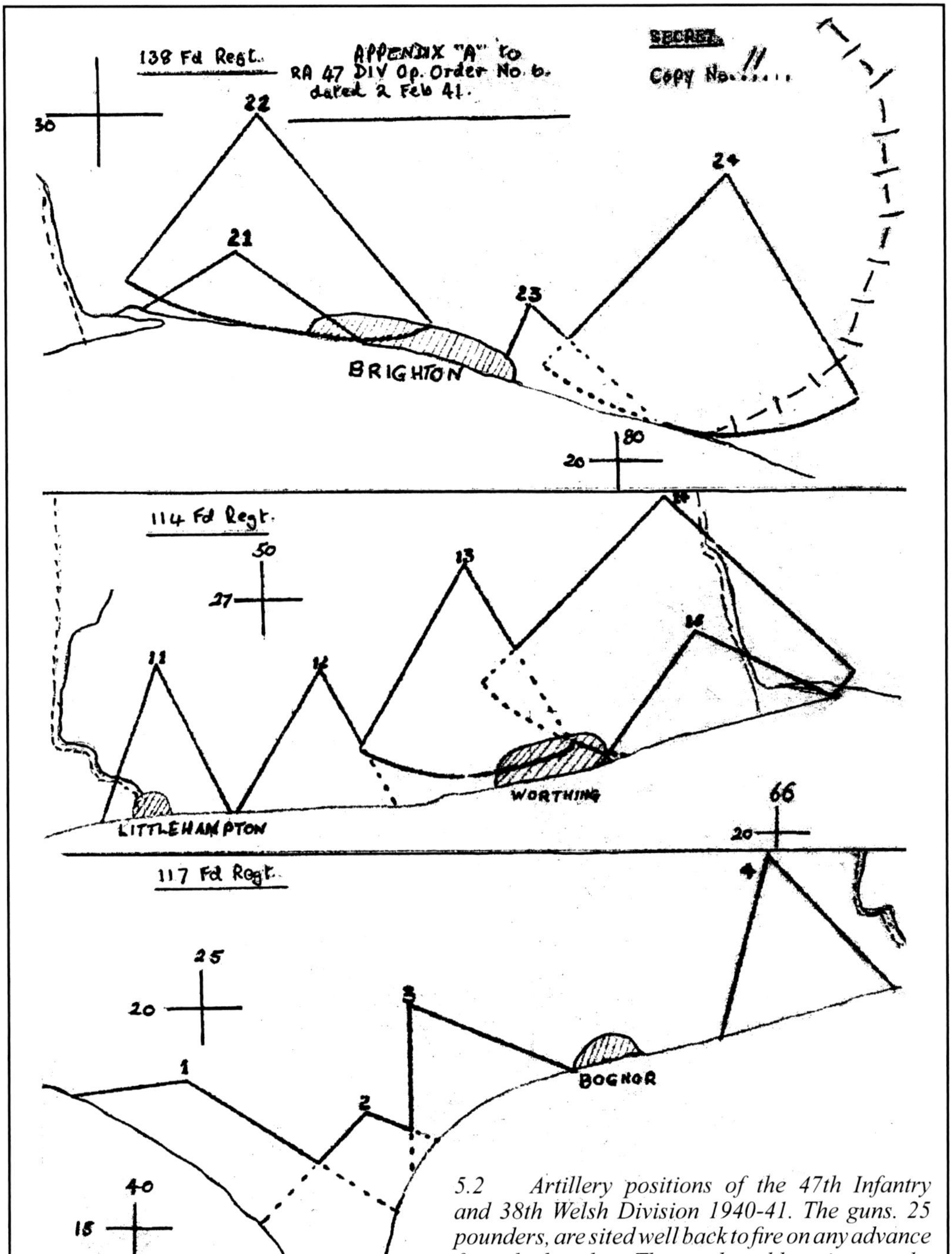

5.2 Artillery positions of the 47th Infantry and 38th Welsh Division 1940-41. The guns. 25 pounders, are sited well back to fire on any advance from the beaches. The numbered locations on the South Downs are given in Chapter 5.

5.3 Armoured Quad vehicles with bullet proof windscreens towing howitzers across a field

5.4 A universal carrier armed with a Bren gun and fitted with a radio acts as an armoured observation post for artillery. Hidden under trees near the coast

5.5 In 1940 two 9.2 howitzers stood under trees in Oaklands Park, Chichester.

5.6 In 1940 12 inch howitzer railway guns of the Super Heavy Battery moved along the lines to firing positions between Rye and Chichester.

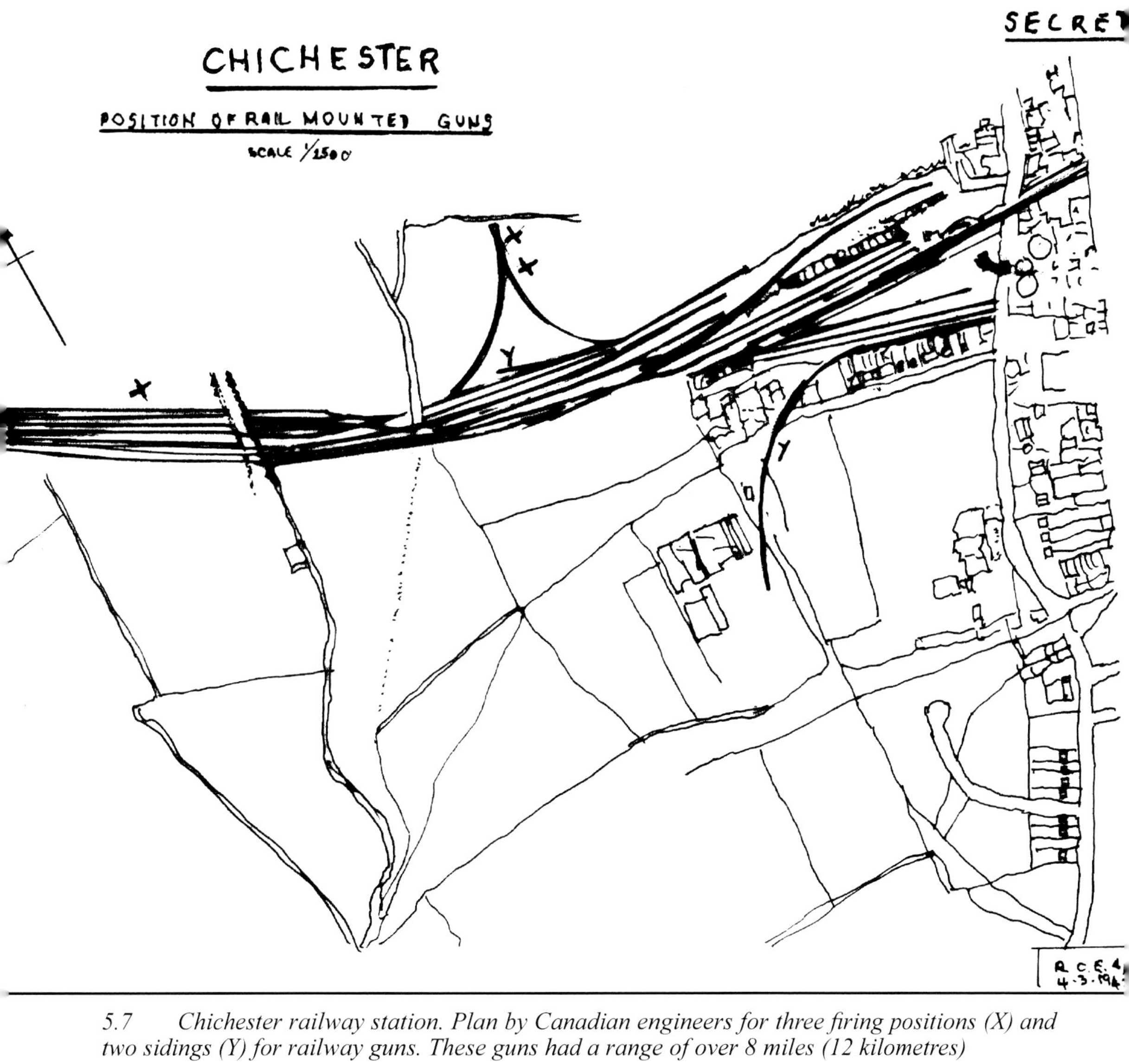

5.7 Chichester railway station. Plan by Canadian engineers for three firing positions (X) and two sidings (Y) for railway guns. These guns had a range of over 8 miles (12 kilometres)

5.8 A rail gun with its spade arms out and cables fixed to steady the gun platform as it fires

5.9 The armoured train F with a 3-inch gun front and back which patrolled along the railway lines Ashford, Dungeness and Lewes

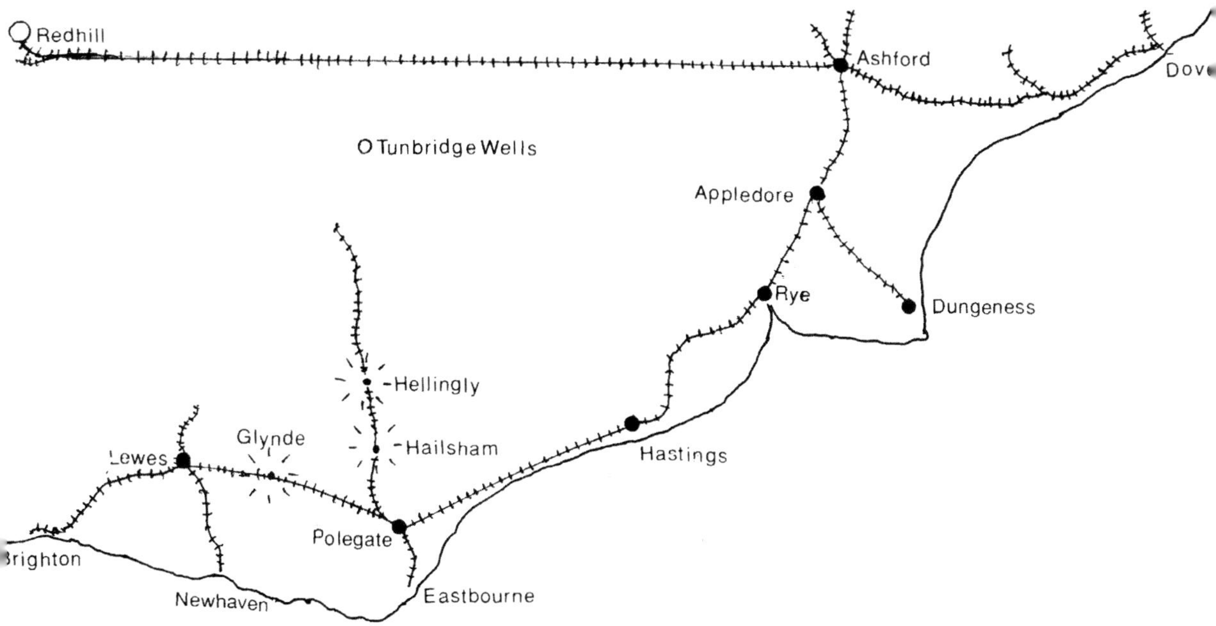

5.10 The firing positions, (starred) for 12 inch howitzer railway guns at Hailsham, Hellingly and Glynde. The patrol route of armoured train F is also shown, (see Chapter 5)

Chapter 6

DEPLOYMENT OF AN INFANTRY DIVISION: Selsey Bill to Newhaven

In April 1941 the 38th Welsh Infantry Division with its complement of men, artillery and armour replaced 47th Infantry Division and took over responsibility for defending the Sussex coast between Selsey Bill and Newhaven, and the hinterland up to the northern ramparts of the South Downs. By this date most of the fixed concrete defences (pill boxes and gun emplacements) had been built, but were falling out of favour because of the inflexibility they imposed on commanders in the field. General Montgomery, who had recently taken over, expected infantry brigades in coastal areas to hold their positions in well wired localities from which to attack. He pressed for the establishment of 'defended localities' to provide well organised defence in depth behind the coast. In his view the lack of this had led to the success of the speedy German advance through France. Much of this new thinking was included in the 38th Division Operation Order which spelt out in detail how the major part of the defence of Sussex was to be organised. It is an interesting example of how detailed Divisional Orders had to be so that every unit involved carried out their commander's orders in the way he wanted.

The Divisional objectives were:-

1 To prevent an enemy landing in Sussex
2 To annihilate any enemy within the divisional boundaries
3 To stop the enemy from reaching the South Downs.

Warning of an Invasion

It was anticipated that all units in the field would receive 48 hours warning of a serious invasion threat.

Operational Control

The area occupied by 38th Welsh Division was divided into three sectors - *Western, Central and Eastern* covering an area of approximately 600 square miles.

The available troops were allocated to these sectors :-

Western

Selsey to Littlehampton: 114th Infantry Brigade: 3 battalions on the coast.

Central

Littlehampton to Shoreham by Sea: 115th Infantry Brigade: 2 battalions on the coast and 1 battalion on the Downs.

Eastern

Shoreham by Sea to Newhaven: 113th Infantry Brigade: 2 battalions on the coast and 1 battalion on the South Downs.

Military Airfields

For the defence of Tangmere and Ford aerodromes, 140 Infantry Brigade was stationed near Chichester and its fighting troops were camped around Goodwood, Halnaker and Shopwyke.

Home Guard

When 'Action Stations' was declared, all Home Guard companies came under the authority of the army commander in the sector where the men lived.

Organisation of the Defence

First defence zone (on the coast)

In the coastal zone, the defence consisted of a series of platoon localities prepared for all round protection and sited to bring a continuous belt of fire down along the entire front.

The platoon frontages were reinforced with static machine guns and 2 inch mortars. But the long length of front to be held meant that the garrisons had to be dispersed into rifle, light machine gun and medium machine gun posts with wide gaps between. It seems that the building of pill boxes had gone too far to make any serious change possible to fit the defence strategy and so those pill boxes which were disused or not wanted were to be made to look as if occupied.

The only guns permitted to fire along fixed lines were medium machine guns sited to cover the beaches, and some in defended localities on the South Downs. Others were to be kept free so that they could be moved to wherever they were needed most.

Second zone (behind the coast up to the South Downs)

Between the sea and the South Downs infantry positions for all round defence were to be established. Their objective was:-

(a) to destroy any enemy trying to penetrate inland from the coast

(b) to prevent the enlargement of the bridgehead

(c) to secure the rear of the coastal zone (the South Downs) from attack.

The defence line to be held, which was mainly trenches, foxholes, loop holed walls and roadblocks began at Birdham on the Chichester Channel and followed the disused canal through Donnington to Barnham. It ran behind the railway line as far as the River Arun where it turned north through Lyminster, Poling, Angmering and Highdown Hill. It then roughly followed the road around the back of Worthing to Sompting, Lancing Ring, Lancing Hill, Mill Hill, Slonk Hill at Shoreham and the old fever hospital at the back of Portslade. From there the defence line went close to Port Hall, (Brighton) and on to Race Hill Farm where it turned further inland to Mount Pleasant, High Hill, and Mill Hill, overlooking the valley of the Ouse, which ran out to the sea at Newhaven.

Third zone (Chichester and along the South Downs)

This zone comprised the city of Chichester to the west of the Divisional area and the South Downs at the back of the second zone. Defended localities were protected by barbed wire and earthworks and sited on the northern edge of the Downs. Each was to be garrisoned with of one company of infantry and as many machine guns as could be made available; 2 pounder anti-tank guns were set up to protect the positions against armoured fighting vehicles (AFVs).

The positions on the Downs were to be be concealed from the air and where possible dummy ones were to be constructed to mislead the enemy. Barbed wire around positions was not be circular but was to fit in as far as possible with hedges and edges of fields and woods.

Divisional artillery

The fire plan for artillery drawn up earlier in February 1941 by the 47th Division was to be followed as far as possible; the guns of the 38th Welsh Division taking over the same positions occupied by their predecessor. As, however, the latter were better equipped with more fire power and were assisted by 5 Defence Regiment, Royal Artillery, for beach defence, they were able to provide better cover especially over likely landing places to the east and west of Littlehampton.

Defence of large towns

The inner part of large coastal towns was to be defended by local Home Guard Units. But these were not expected to be very effective and Divisional troops were to man trenches and foxholes around the perimeter of towns.

Defended Localities in the Divisional Area

Organised defended localities, stop lines and category A Nodal points (capable of resistance of six days or longer) were set out on grid lines and identified with a code letter. and are shown on a map with a short explanation as follows. Some of these planned lines of resistance were effective with concrete road blocks, pill boxes and gun positions. Other lines were less well developed and existed on paper only:-

BK - BF - BA

A 4 Corps stop line from Rudgwick ran through Horsham and Ardingly station and eastwards out of the Divisional area. It was a developed line with tank obstacles and concrete pill boxes for light machine guns and anti tank rifles.

BM - BG - BH - BC - WY

This was the Divisional stop line from Pulborough, Floodgate Farm, Bines Green, Burgess Hill, River Rother to Mill. It was partially developed with road blocks and local defences but no continuous tank obstacles.

BR - BM - BK

This line of defences followed the River Arun from Littlehampton, Pulborough, Rudgwick and northwards out of the area. Although the river was a tank obstacle, crossings were blocked and emplacements for anti-tank guns were also prepared.

BI - BH - BG - BF

This was only a partially developed position. Along the River Adur from Shoreham to Bines Green, Floodgate Farm, Nuthurst, Horsham and north towards Dorking. There were no continuous tank obstacles except on the River Adur. Crossings were blocked and there were emplacements for anti-tank guns.

BC - BA

This line followed the railway from Burgess Hill to Ardingly railway station. It was a partially developed position with some road blocks.

Unlettered

Chichester to Midhurst. The line followed the valley of the River Lavant. The river was not a tank obstacle, but the railway cuttings and woods favoured the defence.

Tanks

The task of the 43rd Royal Tank Regiment was to support the infantry in the Divisional area. It was also charged with taking offensive action against any enemy, who managed to reach the South Downs either by penetrating through the forward defences or by airborne landings.

In each tank regiment area a squadron of tanks was to be based in a battle position which was tactically the most important part of the sector. In most cases this was close to a defended locality so that they could receive protection from the infantry around them.

Anti-Aircraft Defence

As the area covered by 38th Welsh Division was in a 'Fighter Zone' there were no permanent anti-aircraft defences in position.

Experience had shown that troop positions were likely to be bombed at any time and particularly before dusk. Thus to counter any attack all anti-aircraft light machine guns were to be kept mounted and manned on receipt of an air raid warning.

In order to avoid mistake, aircraft were not to be engaged at night until they had committed a definitely hostile act, or by day until there was no doubt that they were hostile.

Anti-Tank Guns

The anti-tank guns of 38th Division were :-

(a) to protect the infantry locations on the South Downs

(b) to deal with tanks attacking the forward locations in the coastal belt

(c) to engage with any reserve guns, enemy AFVs moving north from the South Downs

(d) to supplement the anti-tank defences within the coastal belt where obstacles were inadequate or approaches especially favourable for tanks.

Machine Guns

There was a surplus of 131 machine guns above the normal establishment within the Division. Of these 14 were allotted to 1/8 Middlesex Machine Gun Battalion. On 'Action Stations, this unit was to go to the Divisional Headquarters in the Steyning, Upper Beeding and Bramber Nodal Point area. The remaining extra guns were issued for use in static positions on beaches and the Downs. About 40 had been sent to each zone.

Divisional Reserves

Because of the long front held by the Division there was no Divisional reserve. However, there was a third division held in the Corps reserve and an Armoured Division was also held back to deal with counter attacks.

Demolitions

The following demolitions were prepared and the responsibility for maintenance and manning these was given to 284, 502, 561 and 283 Field Companies of the Royal Engineers:-

Brighton West Pier
Brighton Palace Pier
Shoreham Bridge
Causeway to Thorney Island
Selsey Causeway
Selsey Lifeboat Station walkaway

Barbed Wire

The standard wire obstacle in the Divisional area was to be two double apron fences having between them contiguously a triple concertina fence, the later being supported by horizontal wires stretched between eight foot (2.4 metres) forestry pickets. Horizontal wire was also to be correctly fixed to the two bottom coils. Screw pickets were not to be used in any future fences. Where this type of picket was already in place the fence was to be straightened at least every third bay by the addition of forestry or angle iron pickets which should be wired with additional wire. All correctly sited wire obstacles in the Divisional area were to be brought up to this standard as soon as possible and properly maintained. Where necessary a single strand of cattle wire three feet (1 metre) high was to be erected to prevent beasts damaging themselves on the fences.

Civilian population

In the invasion areas the civilian population was to be ordered to stay put.

Nodal Points (Defended Areas)

A complete list of the Nodal Points in the 38th Division area of Sussex is too numerous to be given here. The intention was that most towns, villages, road junctions, bridges and stations should be turned into defended areas and garrisoned by the Home Guard in support of the army. Thus in the rural district of Midhurst there were 21 Nodal points which gives some idea of the coverage. As late as 1943 one Home Guard commander was complaining of a long list of places which had been surveyed but where no defences had been built. Thus like the partly completed army stop lines the Nodal Points and defended area scheme was never fully implemented as its planners intended and was eventually found not to be needed.

The maps and plans which accompany this chapter have either been copied from those in 38th Divisional Defence Scheme of 23rd July 1941 or are based on information they and Sussex records contain.

War Office manuals of instruction dating from 1937 onwards were issued to all infantry battalion officers and dealt with training troops in fieldcraft and battle tactics. These included guidance on the importance of observation, the use of ground, cover, camouflage, protection from fire, and village and street fighting. Pictorial examples helped in the training and a few examples are given in the book.

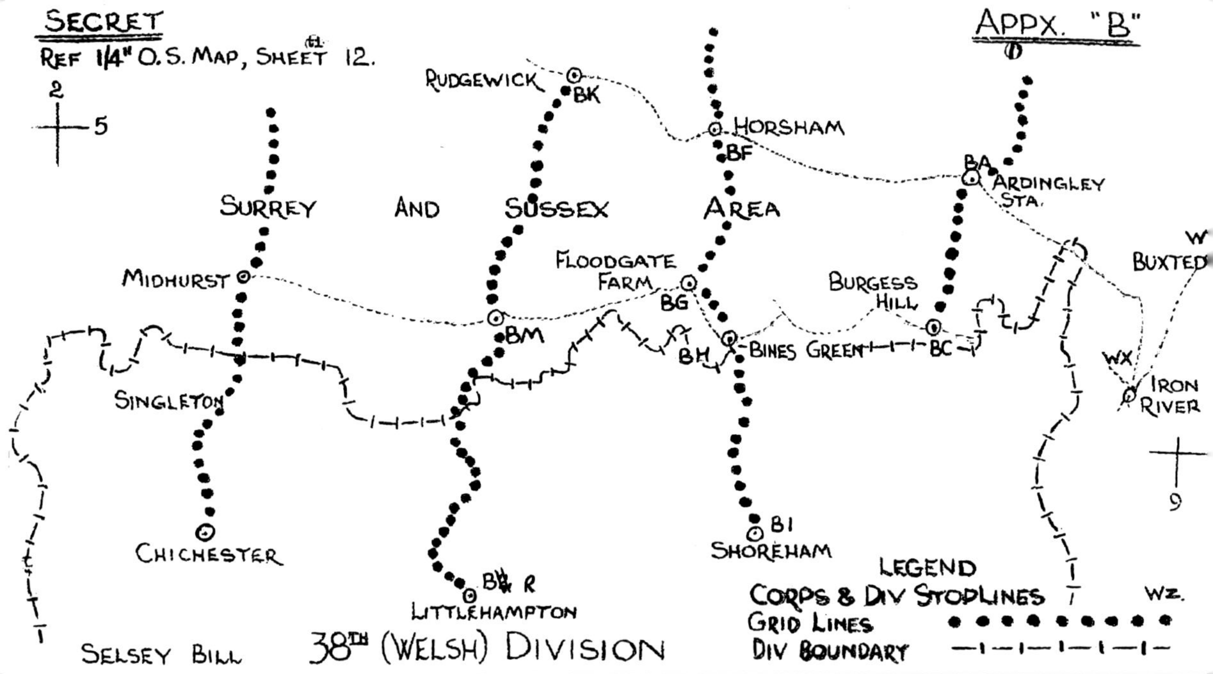

6.1 Corps and Division stop lines in the 38th Welsh Divisional area. See Chapter 6 for an explanation of progress in building the stop lines between the points identified with code letters

6.2 The Brigade areas between Selsey Bill and Newhaven in June 1941. The dotted area, 3 miles (4 kilometres) in depth was for road blocks. The shaded area, (South Downs) was kept free from the public for tanks and troops

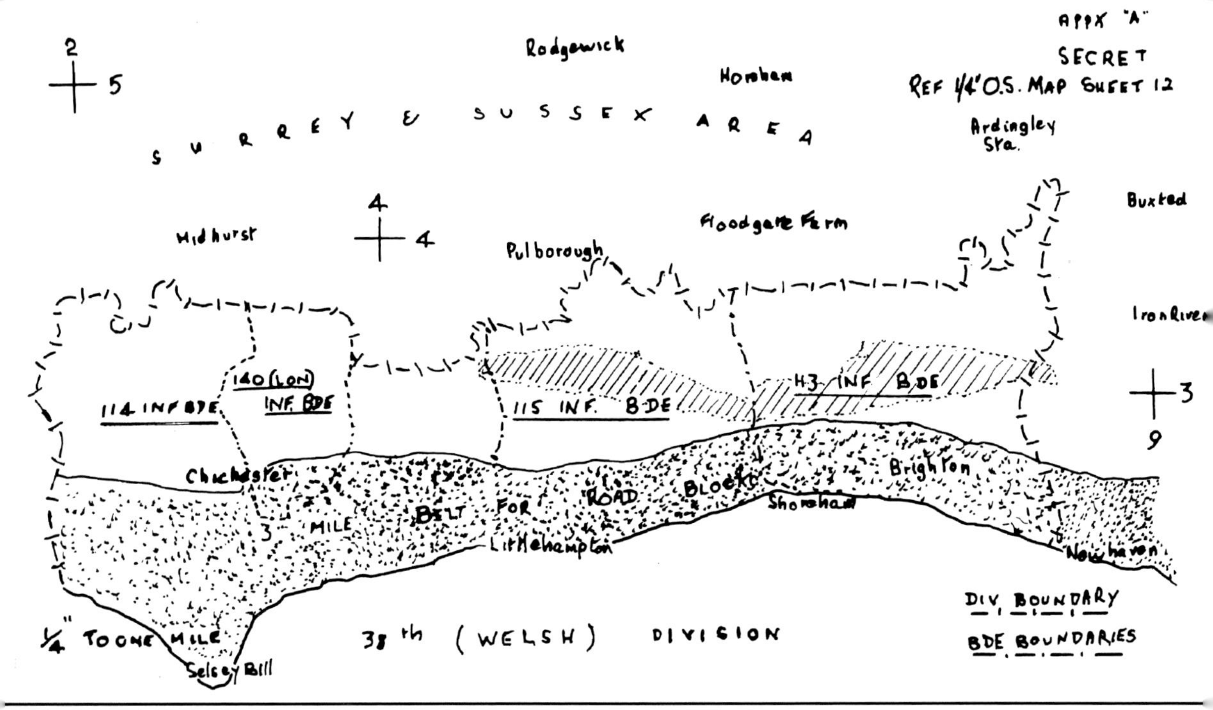

6.3 A pill box stands in a garden overlooking the beach at Lancing. The entrance and gun slits are blocked.

6.4 At the foot of the Downs men load shells into a 2 pounder anti-tank gun. Made by Vickers Armstrong it was better than the German 37 mm gun.

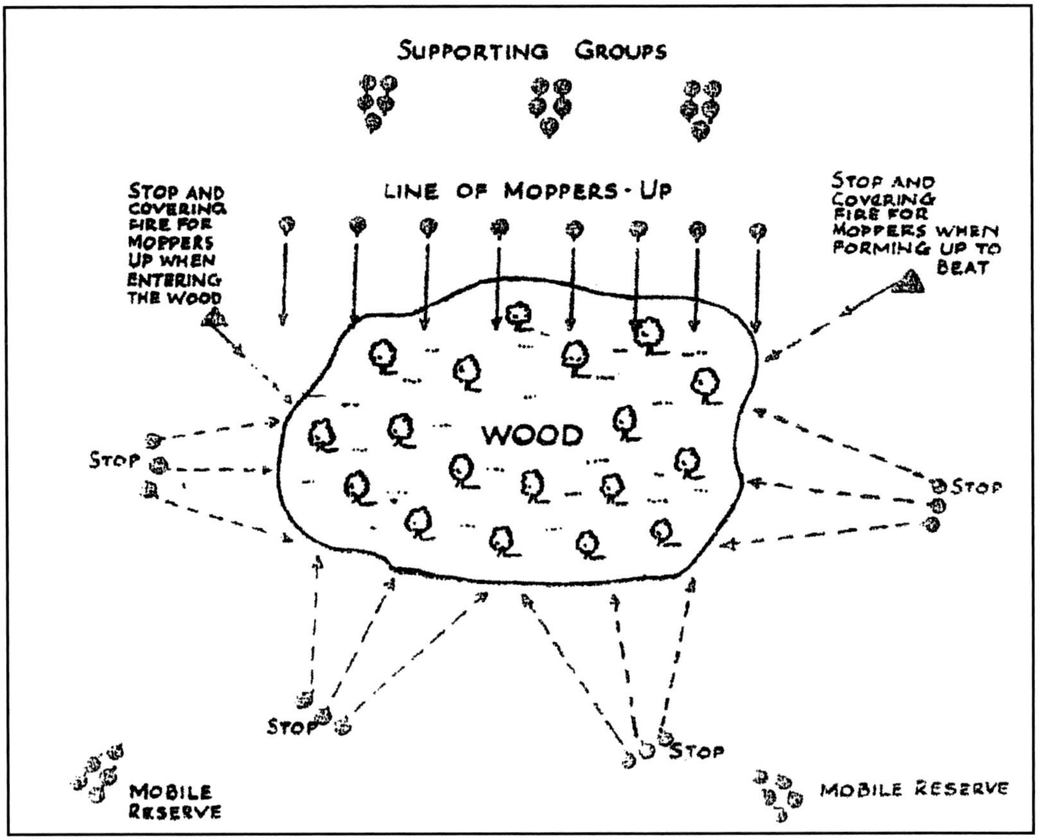

6.5 Infantry Training Notes, 1937, revised in 1941, advised Platoon Commanders how to clear a wood of parachutists.

6.6 A 6 pounder anti-tank gun being fire off Bognor beach east of the Pier in 1941. These guns were expected to engage tanks at short range.

6.7 Fieldcraft. An infantry platoon advancing in diamond formation. Good for all round observation and fire, but makes a good target if spotted.

Chapter 7

THE RUSH TO BUILD OBSTACLES

Only those who lived during 1940 can remember the horror experienced when the German army captured the French Channel ports and were close to invading Britain. There was widespread apprehension on the Sussex coast and those that could fled. Fear of a landing by parachutists and gliders was heightened at night by the blackout, and the endless drone of enemy aircraft overhead. No one really knew what was going on or what to expect except the worst. Another worry was over the superiority of German tanks and infantry which had swept successfully across Europe without being stopped. People had seen the pictures and feared what was coming.

Overnight the once friendly beaches, parks and fields seemed very open and vulnerable to enemy infantry and tanks which were not only expected to appear over the horizon but also to descend from the sky.

In 1937 the War Office issued a Military Engineering Volume on 'Defences'. It gave wide ranging if generalised guidance on the defence of infantry and artillery positions, command posts and railways. There were several pages of historical references going back to the Napoleonic wars, which did not help much. Tanks got a brief mention but there was little about dealing with parachutists and gliders. Subsequently, as a result of battle experience and blitzkrieg tactics in France there was a flurry of new advice about road blocks, and methods of disabling and stopping tanks.

Early in 1940, army engineers had to improvise and work fast to fortify the beaches and the countryside with concrete blockhouses, barbed wire and anti-landing scaffolding. This chapter gives examples of some of the defences which quickly appeared on the roads, fields and beaches of Sussex.

Pill Boxes

Pill boxes and blockhouses are hardened defence works allowing infantry inside to kill the enemy outside without being harmed. That is the theory behind all fortification, but it only works, sometimes. They could be death traps. No one knows how many pill boxes were built throughout Sussex until the eighteen months after May 1940 when construction was stopped. Pill boxes could be small and armed with two men with rifles and Bren guns, or larger with heavier weapons. Sometimes there was provision for anti-aircraft machine guns.

The main defensive stop line of pill boxes to protect London, (the GHQ line) approved by General Ironside, and sealing off the South Coast, stretched across the top of Sussex between Rudgwick and Peasmarsh with a spur line reaching down the banks of the River Ouse to Newhaven. A similar containment line along the River Arun at Arundel was never completed. Otherwise pill boxes seem to have been built throughout the county singly or in clusters (Selsey, Cuckmere Haven, Seaford): to protect airfields, (Shoreham by Sea); river bridges; (Bodiam), cliff exits (Birling Gap and Cuckmere Haven), and road junctions (Worthing and Eastbourne). The perimeters of towns and villages designated as Nodal Points or defended areas were often so protected, (Lewes). On some of the beaches they were fairly numerous, (see Chapter 8) but an untold number at Worthing, Brighton, Eastbourne, Hastings and other seaside places were removed even before the end of the war, and evidence of their existence is now hard to find.

Pill boxes could be square, oblong, circular, hexagonal, and almost any shape you can think of. This has made it difficult to classify them and sometimes even decide why they were sited where they were; perhaps because of some long forgotten local defence scheme. They can be found tall and conspicuous, or closely tucked into the ground, behind garden walls, in open fields, or concealed in the hedgerows and woods. Usually they were built of thick reinforced concrete, but as there was a shortage of cement, stone, brick and wood was also used. Some were designed by contractors and fashioned from prefabricated panels. Camouflage was usually earth or paint, sometimes a mock up of similar buildings nearby. That said most of them were death traps and could be surrounded or attacked by flame throwers and hand grenades unless they were grouped to give each other supporting fire. Civilian contractors under direction of the army engineers carried out most of the building work to a few standard plans issued by the War Office. Because of haste there was often a free for all. Often the basic design was modified by a local builder or perhaps changed to meet the needs of the site and give a clear field of fire. The urgency of the time and labour shortages resulted in some unorthodox structures. Most pill boxes have now been demolished, but a few remain visible, some covered in undergrowth, and there will be others now forgotten about, but one day to be found again.

There are several excellent books which go into great detail about pill boxes in Sussex, their construction, purpose and where they can be seen, and the photographs in this account serve only as examples of those which remain.

Barbed wire

Nasty stuff to handle, but versatile and absolutely essential to protect infantry positions from attack. Barbed wire was used extensively by all armies in trench warfare during World War I. In 1940-41 strong points, road blocks and mile after mile of the Sussex coast was festooned with it in belts several yards wide. Hundreds of tons of wire were despatched for the use of infantry and Home Guard units. Cheap to produce in 12.5 and 14 SWG (Standard Wire Gauge) it was delivered in 130 or 176 yard coils weighing between 32 and 42 pounds each.

War Office instructions specified how it should be used in different patterns and Dannert Concertina wire, which came in great circular rolls, merited special guidance showing infantry how it should be fixed. A team of ten men were expected to put up a 100 yard (91 metres) stretch in one hour. For Sussex beaches and esplanades two belts of concertina one yard apart were recommended. Wire entangled in hedgerows or stretched at knee height in a pattern between pickets across fields would delay surprise attacks at night. Field gaps and roads were blocked by wire knife rests. Most wire was removed quickly at the end of the war but some photographs show it in place often festooned with sea weed on the beaches and grass covered in the fields.

Landing craft, Glider, and Anti Tank obstacles

Most of the beaches in East and West Sussex where a landing was likely had rows of 3 inch steel tubular scaffolding fixed to base plates 18 inches square standing in sea up to four feet deep when the tide came in. To make life more difficult for the invader, Dannert wire and mines were strung between the poles. often draped in seaweed. Scaffolding was supplied up to 18 feet in length and was used extensively to obstruct infantry carrying gliders and transports from landing on open fields, beaches, and parks. As the pictures show it needed to be erected high to be effective.

To impede a tank's progress a line of reinforced concrete cubes approximately 5 feet square (1.5 sq. metres) were cast in situ about 3 feet (91 cm) apart and sunk 12 (30 cm) inches into the ground. They could stop a 16 ton tank and were best placed with a corner facing the direction of attack. The design made the tank rear up and expose its underside if it attempted to ride over the obstacle. Under the direction of army engineers, long stretches of blocks were built by civilian contractors along the coast, and at road junctions and bridges. They were said to be proof against the fire of 2 pounder anti-tank guns. To be properly effective two rows of blocks were recommended, but scarcity of materials sometimes made this impossible. Concrete cylinders 2 feet (1.8 metres) in diameter and staggered in groups of three served a similar purpose. Smaller blocks known as pimples were tetrahedron shaped chunks of concrete, used to fill access gaps in the main defensive line.

Another barrier to tanks was the use of five staggered rows of 90 pound rails about four feet apart and 3 - 4 feet high put into timber lined sockets across a road. These formed a useful barricade as did V shaped welded bent rails.

Ditches, Banks and Rivers

Most tanks would be stopped by a river or waterway if it was at least 50 feet (46 metres) wide with a depth of five feet (1.5 metres). Earth banks with a slope of at least 60 degrees were reckoned to be tank proof and could sometimes be graded to meet this requirement. The few rivers in Sussex being tidal hardly met the approved standard but could still form a useful obstacle if the tide was in. Tree stumps about two feet in diameter (2 metres) and of the same height would also deter a tank. Anti-tank ditches were a more useful barrier. These were excavated all over Sussex to protect towns and defended areas, although they quickly fell in without proper revetment and this was not always possible to do. Because of their temporary nature they have largely been forgotten about but can sometimes be seen as a disturbance in the ground There was such a ditch in open ground around part of the perimeter of Worthing and fortunately a map of it survives. At Courtlands, Goring by Sea, it went north to Columbia Drive, through open ground. A further short ditch stretched from Pond lane to Bramble Lane. On the northern edge of the town it descended from Mill Lane to Findon Road and then followed an irregular line from the Links Road golf clubhouse to the top of Hill Barn lane. It began again in Charmandean Lane where sockets in concrete paving are visible and then ran eastwards through the Sainsbury site to end in water meadows at the end of Clarenden Road, Broadwater. The purpose of the ditch is a bit obscure. It may have been designed to close off the main routes into the town. But there are gaps which suggest it was not completed for some reason. An alternative explanation may be that it was feared enemy troops would land on the Downs and attack the rear of the forward troops on the beaches.

Similar smaller anti-tank ditches were dug around other Sussex towns, on the Crumbles near Eastbourne, and across the valley of Cuckmere Haven.

Perhaps more than anything else the remains of old defences are a reminder of those dangerous days. Bits of rusty wire and chunks of concrete lie scattered in out of the way places, pill boxes hidden in hedgerows, foundations littering the beaches, and suggestive dips in the ground will remain as a decaying monuments of those times for years to come.

7.1 One of a group of circular pill boxes on the edge of Seaford Golf course.

7.2 *Instructions to troops from the War Office specified how to handle barbed wire and design road blocks.*

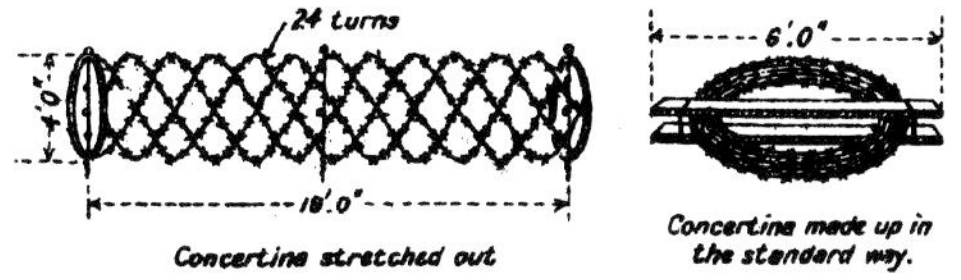

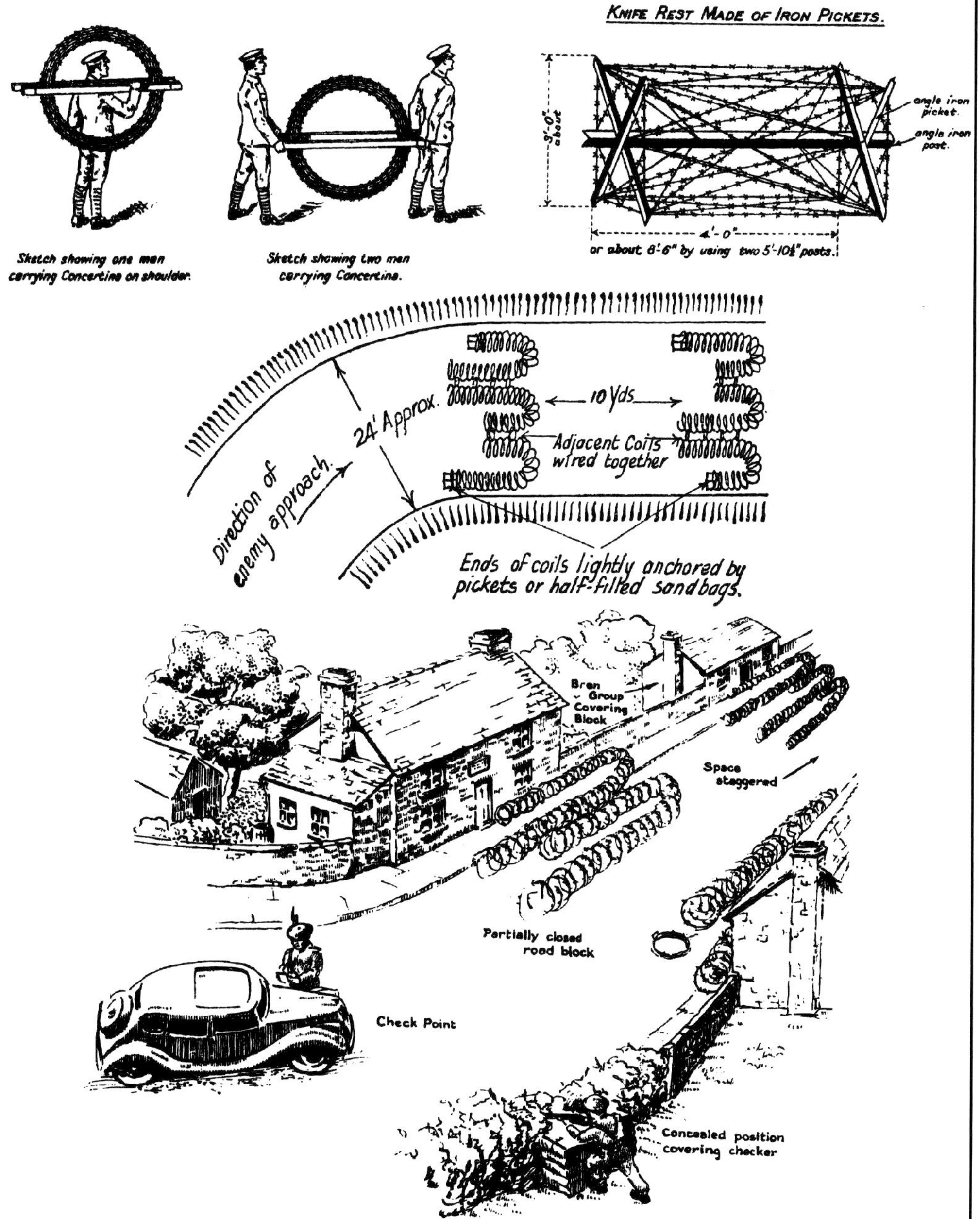

7.3 Dannert concertina wire along Brighton beach and on the upper promenade road protecting the gun battery nearby.

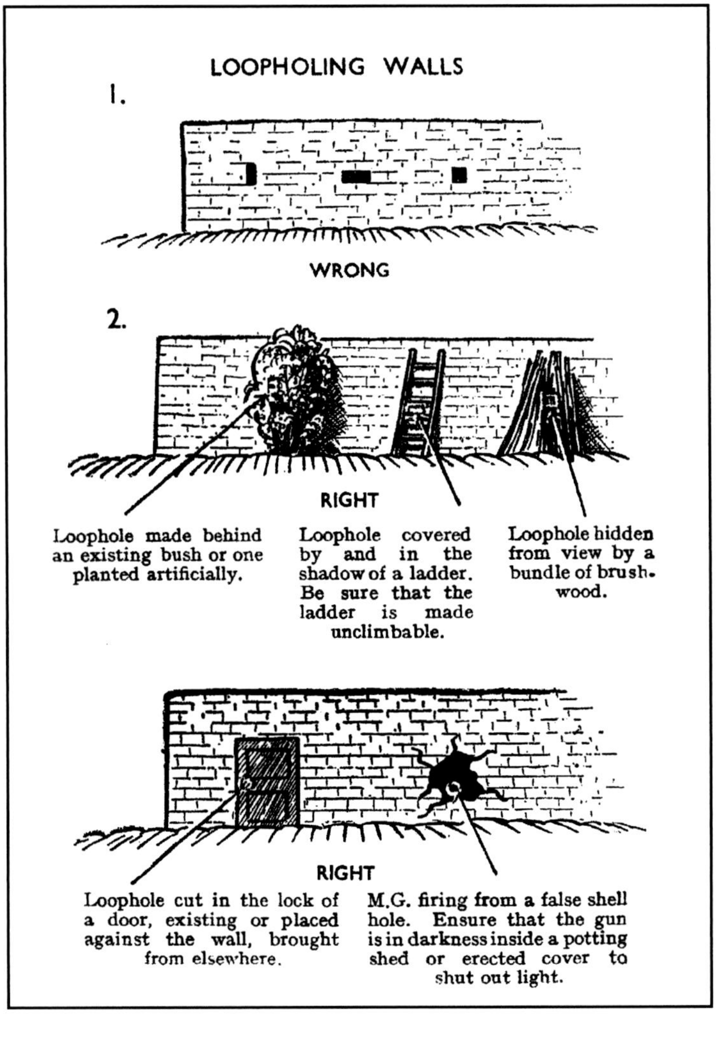

7.4 War Office Notes to Platoon Commanders 1941. Knocking loop holes in walls.

7.5 Loopholes can still be seen in a garden wall at Holywell Road, Eastbourne behind the sea front.

7.6 This pill box built behind a garden wall on Seaford sea front protected 343 Coast Battery which stood nearby.

7.7 An anti-tank ditch leads up to the blocks and V shaped rails are slotted in holes in the road to complete the barrier.

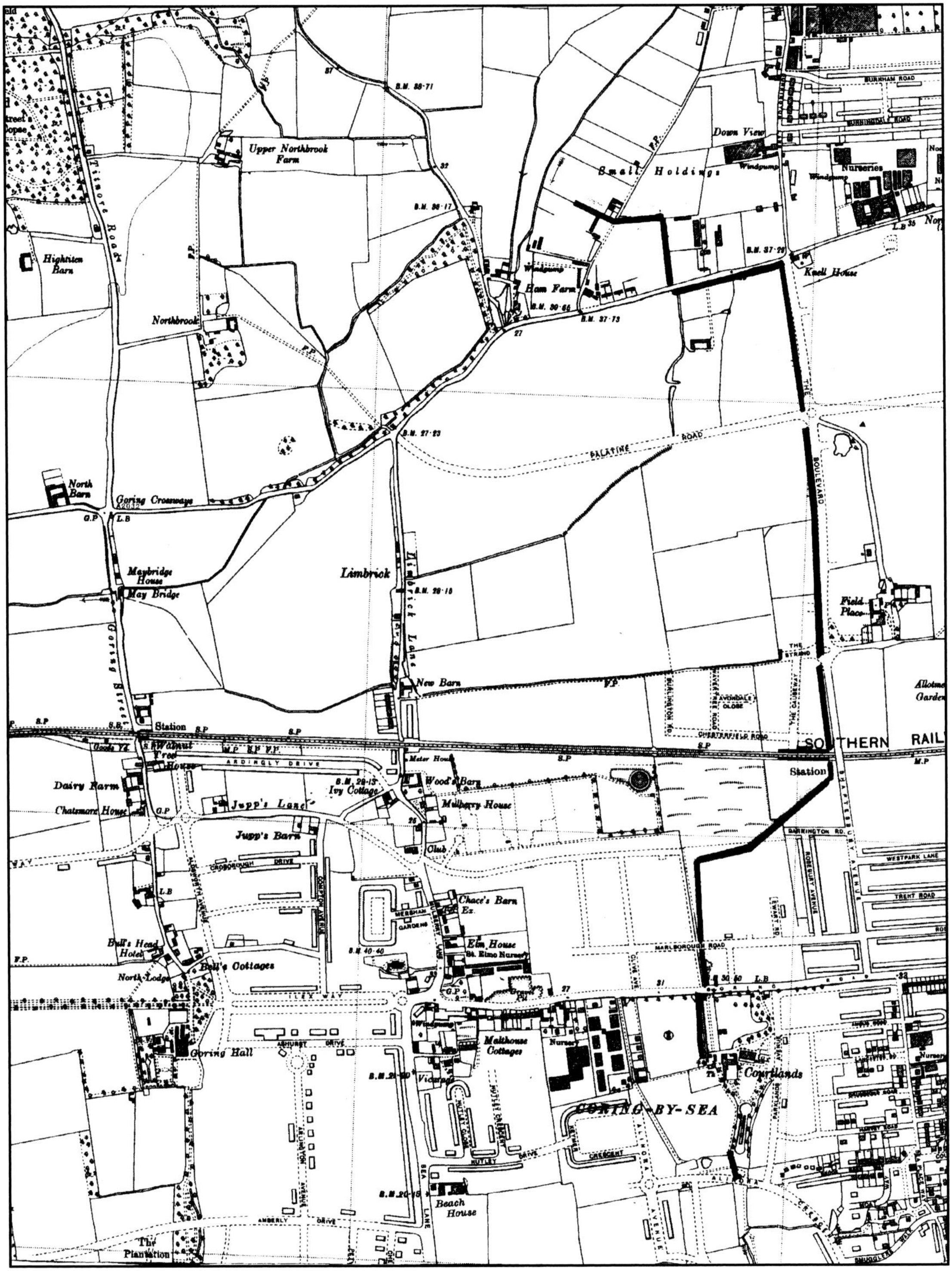

7.8 The black line marks the course of the anti-tank ditch across vacant ground from Courtlands, Goring, to fields near Titnore Lane, Durrington.

7.9 An anti-tank ditch around a defended area at Eastbourne now under housing.

Chapter 8

FORTIFICATION OF A SUSSEX SEA FRONT

In 1938 the population of Worthing Municipal Borough, the largest town in West Sussex, was 46,000. Its beaches stretched for over six miles with a large expanse of smooth sand which at low tide receded for about half a mile and made it a popular holiday place for families. Given the right weather conditions its beaches were very suitable for an invasion, and later when details of the enemy's plans were known, the German 9th Army intended to land three divisions along this part of the coast.

In common with other parts of Sussex suitable for landing men and tanks hasty preparations began in the summer of 1940 to prohibit public access to the beaches and to fortify them against attack.

Orders had been issued from the War Office authorising the building of pill boxes and blockhouses of different designs. Two examples based on WW I experience were included in a War Office manual on 'Defences' issued for the guidance of troops and engineers in 1937.

But any sort of defence structure has to be modified to fit the geography of the site and its purpose. For this reason many weird and wonderful concrete and brick structures were built which bear little relationship to the plans. After the experience of the British Expeditionary Force (BEF) in France there was a great fear of the danger posed by parachutists and troop carrying gliders, and this led to long rows of steel scaffolding being built across fields, roads and open spaces close to the beach. Scaffolding was also erected in the sea at the end of the groynes and then mined to obstruct tanks and landing craft.

All seaside towns in Sussex were fortified with similar measures, although the task took many months and was not completed until 1941.

When the threat of invasion passed and before the end of the war in 1945 most defence structures were removed or demolished down to ground level. Access to the beaches was then held up for some time until all the mines were lifted. A daunting task because movement of the tides had shifted some and others could not be found because the records were wrong or had been lost.

Fortunately for Worthing, plans survive of the design and exact locations of the pill boxes, gun sites, scaffolding and anti-tank defences which were built along the sea front, but space allows only three to be included here.

There were sixteen structures of various shapes, for different weapons for beach defence; two six inch coast batteries and three concrete anti-aircraft battery sites. To delay tanks attempting to storm the beaches there were 391 concrete cubes which were cast on the ground where they stood.

The defences start from the municipal boundary with Ferring in the west and end at the Lancing border in the east. The area covered with belts of barbed wire is shown as XXXX. Scaffolding to deter gliders landing is represented by a series of gates. Concrete blocks are shown as open cubes. The block numbers on the map are of no significance as they refer to instructions for removal, but they are useful for pinpointing the sites of blockhouses and gun positions. The number and letter combinations for the pill boxes and gun emplacements below correspond to those on the maps and plans. The following list shows the extent of the fortifications along the sea front which was cluttered with all manner of concrete defence works.

Worthing Beach Defences.

Sea Lane, Ferring to Bodiam Avenue (blocks A1 - A12)
Near Block A1 - a concrete blockhouse for a 3 inch gun
2E - a concrete block house for machine guns
Aldsworth Avenue to Chelwood Avenue (blocks A14 - A24)
2G - a concrete pill box for machine guns
3C1 and 3C2 - concrete pill boxes for machine guns
Sea Lane, Goring by Sea to Patricia Avenue (blocks A25 - B9)
7B, and 7D - pill boxes built with timber sleepers
8 - a double concrete pill box for machine guns
9 - a concrete and brick emplacement for a 4 inch gun with an observation post on the roof
12B - a concrete pill box with a timber store
16 - a concrete pill box. The base can still be seen
Seafield Avenue to Eirene Avenue (blocks B10 - B19)
15F - a concrete pill box and an unidentified structure
George V Avenue to Rye Close (blocks B20 - C9)
23 - a concrete pill box for rifles and machine guns
27B - a concrete pill box for rifles and machine guns
27C - a concrete emplacement for a 4 inch gun
Grand Avenue to Heene Road (blocks C10 - C27)
27D - a brick and concrete emplacement for a 60 cm searchlight
27G - a circular brick and concrete emplacement for an anti-aircraft gun
27H - a brick and concrete pill box with a light anti-aircraft gun
28 and 28A - Brick and concrete heavy surface emplacements for 6 inch coastal guns
28C -a brick and concrete light anti-aircraft gun emplacement
28E - a brick and concrete emplacement for a 60 cm searchlight
Heene Road to Queen's road (blocks 28 - 37)
36E - a concrete pill box
Western Place to the Bandstand and Pier (blocks 38 - 52)
No defences shown, but they may have been removed at an earlier date.
Pier to Beach House Grounds (blocks C56 - C76)
39D - a brick and concrete 4 inch gun emplacement covering the sea
39E - a brick and concrete 4 inch gun emplacement firing east
Boating Pool to Ham Road (blocks C77 - C92)
39G- a concrete emplacement for a 4 inch gun
Near block 85 was a sandbagged anti-aircraft machine gun position
Ham Road to Thalassa Road (blocks C93 - C105)
46C - a concrete pill box for machine guns
47B - a concrete pill box for machine guns
Brougham Road to Western Road, Lancing (blocks C106 - 120)
46E - a concrete Bofors anti-aircraft gun position

During 1940-42 there were also slit trenches and sand bag emplacements for machine guns on the promenade, but these had mostly disappeared by 1945 when the public were allowed on the sea front again.

8.1 A square pill box with loop holes now blocked stood overlooking the beach at Ferring and had its entrance through a grass bank in the rear.

8.2 The post war Sea Lane Café on Goring sea front at Worthing stands close to a 4.7 gun site (9) with pill boxes (7B, 7D) in support, and a double pill box (8) facing west, Another pill box (12B) straddled the café car park and shingle bank, (See Chapter 8)

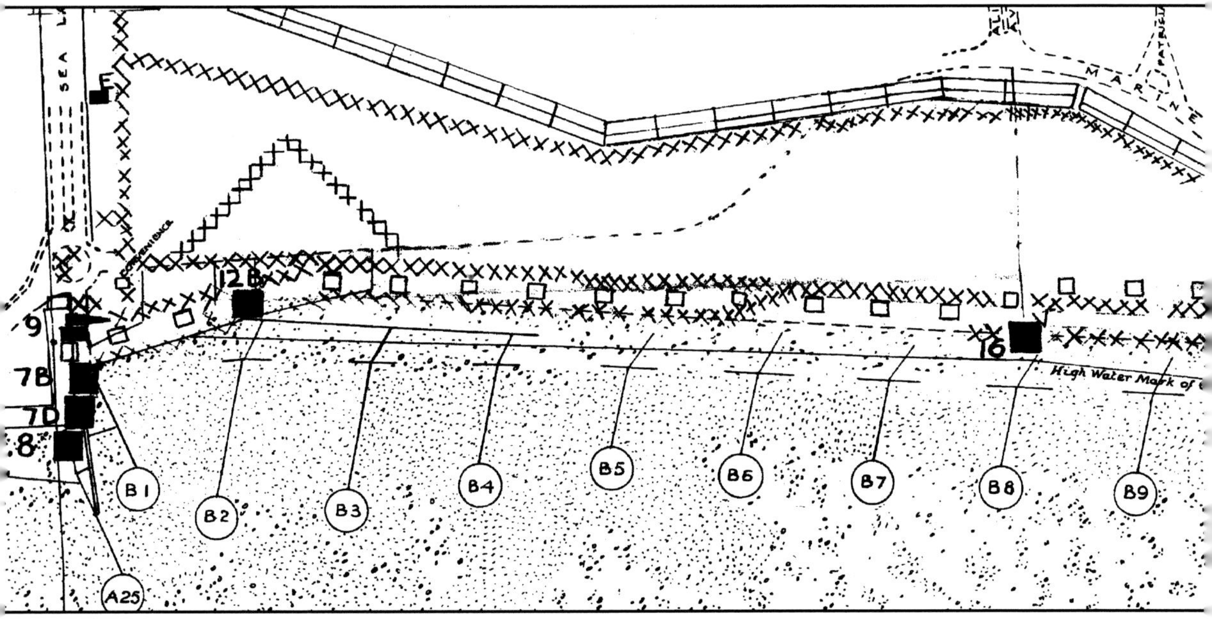

8.3 The Sea Lane Café today. It stands close to a kink in the coastline which made it an ideal place in 1940 to site guns covering the sea and beach east and west.

8.4 At Grand Avenue, Worthing there were searchlights (27D, 28E). 6 inch guns (28, 28A) and anti-aircraft light machine guns (27H, 28C). There were extensive belts of wire around the battery.

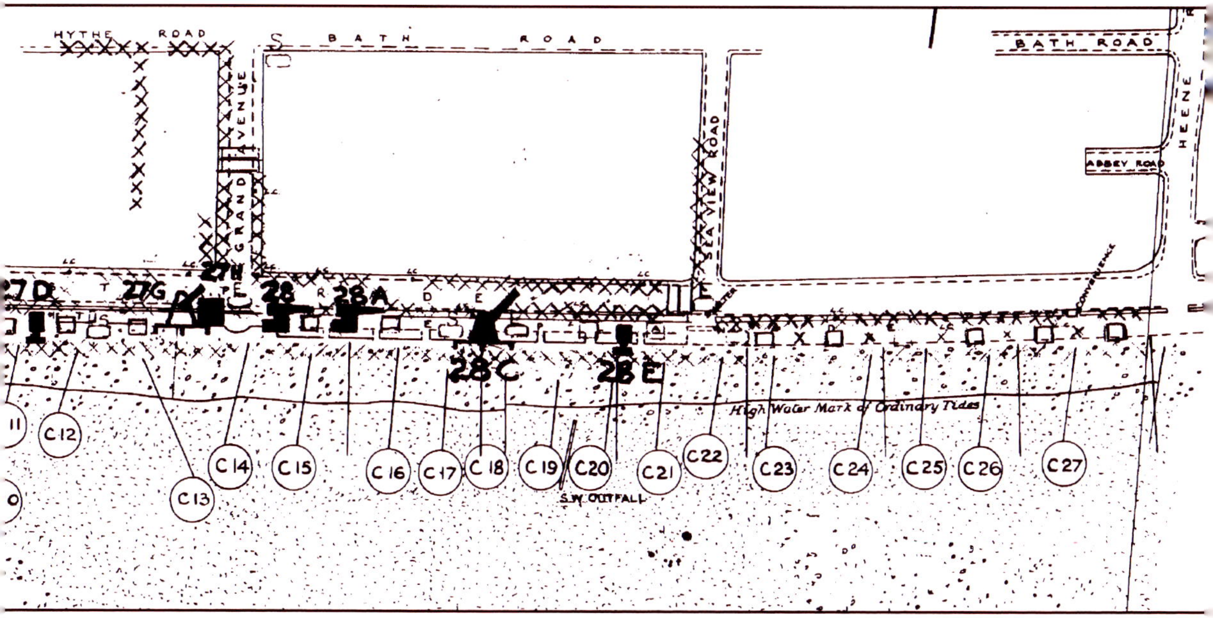

8.5 A Lewis gun in a sandbag enclosure protects the coast battery.

8.6 A machine gun post dug into Worthing promenade east of the Pier Pavilion. On the left concrete anti-tank blocks appear as a solid wall.

8.7 Anti-landing scaffolding erected in the sea at Worthing and Bognor Regis.

8.8 From Worthing Pier to Beach House Gardens there was much wire and many anti-tank blocks. 4 inch Guns at (39D, 39E) fired eastwards and out to sea.

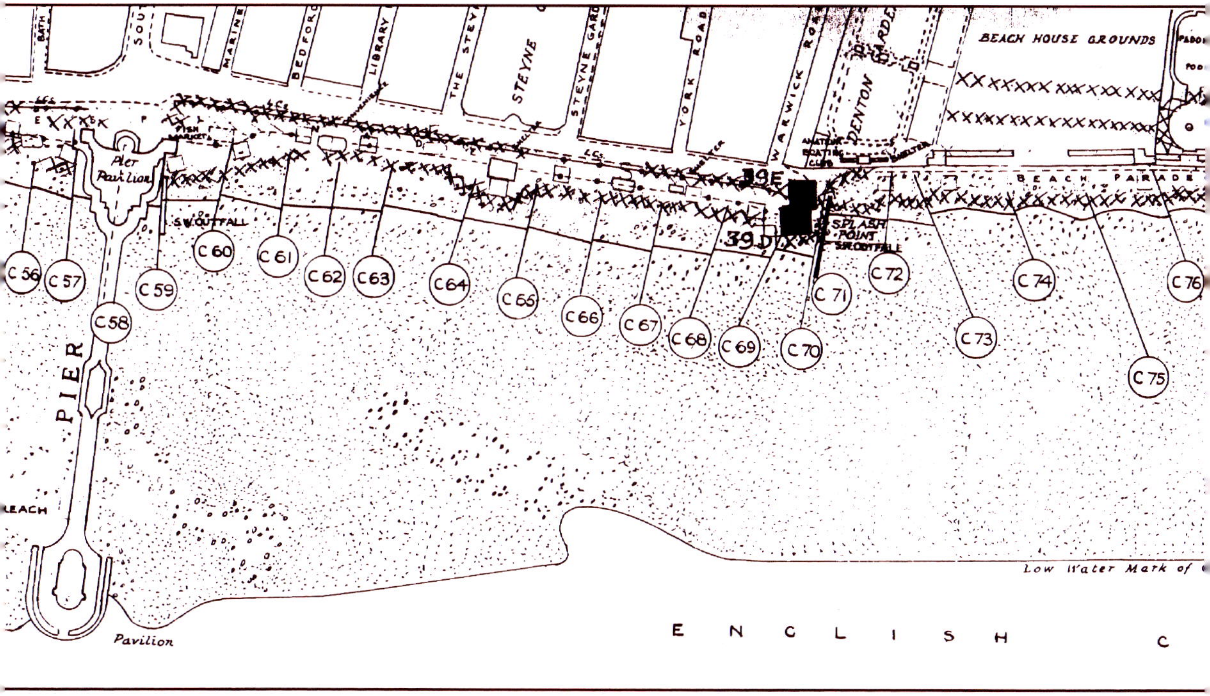

8.9 Rear view of the gun batteries, (39D, 39E) at Splash Point, Worthing in 1945. There was also a blockhouse and observation post in the complex.

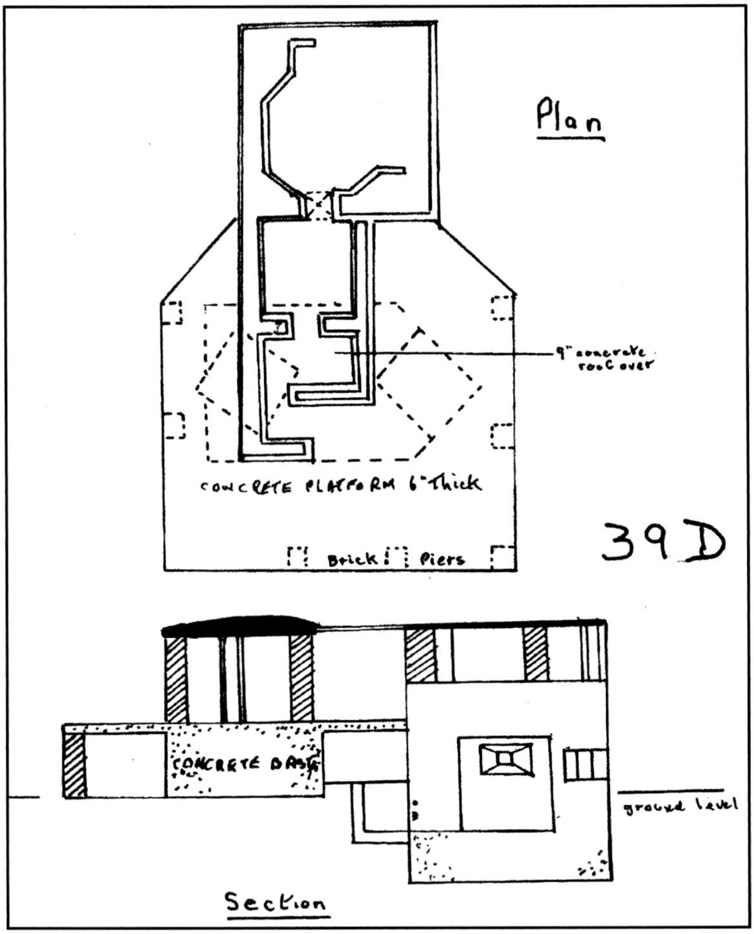

8.10 An engineer's drawing of the two gun batteries, (39D, 39E) at Splash Point.

8.11 The 40 mm Bofors anti-aircraft gun and protective machine gun post close to Selden Lawns, Worthing. The gap cut in the Pier is barely visible in the distance.

Chapter 9

THE EMERGENCY COAST DEFENCE BATTERIES SELSEY BILL TO DUNGENESS

The speedy and successful German advance across the Netherlands in May 1940 galvanised the government into taking action to protect the British coastline against an enemy invasion. The collapse of French resistance in June hastened the preparations even more. The Home Defence Executive chaired by the Commander in Chief of the army had already agreed that the Kent and Sussex coast was most at risk. Their assessment of the situation was that an immediate invasion was unlikely until the German army had regrouped and consolidated their gains in France. But time was short and there was much to be done.

The permanent coast defences, (those at the major ports, including Portsmouth and Newhaven) had been on a precautionary warning alert since August 1939. Not that this was of much significance in Sussex. The minor harbours of Rye, Shoreham and Littlehampton had never been armed since the Napoleonic wars. Even the cross Channel port of Newhaven had only two old six inch guns and two twelve pounders. For over one hundred years there had never been any necessity or urgency to build any proper defences on the long Sussex coastline, so open and vulnerable to attack from the rest of Europe.

The collapse of France was to hasten the building of new gun batteries, the laid down ration being two six inch guns for every six miles of coast, although this target was never to be achieved. There were not sufficient guns available. The shortage of guns and trained men to man them meant that an offer by the Royal Navy to supply guns taken from old warships and kept in Portsmouth dockyard was taken up and 150 were made available, some of which were allocated to Sussex. The Navy also sent Royal Marine Gun crews to man batteries at Seaford, Shoreham, Worthing and Littlehampton. This was a short term measure (weeks) and by June 1940 the army had managed to sort itself out and replaced the marines by men from the Royal Artillery Regiment.

The title “Emergency Coast Defence Batteries” was given to distinguish them from the guns in permanent fortifications of which there was only one in Sussex, at Newhaven Fort. In their close defence role the Sussex batteries were expected to engage targets up to 6,000 yards (5,500 metres) off shore. It was assumed these would be vessels not larger than destroyers. Orders to the gunners were to sink all unfriendly shipping approaching the shore for a landing.

Selection of sites

The choice of the best site for each six inch battery on the Sussex coast was made by convening a ‘Siting Board’ of artillery and engineer officers since the expertise of both was necessary to come to the best decision. The average distance between batteries on the flat parts of the coast was about 9,000 yards, (5.5 miles). Visibility along the coast and out to sea, and the ability to support the fire of adjacent batteries were important factors affecting the choice of site. Apart from the guns defending Newhaven harbour high, on the cliffs, the batteries were built as close as possible to the beach. The Battery Observation Post, (BOP) had to be high enough for the fall of shot to be seen so that corrections could be made.

From Inspection reports it is clear that most of the new batteries were ready for action about June 1940. The six inch guns were mounted in pairs. Most had been made before 1914 and were not the most efficient of their kind. They stood temporarily in sandbagged emplacements until proper protected gun houses and magazines could be built.

The Coast Battery

Each battery comprised a pair of six inch guns in open fronted brick and concrete built gun houses about 100 yards (91 metres) apart. When not in use for protection against the weather the open front was closed with a tarpaulin and camouflage netting. The roof was a slab of concrete nine inches (228 mm) thick. This gave some protection from air attack to the gun crews and the ready use ammunition store. A reinforced concrete magazine for high explosive shells was close by. At the Eastbourne battery the shells were kept in the basement of the Martello Tower, but this was marked unsatisfactory by an inspecting officer. A short distance away on each side of the battery was a small brick shelter with wooden or metal shutters to house the 90 cm searchlight. These had a range of two miles (3 km) depending on visibility at sea. The buildings of the battery site were concealed as much as possible from air attack and usually resembled a huddle of seaside huts and fishermen's shacks.

The battery equipment included a Lister generator in a brick built engine house to power the searchlights, range finding equipment by Barr and Stroud which used a vertical base system for low sites, a depression position finder and various plotting boards and communication equipment.

The Battery Observation Post (BOP) was the eyes and ears of the battery. At Worthing it was in a high block of flats with look out slits cut in the end wall. At Littlehampton, Winchelsea and Cooden brick towers were built, but at Cooden the tower was said to be too high at 37 feet (11 metres) and had to be reduced to make it less conspicuous. The guns at Eastbourne and Pevensey Bay stood near Martello Towers and concrete BOPs were built on top of their roofs. At Bognor an inspection found that a summer house was being used as a BOP. This was recorded as unsatisfactory but it is unclear whether a better one was built.

Gunnery officers needed a pair of binoculars to gauge the fall of shot in the sea and thereby hangs a tale of the desperation of the times. Supplies of binoculars were scarce and in October 1940 the Ministry of Supply launched a publicity campaign asking the public to give up their binoculars to the armed services. Compensation of from £17 to £27 was paid according to the type. The public responded well and by April 1941, 70,000 binoculars had been sent in and some of these ended up in the coast batteries. According to an equipment list issued in 1941, Binoculars Mark I were issued to the Sussex coast batteries even though they were reckoned to be obsolete for the purpose. Prismatic Binoculars No 5 Marks 1 and 2 were recommended when supplies became available. It seems you had to make do with what you got,

Each battery usually had some form of protection other than rifles against low flying aircraft who were likely to swoop in over the sea and bomb or machine gun the area. There was either one or two Bofors or Lewis guns in a sandbag emplacement close by to keep attackers away.

The perimeter of the battery area was defended against land or sea attack with wire, mines, spigot mortars, weapon pits and machine gun posts, but it is unlikely that they could have held out long without being reinforced. Such defence precautions were patchy in built up areas.

Activity at the Coast battery

The war time staffing establishment for a coast battery was three officers and 108 men, although this was later reduced to 80 men. To operate a six inch gun took one Non Commissioned Officer (NCO) and six gunners. Thus it took 42 NCOs and men to man two guns in three watches. Local battery orders said that there had to be sufficient men on duty day and night to open fire and keep it up until reserves arrived, The men were housed in huts or empty hotels and houses for there were plenty of these when life on the coast became hazardous. No civilians were allowed near the batteries and coast roads were often closed to vehicles which caused some inconvenience locally.

Each battery kept a daily War Diary in which everything of interest was recorded. Unfortunately the diaries of most of the Sussex batteries have not survived and those that have contain a dreary list of weather reports and changes in the battery personnel. But in the long periods of tedium there were bursts of activity most of it in the sky. No Sussex batteries were in action against ships, but they were fired on and bombed by aircraft. Because they were under the flight path of bombers returning from raids on Europe they also helped in rescue attempts. A Spitfire crash landed near the Pevensey Bay battery and the pilot was saved from the sea. The battery also shot down a Fokker Wolf 190 and later that year two American Flying fortresses and a Liberator bomber landed on the sea in front of the battery.

In the 1940s everything happened under a blanket of secrecy and few knew what was going on outside their own daily experience. Thus one battery reported the enemy landing suspected spies at Dungeness one night, another the presence of German wreckage off the shore. The Cooden battery reported sighting suspected German E boats, and also the landing of five French boys from a small boat. At night the blackout added to the isolation and numerous flashes, bangs, whistles and engine noises usually remained unexplained. There were also humorous entries in the diaries. One report mentioned a powerful smell along the beach and at Winchelsea the battery was over run by marsh flies. When an officer visited to inspect the battery he found that when the No 1 gun fired the Battery Observation Post was blinded by its smoke and needed to be resited.

It is hard to avoid the impression that life in the coast batteries was tedious, cold and boring without much happening for most of the time. Later in the war when the threat of invasion had mostly gone away the coast batteries were manned by local Home Guard units after they had had special training for the task.

Battery Locations

The sites of the Sussex coast batteries have been plotted on War Revision One Inch Ordnance Survey Maps, (Military Grid), sheets 133, 134, 135, 183, 184. and set out below. The target area of the guns was the sea in an arc in front of the battery and unless otherwise stated the guns were all six inch. For simplification mostly one battery designation is given.

Selsey Bill

There were no permanent coast defence batteries on Selsey Bill. The east side was covered by the guns of the Bognor battery and the west side lay within range of the long range batteries at Portsmouth and the Isle of Wight. This artillery was also supported by a battery of two 9.2 inch guns with a range of 13,000 yards in Oaklands Park, Chichester close to where the Festival Theatre now stands. Early in 1942 these guns were replaced by two 12 inch railway guns sited in the goods yard at Chichester railway station. Their role was to neutralise the Selsey area and the airfield on Thorney Island.

Bognor: 238 Coast Defence Battery (553 Coast Regiment)

This battery was actually in Aldwick about 500 yards from Bognor town centre. It stood overlooking the beach in the gardens of houses in Aldwick Avenue. It was one of only two batteries in Sussex armed with two 5.5 guns. These were old short range guns and unsuitable for coast defence purposes. It seems they were never replaced by the more powerful 6 inch guns because the likelihood of an attack diminished over time.

Littlehampton: 346 Coast Defence Battery (553 Coast Regiment)

This battery stood on the edge of the promenade near the former Beach Hotel since replaced by a block of flats. Two brick recesses with seats mark the site of the emplacements. The Battery Observation Post (BOP) still remains in its original position, but has been much altered. It was built in June 1940.

Angmering-on-Sea: 149 Coast Defence Battery (553 Coast Regiment)

Just west of Kingston Gorse on a private estate in Angmering-on-Sea this battery stood in the garden of a house in South Strand named "Pergolas" then owned by Colonel Sir John Perring. It was a slightly later battery set up in February 1941.

Worthing: 345 Coast Defence Battery (553 Coast Regiment)

Set up in June 1940 on the promenade in front of West Parade at its junction with Grand Avenue. The BOP was in the high block of flats behind at that date known as "The Towers"

Shoreham-by-Sea: 344 Coast Defence Battery (553 Coast Regiment)

This battery was established in June 1940 on the beach, the guns being either side of the old disused fort built in 1857. One of the houses on the beach served as a BOP.

Brighton: 359 Coast Defence Battery (553 Coast Regiment)

This battery stood on a level stretch of ground at the top of Duke's Mound opposite the houses at 14 Chichester Terrace and 1 Lewes Crescent.

Newhaven Fort and Castle Hill Battery (521 Coast Regiment)

Although Newhaven Fort was a permanent fortification it was mainly garrisoned by emergency batteries. In September 1939 the fort was manned by 159 Heavy Battery Royal Artillery (TA). Later 100 Coast Defence Battery took over until September 1943 when it was supplanted by 193 Coastal Defence Battery. The two six inch guns were mounted on the sea front ramparts of the Victorian fort built in the late 1860s. The BOP was in the fort.

Building of a new battery for three 6 six inch guns further up Castle Hill began in November 1941 but was not completed until June 1943. It is possible that 101 Independent Battery was also stationed at Newhaven until the new battery position was ready. Both batteries had separate BOPs.

Seaford: 343 Coast Defence Battery (521 Coast Regiment)

The gun houses for this battery were sited either in the gardens of the houses fronting Marine Drive, west of Connaught Road, or on the sea-front itself. A pill box which once stood on the corner of Connaught Road was part of the perimeter defences for this battery.

Eastbourne : 342 Coast Defence Battery (552 Coast Regiment)

Two six inch naval guns (built in 1910 and 1911) stood on the promenade below the Martello Tower No 73 known as the Wish Tower. The battery was responsible for the defence of the coast from Langney Point in the east to the cliffs of Beachy Head in the west.

Pevensey Bay: 237 Coast Defence Battery (552 Coast Regiment)

One of four batteries covering the wide expanse of Pevensey Bay. This battery dates from March 1941. Two 5.5 inch guns stood close to Martello tower No. 61 bordering the present Valprinseps and Norman Roads. It seems that these unsuitable guns were not replaced with six inch guns later. There was, however a battery of two 4.5 howitzers at their rear ranged on Westham, Pevensey village and station, and Norman's Bay halt.

Norman's Bay: 375 Coast Defence Battery (552 Coast Regiment)

A battery of two 4.7 inch guns probably dating from early 1941. The battery was on the shore south of the railway line and sited between the west and east sluices of Waller's Haven. The west sluice has now been filled in and only the east sluice is operative.

Cooden Beach: 221 Coast Defence Battery (552 Coast Regiment)

Two six inch guns were emplaced south of the railway line in the gardens of large houses whose backs faced the sea in Cooden Drive, on the outskirts of Bexhill. Two houses then called 'Three Chimney' and 'The Gate House' were part of the site.

Bexhill: 385 Coast Defence Battery (552 Coast Regiment)

A battery of two four inch guns which may have been replaced later by six inch guns when supplies became available. It stood at the eastern end of Bexhill in the vicinity of 'My Lord's Rock'.

Hastings: 341 Coast Defence Battery (552 Coast Regiment)

Two six inch guns were sited on Hastings sea front. Their location is uncertain but may have been on the promenade in the vicinity of Pelham Place. Set up in June 1940.

Cliff End: 194 and or 374 Coast Defence Batteries (552 Coast Regiment)

Before the cliffs rise sharply from the marshes towards Hastings there is a knoll about 200 yards back from the sea on which this battery was built. It looks out across the sea and the Pett Levels and the western end of the Royal Military Canal which is now closed off from the beach. The gun house, magazines and a pill box are in a fair state of preservation.

Winchelsea 360 and or 341 Coast Defence Batteries (552 Coast Regiment)

This site was on the sea shore at Winchelsea Beach which is about a mile south of the ancient town of Winchelsea. Its guns swept the approach to Rye harbour and supported the fire of Cliff End battery to the west. Some remains of military buildings have been incorporated into post-war housing in the Dogs Hill Road area and the BOP is clearly visible in a garden in Smeatons Lane.

Jury's Gap: 336 Coast Defence Battery (551 Coast Regiment)

The guns fired across the sands into Rye Bay and the battery site was close to the sewer which drained the marshes, just outside the Sussex border which ended at Camber Sands.

Dungeness (552 Coast Regiment)

In 1940 no provision was made for guns to be sited on Dungeness Point as there was a Mobile Naval Base Defence Organisation battery stationed there. Later, and presumably when more artillery became available, 213 Coast Defence Battery of two 4.7 inch guns and 374 Coast defence Battery of three six inch guns are shown in the records as being stationed near the point. These batteries commanded the good holding ground and anchorage on the west flank of Dungeness Peninsular, the entrance the Rye harbour, and also supported the other batteries in the bay. The Dungeness Peninsular was not easy to defend and any fixed guns on it could easily be over run.

Note

The information in this chapter comes from many sources and should not be regarded as complete. In the early and unsettled days of 1940-1941 batteries were often switched between sites to reflect defence priorities and changing needs. Also on 23rd September 1941 artillery siting boards were convened to choose additional sites for gun batteries at Hove, Lancing and Middleton, but there is no firm evidence that these were ever built and armed.

9.1 A gunner on watch outside his coast battery scans sea and sky.

9.2 This is a view of Cliff End Battery near Fairlight east of Hastings. Most of the buildings remain and the Battery Observation Post has excellent views across Rye Bay to Dungeness.

9.3 The rear of 345 Coast Defence Battery on the promenade at Grand Avenue, Worthing.

9.4 A close up inside one of the 6 inch guns at the Worthing Battery.

9.5 A War Revision Ordnance Survey map marked with the site of the Coast Defence Batteries between Eastbourne and Bexhill on Sea.

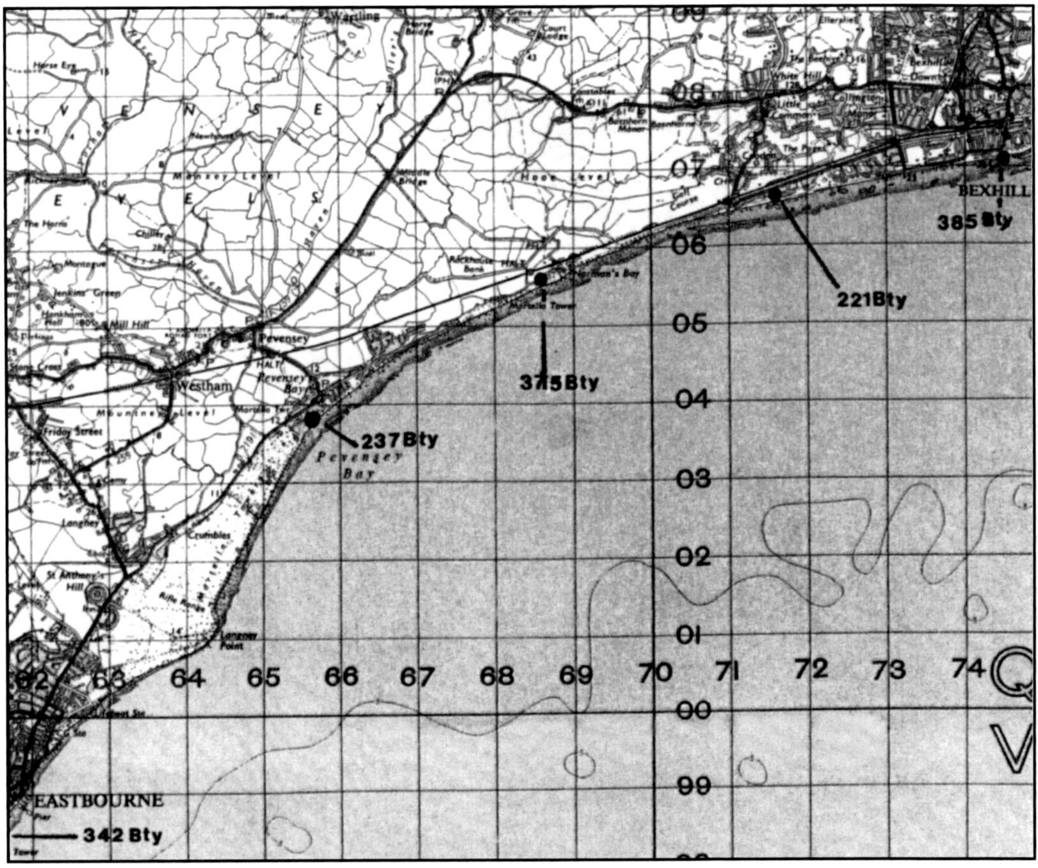

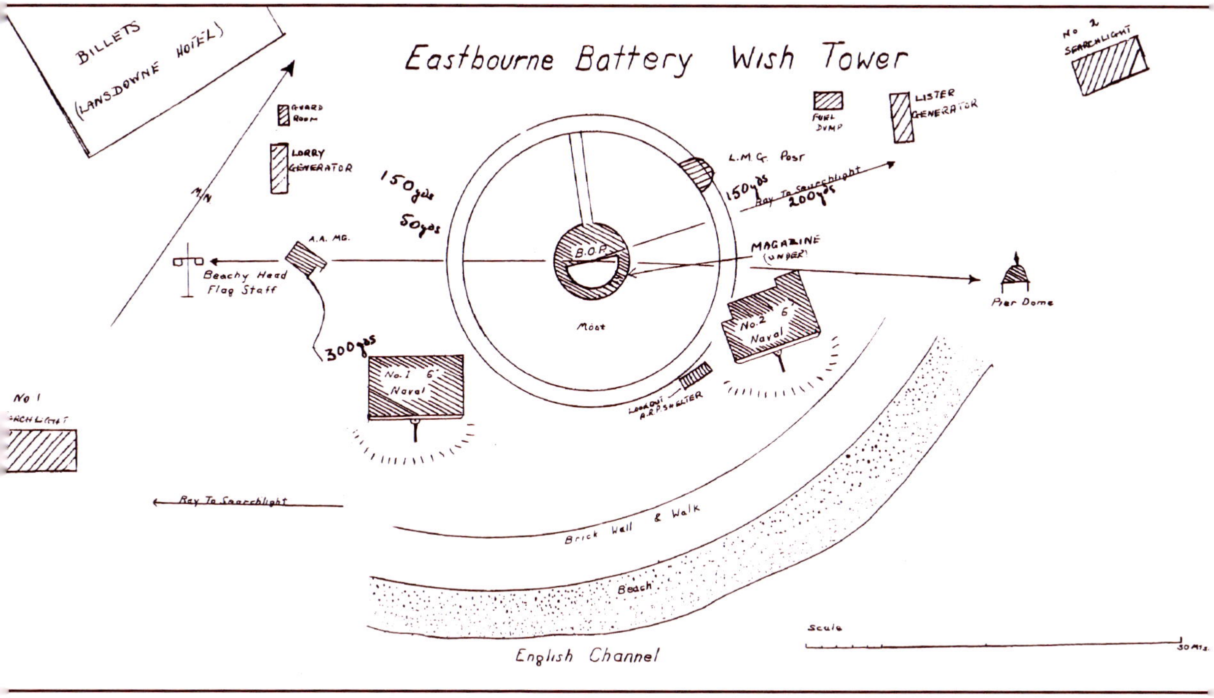

9.6 War Diary plan of 342 Coast Defence Battery at the Wish Tower, Eastbourne.

9.7 Gunners loading one of the 6 inch guns at the Eastbourne Battery.

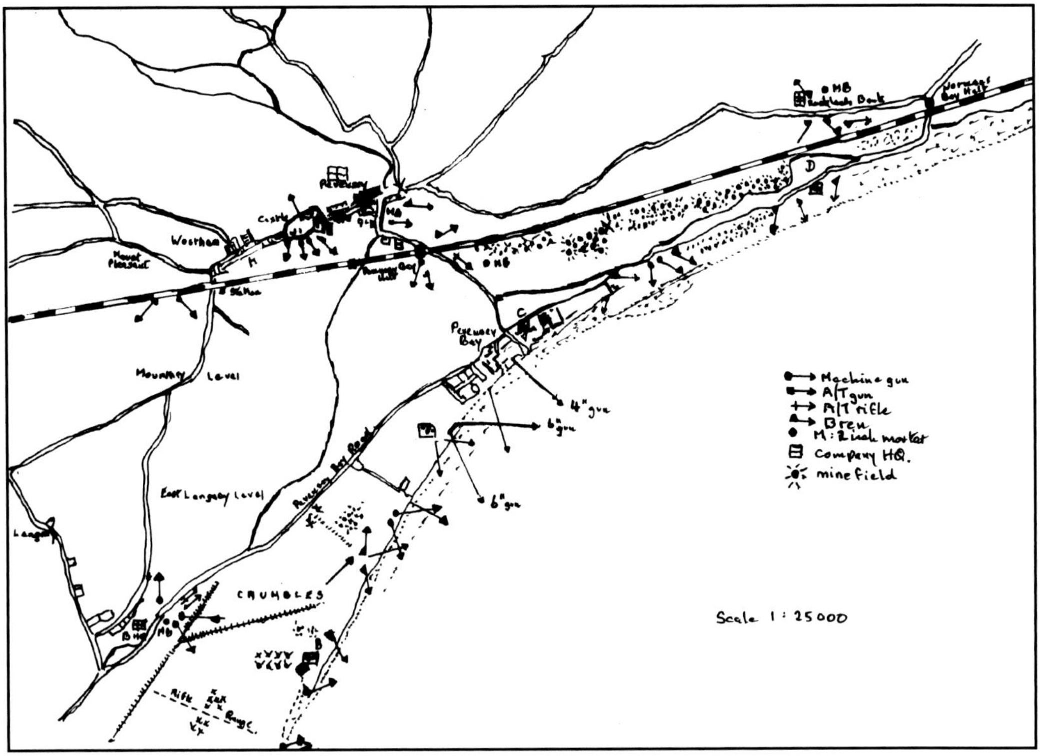

9.8 *Plan of the perimeter defences at 237 Coast Defence Battery at Pevensey Bay.*

9.9 *Drawing by an unknown gunner of the view on the left flank of the Pevensey Bay Battery.*

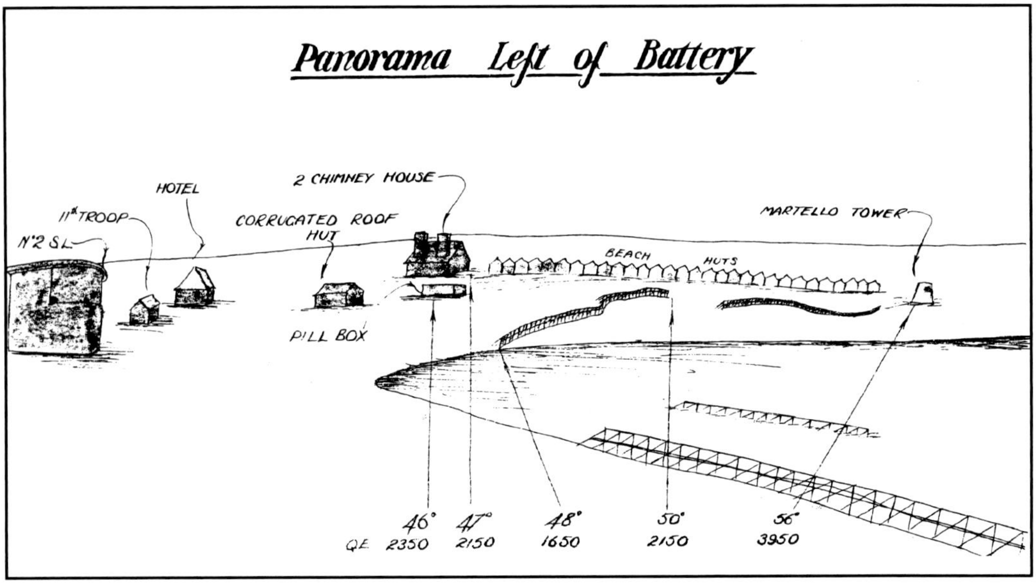

9.10 Gunners passing No 1 gun at the Pevensey Bay battery. No 2 searchlight house stands right in the background with anti-tank obstacles on the beach.

9.11 A rare surviving 90cm searchlight with fan for coast batteries found in a junk yard.

9.12 The Battery Observation Post on top of the Martello Tower at Pevensey Bay now used as a residence. The gun battery stood in front on the beach.

9.13 *Gun drill at 385 Coast Defence Battery at My Lord's Rock, Bexhill on Sea.*

9.14 *Gunners fusing shells at 341 Coast Defence Battery on Hastings sea front.*

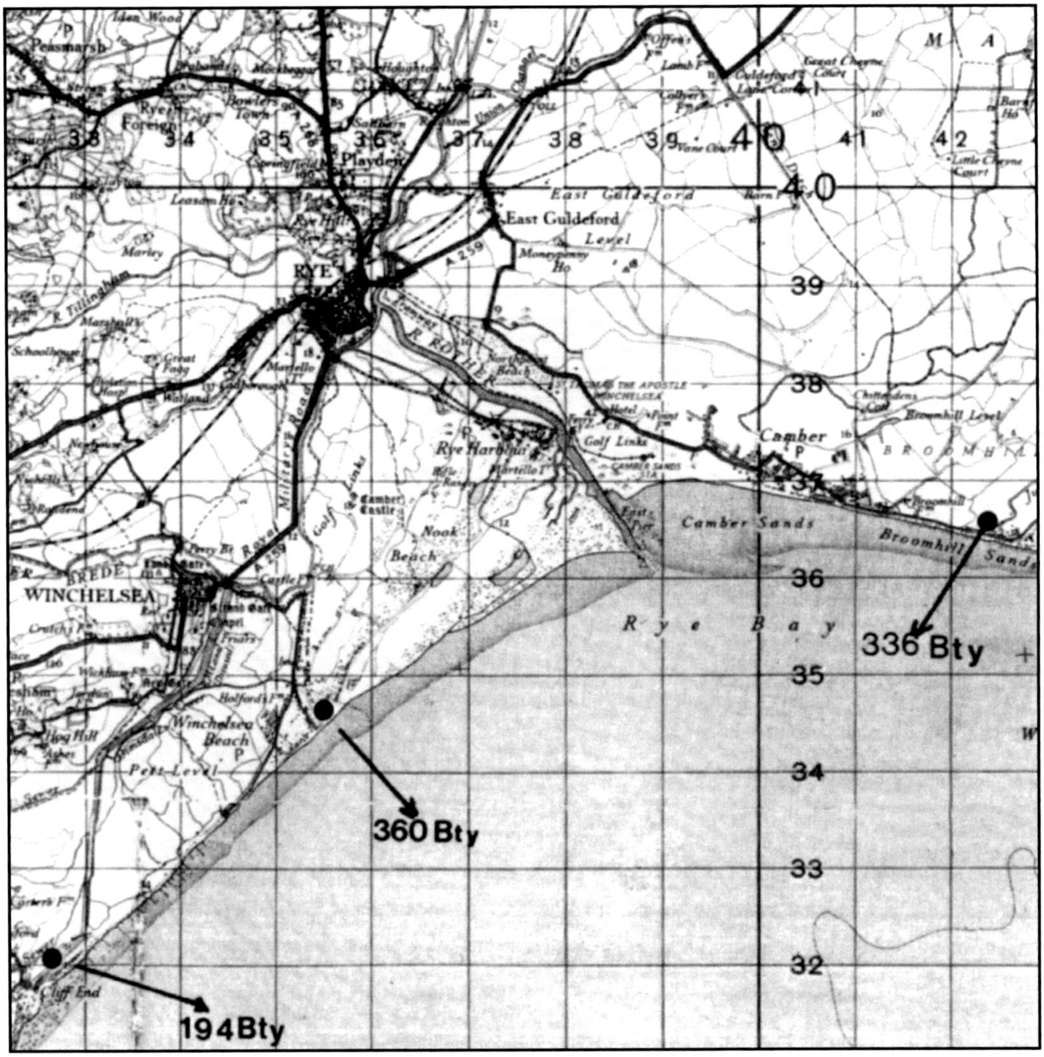

9.15 *The Coast Defence Batteries between Cliff End, Hastings and Camber east of Rye.*

9.16 The Battery Observation Post for 360 Coast Defence Battery at Winchelsea Beach. It now stands back from the sea in a garden in Smeatons Lane in 2010.

9.17 Ministry of Supply poster seeking binoculars from the public.

CHAPTER 10

OLD NEWHAVEN FORT AND ITS ROLE IN THE 1940s

Newhaven port is the only Sussex deep water port to have a cross Channel service to France. Since 1847, there has been a direct rail link to London hence its double usefulness to an enemy intent on invasion. In 1939 the Admiralty designated Newhaven as a Commercial Port and sent a small party of naval ratings there to set up a trawler and mine sweeping base. It was also scheduled to be a casualty clearing station ready to unload war casualties from France, and there was even some discussion as to whether it could be classified as an open port under the Geneva Red Cross Convention. During the winter of 1939-40 orders were apparently issued that it was not to be defended, but air raids and the Dunkirk invasion led to it being militarised and listed as a defended port.

The port and its facilities developed rapidly. A War Signal Station and Examination Service to interrogate incoming vessels was set up and auxiliary patrols and motor launch flotillas were sent out into the English Channel. A large underground joint naval and army communication centre was dug into the hillside at Denton across the river valley, and this together with the naval base was commissioned as HMS Forward.

Following the publication of a Royal Commission report in 1860 a decision was taken to strengthen the defences of the major naval ports by the building of expensive fortifications to protect them against attack. Although not then a naval port, the importance of Newhaven as a ferry terminal with a direct rail link to London was recognised. The building of a powerful new fort to replace an existing obsolete battery was begun but not completed and armed until over ten years later.

The fort is a substantial work enclosing nearly sixteen acres of the lower slopes of Castle Hill, overlooking the entrance to the River Ouse and the harbour. Built along the 100 foot (30 metre) contour and sunk into chalk downland its profile is almost invisible from the sea. It is protected by a ditch 39 feet (12 metres) wide and 29 feet (9 metres) deep. Both walls are faced with concrete - the first fortification in Britain to use concrete instead of brick for the purpose. Entrance to the fort is over a fixed drawbridge and through a tunnel in the rampart. Although obsolete since 1900 it was a sufficiently strong defensive position to resist any land attack on the guns mounted on the rampart facing the sea in 1940.

On the outbreak of war there were two six inch guns in the fort and some months later two 12 pounders were added. The gun emplacements were roofed over after the Spanish Civil War experience of successful and disastrous attacks by German Stuka dive bombers. Ammunition was supplied to the guns from the Victorian magazines below, modified with automatic lifts. Canadian engineers dug a primitive tunnel through the southern rampart which was lined with corrugated iron sheeting and hoops. This led to two lookouts cut in the chalk cliff face. This tunnel has now been closed off as unsafe. Magazines, laboratories, and casemates once capable of holding 250 men and their stores easily accommodated the much smaller garrison needed to defend the fort and work the modern guns. When the fort was built it had a long and steep tunnel driven down through the cliff to a large caponnier (blockhouse) built in brick, with loopholes to give flanking fire along the base of the cliff. A branch tunnel led to a sally port behind the Hope Inn. At some date the blockhouse was filled with large iron oil tanks with an array of pipe work which is believed to have been connected to a fire boom laid across the Narrows of the harbour. It seems to have been faulty because it was removed later after an accident. The strength of the fort was enhanced by building into its ramparts 17 Bren gun posts and rifle pits. There were four pill boxes, including one in a very conspicuous position over the main gate and a Blacker Bombard (mortar) in the north west corner.

The task of the guns in the fort was to sink enemy shipping approaching the shore and attempting a landing in Seaford Bay or the capture of the port. It was accepted that the six inch guns in the fort had limitations inasmuch as they had restricted fire coverage over the sea westwards towards Brighton. In November 1941 work began on a second battery of three six inch guns outside the fort and higher up Castle Hill. The guns of this new battery. were to have 45 degree elevation which increased their range to 24,000 yards (13.6 miles). They were not expected, however, to effectively engage ships more heavily armed than light cruisers and armed merchant ships. Each emplacement had an underground magazine which supplied the guns.

Access to the new battery from the fort was by a footbridge across the moat from the western rampart, and the rear of the battery was protected by belts of barbed wire. For some reason the new battery was not finished and armed until August 1943, by which time there was no serious threat to this part of the coast.

The three concrete gun positions lie disused today with their magazines sealed beneath. A high Coast Guard tower has been built over the magazines of the middle one.

There were many changes in the regiments manning the guns at Newhaven. In September 1939, 159 Heavy Battery (Royal Artillery) (Territorial Army) formed the garrison. Then Coast Defence Batteries, 160, 193, and 100 of 521 Coast Defence Regiment took over the duty. Following the abolition of coastal artillery in 1956 the fort was sold to the Local Authority seven years later. It had been neglected and vandalised but after extensive repairs it was opened to the public as a tourist attraction. Most of the underground passages, magazines, casemates and gun positions of the original Victorian fort can be seen and some of the WW2 additions are obvious even if their purpose today is obscure. Newhaven Fort has survived for over one hundred years and its sheer bulk suggests that it will remain much the same for as long as the chalk cliffs beneath it exist.

10.1 Newhaven Fort from the east in 1939 when it was still a military station.

10.2 The drawbridge and entrance to Newhaven Fort. The pill box over the entrance was added in 1940

10.3 The army left Newhaven Fort in 1956. This was its vandalised interior in 1971

10.4 An old 6 inch gun on Newhaven Fort with the overhead protection removed. There was a 12 pounder Quick firing gun in the background building.

10.5 Newhaven Fort in 1940 showing the perimeter defences and the proposed new battery outside the fort ditch.

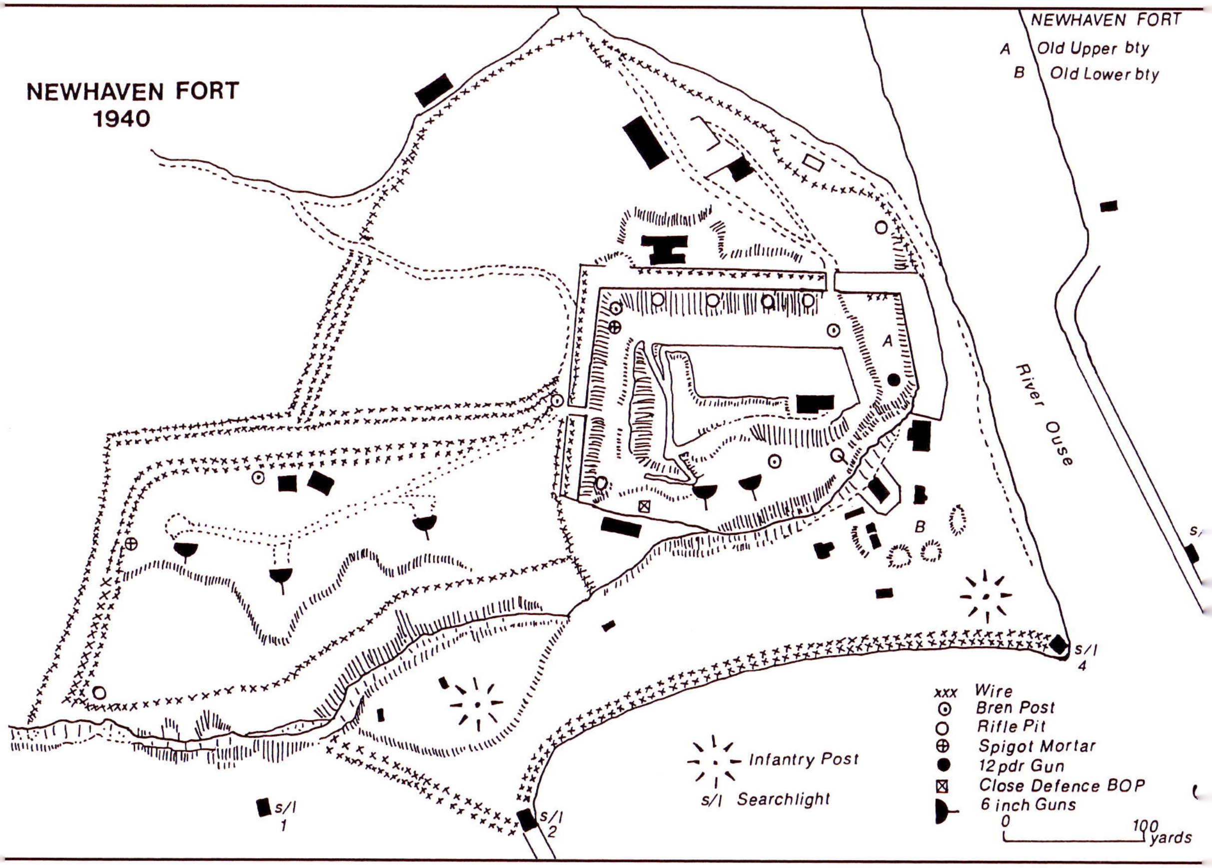

10.6 The Battery Observation Post on top of the Fort.

10.7 A tunnel dug by Canadian engineers through the chalk cliff to an observation loophole overlooking the harbour.

↗ 10.8 Site of the batteries covering Seaford Bay and the entrance to Newhaven harbour.

→ 10.9 Site of one of the new 6-inch emplacements completed in 1943. The magazine is partly sunk into the hillside at the rear.

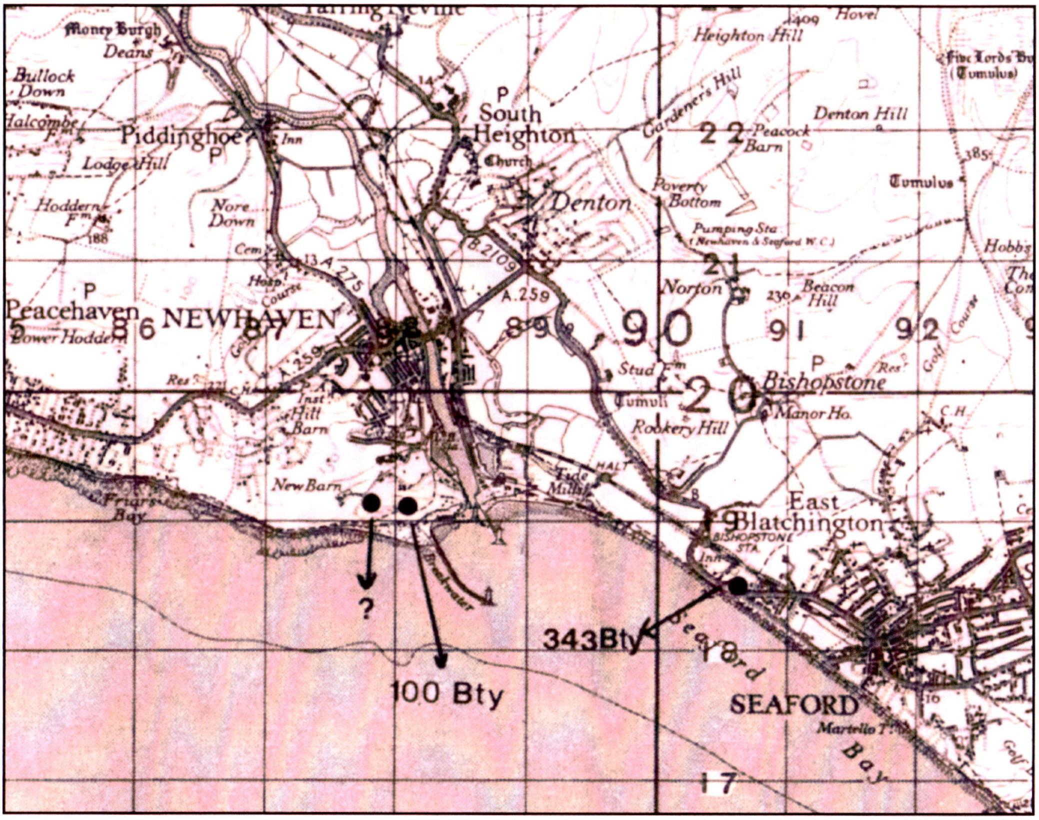
Heighton Hill
Bullock Down
South Heighton
Piddinghoe
Lodge Hill
Denton
Denton Hill
Peacock Barn
Tumulus
Nore Down
Poverty Bottom
Pumping Sta
Peacehaven
NEWHAVEN
Norton
Beacon Hill
Stud Fm
Bishopstone
Manor Ho.
Rookery Hill
New Barn
Tide Mills
East Blatchington
?
343Bty
100 Bty
SEAFORD
Seaford Bay
Martello T

10.10 The 1874 caponnier for infantry to protect the base of the cliff from mining operations.

10.11 The interior of the caponnier filled with oil tanks to supply the fire barrier installed across the harbour mouth.

Chapter 11

HMS FORWARD AN UNDERGROUND HEADQUARTERS

By 1941 many of the new gun batteries along the Kent and Sussex coast were in various stages of completion. Between Dover and Portsmouth it was left entirely to the discretion of the local battery commanders when they fired their guns at ships out at sea. The Admiralty was understandably unhappy with this absence of any centralised control. With so many of their ships in the English Channel the danger of their being sunk by trigger happy gunners because of mistaken identity was too great. They were also insistent that their freedom of movement about the Channel should not be restricted.

The matter was referred to London and the Chiefs of Staff decided that the Admiralty and War Office should arrange for joint control over when the coast batteries should be allowed to fire. This could only be done by putting the two services together. Approval was given to building combined plotting rooms for the purpose and because of their importance they were to be blast and splinter proof and preferably underground.

Since the beginning of the war there had been a naval presence at Newhaven port and with an increase of naval activity there it was decided to build a joint naval and army plotting room outside the port, both areas being commissioned, in the naval fashion, as land based HMS Forward. The site chosen was at South Heighton, a small village on a shoulder of chalk downland below Denton village. It lies on the east bank of the Ouse valley just over two miles from Newhaven harbour. It was excavated in haste by sappers of the Royal Engineers and was a rough and ready affair which today is in a deteriorating condition sealed off from public access.

Two very long entrance tunnels were dug into the centre of the chalk hillside. At the lower level tunnel T1 starts from a blocked brick doorway beneath a pill box in Avis Road, (A26), and a second tunnel T7 began under Room 16 at Denton House, (Guinness Trust Estate) which stood between Denton Road and Heighton Road. After the war Room 16 was demolished and today this former entrance to the tunnels is a padlocked manhole in a private garden.

The operational centre of the complex, where the tunnels come together, is about seventy feet down (21 metres) inside the hill. There are two wider parallel tunnels, T2 and T3 linked by five branch tunnels, C1 - 5 all about nine feet (3 metres) wide. As chalk is a very stable material the tunnels were lined with H section mine arches backed with galvanised corrugated iron sheeting. Plywood was used to line the walls which were white washed to make the working areas lighter.

Inside the main tunnels breeze block and wooded partitions were installed to give some privacy to the various working areas. In these were the telephone switchboards, teleprinters, coding machines and the separate but adjacent naval and army plotting rooms. There was sleeping accommodation for the male and female day and night watches. The smaller offshoot tunnels housed Elsan toilets, wash rooms, a galley and air conditioning equipment. Special daylight lighting was installed and airlocks at the entrances kept the temperature at a constant 65 degrees. Working in a confined space and an artificial atmosphere was not pleasant and perhaps the only compensation was that at night they were safe from enemy bombing.

Probably there were up to 20-30 service personnel working underground at any one time. The army contingent included a plotting officer from a coast artillery regiment. four plotters and four telephonists all from the Auxiliary Territorial Services, (ATS). Their duties were shared with the Women's Royal Naval Service, (WRENS) who worked in the naval section.

The advantage of the combined plotting room to the army was that it enabled them to keep all the coast artillery batteries informed about the movements of shipping whether friendly or hostile. How the system worked was that the bearing range and position of vessels at sea would be passed from ships, radar stations, the coast watching organisation and other intelligence to the staff in the naval plotting room. If the ship was a 'doubtful' or hostile it was given a number and the details passed to the adjacent army plotting room. Both navy and army plotting rooms then checked the position of the suspect ship at short intervals (minutes) and transmitted details of its range and bearing to coast batteries and naval vessels in the vicinity. Coast batteries were forbidden to engage a ship until the naval duty officer authorised his army counterpart to give the order to fire.

A military map dated November 1941 shows the locations of the Coast Defence Chain Home Low radar stations manned by the army and linked to the joint naval and army plotting rooms at Newhaven and Portsmouth. They kept watch over traffic in the English Channel and, as a result of the information they provided, six enemy ships were sunk and one damaged.

During the building of the underground centre some thought had been given to its protection. The main threat was expected to come from saboteurs, but enemy commando type raids on the coast could not be ruled out. The two entrances were guarded by sentries behind iron gates and there were also four pill boxes and an observation post ST6 with a good view of the harbour and surrounding countryside. Entrance into these was by ladders fixed to shafts from inside the complex. These had been drilled by Canadian engineers soon after they arrived in this country. At the bottom of tunnel ST 7 leading down from the top of the hill was a pit to catch any grenades rolled down and there were also internal gates and machine gun positions. For a time the pill boxes were manned by the Home Guard armed with Vickers machine guns.

It is clear from correspondence with the Admiralty that it regarded the protection of this underground headquarters as of grade A importance and expected the army to take responsibility for it. The latter were less sure being unwilling to tie men up on static guard duties. Their view was that the entire area around was a closed military zone with plenty of divisional troops in the vicinity. The Admiralty apparently lost out for the matter seems to have been resolved in 1942 with a small marine guard taking over responsibility for defence.

The joint naval and army plotting rooms closed when the war ended and all that remains today is a series of empty tunnels sealed off and gradually decaying away. A housing estate was built across the top of it in 1979.

11.1 South Heighton from the north west. The tunnel complex lies buried beneath the low hillside in the centre of the picture.

11.2 Plan of HMS Forward: Plotting Rooms (T2). Codes and Signals (T3). Switchboards (C4/ C5) Toilets (RM 1/2) Galley (RM3) Pillboxes (P) Slopes (ST).

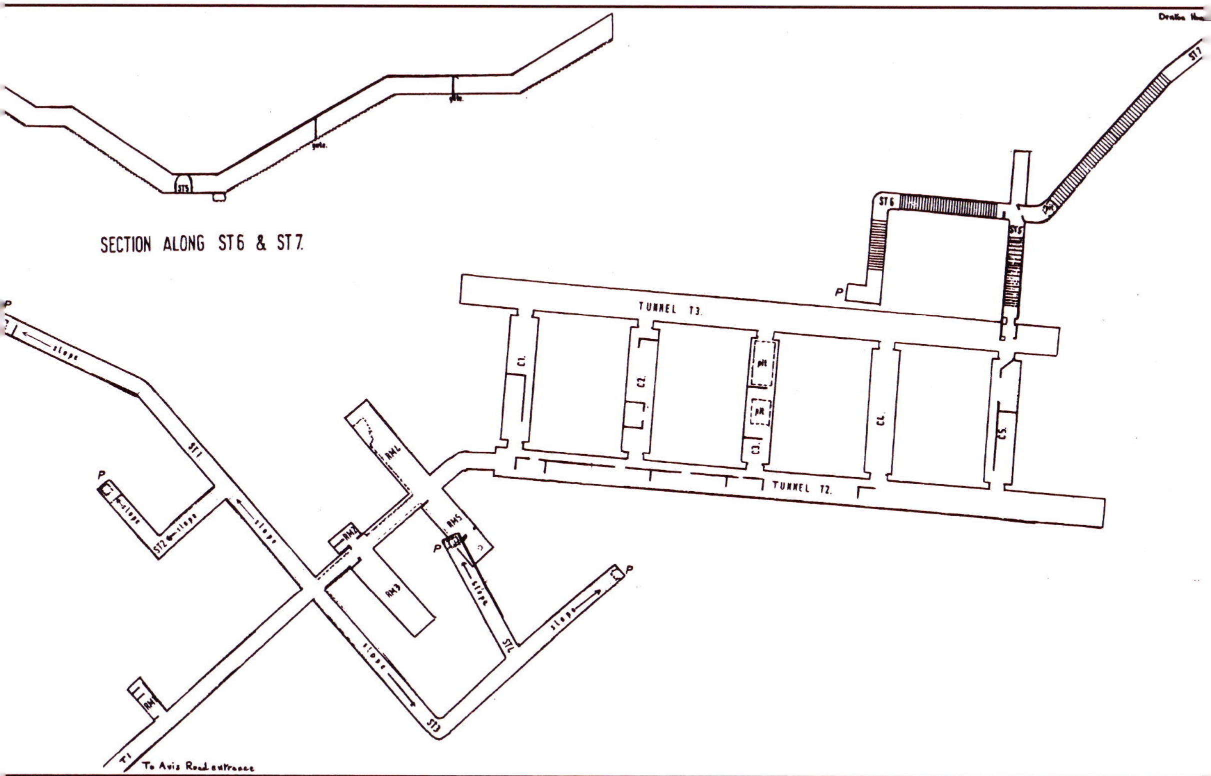

11.3 A naval plotting room in operation during the war.

11.4 Surveying the tunnels at South Heighton.

↗ *11.5 South Heighton. A tunnel junction with badly corroded ironwork.*

→ *11.6 South Heighton. Some of the ventilation trunking is still in place.*

Chapter 12

MILITARY SIGNALS BETWEEN LONDON AND THE SOUTH COAST

Generals faced with deploying armies to counter an invasion of the South Coast of England have over the centuries had to decide where the invader is going to land. The key to making the right decision was communication from the coast to the headquarters of the military and civil authorities. In 1587 Queen Elizabeth's Ministers established a chain of fire (actually smoke) beacons from the coast to London to signal the Spanish Armada was approaching. When Napoleon threatened invasion in 1803, naval signal posts using flags and a special army telegraph system served the same purpose.

The German threat to the Sussex and Kent coast in 1940 meant that the existing public telephone system had to be augmented with a new network of cables linking all three services. An extensive wireless network was also needed but gave rise to problems.

Fortunately, a special Defence Telegraph Network had been set up in 1938. Based on a number of major switching centres for telephones and teleprinters it connected all the static headquarters of the three services. It was installed by the Post Office, but manned by service personnel and used mainly for service administrative traffic. It was recognised that in wartime most military units would also have access to the public telephone system and so extra cables were laid below ground to provide alternative routes around centres which might be affected by bombing or land attacks.

There turned out to be difficulties in setting up a wireless network which was needed to pass priority, sometimes secret, messages to all the military units in South Eastern Command. The problem of sufficient channels for army signals was made worse by the shortage of equipment after the Dunkirk retreat. Eventually an extensive wireless network for the Hampshire to Kent area came into being and fortunately a diagram of this has survived. It shows how information from infantry divisions and tank brigades along the coast, reported through their Corps headquarters, (4, 5, and 12 Corps) to the South East Command Centre and thence to the War Office, and GHQ Home Forces. There were parallel links to RAF squadrons at Odiham (Hants), Gatwick, and Croydon (Surrey), and to the RAF Army Co-operation Command who oversaw 34, 35 and 36 Wings. Also connected to the network was the Canadian Corps with its three divisions, north of Aldershot.

On the coast there was a joint army and naval wireless link connecting the naval staff at Portsmouth and Dover with HMS Forward at Denton, Newhaven, to ensure that the action of the army coast defence batteries was co-ordinated with the movement of naval ships in the English Channel when an enemy was sighted.

It has already been mentioned that because so much wireless equipment was lost in the retreat from France, what remained was not always fit for the job. Most of the wireless sets in use were No 9 and No 11 sets, both with a too short range of 50 miles and a limited number of channels. The No 3 set at the the War Office and South Eastern Command Centre needed a 70 foot high mast. As this made the site conspicuous it had to be built three miles away from the field headquarters and operated by remote control. There were so many doubts about the efficiency of the whole system if invasion came that portable radios were issued to units over which coded invasion warnings would be sent if all else failed. A backup pigeon service was also held in reserve. This was never used but birds had to be requisitioned from reluctant private owners and trained to work from fixed and mobile lofts.

Invasion Warnings

A set of fairly basic signals warning of the probable start of an invasion was issued to the navy, army and air force.

For the navy three or more white rockets burning for about 7 seconds meant that enemy ships had been sighted. One red flare meant large numbers of aircraft were flying towards the shore.

For the army forward troops were told to fire two Verey lights which signified that enemy troops were landing.

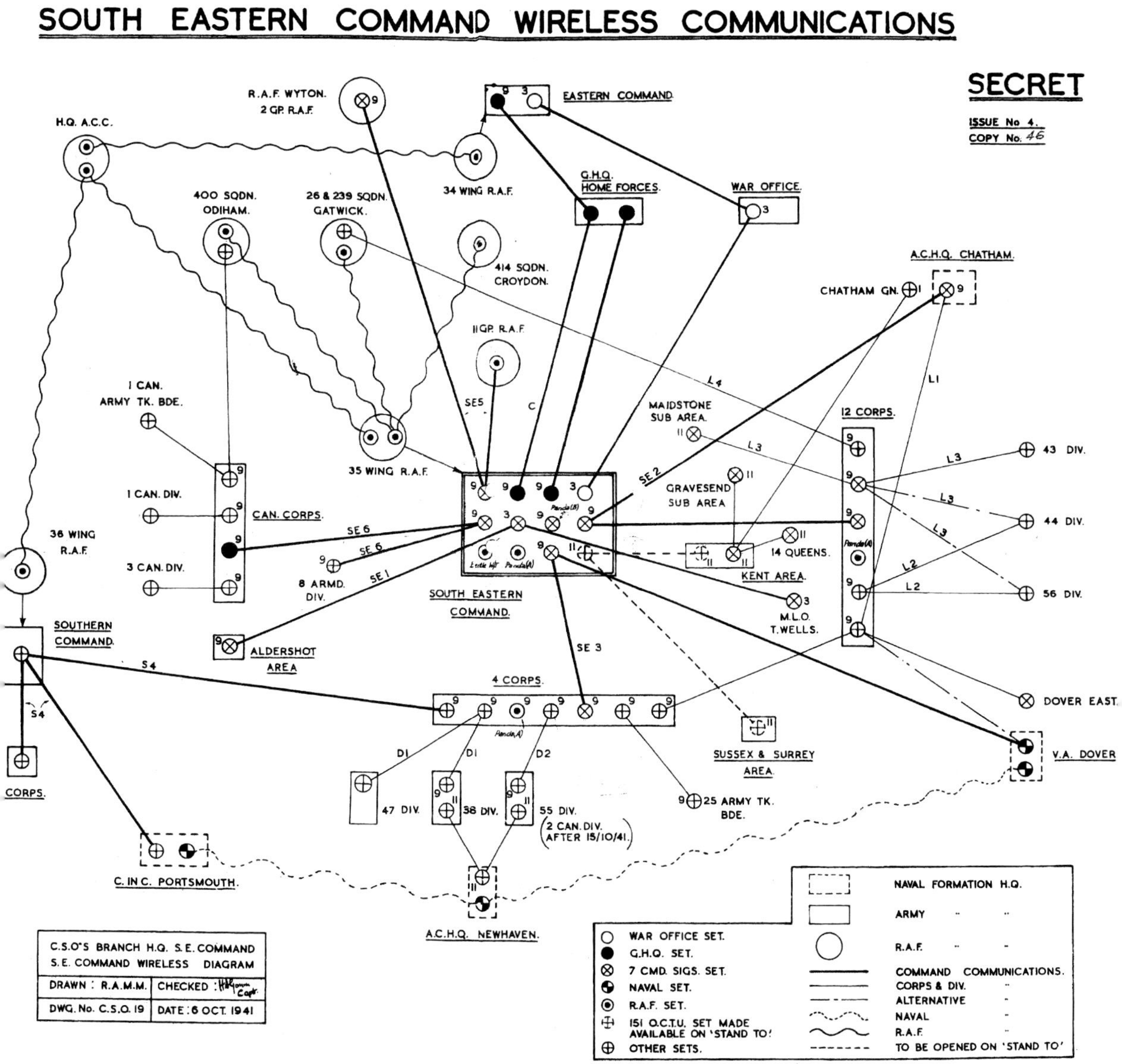

12.1 The wireless communication network between London and the coast in 1941.

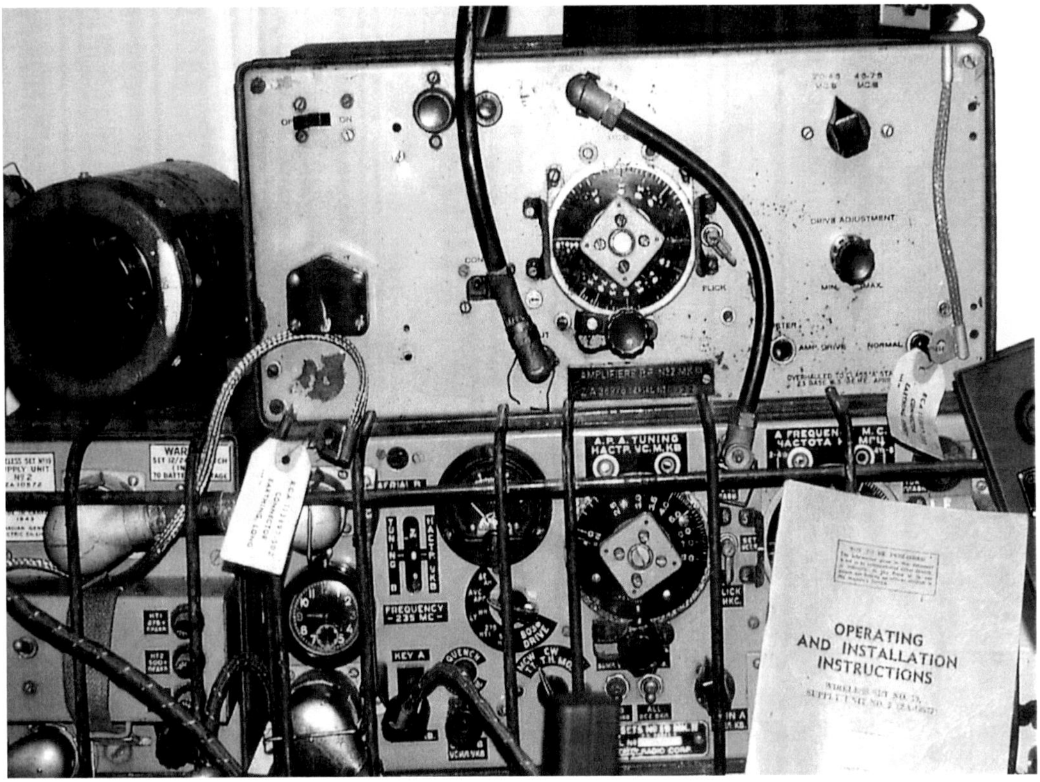

12.2 There were many types of wireless sets used by the army. This is probably a No 19 set operated by Royal Signals personnel.

12.3 Standard civilian Post Office switchboards of this type were installed in army headquarters and manned by Royal Signals personnel.

Chapter 13

Nets, Fire Booms and Minefields

The prepared defence of Sussex against invasion began some twenty miles from land out at sea, and was undertaken when the military situation became critical after the evacuation from France. It was essential to stop troop carrying barges from approaching the coast and enemy submarines had to be deterred from sneaking close to the shore to make a reconnaissance.

Floating Net Barriers

The Admiralty code name for this operation was "Tablecloth". Light horizontal coiled anti-submarine wire nets were suspended from floating canvas tubes filled with kapok. The net barrier followed the line of the coast and was anchored about twenty-two miles out at sea. One such barrier was installed off St Leonards and stretched 13 miles to Holywell Bank off the Wish Tower at Eastbourne. This work was completed before May 1941. The Army Headquarters of 4 Corps under South Eastern Command asked for two miles of a similar net to be put in the sea off Seaford, and a half a mile of net barrier to cover the entrance to the Cuckmere River. This request was referred to the Naval Officer at Newhaven for his views and given the area's importance it was probably agreed to and acted on. Further west along the Sussex Coast, another barrier nearly 9 miles long stretched between Black Rock at Brighton and close to a patch of sea, known as Grass Banks, about one mile off Worthing. This barrier had also been finished before May 1941.

Between the net barrier and the shore there was sufficient sea room for lighter vessels to patrol and report the approach of enemy submarines and ships. After Dunkirk auxiliary patrols were organised for this purpose. Five sections were formed with six boats, (of various types) in each, and they sailed out of Littlehampton, Shoreham, Newhaven and Rye harbours. The craft were not very suitable for this work in winter, although the inshore patrols were kept up.

Sea Mines and Fire Booms

No minefields off the Sussex coast seem to have been laid before the summer of 1940 because the German Navy was not active in this part of the Channel. When a minefield was laid the sea ways between it and and the shore were kept free for coastal shipping and anti submarine patrols.

Booms and or controlled minefields (ie fired from the shore) were subsequently installed at Chichester Bar, Pagham Harbour, the entrance to the River Arun at Lttlehampton, Shoreham Harbour inner basin, and the entrances to Newhaven port and Rye harbour. At Newhaven and Shoreham vessels were sunk to narrow the channel and a block ship was available to be pulled across and close the gap if necessary.

Arrangements for a fire boom were made ready at Newhaven although this resulted in local difficulties and had to be removed. Some booms at the smaller harbours were kept ready in case they were needed. They were rudimentary structures comprising timber spars and wire.

The working harbours were protected by controlled minefields with mines supplied from the depot at Frater near Gosport. Controlled minefields worked on the loop system. A loop of electric cable was laid on the sea bed enclosing an area 600 yards by 25 yards, A ship crossing the area induced a small current in the loop which showed up in the control station on shore as a spot of light on a screen. Mines laid down the centre of the loop could all be fired simultaneously from the shore. The harbour defence scheme would comprises several loops, some without mines to give an early signal of the approach of a ship. This was particularly helpful at night along a darkened coastline. The Newhaven controlled minefield was operated from within the fort. Mine watching posts for loose mines detached by the tides and of danger to shipping were set up on West Quay and manned by Southern Railway workers.

Police reports show that during 1939-42 about 120 sea mines came close inshore between Selsey and Winchelsea and were exploded by machine guns, rifle, or gun fire. Most were German, but there were some British and four French mines. There were some casualties when they were destroyed.

Minefields on beaches, sea front roads and fields behind

There were several different marks of anti-personal and anti-tank mines used by infantry and armoured divisions stationed in Sussex in the 1940s. The former were laid according to the Divisional Commanders policy the latter by local commanders, in a density of one mine per yard of front and buried at various depths, usually above the high water mark. The East and West Sussex Police Archives include several hundred documents, plans and drawings relating to the type and laying of mines on the beaches, fields and roads of the county. Mine laying was carried out in November 1941 and records of what was done have survived because when clearance was undertaken by the army in 1944-45 safety certificates had to be given by the army authorities to the local police.

The Canadian Engineers of the No 1 Tunnelling Company Canadian army laid many of the minefields. Pipe mines were often referred to as McNaughton Tubes after General McNaughton who commanded the 1st Canadian Division. These were metal pipes packed with an explosive known as PBG (Polar Blasting Gelatine). Most of the roads and bridges leading inland from the coast had pipe mines buried underneath.

The mine clearance certificates often cautioned that disposal was hampered by movement of the sea, wind blown sand, cliff falls and the effects of enemy action. Drawings of mined areas in East Sussex on Brighton sea front and Birling Gap, are reproduced as examples. There were over several hundred mined areas on or close to the beaches. Some of the longest stretches were on the Lawns on Hove sea front; from Burrow Head, Newhaven, to Tide Mills; in the fields behind the beaches south of the railway Eastbourne to Bexhill; and from Fairlight to Winchelsea and the Kent border. Some minefields were up to 80 yards wide and most were accompanied by belts of wire and steel anti-tank scaffolding.

In West Sussex, with its long flat open beaches and no cliffs or hills behind there were over 100 separate mine belts stretching for mile after mile from Shoreham by Sea to Selsey Bill and Thorney Island. Two maps show the mined areas on Worthing sea front and adjacent to the mouth of the River Arun at Littlehampton.

A copy of the Mine Clearance Certificate for minefield No 55A to the northwest of the old west bank fort at Littlehampton shows that this small area of 4,800 square yards between two gaps to reach the defence positions in the fort, was sewn with mines. The certificate also expresses doubts about the exact number of mines laid.

The records were not always accurate and in 1947, Mr Rand a City of London police sergeant, was on holiday at East Beach, Selsey and while out walking with his dog near Park Lane trod on a mine under some tamarisk trees, which exploded, only the dog survived! There were similar unfortunate incidents in East Sussex, usually reported in local newspapers. Given the number of mines laid in Sussex it is perhaps remarkable that there were so few casualties and thanks must be given to the engineers who cleared the minefields when the war ended.

13.1 Diagram of a minefield at sea. 'Influence' mines detect the approach of a ship and explode when a ship passes by.

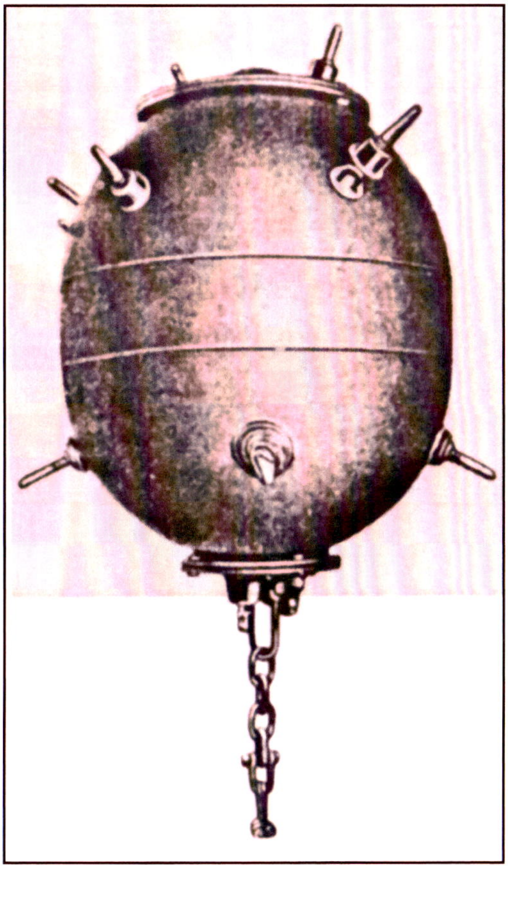

13.2 This is a standard British Mark XIV contact mine which was moored by a chain to the sea bed

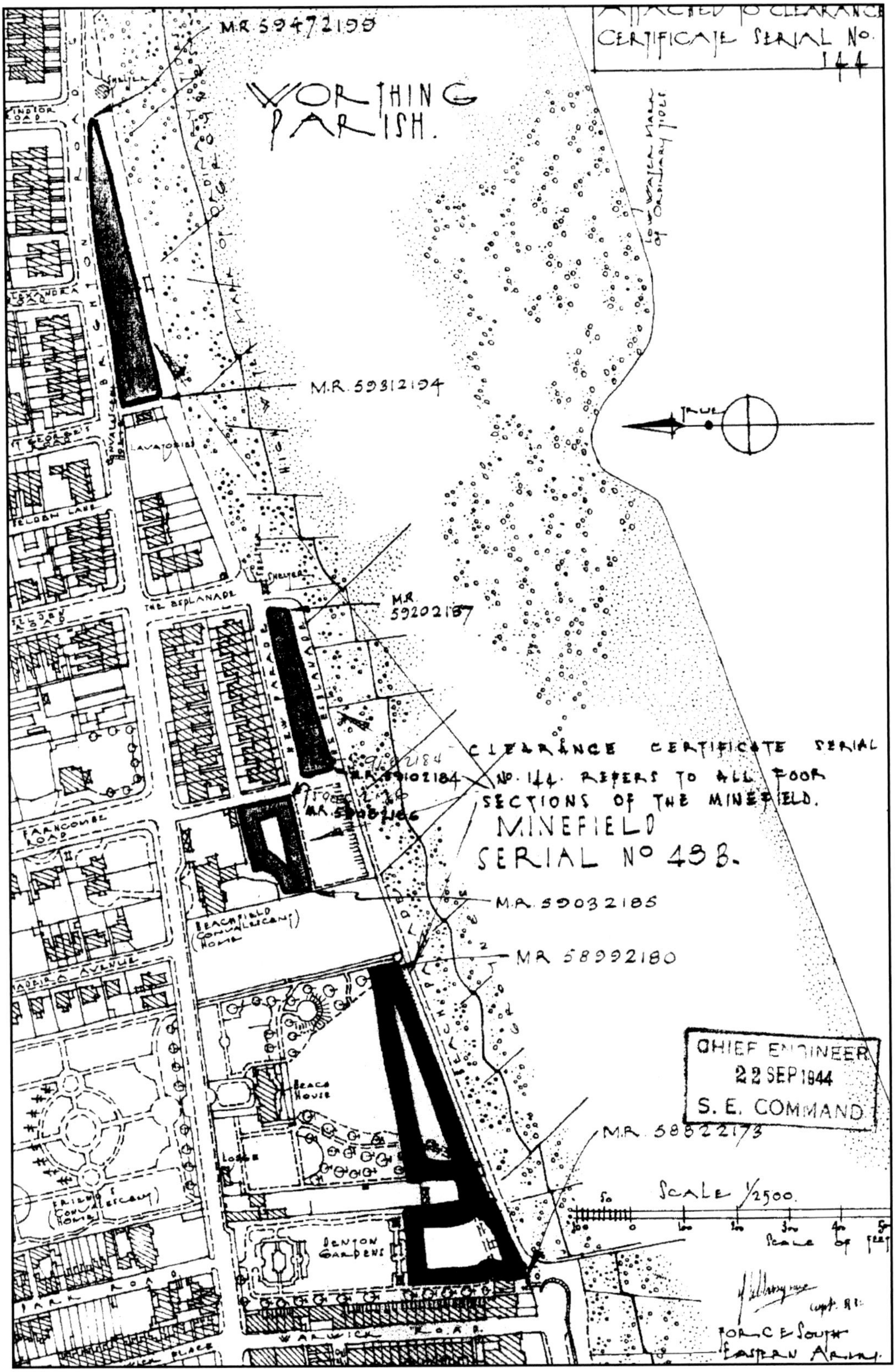
ATTACHED TO CLEARANCE CERTIFICATE SERIAL No. 144
WORTHING PARISH.
M.R. 59472199
M.R. 59312194
M.R. 59202187
M.R. 59102184
M.R. 59032185
M.R 58992180
M.R. 58822173
CLEARANCE CERTIFICATE SERIAL No. 144. REFERS TO ALL FOUR SECTIONS OF THE MINEFIELD.
MINEFIELD SERIAL No 438.
TRUE
LAVATORIES
SHELTER
THE ESPLANADE
BEACH HOUSE
DENTON GARDENS
WARWICK ROAD
SCALE 1/2500
SCALE OF FEET
CHIEF ENGINEER
22 SEP 1944
S. E. COMMAND
FOR C.E. SOUTH EASTERN ARMY.

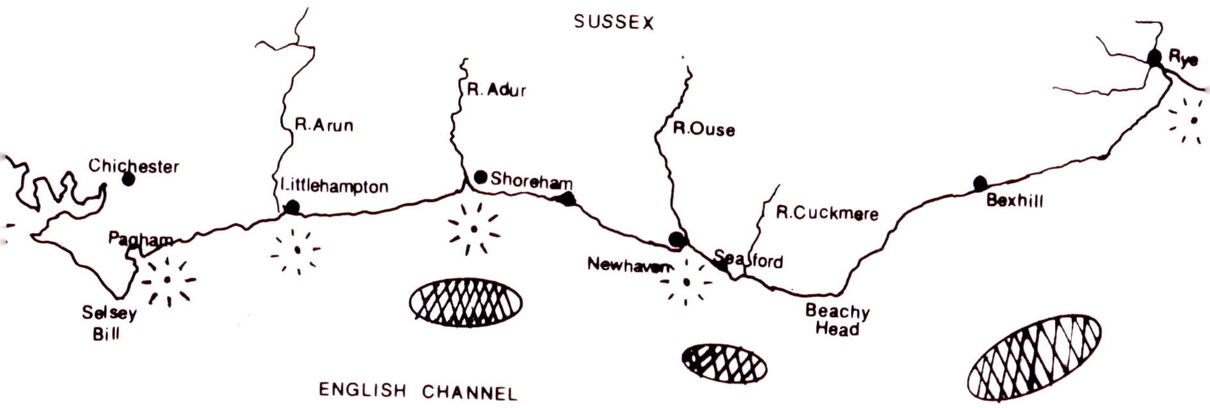

13.3 Controlled mine-fields, fired from the shore, (*) were placed outside all harbours in Sussex. The net barriers (X) were anchored further off the coast.

← 13.4 This map of the sea front east of Worthing Pier shows minefields from Denton Gardens near Splash Point to Windsor Road.

13.5 Types of British anti-tank mines used to blow off the tracks of armoured vehicles. The loss rate of tanks crossing a minefield in WW 2 was about 17%.

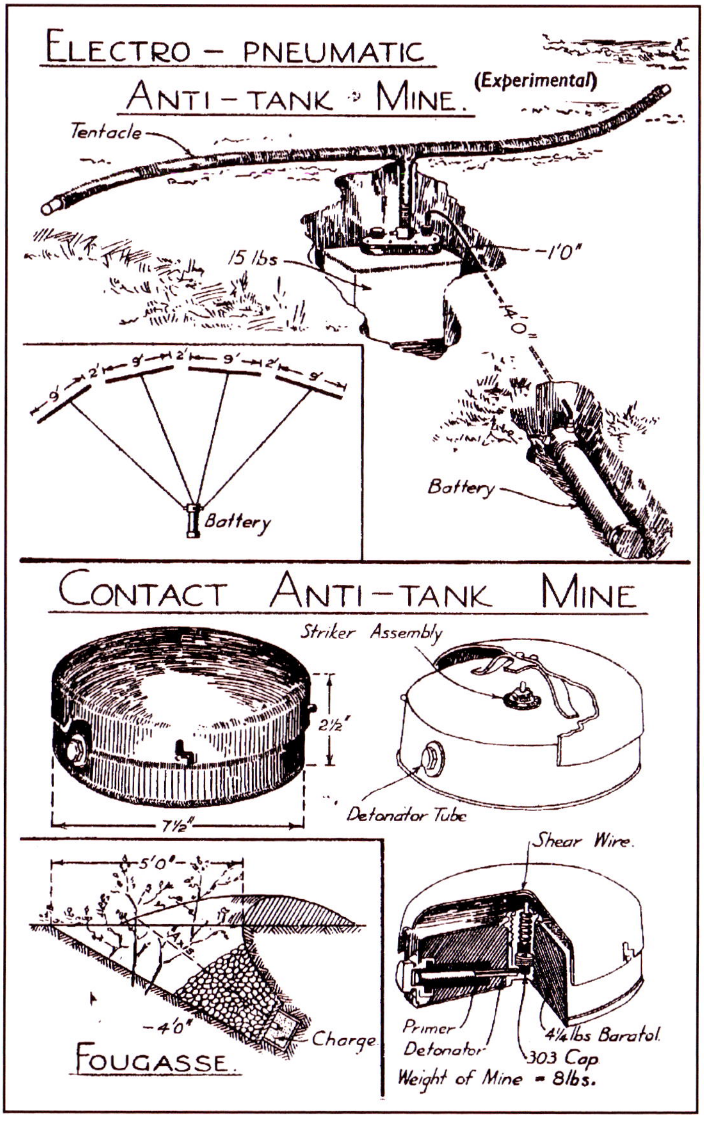

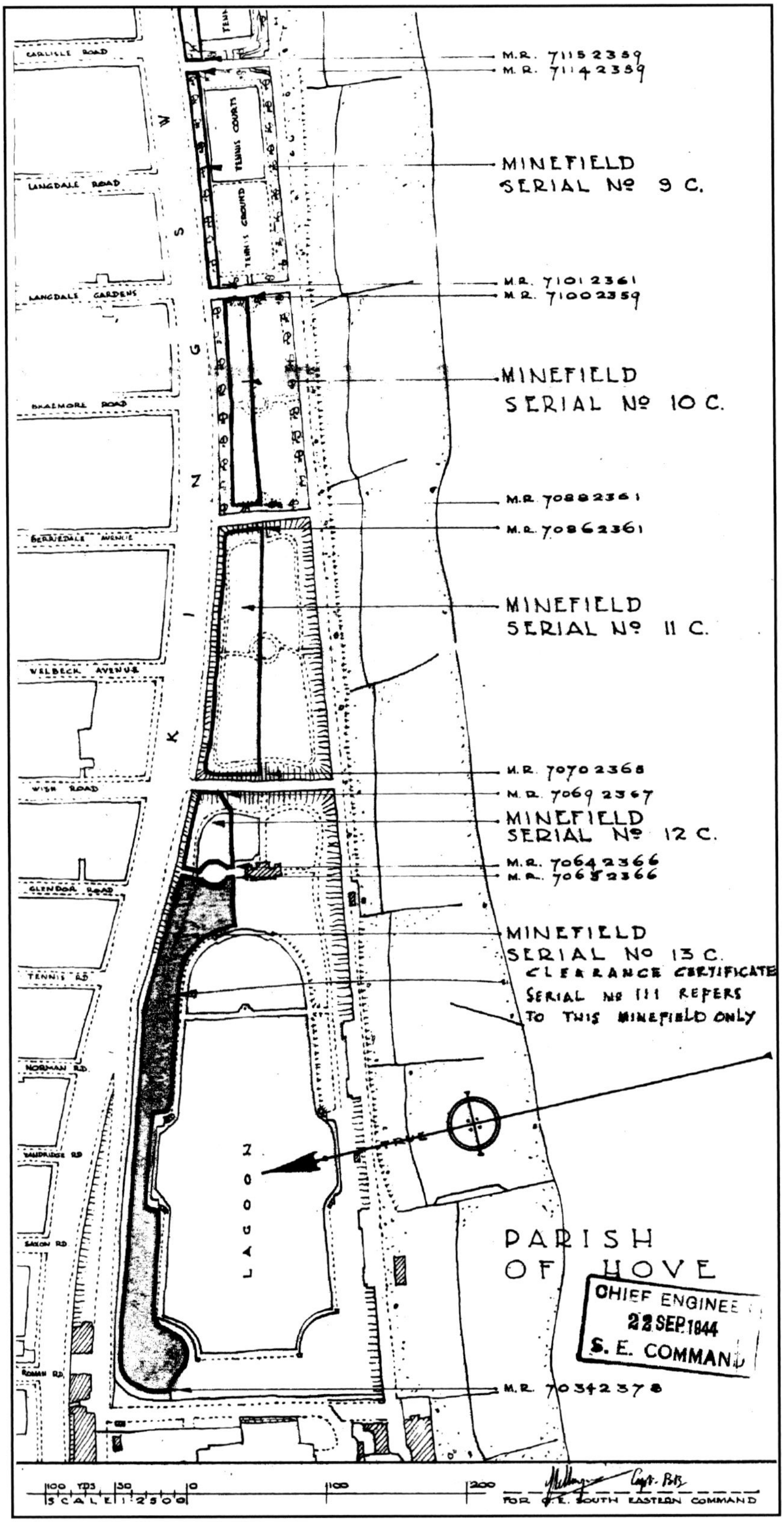

13.6 This minefield in Hove stretched from Carlisle Road to the Lagoon. One mine every yard (metre) in wide belts.

13.7 Birling Gap in 2010, unchanged but with new steps and no minefield.

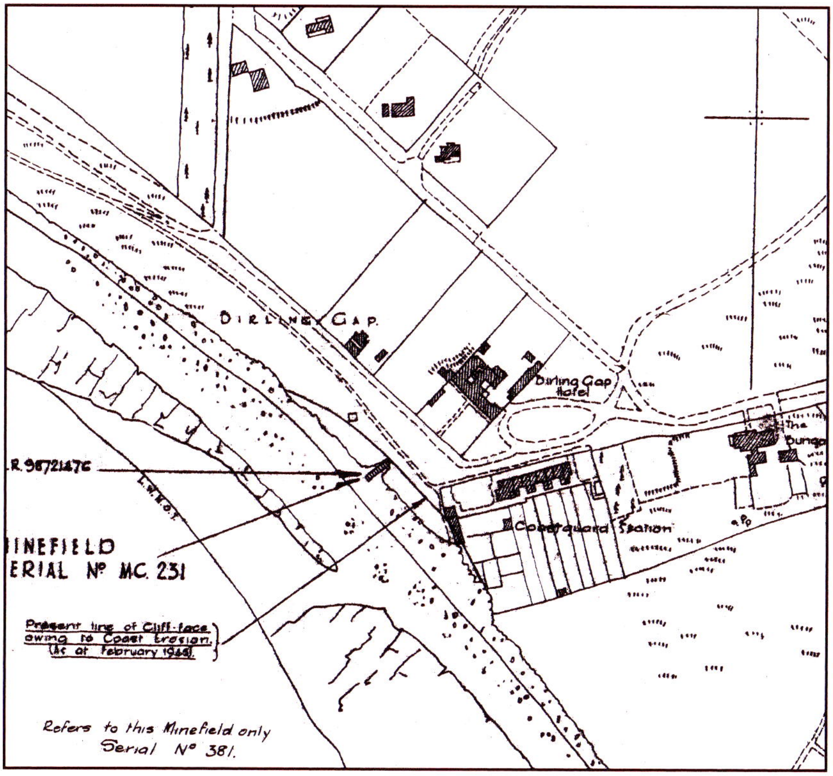

13.8 The minefields at Birling Gap near Eastbourne were around steps from the beach to the cliff top. They were overlooked by pill boxes.

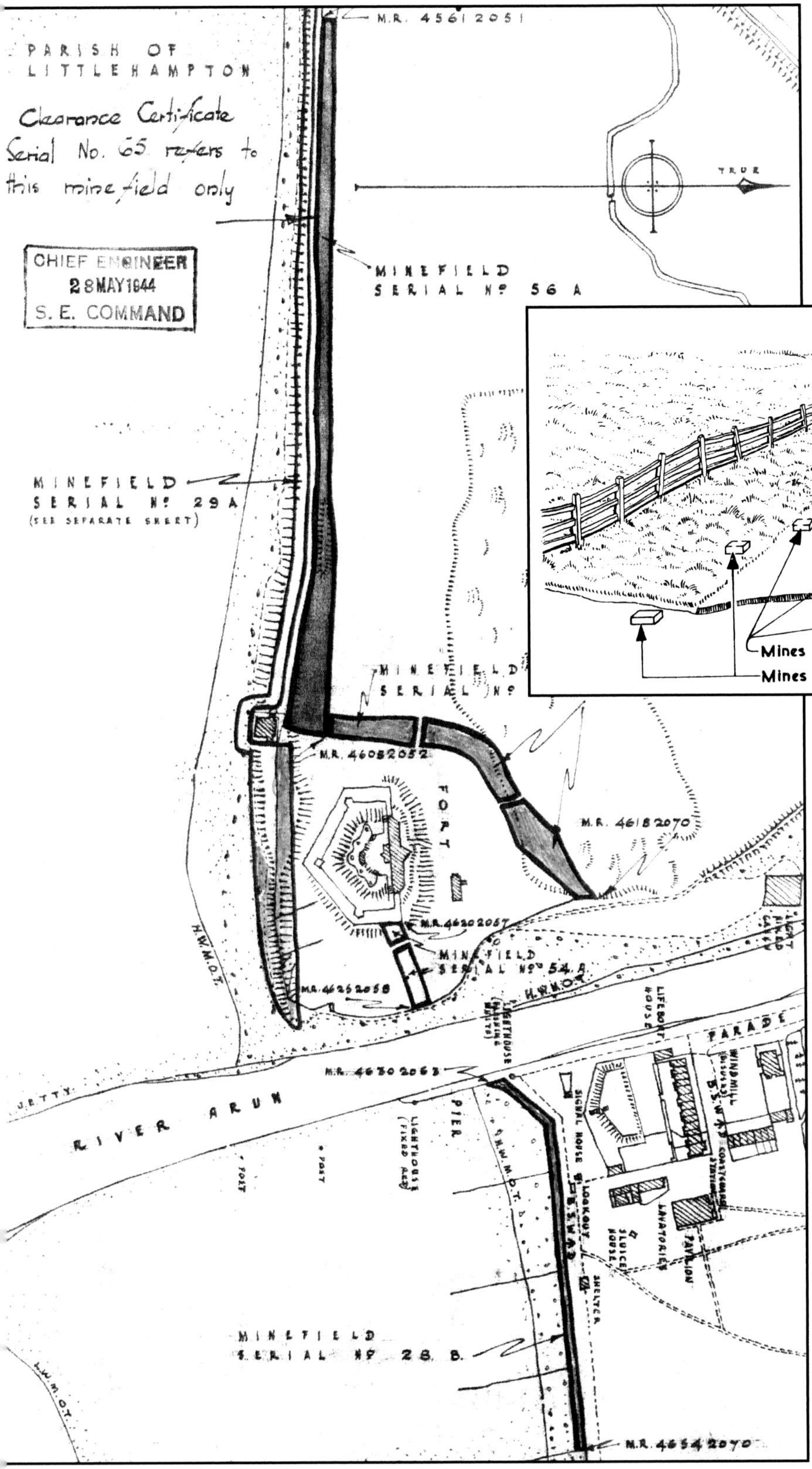

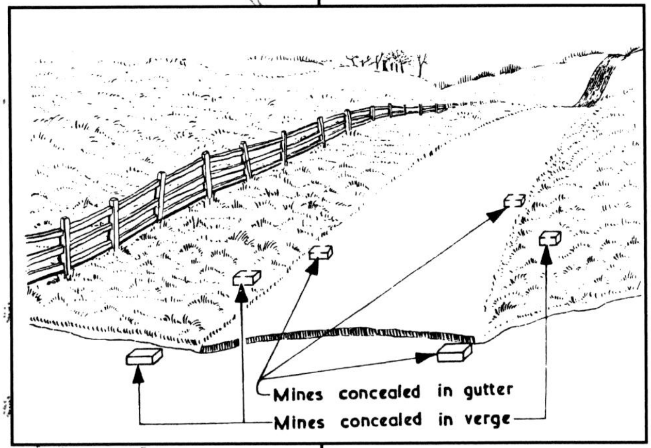

13.9 Anti-personal mines were hidden everywhere. Their purpose was to hold up an attack.

← 13.10 At Littlehampton there were minefields on the beach and around the old fort. Behind Minefield No 28B was 345 Coast Defence Battery

→ 13.11 A Minefield Clearance Certificate for Littlehampton sounds a cautionary note!

Certificate

of the

REMOVAL OF DANGEROUS MILITARY DEFENCE WORKS.

(Issued under the authority and on behalf of G.O.C.-in-C. South Eastern Army.)

GENERAL. *This Certificate will be issued to the Service Department, Government Department, Local Government Authority, or the Civil Authority concerned, and is intended to guarantee, as far as circumstances will permit, the safety of certain Structures, Buildings or Areas of Land which have been made dangerous by the installation of Explosive Devices, but from which such devices have subsequently been removed.*

ADDRESSED TO The Regional Commissioner, No.12 Region.

TYPE OF EXPLOSIVE DEVICE

Minefield.

LOCATION OF STRUCTURE, BUILDING or AREA of LAND

Military Reference Minefield Serial No. 55A.
Map Ref. Sheet 133. 46082052 to 46182070.

Civil

The minefield was situated in the Parish of Littlehampton in the County of Sussex. The minefield lay to the west and north of the old fort on the west of the mouth of the river Arun. The minefield extended from a point 90 yards north of High Tide Level and 40 yards west of the fort northwards for 100 yards and then north eastwards for 140 yards terminating at the top of the bank 60 yards west of the river. The minefield had an average width of 20 yards and covered an area of 4800 square yards.

REPORT BY THE CHIEF ENGINEER, S.E. COMMAND

I have carefully studied the Minefield Records of the above area, available in this office, which records were compiled from the reports of the Engineer Officers engaged in the work of laying the mines. They are accurate only in so far as the circumstances of the time at which the minefields were laid permitted but in the main fairly represent the facts.

I have compared the records with the detailed reports of the Engineer Officers entrusted with the responsibility of clearing the minefields of the above area, and, as a result, I am of the opinion that :—

There is some doubt from the old records as to the number of mines originally laid.

From the report of the officer in charge of clearing the minefield I am satisfied that all mines have been removed from the area shown on the attached plan.

[Stamp:] ... ENGINEER 20 JUN 1944 ... MAND

Date 20 June, 44.

[signature]
Brigadier,
Chief Engineer,
for G.O.C.-in-C.
South Eastern Army.

2 Copy No.

(15721) SECD/4045 1/44 1,000 L. & M. Gp 50.

Chapter 14

THE ARMY COAST WATCHING RADAR AND THE BEACHY HEAD ROTOR BUNKER

The first early warning radar stations in Sussex to detect the approach of enemy aircraft were in place shortly before WW 2 began. They were an important part of the reporting system for RAF fighters in the Battle of Britain in 1940 and were conspicuous by high lattice work transmitting and receiving towers. These first stations were built at Rye, (Guldeford Lane); Rickney, (Church Acre north west of Pevensey); and Poling north of Littlehampton. All these stations stood on low open lying ground and 200 foot high steel or wooden Merryweather towers for transmitting and receiving signals were necessary. Royal Air Force staff operated the stations and lived in huts close by.

Experimental work on the RAF Chain Home (CH) equipment resulted in the development of a coast defence radar, which could track ships at sea as well as low flying aircraft. The army's interest in this radar for detecting enemy ships and troop transports approaching landing beaches was obvious. From late 1940 until 1941 coast watching radar sets were gradually made available for army use. New radar stations were set up along the South Coast, each given the prefix M, and there were at least nine (M7 - M15) in Sussex. No 1 was at Fanhole near South Foreland in Kent. Some of the sites selected were those also used for RAF radar stations. The coast watching stations were operated by men from the Royal Artillery (RA), Royal Army Ordnance Corps (RAOC) and the Royal Electrical and Mechanical Engineers (REME) until 1942 when all radar installations became the responsibility of the RAF.

The radar equipment was housed in transportable cabins, or in purpose built oblong concrete buildings with flat roofs. A turntable stood on the roof with a large rotating aerial. There were several different aerial arrangements. The coast watching stations needed to be on cliff tops, high down land, or with masts 200 feet above sea level. They did not have to be close to gun batteries.

A secret report of November 1941 shows the following coast defence radar stations in Sussex:-

M.7 Hastings (Fairlight)
M.8 St Leonards-on-Sea
M.9 Bexhill-on-Sea
M.10 Beachy Head
M.11 Seaford. First at High and Over, then at Seaford Head
M.12 Newhaven (Friars Bay)
M.13 Brighton (Portobello)
M.14 Shoreham by Sea
M.15 Poling

Reports went by telephone landline to the joint naval and army control centre at Newhaven, except for the Beachy Head and Shoreham-by-Sea stations whose reports went initially to Dover or Portsmouth respectively. The Brighton radar was then found to have poor reception and be badly sited, and because there was dead ground in front of the Shoreham radar it was recommended that these two stations should be closed as the one on Truleigh Hill, at the back of Shoreham, could be adapted to give better results and this was done.

Newhaven deserves a special mention because when a new six inch 42 degree counter bombardment battery on Castle Hill was completed in 1942, changes were needed to the operation of the M12 station at Friars Bay further west of Newhaven fort. It was equipped with a different type of radar and was redesignated a B 17 station. It is unclear whether this radar took the place of M12 or was just sited nearby. It was a special type of radar developed for coast batteries to improve the direction of the gun when it fired and also record the fall of shot.

As radar technology developed, particularly in regard to air and sea warfare, other radar stations, some experimental, some serving the needs of the RAF, Royal Navy and United States Airforce were established in Sussex. Mr Owen of Leigh on Sea remembers a number of RAF lorries suddenly appearing near his home in Durrington. They were towing trailers reminiscent of strange bird cages which revolved. These were mobile units assembled to form a new GCI night fighter radar interception station.

The most favourite site for radar activity was Beachy Head because of its location and height, and at one time there were at least ten radar and radio direction finding stations functioning on the headland for various branches of the armed services.

Of all the defence structures built along the coast during the war the RAF radar stations remained operational the longest. After World War 2 ended they continued to be necessary for protection against nuclear attacks during the Cold War, and some of the Sussex wartime sites were rebuilt to house advanced radar equipment. In the 1950s under a scheme with the code name of ROTOR a reduced number of existing radar stations were strengthened against attack from the air. In Sussex there were to be only five stations. A new single level deep bunker was constructed underground on Beachy Head for a control and early warning radar (CEW). At Wartling there was a new three level underground bunker for ground control of interception equipment (GCI). Fairlight and Truleigh Hill remained Chain Home Extra Low (CHEL) radar stations, but the equipment was housed below ground. Poling continued as an existing Chain Home (CH) station. Although most of the expensive excavation and conversion work at these sites had been completed by 1960, newer technology eventually made them redundant. The ROTOR plan was scrapped and Beachy Head's role as a radar centre was taken over by RAF Wartling until 1964, when it too was closed.

The Sussex coast played a significant role in the operation of various types of radar to keep Britain safe from attack, by air and sea. There is not much left to show for it now, other than a few concreted areas where the masts and buildings stood and where the operators worked and lived. At Fairlight, Truleigh Hill and Wartling the underground bunkers remain buried and after having been used for other purposes are in a waterlogged and distressed state. The old M.12 site at Friars Bay was used as a test site for some years but some of the buildings along the chalk cliff top are in danger of slipping into the sea and the survival of the rest of the ruin is problematical. At Durrington there is still a large sealed bunker underneath a junior school in Palatine Road. The most impressive Beachy Head ROTOR bunker built in the 1950s for two million pounds still lies deep under the chalk cliff and is now sealed off. When I last visited in 1994 it had to be opened up and tested for methane gas. Because of its ten foot thick bombproof walls it was reasonably dry although littered with rubble and trunking which had come down from the ceiling and off the walls. Without its equipment it was a disappointing arrangement of empty rooms. It was also full of dangerous asbestos. It is currently owned by Eastbourne Local Authority who have difficulty in finding a use for it.

Note

The nomenclature of the various radar types can be confusing as equipment was produced in a hurry and rushed into service. Hence alternative descriptions of the equipment was given by the services, depending on the purpose for which it was used. AMES was included in some titles and means Air Ministry Experimental Station although these subsequently became fully operational.

1. Chain Home (CH) radar. or AMES Type 1. Used by RAF.

2. CD/CHL Coast Defence/Chain Home Low radar or Ames Type 2. Used by the Army.

3. CA No 1. Coast Artillery radar. Used by the Army.

4. CEW Coastal Early Warning. Used by the RAF,

5. GCI Ground Control of Interception. or AMES Type 7. For RAF use.

6. CHEL Chain Home Extra Low. For RAF use.

RAOC and REME: the Royal Army Ordnance Corps. (later renamed Royal Electrical and Mechanical Engineers were initially responsible for maintaining radar equipment.

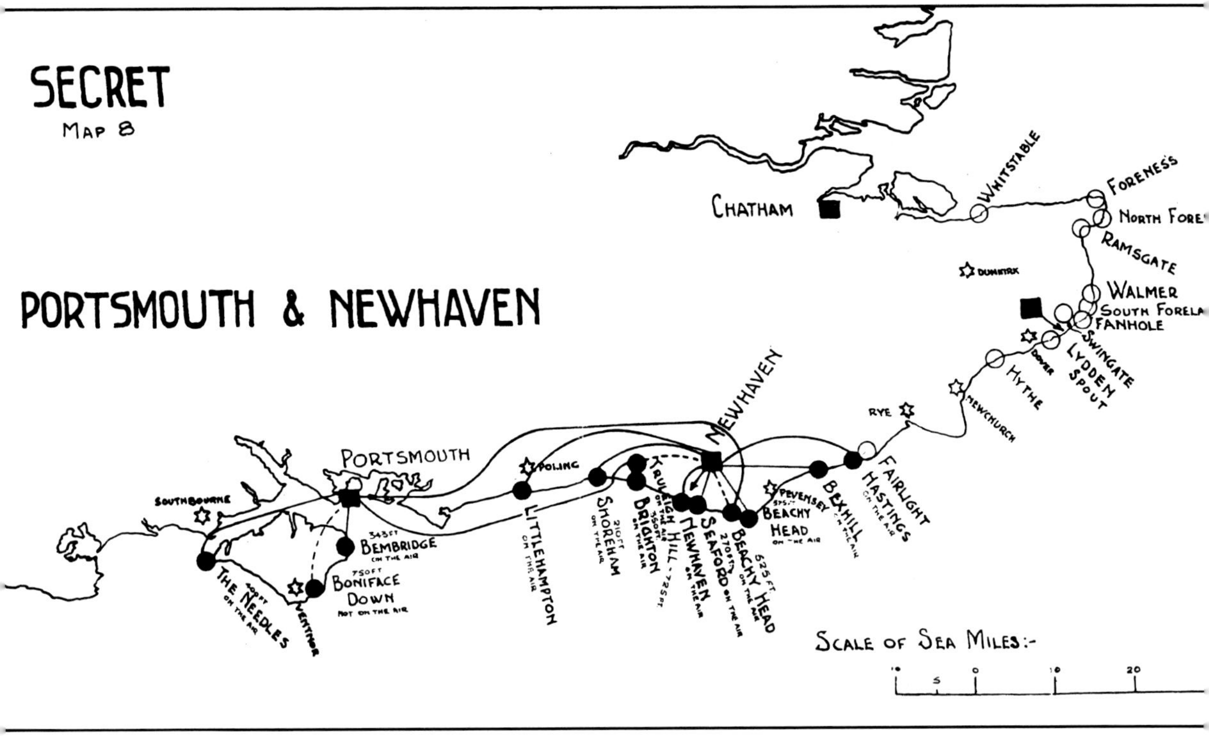

14.1 Army Coast Defence Radar stations (black circles) were linked to joint Naval and Army plotting centres at Portsmouth, Newhaven and Dover (black squares)

14.2 Friars' Bay Army Coast Watching radar station. Plan of the south elevation and matching photograph of the building on the cliff edge.

14.3 The Army Radar Operations Room manned by the ATS in Newhaven Fort

14.4 The 1950s ROTOR radar bunker is inside Beachy Head. A depression near the crest marks the entrance to the rear escape tunnel

14.5 When the guard hut was demolished only a hatch (now grassed over) marks the entrance to the bunker inside Beachy Head.

14.6 A site plan of the Beachy Head bunker now disused and sealed off.

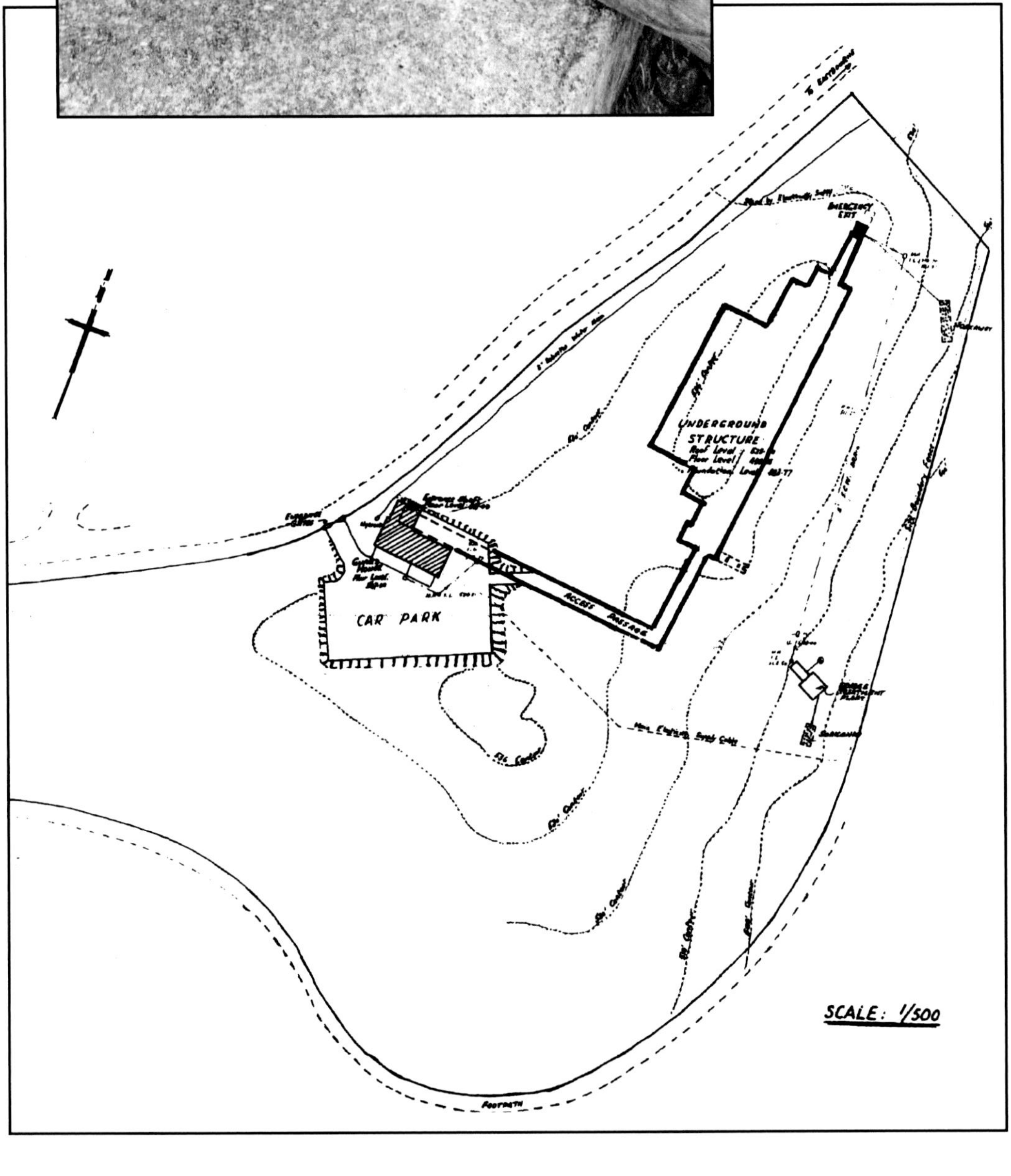

14.7 The central corridor of the Beachy Head bunker.

14.8 The derelict operations room in the Beachy Head bunker.

INDEX

Page numbers of illustrations are shown in bold type

Alanbrooke, General 5, 15, 17
Anti-aircraft defence 40
Anti-tank obstacles **51, 52, 53**
Anti-tank guns **43, 44**
Angmering on Sea (CD) Battery 64
Armoured cars **7, 9**
Armoured train 30, 31, **36**
Artillery
  Guns available (1940) 29, **31, 33**
  Locations 29, 30, **32**
  Rail guns **34, 36, 37**
  Super Heavy Battery 30, **34**
  Quads **33**

Barbed wire 41, 47, **49**
Battle craft **21, 44, 45**
Beach defences 55, **56, 57, 58, 59, 60, 61**
Beachy Head **103**
Bexhill on Sea (CD) Battery 65, **73**
Binoculars 63, **75**
Birling Gap **23, 97**
Bognor (CD) Battery 64
Brighton (CD) Battery **50,** 65
British Army Units
  1st Armoured Division 15, 24
  1st Army Tank Brigade 15, 24
  25th Army Tank Brigade 15
  31st Army Tank Brigade 12, 24
  43rd Royal Tank Regiment 40
  1st London Division 15
  38th Welsh Division 15, 30, 38, 39
  45th Infantry Division 15
  47th Infantry Division 29, 39
  52nd Infantry Division 15
  55th West Lancs. Division 15
  29th Independent Inf. Brigade 15
  5th Defence Regiment R.A. 39
  1/8th Middlesex Machine Gun Battalion 41
  113th Infantry Brigade 38
  114th Infantry Brigade 38
  115th Infantry Brigade 38
  140th Infantry Brigade 38
  283, 284, 502, 561, Field Companies R.E. 41

Canadian Divisions 15, 16, 92
Castle Hill Battery 65, 77
Chichester **35**
Churchill, Winston 4
Cissbury Ring **28**
Cliff End (CD) Battery 65, **67**
Coast Defence Battery maps **68, 74, 81**
Cooden Beach (CD) Battery 65
Cuckfield Nodal Point **8**

Defence zones 38, 39
Defence of large towns 39
Defended localities **19**
Defence Telegraph Network 88
Demolitions 41
Denton 83
Dungeness (CD) Battery 66

Eastbourne (CD) Battery 65, **69**
  Loop holed walls **50, 51**
  Anti-tank ditch **52, 53**

Fire Booms 76, 91
Flame Thrower **14**
Ford 38
Friar's Bay 100, **102**

German Intelligence 6, 11
GHQ Line 46
Glider obstructions 47, 54
Grenade throwing **22**

Hastings (CD) Battery 65, **73**
HMS Forward 83
  Plan **85**
  Plotting Room **86**
  Tunnels **86, 87**
Home Guard **10,** 16, **18, 23,** 38
Hove 66, **96**

Infantryman and kit **13, 20, 23**
Ironside, General 4
Invasion warnings 38, 88

Jury's Gap (CD) Battery 66

Kirke, General 4

Littlehampton (CD) Battery 64
- Minefield **98, 99**
- Nodal Point **8**

Martello Towers 11
Minefields on land 92, **94, 95, 96, 97, 98, 99**
Minefields at sea 91, **93, 95**
McNaughton, General 92

Net barriers at sea 91, **95**
Newhaven Fort
- Batteries 77, **79**
- In ruins **78**
- New guns 81
- Plan of work **79**
- Views of fort **77, 78, 80, 82**

Nodal Points 4, 5, 41, **8**
Norman's Bay (CD) Battery 65

Padgent, General 5
Parachute troops **14, 44**
Pevensey Bay (CD) Battery 65, **70, 72**
Pevensey Castle **9, 10**
PIAT gun **20**
Pigeon service 88
Pill boxes **19, 43,** 46, **48, 51,** 54, **56**
Plotting Room 83

Radar
- Army Coast Watch Stations 100, **102**
- Beachy Head (ROTOR) **103, 104, 105**

Rail Guns **34, 36, 37**
Road blocks **49, 51**

Seaford (CD) Battery 65
Sealion
- German landing area 5, 6, **12**
- Invasion cancelled 6
- Planning document 11

Searchlight **71**
Selsey Bill 64
Shoreham by Sea (CD) Battery 64
South Eastern Command 15
Southwick Home Guard **18**
Stop Lines **42,** 46

Tangmere 38
Tanks
- Mark II **25**
- Cruiser **25, 27**
- Infantry (I) **28**
- Matilda **26, 28**
- Medium **27**

Telegraph Network 88, **90**
Training for battle 17

Williams, General 15
Winchelsea (CD) Battery 66, **75**
Wireless Network 88, **89**
Worthing
- 345 (CD) Battery 64, **67, 68**
- Anti-tank ditch 52
- Beach defences 55, **56, 57, 58, 59, 60, 61**
- Minefield **94**

FURTHER READING

Alexander, C. Ironside's Line, 1998
Balfour, G. The Armoured Train. 1981
Batchelor, J. and Hogg I. Rail Guns, 1973
Butler, C. East Sussex under Attack, 1500-1990 2007
Campbell. D. War Plans UK, 1982
Cobb, P. Coastal Batteries of England, Wales and Scotland, (MSS)
Collier, B. The defence of the UK, 1957
Crook, P. Sussex Home Guard
Cumming, M. Radar Reflections, 2000
Danchev, A and Todman, D. Alanbrooke War Diaries, 2001
Darwin, B. War on the line
Dobinson, C. Monuments of War series, Volumes 1-7
Doherty, R. Ubique. The Royal Artillery in WW 2, 2008
Ellis. G. Secret Tunnels of South Heighton, 1996
Foot, W. Beaches, Fields, Streets and Hills, 2006
Goodwin, J. Pevensey, Eastbourne and Newhaven Defences, 1994
Goodwin, J. , Military Defence of West Sussex, 1985
Gough, J. Watching the Skies, 1993
Goulden, R.J. and Kemp A. Newhaven and Seaford Coastal Forts, 1974
Graves, C., Home Guard of Britain, 1943
Hamilton. N. Montgomery of Alamein1881-1942, 2001
Henslow. M, Miracle of Radar, 1946
Ismay, Lord Memories, 1960
Longstaff Tyrell, P, A Sussex Sunset. Pevensey and Wartling, 1998
Longstaff Tyrell, P. Destination Fowington, 2000
Longstaff Tyrell, P. Operation Cuckmere Haven, 2001
Longstaff Tyrell, P. Maple Leaf Army in Britain, 2002
Longstaff Tyrell, P. Tyrells List. 1998
Longstaff Tyrell, P. Barracks to Bunkers. 2002
Mace, M.F. Sussex Wartime Relics and Memorials, 1997
Mace, M.F. Frontline Sussex 1939-45, 1996
Mackenzie, S.P. The Home Guard
Macleod, R. Col. The Ironside Diaries 1937-40, 1962
Ockenden, M. Cannucks by the Sea, 2006
Osbourne, M. Pill Boxes of England and Ireland, 2008
Padget, J. The Crusading General; Gen. Sir Bernard Padget, 2008
Schenk, P. Invasion of England 1940, 1990
Stacy, C.P. Wilson, B.M. Half a Million Canadians in Britain, 1987
U.S. War Department, German Military Dictionary, 1944
Wills, H. Pill Boxes. A Study of UK Defences 1940, 1990

PRINCIPAL SOURCES CONSULTED

ADM: Admiralty
CAB Cabinet Office
ESRO: East Sussex Records Office
WM Worthing Museum
NA: National Archives
NAM: National Army Museum
SIAC Sussex Industrial Archaeology Society
WO: War Office
WSRO: West Sussex Records Office

Chapter 1 Invasion Threatens and plans change
ESRO SPA 2/23/8 Nodal Points
ESRO SPA 2/28 Nodal Points
NA WO 166/482 Nodal Points and the grid system
WSRO BO/AR/24/3/5 Yellow Booklet
NA ADM 199/569 Military defence of UK in 1940
NA WO 199/909 Invasion appreciation 1941
WSRO MSS 48201 45th Div, Invasion signals
NA WO 196/33 UK Munitions state, June 1940
ADM Copy No 006054. Fuehrer Conference on Naval affairs
Sussex extracts translated by Martienssen in 1947

Chapter 2 German Intelligence about the Sussex Defences
Copy 005730. Specific and technical data of the English fortifications and defences. German High Command. 1940 held by the author

Chapter 3 The Infantry behind the Beaches
CAB War Establishment of Infantry Divisions, 1939-45
Langdon-Davis J, Home Guard Training Manual 1940
Pridham C. H. B . Lewis Gun 1940
Stokes H.G. Signalling and Map reading for the Home Guard 1941
WO Infantry Training for War 1937
WO Infantry Section Leading 1938
WO Training Pamphlets 23 and 33 1940-41
WO Weapon Training 1942
WO Infantry Division in the Defence 1942
WO Regulations for the Home guard 1942
WO Grenades, All Arms 1951
WO PIAT Gun 1943

Chapter 4 Armoured Divisions and Tank Brigades
CAB War Establishment of Armoured Divisions 1939-45

Chapter 5 Artillery, Rail Guns and Armoured Trains
NA WO 199/1423 Artillery policy 1940
NA WO 196/33 Artillery availability 1940

NA WO WO 166/569 Artillery sites on the South Downs 1941
NA WO 166/482 Artillery sites for 38th Welsh Division 1941
NA WO 199/523 Heavy artillery in East Sussex
NA WO 166/562 47th Division Artillery War Diary
NA WO 166/145 Super heavy battery, Hailsham
NA WO 166/674 4 inch guns on beaches
NA WO 192/71 Artillery at Seaford and Beachy Head.
Gittus W E G. Chichester Rail Guns, correspondence 1983
NAM RE drawing Chichester Rail Gun sidings
Balfour G. Correspondence on Armoured Trains and Rail Guns 1986

Chapter 6 Deployment of an Infantry Division: Selsey Bill - Newhaven

NA WO 166/482 Operation Orders 1941
NA WO 166/569 47th Division Fire plan 1941
WO Manual of Field Works. Defended Localities 1925
WO Fieldcraft - All Arms 1948
WO Infantry Training Vol IV 1950
WO Home Guard Training 1952

Chapter 7 The Rush to Build Obstacles

WO Manual of Field Works 1921
WO Military Engineering - Scaffolding 1931
WO Military Engineering. Defences 1937
WO Dannert Concertina Wire 1939
WO Field Engineering: Protective Works 1941
WO Camouflage. 1941
WO Military Engineering Vol XIV, Concrete 1944
WM Anti-tank Ditches, Worthing - Perimeter Defences

Chapter 8 Fortification of a Sussex Sea Front

WSRO B/O 40 12/2 and 12/3 Removal of Defence Works 1954

Chapter 9 Coast Defence Batteries Selsey Bill - Dungeness

The following is only a small selection of the many War Office files in the National Archives about the siting and operation of Coast batteries on the Sussex Coast

NA WO 166/1751 Battery locations
NA WO 199/945 551 Coast Regiment
NA WO 166/1828 552 Coast Regiment
NA WO 166/1752 553 Coast Regiment
NA WO 199/1111 Cliff End Battery
NA WO 166/1850 Bexhill Battery
NA WO 192/69 Cooden Battery
NA WO 199/946 Inspection of Sussex batteries
NA WO 192/80 Shoreham Fort
NA WO 199/78 Newhaven new battery
NA WO 166/1838 Brighton Battery
NA WO 199/2558 Availability of guns
NA WO 199/946 Home Guard to man batteries
WO Coast Artillery Training Vols 1 and 2 1938

Chapter 10 Old Newhaven Fort. Its Coast Defence Role in 1940
NA ADM 1/18136 Newhaven Sub Command 1939-45
NA WO 192/220 Newhaven Fort
NA WO 199/78 Newhaven new battery
NA WO 199/1172 Newhaven fort defence scheme

Chapter 11 HMS Forward. An underground HQ
NA ADM 1/1306 Correspondence
NA ADM 1/18136 History
NA WO 199/1109 Army Plotting Rooms
NA WO 166/689 War Diaries
NA WO 199/1172 Staff appointments
Architect's report and survey 1979-82 (author)

Chapter 12 Military Signals London - South Coast
NA WO 166/145 Wireless Communications Chart 1941
WO Signal Training, Organisation Vol 5 1938

Chapter 13 Nets, Fire Booms and Minefields
ESRO SPA 2/21/46 Minefields in East Sussex
WSRO Pol 25/6/47 Minefields in West Sussex
WSRO Pol W/HQ 15/7 Police reports
Cobb P Net Barriers, Loopholes No 8 1994
WO RE Pocket Book Chapter VI Section 42

Chapter 14 Army Coast Radar and the Beachy Head Bunker
NA ADM 179/151 Coast Defence Radar (Sussex) 1941
NA WO 199/530 Coast Defence Radar (Sussex) 1941
NA WO 199/534 M and K Radars in East Sussex 1942
NA WO 199/1172 Seaford Radar 1942
NA WO 199/532 Beachy Head Radars 1942
NA WO 199/63 Beachy Head Radars 1943
NA WO 192/220 Friars Bay Radar station
Martin R G Friars Bay Radar correspondence 1995
Martin R G Friars Bay Radar, report (SIAS)
Pearson M Coast Defence Radar, Fort Vol 19 1991